THE WHIRLWIND WAR

The United States Army in Operations
DESERT SHIELD and *DESERT STORM*

Frank N. Schubert and Theresa L. Kraus
General Editors

CENTER OF MILITARY HISTORY
UNITED STATES ARMY
WASHINGTON, D.C., 1995

Library of Congress Cataloging-in-Publication Data

The whirlwind war : the United States Army in operations Desert Shield
    and Desert Storm / Frank N. Schubert and Theresa L. Kraus, general
    editors.
            p. cm. — (CMH pub ; 70–30)
        Includes index.
        1. Persian Gulf War, 1993—United States. 2. United States.
    Army—History—Persian Gulf War, 1991. I. Series.
    DS79.724.U6W48 1994
    956.7044'2373—dc20   93–43205
                                                                              CIP

CMH Pub 70–30–1

For sale by the U.S. Government Printing Office
Superintendent of Documents, Mail Stop: SSOP, Washington, DC 20402-9328
ISBN 0-16-042954-4

. . . to Those Who Served

FOREWORD

In 1990–1991 an international coalition reversed the results of Iraqi aggression against Kuwait. The United States provided the bulk of the forces arrayed against Iraq, with the U.S. Army contributing the greatest portion of the ground force.

Successful participation in this historic endeavor marked both an end and a beginning for the Army. At an end was the long and sometimes arduous transition from the Vietnam-era Army. What emerged was a small, superbly equipped, highly skilled, well-trained, and extremely mobile force, composed of units from both the active and reserve components. Its overall excellent performance in Southwest Asia reflected the attention that successive Army Chiefs of Staff had paid to leader development—the effort to professionalize the service's officer and noncommissioned officer corps. In this major test, the Army clearly demonstrated that it could project its power effectively. One of the resounding lessons for the Army in Operations DESERT SHIELD and DESERT STORM was that it could operate as part of a multinational force with great success. Even as these operations were taking place, the Army addressed those steps necessary to prepare for its critical role as a key member of America's armed forces of the future.

The Whirlwind War tells the story of this pivotal chapter in the Army's history. It shows the various strands that came together to produce the Army of the 1990s and how that Army in turn performed under fire and in the glare of world attention. Drafted soon after the end of Operation DESERT STORM, the book retains a sense of immediacy in its approach. Yet the manuscript also went through a series of reviews, and the maps were subsequently carefully researched and compiled as original documents in their own right. The result is a volume that takes its place in the first round of the historical analysis of the events described. More definitive studies will undoubtedly follow, as ever more documents are assessed. But this book is intended to bridge that gap, and I commend it to all readers interested in the current and future role of American ground forces.

Washington, D.C.
June 1995

JOHN W. MOUNTCASTLE
Brigadier General, USA
Chief of Military History

CONTRIBUTORS

Charles R. Anderson is an Asian specialist and former Marine Corps officer who has published personal accounts of the Vietnam War and, for the U.S. Army Center of Military History, has written narratives on Army operations in World War II. He has an M.A. in Asian studies from Western Michigan University and is currently employed as a historian in the Histories Division at the Center.

Judith L. Bellafaire holds a Ph.D. in American history from the University of Delaware. She has taught history at a number of colleges and is now a historian with the Field and International Division of the U.S. Army Center of Military History. Her areas of specialization include World War II and women in the military.

Christopher N. Choppelas is an Army reservist at the Presidio of San Francisco. As a journalist for the 51st Military History Detachment, he participated in the writing of the history of Department of Defense involvement in the 1989 Loma Prieta (California) earthquake. He is a full-time student at San Francisco State University and a microcomputer network specialist working for Hitachi America, Limited.

Charles A. Endress is professor and head of the Department of History at Angelo State University, San Angelo, Texas. He has taught at the United States Military Academy, West Point, and as a Visiting Professor of Military History and Strategy at the Air War College. He holds a Ph.D. in history from Tulane University and retired as a colonel in the United States Army Reserve.

William W. Epley, now retired from the United States Army, was a historian in the Research and Analysis Division at the U.S. Army Center of Military History. He has an M.A. in history from the University of Michigan and has taught European history at the United States Military Academy. In August 1990 he served briefly in the history office of U.S. Central Command at MacDill Air Force Base, Florida. During February–April 1991 he was a historian for the 22d Support Command in Saudi Arabia.

Glen R. Hawkins has an M.A. in international relations from the University of Southern California and an M.A. in history from Harvard University. He retired from the U.S. Army in 1993. He worked as a historian in the Research and Analysis Division of the U.S. Army Center of Military History. During December 1990–March 1991 he was a historian for the 22d Support Command in Saudi Arabia.

Mary L. Haynes is a historian in the Research and Analysis Division of the U.S. Army Center of Military History. She holds an M.A. degree in history from Georgetown University and has been an Army historian for twenty years.

David W. Hogan is a historian in the Histories Division at the U.S. Army Center of Military History. He has a Ph.D. in history from Duke University and has taught American military history at Elon College. His book, *U.S. Army Special Operations in World War II*, was published in 1992.

John H. King, a lieutenant colonel in the U.S. Army Reserve, commanded the 51st Military History Detachment from 1987 to 1992. His detachment was mobilized in 1991 for duty at the U.S. Army Center of Military History during the war in the Persian Gulf. He has an M.B.A. from Golden Gate University. As a civilian he specializes in economic development marketing for Loudoun County, Virginia.

Charles E. Kirkpatrick was a historian in the Histories Division of the U.S. Army Center of Military History. He holds a Ph.D. in history from Emory University. He retired from the U.S. Army in the summer of 1991 and as a civilian is now command historian at V Corps in Frankfurt, Germany. His books include *An Unknown Future and a Doubtful Present: Writing the Victory Plan of 1941* (1991).

Theresa L. Kraus is a historian with the Federal Aviation Administration and holds a Ph.D. in history from the University of Maryland. During preparation of this volume she was a historian in the Research and Analysis Division of the U.S. Army Center of Military History. She has written on a variety of military topics.

J. Britt McCarley is the command historian for the U.S. Army Test and Evaluation Command at Aberdeen Proving Ground, Maryland. He has a Ph.D. in history from Temple University and served as the Air Defense Artillery branch historian at Fort Bliss, Texas, during preparation of this book.

Thomas A. Popa was a historian in the Research and Analysis Division at the U.S. Army Center of Military History until he retired from the Army in 1993. He has an M.A. in history from Kansas State University and is an honor graduate of the Army's Command and General Staff College at Fort Leavenworth, Kansas.

Frank N. Schubert was chief of the Military Studies Branch of the Research and Analysis Division at the U.S. Army Center of Military History. He has a Ph.D. in history from the University of Toledo. His most recent books are *Building Air Bases in the Negev: The U.S. Army Corps of Engineers in Israel, 1979–1982* (1992) and *Buffalo Soldiers, Braves and the Brass: The Story of Fort Robinson, Nebraska* (1993).

James A. Speraw, Jr., is a museum specialist in the Museum Division at the U.S. Army Center of Military History. He has a B.A. in history from the University of Maryland and serves as a staff sergeant in the 158th Cavalry, Maryland National Guard. He was deployed to Southwest Asia as a member of the Special Property Recovery Team, the first unit in the history of the Army to systematically recover materiel from the battlefield for historical documentation.

PREFACE

This narrative is designed to provide an overview of the role of the United States Army in the conflict with Iraq that took place from August 1990 through February 1991. We hope that this study will fill an immediate need by charting the major changes in the Army since the Vietnam years, by showing the scope of the Army's involvement in the Gulf war, and by highlighting the most significant aspects of that participation, to the extent that we could recognize them just after the war.

The initial draft of the manuscript was completed by a team of historians late in 1991, less than one year after the war ended. With one exception, all of the authors were employed at the U.S. Army Center of Military History. The team was divided nearly evenly between civilian and uniformed historians.

This work is based on such sources as were immediately available to the authors. Members of the team used a broad range of official documents and interviews as well as press accounts in assembling this narrative. Each author created a specialized collection of records and other materials according to the needs of each section and the individual author's approach to research. Unless otherwise indicated in the notes, all of the unpublished documents cited remain on file at the Center of Military History.

We do not consider this work definitive. As more documentation becomes available and the passage of time provides different perspectives, other researchers will probe more fully some of the topics and issues mentioned in this book. In fact, it is already plain that questions we did not even raise are becoming the focus of considerable discussion and analysis. Nevertheless, we hope that this volume adequately explains the broad outlines of Army participation in the war and shows the way to further research.

Our involvement in this project was very gratifying. We thank Brig. Gen. Harold W. Nelson, Chief of Military History, 1989–1994, for the opportunity to participate in this endeavor. We also thank the authors and the numerous others without whom it would have been impossible to do the book so quickly or to do it well. We have tried to list in our acknowledgments all of the people who helped, knowing that such mention is in many cases inadequate, but we are indebted to so many people that we saw no reasonable alternative. We alone are responsible for any errors. The views expressed in this book are those of the authors and do not reflect the official policy or position of the Department of Defense or the U.S. government.

FRANK N. SCHUBERT
THERESA L. KRAUS

CONTENTS

Tables

Charts

Maps

Illustrations

THE WHIRLWIND WAR

"It's going to be fast. It's not going to be like Vietnam. It's going to be like nothing you've ever seen."

General John R. Galvin
Stars and Stripes
30 December 1990

Chapter 1
Background To War

The geopolitical problems, border disputes, tribal rivalries, uneven economic growth, and lack of social and political reforms within the Persian Gulf nations are largely the result of developments in Southwest Asia since World War I. The collapse of the Ottoman Empire during the war and the discovery of oil in the Gulf region created the conditions not only for internal chaos but also for external competition among the world's most powerful nations for control of those immense oil resources. Late twentieth-century developments in the area are the direct result of that big power rivalry and its effect on the political development of the states involved.

Emergence of the Post–World War I Persian Gulf States

With the defeat of the Central Powers during World War I, the Ottoman Empire quickly disintegrated. While the United States watched, the European members of the victorious allied coalition, France and Great Britain, reshaped the pieces into spheres of influence, drew boundaries, and set up dynasties. The years immediately after the war saw the emergence of a spate of new Middle Eastern kingdoms and protectorates.

At least twelve of the new political entities that emerged on the Arabian Peninsula after World War I faced problems regarding acceptance of their borders by native inhabitants as well as neighbors. Many traditional tribal and ethnic areas, including regions crossed by nomads, were disrupted by the post–World War I borders. At least twenty-two boundary disputes developed in the region after the war, with armed conflict arising at least twenty-one times and some disputes being settled only to erupt anew. Overlapping claims to grazing land or water, interfamily rivalries, and assertions of historical rights by aggrieved groups all worked against peaceful negotiations. In Iraq's case, the border with Kuwait was one of a number of areas in dispute. Conflicts over the neutral zone between Iraq and Saudi Arabia lasted until 1975, as did border disputes with Iran. The Iraqi-Jordanian border remained in dispute until 1984.[1]

[1] Christine Moss Helms, *Iraq: Eastern Flank of the Arab World* (Washington, D.C.: Brookings Institution, 1984), pp. 42, 44–45; Paul D. Wolfowitz, "Remarks on the Conclusion of the Gulf War," *American-Arab Affairs*, no. 35 (Winter 1990–91): 6; Phebe Marr, *The Modern History of Iraq* (Boulder, Colo.: Westview Press, 1985), p. 1.

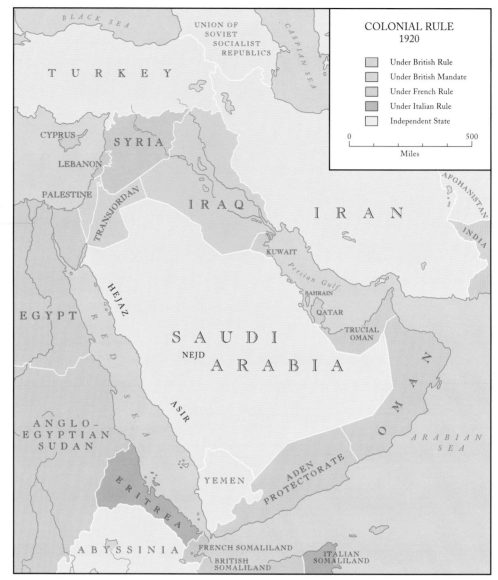

Map 1

Great Britain was the most active of the European imperial powers in the establishment of nations and dynasties. On 18 December 1914, Britain declared Egypt a protectorate, making that country nominally independent. The British also set up monarchies for the offspring of their former ally, the Hashemite Sherif Hussein ibn Ali of Mecca, who had been deposed during the consolidation of Saud family rule in Arabia. They established a protectorate called Iraq and enthroned one son, Feisal, there. They also split off Transjordan (later Jordan), the portion of Palestine that lay east of the Jordan River, from the western part between the river and the Mediterranean Sea, and installed Feisal's brother Abdullah on the throne. In the western portion the British committed themselves to establishment of a national home for Jews. The flurry of coronations ignored only the

Kurds, whose homeland included parts of the newly formed states of Iraq, Syria, Turkey, and Persia (later Iran). Kurdish independence had been on the wartime agenda of the allies, who now decided to postpone action.[2]

The British adopted a pragmatic approach to control of the region. Because of the immense oil potential and important pipeline and transportation routes, political stability was paramount. The best way to achieve that goal was through the establishment of indigenous constitutional monarchies, buttressed and dominated by Britain under the cloak of League of Nations mandates. That approach proved less costly than direct rule (*Map 1*).[3]

The Great War had changed things, underlining the importance of oil for the continued power and prosperity of the industrial world. As early as 1914 the government of Great Britain, quicker than other industrial powers to see the potential importance of oil, had already become majority owner of the Anglo-Persian Oil Company, which controlled major oil fields in Persia. Postwar competition for oil, which pitted France against Britain and later drew in the United States, would go beyond mere commercial rivalries. At stake was the future of the West. The effort to reconstruct the Persian Gulf region represented the beginnings of a global power struggle to secure the oil resources of the Middle East.[4]

Initially the contest for Middle Eastern oil focused largely on Mesopotamia. The Great Power competition for concessions in neighboring Persia had spread westward, stimulated by favorable prewar reports of Mesopotamian oil potential. In fact, one of the major factors in defining Iraq's boundaries was the prospect of a secure pipeline as well as rail and air routes to Palestine and the Mediterranean. Together, Iraq and Transjordan formed a strategic corridor for Britain, linking the Persian Gulf and Anglo-Persian oil production to the British mandate of Palestine and the West. The route across northern Arabia seemed secure, with members of the Hashemite family on the Iraqi and Transjordanian thrones.[5]

In 1930 relations between Iraq and Great Britain underwent a basic change. A treaty widened Iraqi nominal independence considerably, although it left Britain with a major role in foreign policy and granted Britain base rights in Iraq. Still, in 1932 Iraq became the first former mandate to gain a seat in the League of Nations, and a British ambassador replaced the high commissioner.[6]

The first decade of nominal independence for Iraq coincided with a critical period in the development of the oil economies of the Persian Gulf region. In 1932 the Bahrain Petroleum Company struck oil on that rather obscure Gulf island. The modest discovery brought American oil interests in the form of Standard Oil of California (SOCAL) into the Gulf and, more significantly, turned the attention of surveyors to the Arabian mainland, only 20 miles away, where the geological structure was identical to that of Bahrain. The news was especially welcome in Kuwait, where the economy faced ruin as the Japanese success with artificially cultivated pearls destroyed the demand for natural pearls brought up by

[2] David Fromkin, *A Peace To End All Peace: Creating the Modern Middle East 1914–1922* (New York: Henry Holt and Co., 1989), p. 560.

[3] Daniel Yergin, *The Prize: The Epic Quest for Oil, Money, and Power* (New York: Simon and Schuster, 1991), p. 201.

[4] Ibid., pp. 160–64, 184–85.

[5] Helms, *Iraq*, pp. 40–41; Yergin, *The Prize*, p. 185.

[6] Marr, *Modern History of Iraq*, p. 51.

divers in Kuwaiti coastal waters. Kuwait desperately needed new sources of income, and the oil discoveries held out hope for the future.[7]

The rest of the decade saw a succession of oil discoveries and agreements. In May 1933 Standard Oil and Saudi Arabia signed a concession for exploiting local petroleum deposits. In the next year, the Kuwait Oil Company, a joint company formed by Gulf Oil Corporation of the United States and the British Petroleum Company of Great Britain, made a similar deal with the emir of Kuwait. The first big strikes in Kuwait and Saudi Arabia came in 1938. The interdependence of the industrialized world with the oil economies of the Persian Gulf was just beginning.[8]

World War II and the Persian Gulf Region

World War II sped up the process by which the former parts of the Ottoman Empire became nation-states. After that war, and especially after the loss of India in 1947, Great Britain's priorities in the Gulf changed. It found the region no longer necessary as a military frontier to protect its Indian interests but hoped to maintain a presence in the region because of its growing economic involvement in the oil fields.

In much of the Persian Gulf the change to nationhood was preceded by a period of more explicit Western control. In Iraq, Britain put down a wartime attempt to sever its control and depose the monarchy. British occupation of Iraq for the duration of the war followed.

The United States too became directly involved in the Gulf as part of its effort to send supplies to the Soviet Union for the war against Germany.[9] When the United States Army occupied much of Iran and set up the Persian Gulf command in 1942, ignorance of the region was widespread among Americans, policy makers as well as the public. The War Department had no maps of Persia when the decision was made to move into the country, and the State Department's Division of Near-Eastern Affairs had a staff of thirteen, only three of whom spoke some regional language. Initially there seemed little reason for concern. At the time, the United States produced over 60 percent of the world's oil, and the Gulf region, including Iran, Iraq, and Arabian Peninsula, pumped only 5 percent. Wartime demands for oil began the long-term shift of the industry's center of gravity from the Gulf of Mexico and Caribbean to the Middle East, and Americans were quick to adjust.[10]

As U.S. interest in the region grew, European control began to wane. Both the winners and losers in the war were too weary to contest the Middle East's drive for complete independence. Syria gained freedom from France in 1945. Jordan kept the Hashemite monarchy but broke its tie with Britain in 1946. In the most dramatic and traumatic act of nation-building of the period, the Jewish state of Israel emerged from the shambles of the Palestine mandate in 1948. The British decline in the region, under way from about the start of World War II, was gathering momentum.[11]

[7] Yergin, *The Prize*, pp. 283, 292–94.

[8] Ibid., pp. 291, 297, 300.

[9] Francis Robinson, *Atlas of the Islamic World Since 1500* (New York: Facts on File, 1982), p. 158; Marr, *Modern History of Iraq*, pp. 86–87.

[10] Robert Lacey, *The Kingdom: Arabia & the House of Sa'ud* (New York: Harcourt Brace Jovanovich, 1981), p. 261; William B. Quandt, *Saudi Arabia in the 1980s: Foreign Policy, Security, and Oil* (Washington, D.C.: Brookings Institution, 1981), p. 47; Yergin, *The Prize*, p. 393.

[11] Robinson, *Atlas of the Islamic World*, p. 158; John E. Peterson, *Defending Arabia* (New York: St. Martin's Press, 1986), p. 4.

Supply train in the Persian corridor en route to the Soviet Union, loaded with armored vehicles

The Rising Tide of Nationalism

The 1950s evolved as a revolutionary decade in the Middle East. The first shock came in September 1951 when the Iranian government abruptly nationalized the former Anglo-Persian Oil Company—the oldest of the Western concessions. The change was brief. In 1954 the government of Iranian Prime Minister Mohammed Mossadegh was overthrown with U.S. assistance, and a new consortium of Western companies took over the oil concession in October 1954. Americans dominated the new group, with substantial British and lesser French minority interests. The United States was emerging as the dominant Western influence in the region, particularly in the oil industry.[12]

Britain withdrew from Egypt in 1954, and two years later President Gamal Abdul Nasser nationalized the Suez Canal, triggering an ill-conceived effort in 1956 by Britain and France, along with Israel, to destabilize and overthrow the Egyptian government. The Suez crisis may have taught Western powers much about the volatility of the Middle East, but it also confirmed Middle Eastern suspicions of foreign imperialism.

Also in 1956 the youthful Hashemite King Hussein of Jordan dismissed the British commander of his army. In 1958 Egypt and Syria formed the short-lived United Arab Republic, a brief experiment in Pan-Arabism. The revolutionary tide reached Iraq in the same year. A bloody military uprising overthrew Hussein's relatives and revoked the alliance with Britain.[13]

[12] Yergin, *The Prize*, pp. 463–64, 475, 477, 783.

[13] Ibid., pp. 498, 508; Robinson, *Atlas of the Islamic World*, p. 159; Marr, *Modern History of Iraq*, p. 195; Helms, *Iraq*, p. 1.

The 1958 coup by elements of the Iraqi armed forces known as "the Free Officers" brought Brigadier Abd al-Karim Qasim to power. Qasim replaced a regime that had never built viable political institutions to sustain its rule and depended, much like the late Ottoman regime, on the army and bureaucracy as well as family and personal ties for support. Although the work of a small group, the coup reflected widespread discontent with the monarchy's foreign policy, particularly the strong ties to the West and the lack of domestic reform. The new regime's agenda became clear when it demanded major revisions in the nation's relationship with the Iraq Petroleum Company.[14]

In Iraq and elsewhere in the Middle East, oil became the focus of the Arab nationalist tide of the 1950s and 1960s. A 1957 conference of Arab oil experts broached the possibility of an organization of oil-exporting states. Three years later, in September 1960, those states created the Organization of Petroleum Exporting Countries (OPEC) at a meeting in Baghdad, marking the start of a new period of growing assertiveness among oil producers in the Middle East.[15] Nationalizations of oil industries in Libya and Algeria followed as producing countries everywhere took on dominant roles in their relations with oil companies, a transition that climaxed in the OPEC embargo of oil to the West during the October 1973 Arab-Israeli War.

By the 1960s the political order established by Britain in the Middle East had fallen apart. The British had created an imposing institutional facade but had not put down many deep roots. Perhaps their most lasting legacy was an accelerated drive for modernization, financed by the revenues from the oil industry that they had helped nurture. With an overall colonial policy that envisioned gradual conversion of colonies to membership in the Commonwealth, the British had also encouraged indigenous involvement in public administration and created the context in which the nationalist movements could develop. However, this gradualist approach ultimately foundered in the face of Arab and Jewish nationalism. In 1969, already long preoccupied with its economic problems, Britain announced its intent to withdraw its remaining forces from the Middle East. Two years later, the last British troops left Aden at the southern tip of the Arabian Peninsula, leaving the region devoid of the sometimes unwelcome stabilizing power that Great Britain had provided.[16]

The Qasim Regime and the Kuwaiti Border

The 1958 coup marked the beginning of political instability in Iraq. Despite economic and social reforms, Qasim alienated Arab nationalists as well as Western conservatives. He angered the United States by his flirtations with communism and the British by his oil policy. Syria and Egypt resented his harsh treatment of domestic opponents, who included the members of the new Ba'th, or Renaissance, party. That group, initially

[14] Marr, *Modern History of Iraq*, pp. 123, 125, 153; Yergin, *The Prize*, p. 509.

[15] Yergin, *The Prize*, p. 523.

[16] Marr, *Modern History of Iraq*, p. 29; William Jackson, *Withdrawal from Empire, A Military View* (London: Batsford, Ltd., 1986), p. 125; Yergin, *The Prize*, pp. 565–66; Fromkin, *A Peace To End All Peace*, pp. 562–63.

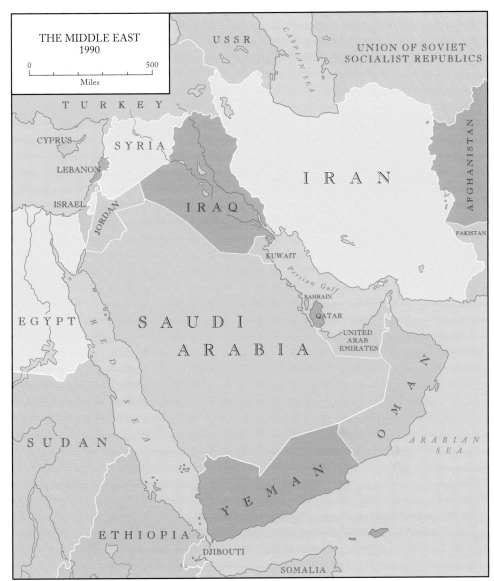

Map 2

organized in Syria just after World War II, combined in its program the two main threads of Arab political thought, Pan-Arabism and radical social change. The Ba'th's tight cellular organization made the party one of the most effective political groups in the region. Disturbed by the growing prominence of Communists in Qasim's government and the failure of a nationalist anti-Communist uprising in northern Iraq, Ba'th leaders concluded that Qasim had to go.[17]

The growing internal and external opposition to the Qasim government reached its climax in 1961. During that year, a revolt among the Kurds in northern Iraq gave the Ba'th allies in its struggle with the regime. But even more serious was Qasim's reaction to Kuwaiti independence. A 1913 treaty between Turkish and British officials had fixed the boundary

[17] Marr, *Modern History of Iraq*, pp. 123, 162–64, 175, 180.

between Kuwait and the Ottoman Empire. However, the outbreak of the World War kept the Ottoman government from formally ratifying the agreement. Iraq accepted that demarcation upon its independence in 1932 but soon changed its mind and asserted its rights to parts of Kuwait. The claim reflected the nation's concern with its limited access to the sea, by way of its 48-mile coastline on the Persian Gulf.[18]

After the 1958 coup, Iraqi leaders actively promoted political instability in the oil-rich monarchies of the Arabian Peninsula. That policy had its roots in antimonarchical fervor and rivalry with Iran for influence in the Gulf. In Kuwait the long-standing border dispute exacerbated the conflict between the radical Iraqi regime and the traditional sheikhdom. Iraq based its maximum original claim to all of Kuwait on the sheikhdom's Ottoman past. The more recent minimum version focused on the islands of Warbah and Būbiyān, which dominated the approach to the Iraqi port of Umm Qaṣr. Iraq claimed those as former parts of the Ottoman province of Al Basrah.[19]

President Qasim revived the larger claim in 1961, asserting that all of Kuwait had once been part of Baṣrah Province. Kuwait, he declared, was an arbitrary creation of the British. Six days after Britain granted Kuwait independence on 19 June 1961, Iraq claimed the entire sheikhdom and prepared an invasion. The Arab League supported Kuwait, admitting the emirate to membership on 20 July, but Iraq backed off only after Britain responded to pleas from its former colony by sending troops. Forces from Arab League members also entered Kuwait in September, stayed into the following year, and departed only when the danger seemed to be past.[20]

The affair proved disastrous for Iraq. Qasim severed ties with the Arab League and broke relations with nations that recognized the former British protectorate, among them Jordan, Lebanon, Tunisia, and the United States. The result completed his isolation from the international community and immensely increased the vulnerability of his regime.[21]

The Ba'th Regime

Qasim's government lasted five years before an Arab nationalist coup organized by the Ba'th ended his rule in 1963. The new regime fell apart within a year, but the Ba'th regrouped to lead a coalition back into power on 17 July 1968. Under Ba'th leadership, Iraq moved toward a more narrow, regional orientation, away from the West and Egyptian-sponsored Pan-Arabism. The Hashemite connection to Jordan was broken permanently, as was any meaningful relationship between the Iraqi Ba'th and the Syrian branch of the party. The Ba'thists also increasingly came to identify the United States as the major supporter of the conservative monarchies in the Gulf and as an enemy of reform.[22]

By the time of the July 1968 coup, a clique of leaders from the town of Tikrīt, among them Saddam Hussein, who was the assistant secretary gen-

[18] Richard F. Nyrop, ed., *Iraq: A Country Study* (Washington, D.C.: Government Printing Office, 1979), p. 68; Yergin, *The Prize*, pp. 236–37.

[19] Nyrop, ed., *Iraq: A Country Study*, p. 236.

[20] Yergin, *The Prize*, p. 524; Trevor N. Dupuy, *How To Defeat Saddam Hussein* (New York: Warner Books, 1991), p. 9; Marr, *Modern History of Iraq*, pp. 180–81; Thomas L. McNaugher, "Arms and Allies on the Arabian Peninsula," *Orbis* (Fall 1984): 519.

[21] Marr, *Modern History of Iraq*, pp. 178–81.

[22] Ibid., pp. 183, 191, 205, 207–08; Helms, *Iraq*, pp. 138–39.

eral, dominated the Iraqi Ba'th party. Although not alone in bringing about the coup, the Ba'th soon took full control and significantly changed the structure and orientation of the Iraqi government. A one-party state with an impressive institutional structure emerged, along with gradual consolidation of power in the hands of one man to a degree not seen since the last days of the monarchy. Buttressed after 1972 by arms provided under a treaty with the Soviet Union, the Ba'th created a strong central authority.[23]

Iraq revived the border dispute with Kuwait in 1973, hoping to gain sovereignty over Warbah and Būbiyān islands in an effort to protect its second largest port at Umm Qaṣr. Fighting broke out in March, when Iraqi troops attacked a Kuwaiti border post overlooking the port and naval base of Umm Qaṣr. Three soldiers, one Iraqi and two Kuwaitis, were killed. Iraq demanded a portion of the coast south of the port city and Warbah and Būbiyān, but retracted its demands under international pressure. The situation gradually improved as Iraq became preoccupied with its own development programs and made a general effort to improve relations with its neighbors during the second half of the 1970s (*see Map 2*).[24]

The episode revealed the fragility of Kuwait's position in the face of determined Iraqi aggression and even raised the possibility of an Iraqi menace to Saudi Arabian oil fields. In recognition of the danger to their own interests, the Saudis supported the Kuwaiti government and even sent 15,000 troops to help defend their small neighbor. They also exerted diplomatic pressure through the Arab League. Although Iraq backed down, it did not give up its claims. Tensions remained high for several years, and occasional reports of Iraqi incursions reminded all concerned that the dispute remained unresolved.[25]

The United States and Middle Eastern Oil

As Britain declined as a regional force in the Middle East, the United States became more influential. World War II had raised American awareness of the region's strategic importance, while the growing involvement of American oil companies had made the region more important to American security and prosperity. Gradually the prewar uncommitted benevolence was replaced by more active and explicit involvement.[26]

The initial association of the United States in Arab minds with the principles of self-determination and anticolonialism helped establish American credibility in the Middle East. That early goodwill faded, however, as American support of Israel became evident. Arab states lost confidence in the evenhandedness of the United States and came to view it as an enemy.

American economic interests in Middle Eastern oil remained largely in private hands. The need for direct government involvement did not become clear until profound changes took place in the oil industry, including the final wave of nationalizations that followed the dramatic 1973 price increases. The United States needed assurance of regular supplies and

[23] Marr, *Modern History of Iraq*, pp. 207–08, 211, 214–15; Frederick W. Axelgard, *A New Iraq? The Gulf War and Implications for U.S. Policy*, The Washington Papers, no. 133 (New York: Praeger, 1988), p. 11.

[24] David L. Price, *Oil and Middle East Security*, The Washington Papers, vol. 4, no. 41 (Beverly Hills, Calif.: Sage Publications, for the Center for Strategic and International Studies, Georgetown University, 1976), p. 60; Nyrop, ed., *Iraq: A Country Study*, p. 237.

[25] Nadav Safran, *Saudi Arabia: The Ceaseless Quest for Security* (Ithaca, N.Y.: Cornell University Press, 1985), p. 138.

[26] David Holden and Richard Johns, *The House of Saud: The Rise and Rule of the Most Powerful Dynasty in the Arab World* (New York: Holt, Rinehart and Winston, 1981), p. 149; Robert W. Stookey, *America & the Arab States: An Uneasy Encounter* (New York: John Wiley and Sons, 1975), pp. xiii, 54–55.

The Dhahran civil air terminal

sought to channel the huge oil profits into areas that enhanced the American fiscal stability and prosperity. After Britain withdrew from the region, the United States adopted a "twin pillars" policy, encouraging the development of regional power centers in Saudi Arabia and Iran, which would be relied on to maintain stability and protect American interests.[27] The new American policy also served another purpose—to block Soviet influence in the region.

The United States and Saudi Arabian Defense

With the emergence of the United States as a bulwark against Soviet influence, the government of Saudi Arabia began to turn toward the United States. The success of a small American military training mission late in World War II helped encourage what ultimately became a long-term connection between the armed forces of both nations. The training mission later expanded to several Saudi bases and remained an important part of postwar American assistance to Saudi Arabia. In 1950 President Harry S. Truman explicitly assured King Abdul Aziz of American support for the preservation of Saudi independence and territorial integrity. Closer ties benefited both countries. The United States gained access to and use of the Dhahran airfield. In exchange the United States provided arms and training for the small Saudi army and helped develop the naval and air services.[28]

The work of the United States Army Corps of Engineers was singularly important to the development of that military relationship. The association dated from the last year of the war, when the corps built a military

[27] Stookey, *America & the Arab States*, pp. 54–55, 263; Michael Sterner, "The Gulf Cooperation Council and Persian Gulf Security," in Thomas Naff, ed., *Gulf Security and the Iran-Iraq War* (Washington, D.C.: National Defense University Press and Middle East Research Institute, 1985), pp. 5–6; Yergin, *The Prize*, p. 646.

[28] Peterson, *Defending Arabia*, p. 56; Stookey, *America & the Arab States*, p. 88; Quandt, *Saudi Arabia in the 1980s*, pp. 48–49, 52; Holden and Johns, *The House of Saud*, pp. 157–58; Anthony H. Cordesman, *The Gulf and the West: Strategic Relations and Military Realities* (Boulder, Colo.: Westview Press, 1988), p. 206; Yergin, *The Prize*, pp. 427–28.

airfield at Dhahran, and gradually solidified with completion of massive construction programs that extended into the 1980s. Although mainly military, these efforts also included civil projects such as the facilities for the national television network and the Dhahran civil air terminal. The terminal project in particular, a striking piece of work that won the American Institute of Architects' first honors in 1963 for designer Minoru Yamasaki, established with the Saudi government the corps' reputation for quality engineering and construction. The Engineer Assistance Agreement of 24 May 1965 cemented that relationship and provided the basis for subsequent Corps of Engineers work in the kingdom.[29]

In the 1970s the relationship changed from that of client and patron to a complex interdependence. The Saudis needed American support for their security as well as help in development projects; the United States needed Saudi cooperation regarding the supply and price of oil and the recycling of Saudi oil profits. Early in the decade the Saudis, with one eye on the power vacuum created by the British withdrawal from the Gulf, asked for a special American military mission to study projects related to national security and make recommendations for future assistance. In response, the United States conducted several studies of Saudi defense requirements and began the sale of modern fighters to the Saudi air force. Other large military sales programs followed, as did modernization and training programs, their costs surging along with Saudi oil profits.[30]

As part of the vastly expanded program of assistance, the United States endorsed a Saudi military strategy that envisioned permanent deployment of large portions of Saudi forces in elaborate military cities near threatened frontiers. They consisted of command and control sites, airfields, hangars, depots, maintenance and repair shops, and elaborate cantonments for soldiers, their families, and supporting civilians. The sites included Khamīs Mushayṭ, close to Yemen; Tabūk in the north near Jordan and Israel; and Ḥafar al Bāṭin, next to Kuwait and Iraq.[31]

The last of those, initially called Al Batin Military City but later renamed for King Khalid, began in 1972. Originally intended for three brigades and a tactical airfield and with an estimated price tag of $9 billion, it was the most costly construction project ever undertaken by the Corps of Engineers. In the 1980s declining oil profits forced reduction of the base to two-brigade size and postponed construction of the airfield. However, when the corps turned the city over to the Ministry of Defense and Aviation in 1986, the final cost was still $7 billion.[32]

The relationship between the United States and Saudi Arabia was based on mutual but not identical interests. Saudi survival depended in large measure on the kingdom's ties to the United States, but the government's specific concerns were complex. The Saudis wanted visible American help through the sale of sophisticated weapons and treatment that indicated that they were as important as America's other major regional allies, Israel and Egypt. The major menace to Saudi Arabia came from the Gulf, where both Iraq and Iran were potentially formidable foes.

[29] Stookey, *America & the Arab States*, p. 88; MS, John T. Greenwood, Diplomacy Through Construction: The U.S. Army Corps of Engineers in Saudi Arabia, Office of History, Headquarters, U.S. Army Corps of Engineers [1988], pp. 2–4, 6. All other unpublished documents are in U.S. Army Center of Military History (CMH), Washington, D.C., files unless otherwise stated.

[30] Safran, *Saudi Arabia*, pp. 172–73, 204; Quandt, *Saudi Arabia in the 1980s*, pp. 51–52; Holden and Johns, *The House of Saud*, p. 359.

[31] Safran, *Saudi Arabia*, pp. 208–09; McNaugher, "Arms and Allies on the Arabian Peninsula," p. 507.

[32] MS, Greenwood, Diplomacy Through Construction, pp. 9–10.

VII Corps area, King Khalid Military City

The Saudis counted on Iran to check Iraq and the United States to curb Iran. The Soviet Union represented a more remote danger. When it came to the security of Saudi oil the interests of both the United States and Saudi Arabia were nearly identical.[33]

The Carter Doctrine

A series of events at the end of the 1970s jolted the United States into a more active approach to the region. To the west of Arabia, across the Red Sea, Ethiopia emerged as a Marxist state and almost immediately went to war with neighboring Sudan. In Iran, Mohammed Riza Shah Pahlevi's regime collapsed in early 1979 and a bloody revolution followed, bringing to power Ayatollah Ruhollah Khomeini's intensely anti-American Islamic republic. In November a group of radical Muslims in Saudi Arabia attacked the great mosque in Mecca, calling into question the stability of the Saudi regime, and before the year ended, Soviet tanks rolled into Afghanistan. The entire region seemed to be in turmoil, and American policy demanded reconsideration.[34]

On 23 January 1980, President Jimmy Carter announced what became known as the Carter Doctrine. In the traditional State of the Union speech before Congress, Carter declared that "an attempt by any outside force to gain control of the Persian Gulf region will be regarded as an assault on the vital interests of the United States of America, and such an assault will be repelled by any means necessary, including military force."[35] Although such a position had long been implied by American support of Saudi Arabia, the speech marked a turning point.

[33] Quandt, *Saudi Arabia in the 1980s*, pp. 142, 156; Safran, *Saudi Arabia*, pp. 151, 214; Cordesman, *The Gulf and the West*, p. 240; Peterson, *Defending Arabia*, pp. 7, 118, 145.

[34] Peterson, *Defending Arabia*, pp. 7, 146–47; Maxwell Orme Johnson, *The Military as an Instrument of U.S. Policy in Southwest Asia: The Rapid Deployment Joint Task Force, 1979–1982* (Boulder, Colo.: Westview Press, 1983), pp. 9–10.

[35] Quote from Yergin, *The Prize*, p. 702; Johnson, *The Military as an Instrument of U.S. Policy*, p. 1.

President Carter acted quickly to secure bases that would enable the United States to move forces into the region. The United States gained access in 1980 to the island of Masira from the government of Oman, the only Gulf country to allow American forces on its territory in peacetime, and wartime use of supporting bases in Somalia (Berbera), Kenya (Mombasa), and Egypt (Ras Banas). A rapid deployment force, established in October 1979, was renamed the Rapid Deployment Joint Task Force in March 1980. Although initially without any assigned troop units, the new organization provided the planning staff necessary for more ambitious contingency operations in the Persian Gulf.[36] Exercise BRIGHT STAR 81 in November 1980 was a more concrete gesture. The United States sent a battalion of the 101st Airborne Division (Air Assault) for two weeks of training with Egyptian forces in the desert west of Cairo. A squadron of eight A–7 aircraft and the rapid deployment force headquarters accompanied the battalion. The exercise symbolized the Carter administration's commitment to protect vital American interests in Southwest Asia.[37]

The Onset of the Iran-Iraq War

The tension between Iran and Iraq had deep roots. Long-standing major problems included rivalries between the minority Sunni Muslims who dominated Iraq and the majority Shiites, Kurdish aspirations to nationhood that challenged both countries as well as Turkey and Syria, and disputes over borders that confined Iraq to its narrow and tenuous access to the Persian Gulf by way of the Shatt al Arab waterway. In 1969, when Britain announced its intent to withdraw from the Gulf, Iran and Iraq already seemed poised for war. Iran was concerned over its neighbor's Pan-Arab Ba'th ideology, zeal for revolutionary socialism, and anti-Western orientation. Iraq feared the Shah's aggressive stance, buttressed as it was by a large armament program and support from the United States. That year did see a small confrontation over the boundary along the Gulf, and disputes flared in the 1970s as well, once when Iran occupied three Gulf islands in 1971 and several times later over the border.[38]

Most of those differences appeared to have been put to rest by the Algiers Treaty in 1975. This agreement settled the border dispute over the Shatt al Arab waterway in Iran's favor and ended the Shah's support of Kurdish insurgents in Iraq. At the same time, Iraq renounced a long-standing claim to the southwestern portion of Iran, an area called Arabistan by Iraq and Khūzestān by Iran, and recognized Iranian control of the disputed Gulf islands.

Saddam Hussein, already a dominant force in the Ba'th party, took over the presidency in 1979, the same year that the fundamentalist Shiite regime came to power in Iran. The Iranian revolutionaries revived past disputes and added a new one, Iranian incitement of Shiite discontent in Iraq. When the Iranian monarchy was overthrown, Iraq

[36] Yergin, *The Prize*, p. 702; Johnson, *The Military as an Instrument of U.S. Policy*, pp. 1, 8, 34; Peterson, *Defending Arabia*, p. 6; Majid Khadduri, *The Gulf War: The Origins & Implications of the Iran-Iraq Conflict* (New York: Oxford University Press, 1988), pp. 143–44.

[37] Johnson, *The Military as an Instrument of U.S. Policy*, pp. 98–99.

[38] Khadduri, *The Gulf War*, p. 17; Marr, *Modern History of Iraq*, pp. 211, 229.

denounced the Algiers Treaty and demanded restoration of the eastern bank of the Shatt al Arab as the border. After a period of mutual sporadic border violations and skirmishes, Iraq attacked its neighbor in earnest in the summer of 1980.[39]

The war, extremely ill conceived, resulted directly from President Saddam Hussein's poor political judgment. The situation could have been contained, as it had been in the past, and Iraqi interests could have been promoted short of war. But Iran appeared weak and disorganized, and the Iraqi president thought he could easily win. His miscalculation of his opponent and corresponding overestimate of his own ability to impose a solution proved disastrous. It was exactly the kind of error that a highly personalized leadership lacking institutional checks and balances was inclined to make.[40]

The Reagan Approach

The Ronald W. Reagan administration, which took office in 1981 when the war between Iran and Iraq was only a few months old, built on the Carter Doctrine. Reagan gave permanence and substance to the new approach and expanded the doctrine beyond the original commitment to deal with threats from outside the Gulf to cover any threat to Saudi Arabia. The United States would not, he avowed at a news conference on 1 October 1981, "stand by and see that taken by anyone that would shut off that oil." Moreover, he indicated readiness to keep open the Strait of Hormuz in the event that Iran tried to close the Persian Gulf to shipping.[41]

Reagan's military plans for Gulf security were more ambitious than those of his predecessor. The Reagan administration regarded the lack of an actual American military presence as a tacit invitation to Soviet intervention. The refusal of the Persian Gulf States to accept American military forces frustrated the Reagan government, so the new administration strengthened the rapid deployment concept with significant expenditures for military construction in the Middle East and nearby areas. In the first Reagan administration, the United States spent nearly $1 billion on construction and support facilities, in Morocco, at Lajes Field in the Azores, and on the Indian Ocean island base of Diego Garcia. Reagan also made the first official assignment of forces to the rapid deployment force on 24 April 1981 and gave it a prominent place in the defense establishment.[42]

While the Carter administration had buried the rapid deployment force within the U.S. Army Readiness Command, Reagan gave it visibility and prominence. In October 1981 the connection to the Readiness Command ended, and the task force became a separate command reporting directly to the secretary of defense through the Joint Chiefs of Staff. One month later, Exercise BRIGHT STAR 82 showed the growth of plans and forces, testing a broad range of tactical and logistical capabilities. On 1 January 1983, the force became one of six U.S. multiservice commands. Renamed United States Central Command, its specified theater of

[39] Marr, *Modern History of Iraq*, pp. 234, 245; Khadduri, *The Gulf War*, pp. 83–85.

[40] Marr, *Modern History of Iraq*, pp. 292, 295; Shahram Chubin and Charles Tripp, *Iran and Iraq at War* (Boulder, Colo.: Westview Press, 1988), p. 7.

[41] Peterson, *Defending Arabia*, p. 7; Quote from Johnson, *The Military as an Instrument of U.S. Policy*, p. 40; Harold H. Saunders, "The Iran-Iraq War: Implications for US Policy," in Naff, ed., *Gulf Security and the Iran-Iraq War*, p. 65.

[42] Khadduri, *The Gulf War*, p. 144; Cordesman, *The Gulf and the West*, p. 137; Johnson, *The Military as an Instrument of U.S. Policy*, p. 95.

operations included Southwest Asia and northeast Africa. Its commander was given charge of nearly all American military activity in that part of the world, including planning for contingencies, coordinating joint exercises involving American and other forces, and administering security assistance. The command oversaw the airborne warning and control system (AWACS), the tanker aircraft at Riyadh, and the Navy's five-ship Middle East Force. Its total deployment potential stood at 300,000.[43]

Despite the increase in the size and capability of the deployable force, there were limits to the American ability to move its forces overseas. The United States still needed bases and facilities in the Persian Gulf, and, although it alone in the West could contribute significantly to the defense of the Gulf, it could not transfer a large combat force on short notice. Throughout the 1980s, Central Command planners emphasized helping friendly nations in the Middle East defend themselves through training, arms sales, and military liaison as well as joint maneuvers. The force reassured countries like Saudi Arabia, which rejected an overt American presence but needed to know that support was available in an emergency.[44]

The success of a rapid transfer of U.S. troops to the Persian Gulf depended on Saudi acceptance and support. Whether the threat came from the Soviet Union or an aggressive neighbor such as Iran or Iraq, access to Dhahran and King Khalid Military City were necessary for any major deployment. Bases at Diego Garcia and elsewhere provided peripheral facilities but were too remote to use as operational centers for the defense of the oil facilities of the upper and central Persian Gulf.[45]

The Gulf Cooperation Council

While the rapid deployment force was an ingredient in the American recipe for regional stability, the United States also wanted to foster the establishment of a viable partnership among the Persian Gulf States. When war started between Iran and Iraq in 1980, Saudi Arabia and the states along the southern shore of the Gulf watched warily. Some, Saudi Arabia, Kuwait, and Bahrain among them, had experienced Iranian threats even before the war started.

The Arab states around the Gulf generally backed Iraq. Saudi Arabia and Kuwait were particularly outspoken in their support. Both contributed substantially to the $40 to $50 billion that all the Gulf States provided Iraq. In addition, both allowed Iraq to use their ports for arms shipments and sold oil on behalf of Iraq. Saudi Arabia also allowed Iraq to build and use a pipeline through its territory.[46]

Although Kuwait was among the most generous contributors to the Iraqi cause, there were some things it would not do. Early in the war, Iraq renewed a proposal it had made in 1975 for 99-year leases on the islands of Būbiyan and Warbah. Kuwait refused. In 1984 Saddam Hussein scaled down his request to a 20-year lease in exchange for an agreement to a definitive border. Once more Kuwait declined.[47]

[43] Peterson, *Defending Arabia*, p. 153; Johnson, *The Military as an Instrument of U.S. Policy*, p. 99.

[44] Cordesman, *The Gulf and the West*, pp. 2, 11, 137; Peterson, *Defending Arabia*, pp. 238–39; Quandt, *Saudi Arabia in the 1980s*, p. 56; Khadduri, *The Gulf War*, p. 144.

[45] Cordesman, *The Gulf and the West*, p. 141.

[46] Johnson, *The Military as an Instrument of U.S. Policy*, p. 114; Khadduri, *The Gulf War*, pp. 126–27; Axelgard, *A New Iraq?*, pp. 73–74; Chubin and Tripp, *Iran and Iraq at War*, p. 154.

[47] Axelgard, *A New Iraq?*, p. 75.

Despite their open support of Iraq during the early stages of the war, Kuwait and Saudi Arabia understood that in the long run Iraq threatened their security. With this threat in mind, they led the effort to create the Gulf Cooperation Council, a regional defense alliance that was established in May 1981. In addition to Kuwait and Saudi Arabia, members included Bahrain, Oman, Qatar, and the United Arab Emirates, a confederation made up of the sheikhdoms of Abu Dhabi, Ajmān, Dubai, Fujiera, Ra's al Khaymah, Sharjah, and Umm al Qaywayn. Iraq, which in 1974 had proclaimed itself "the most important and advanced Arab country in the area" and consequently protector of the Gulf "against dangers and encroachments," sought, but was denied, membership. The council tried to contain the war between its powerful neighbors and ultimately bring both sides to the bargaining table.[48]

Militarily, the Saudi armed forces formed the key to the council's limited defensive capabilities. The kingdom was by far the largest and most powerful of the six members. With oil reserves and revenues that dwarfed those of the others, it had the largest armed forces and good lines of communications. However, its military prowess was only imposing in contrast to that of the other members. A lack of manpower severely limited the capabilities of the Saudis, although the military infrastructure built under Corps of Engineers contracts compensated somewhat by enabling the Saudis to take advantage of the most technically advanced weapons.[49]

While Iran and Iraq slugged it out, the Gulf Cooperation Council progressed toward its goal of creating an effective regional security structure. Despite the pointed rejection of the Iraqi application, the members continued to view fundamentalist Iran as the more immediate threat. Saudi Arabia and Kuwait continued in the forefront as providers of material aid to Iraq.[50]

The council expressed interest in cooperation with the United States but still wanted to keep actual forces at arm's length. Member states did not agree with the United States regarding the nature of the threat to regional stability. The United States emphasized the Soviet peril, at least until the middle of the decade, when American policy makers began to put more stress on strengthening the Arab side of the Gulf against a potential Iranian threat to the flow of oil. The council always worried more about its powerful and quarrelsome neighbors and Israel than about the Soviet Union.[51]

The United States and the Iran-Iraq War

During the 1980s confusion in American policy caused a crisis in relations with the Gulf States. In 1984 the United States, concerned that Iran might win the war and become a long-range menace to the supply of oil, reestablished diplomatic relations with Iraq, after a seventeen-year break. At the same time, some American officials embarked on the clandestine sale of arms to Iran, in direct contradiction to the official effort to withhold them from Tehran. They channeled the money from that venture to

[48] Ibid., p. 73; Khadduri, *The Gulf War*, p. 151; Quote from Ba'th Party, *The 1968 Revolution in Iraq, Experience and Prospects*, the Political Report of the Arab Ba'th Socialist Party in Iraq, January 1974, as cited in Efraim Karsh and Inari Rautsi, *Saddam Hussein, A Political Biography* (New York: Free Press, 1991), p. 63.

[49] Peterson, *Defending Arabia*, p. 200; Cordesman, *The Gulf and the West*, pp. 149, 151, 194, 196; McNaugher, "Arms and Allies," pp. 513–18.

[50] Axelgard, *A New Iraq?*, p. 74.

[51] Cordesman, *The Gulf and the West*, p. 4; Peterson, *Defending Arabia*, pp. 8–9, 242–43; Saunders, "The Iran-Iraq War," p. 70.

F–16 fighters at a Saudi air base during DESERT SHIELD

the support of a Nicaraguan insurgency dear to the heart of President Reagan, casting considerable doubt on American purpose and reliability.[52] The United States also sold AWACS to the Saudis and began joint planning for modernization of the Saudi air force, which had started shortly after the fall of the Shah of Iran.[53]

In 1988, when Kuwait responded to Iranian attacks on its shipping by asking the superpowers for protection, it found the United States eager to provide assistance and reassurance of its steadfast support. To restore its position in the Gulf, the United States agreed to reflag and convoy Kuwaiti ships. Protection of the flow of oil was in any case still a paramount American interest, and President Reagan affirmed his commitment to safeguard Gulf exports. Along with the reflagging went a major American naval deployment to protect the tankers.[54]

The United States and Saudi Arabia maintained their close military relationship throughout the Iran-Iraq war. American diplomats continued to enjoy easy access to the ruling family, although they never convinced the Saudis to agree formally to American access to their bases or abandon their opposition to the stationing of American soldiers in the kingdom. The official Saudi position was that both superpowers should keep their forces out of the Persian Gulf. The Saudis, however, never objected to the American naval contingent in Bahrain and other period-

[52] Axelgard, *A New Iraq?*, pp. 14–16; Cordesman, *The Gulf and the West*, p. 313.

[53] Sterner, "The Gulf Cooperation Council," p. 16; Quandt, *Saudi Arabia in the 1980s*, p. 53; Cordesman, *The Gulf and the West*, p. 240.

[54] Cordesman, *The Gulf and the West*, pp. 2, 310, 327; Yergin, *The Prize*, p. 765; Anthony H. Cordesman and Abraham R. Wagner, *The Lessons of Modern War*, vol. II, *The Iran-Iraq War* (Boulder, Colo.: Westview Press, 1990), pp. 289–90, 391–92.

ic displays of American might in threatening situations. Limited American deployments, among them minesweepers, operational aircraft, and the AWACS, were acceptable.[55]

Reinforcement by U.S. forces in an emergency was always a basic component of Saudi defense planning, albeit only in event of a clear and immediate threat. In fact, to many observers, Saudi installations appeared plainly overbuilt, as if actually intended only for other forces. Saudi bases, with their modern infrastructure and service facilities, could accept an American deployment on very short notice. Those bases, combined with the large quantities of American supplies and equipment purchased ostensibly for Saudi use, ultimately constituted the virtual equivalent of American bases in Saudi Arabia, albeit without the American personnel needed to translate their potential into actual combat power.

The Saudi military buildup was principally oriented on aviation facilities. The Saudis had the largest and some of the most modern air bases in the region, with American contractor employees servicing their equipment and American-trained technicians among their own ground crews. Although rejecting any combined maneuvers, they recognized the need for cooperation with a Central Command deployment when necessary. Short of that necessity, however, they insisted that cooperation remain based on Saudi military buildups with American arms and technical assistance.[56]

Saudi purchases from the United States did facilitate a possible deployment of Central Command forces to Southwest Asia. Any expeditionary force would gain an advantage if its weapons, ammunition, and parts were compatible to the equipment used by a potential host nation. The United States achieved a large measure of interchangeability through military assistance to the Gulf States, despite occasional frustration at the hands of American supporters of Israel, who saw the provision of any arms and equipment to an Arab nation in a different light.[57]

From the Iran-Iraq War to the Invasion of Kuwait

The Iran-Iraq war ended in August 1988 with both sides exhausted and Iraq claiming victory but without Iraqi success in achieving control of the Shatt al Arab. Thereafter, the United States and the Gulf States continued to support Iraq, with American policy in the Persian Gulf trying to moderate Iraqi behavior through closer economic ties. Despite human rights abuses and the continuing development of chemical and nuclear weapons, Iraq's secular leadership seemed less threatening than Iran's religious zealots. Meanwhile, the continued financial contributions of Saudi Arabia and the sheikhdoms of the Gulf Cooperation Council enabled Iraq to rebuild its armed forces, which had been mauled by eight years of war.[58]

In spite of the continued support of Iraq, there was a growing perception in the United States that the major near-term threats to the states of the southern Persian Gulf and to Western oil supplies came not from the Soviet Union but from the Gulf region itself. The Iran-Iraq war had

[55] Cordesman, *The Gulf and the West*, pp. 141–42; Quandt, *Saudi Arabia in the 1980s*, pp. 2, 55.

[56] Cordesman, *The Gulf and the West*, pp. 142–43; Quandt, *Saudi Arabia in the 1980s*, p. 156; Peterson, *Defending Arabia*, pp. 148, 203; Khadduri, *The Gulf War*, p. 143.

[57] Cordesman, *The Gulf and the West*, pp. 7, 13.

[58] Helms, *Iraq*, pp. 163–64; Stephen C. Pelletiere, Douglas V. Johnson II, and Leif R. Rosenberger, *Iraqi Power and U.S. Security in the Middle East* (Carlisle Barracks, Pa.: Strategic Studies Institute, Army War College, 1990), pp. 42, 53; Judith Miller and Laurie Mylroie, *Saddam Hussein and the Crisis in the Gulf* (New York: Times Books, 1990), pp. 148–49, 189–90; *New York Times*, 10 Apr 91; Don Oberdorfer, "Mixed Signals in the Middle East," *Washington Post Magazine* (17 March 1991): 20–21.

shown that both combatants had the resources to sustain massive forces, even in the face of sizable losses. Both now had the experience of a decade of war to go with traditions of political instability. Meanwhile, the Iranian revolution represented a constant danger not only to Iraq, but the southern Gulf States and the industrial West as well.[59]

The end of the war left Iraq both remarkably strong and desperately weak. By regional standards, the Iraqi armed forces appeared formidable, and the war seemed to have forged a strong feeling of national cohesion. Iraq believed that it had won the war and defended Arab interests against the traditional Persian threat. Iraq also saw itself as a major oil power with a dominant role in the region. At the same time, it had piled up a debt estimated as high as $70 billion. The $5 to $6 billion in interest that the government paid annually consumed nearly one-third of its oil revenues.[60]

The war crippled Iraq's economic development program and stifled the social mobility that had attended it. The years of fighting left much of the nation's industrial capacity weakened and its ability to export oil severely impaired. Economically, the war also diminished Iraq's international position and forced the regime into a position of dependence on its wealthy neighbors. That reliance actually represented a continuation of the relationship that had sustained Iraq through the war, although Iraq was convinced that it had not received adequate support. Iraqi resentment focused largely on wealthy Kuwait, which held territory that Iraq coveted and considered its own.[61]

Although the states of the southern Gulf did not appreciate the depth of Iraqi bitterness at their supposedly inadequate support, they were not blind to the threat implicit in Iraq's postwar military strength and confidence. The Saudis knew that the border with Iraq was ideal for armor operations and that the entire Arabian Peninsula was vulnerable to attack from the northeast. Major Saudi oil facilities were only 200 miles away. King Khalid Military City, with its two armored brigades, provided only limited security, and other Gulf Cooperation Council members had no military forces of consequence. Any assault on Kuwait might easily become the first stage of a two-phase attack on the rest of the peninsula.[62]

The United States shared Saudi Arabia's concerns. Kuwait, the door to the entire oil-producing region, was very vulnerable. Threats to its stability, either from external or internal pressures, would have wide ramifications, endangering the flow of oil and the economic health of the industrial West (*Map 3*).[63]

In the two years after the fighting between Iran and Iraq ended, Iraq increased its pressure on Kuwait. The war had left the Shatt al Arab approach to Al Başrah and the city itself a shambles. The opening of the waterway to shipping remained in the distant future. Iraq again turned its attention to the border that it shared with Kuwait. In addition to demands for compensation for revenues allegedly lost due to Kuwaiti oil sales in excess of OPEC quotas and for oil pumped from oil

[59] Cordesman, *The Gulf and the West*, p. 81.

[60] Yergin, *The Prize*, p. 767; Pelletiere, Johnson, and Rosenberger, *Iraqi Power and U.S. Security*, p. 53; Tom (Tsutomu) Kono, "Road to the Invasion," *American-Arab Affairs*, no. 34 (Fall 1990): 29–30.

[61] Marr, *Modern History of Iraq*, p. 245; Miller and Mylroie, *Saddam Hussein and the Crisis in the Gulf*, pp. 8–9, 193–94; Kono, "Road to the Invasion," p. 41.

[62] Cordesman, *The Gulf and the West*, pp. 4, 93–94; Safran, *Saudi Arabia*, p. 206; McNaugher, "Arms and Allies," p. 496; Karsh and Rautsi, *Saddam Hussein, A Political Biography*, p. 63.

[63] Cordesman, *The Gulf and the West*, pp. 4, 309; Peterson, *Defending Arabia*, p. 246.

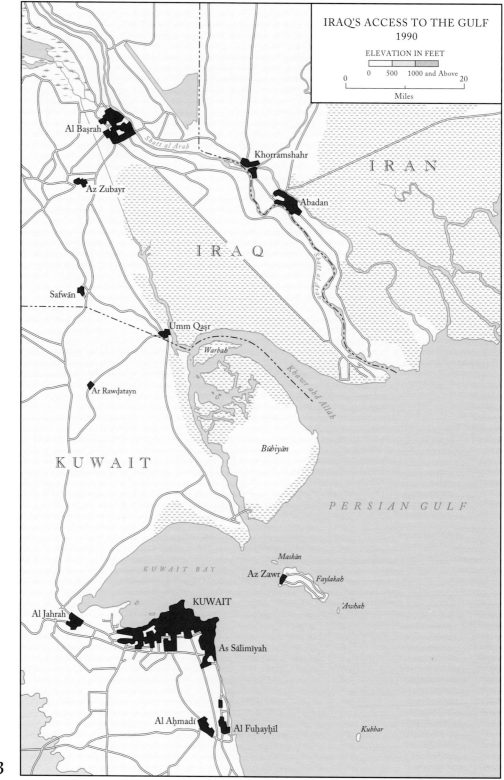

IRAQ'S ACCESS TO THE GULF
1990

ELEVATION IN FEET

0   500   1000 and Above

Miles

I R A N

Al Baṣrah

Shatt al Arab

Khorramshahr

Az Zubayr

Abadan

I R A Q

Shatt al Arab

Safwān

Umm Qaṣr

Warbah

Khawr abd Allah

Ar Rawḍatayn

Būbiyān

K U W A I T

P E R S I A N   G U L F

Maskān

Az Zawr

Faylakah

KUWAIT BAY

KUWAIT

'Awhah

Al Jahrah

As Sālimīyah

Al Aḥmadī   Al Fuḥayḥil

Kubbar

Map 3

fields claimed by Iraq, Saddam Hussein's government renewed its interest in Būbiyān and Warbah islands. He cleared the way for action by
beginning negotiations for a final settlement with Iran, massing troops
on the Kuwaiti border, and sounding out the American reaction to a
possible military move into Kuwait. Saddam appeared to ignore the
restatement of the Carter Doctrine by the administration of President
George H. Bush in National Security Directive 26 of October 1989,
warning that the United States would defend its vital interests by force
if necessary.[64]

Meanwhile, Kuwait struggled to find a counterbalance to the
increasing Iraqi threat. It had a military agreement with Egypt that dated
from the last phase of the Iran-Iraq war and even made an overture
toward Iran, which might again serve as a potential counter to Iraq. But
neither those connections nor the Gulf Cooperation Council had the
potential strength to ward off a determined Iraqi attack. Kuwait needed
protection, like that provided by Great Britain at the turn of the century
and by the United States in 1987. Yet, like Saudi Arabia and other Arab
states, Kuwait accepted American construction support and air defense
missiles but stopped short of inviting an American presence in support
of its own defense. That refusal, grounded in strong feelings of national
pride, race, and religion, reflected an unrealistic assessment of its situation. As historian Theodore Draper wrote during the year of the tanker
war, in which Kuwaiti oil tankers began to fly American flags, "Kuwait
was too rich to be left alone and too weak to defend itself."[65]

During the first seven months of 1990, Iraqi troop movements and
presidential bombast foreshadowed the impending crisis. But, like
Saudi Arabia and Kuwait, the United States did not recognize the
imminence of the Iraqi threat until it was too late.[66] On 2 August 1990,
when Iraqi tanks rolled through Kuwait to the Saudi border and
Saddam Hussein's government declared that Kuwait no longer existed
as an independent country, perceptions quickly changed. President
Bush quickly decided to uphold the Carter Doctrine and commit the
United States to direct military action.

With a large majority of the nations of the world opposed to the
invasion of Kuwait, President Bush built a broad-based coalition in
support of intervention. The United States, which took the lead in
developing and coordinating opposition to Iraq, achieved a diplomatic
triumph of great magnitude and far-reaching consequence. Urged forward by the United States, the United Nations General Assembly
imposed an embargo on Iraq, and the Security Council voted to con-
demn the invasion. Almost immediately coalition forces moved toward
Southwest Asia. By far the largest contributor to the force, the United
States honored commitments to Saudi Arabia first made by President
Truman.[67] The result was Operation DESERT SHIELD, which before it was
over became the DESERT STORM.

[64] National Security Directive 26, *U.S. Policy Toward the Persian Gulf*, 2 Oct 89; Kono, "Road to the Invasion," pp. 41–43; *New York Times*, 21 Mar 91; Oberdorfer, "Mixed Signals," pp. 21, 36.

[65] Kono, "Road to the Invasion," p. 41; Cordesman, *The Gulf and the West*, p. 108; Quote from Miller and Mylroie, *Saddam Hussein and the Crisis in the Gulf*, p. 215.

[66] Oberdorfer, "Mixed Signals," pp. 22–23, 36–41.

[67] Yergin, *The Prize*, p. 772; Dupuy, *How To Defeat Saddam Hussein*, p. 19; Miller and Mylroie, *Saddam Hussein and the Crisis in the Gulf*, pp. 227–28.

Chapter 2
THE ARMY OF DESERT STORM

The Army that deployed in 1990 to Saudi Arabia, the product of almost twenty years of reform and experimentation, bore little resemblance to the Army that left the Republic of Vietnam in 1972. At the end of the Vietnam War some weapon systems were obsolete while others were obsolescent, and conventional mobile warfare had to compete with counterinsurgency operations for military doctrinal, organizational, and training attention. At the same time, indiscipline, drug abuse, racism, and poor training were epidemic within the ranks.[1]

By 1990 those problems were either well in the past or on their way to resolution. Not only were new weapons in place, but military theorists and planners had also broadened the range of possible conflicts to include from small tactical deployments of short duration to a major war over a broad front. Meanwhile, the Army had addressed its internal problems. High standards of recruitment, training, and discipline were in place. In the intervening two decades, the service rebuilt itself around the concept of an all-volunteer force designed to integrate the Army Reserve and Army National Guard into its wartime organization. Army leaders evolved new doctrine for ready forces, focused on the acquisition of new equipment to support that doctrine, tied both together with rigorous training programs, and concentrated on leader development initiatives that increased officer and noncommissioned officer professionalism. By the summer of 1990 the U.S. Army was a technologically sophisticated, highly trained, well-led, and confident force.

New Doctrine

A reassessment of how the Army fought began with President Richard M. Nixon's "Guam Doctrine" of 1969, in which he stated that the United States would maintain a smaller defense establishment able to fight a "1-½ war" contingency. This was generally interpreted to mean that the Army would prepare to engage in a general war, probably in the European theater, and in a minor conflict, presumably a Third World counterinsurgency. The smaller Army envisioned by Nixon faced growing challenges, however. American intelligence agencies in the early 1970s

[1] On problems within the military at the end of the Vietnam War, see William L. Hauser, *America's Army in Crisis* (Baltimore: Johns Hopkins University Press, 1973); Paul L. Savage and Richard A. Gabriel, *Crisis in Command: Mismanagement in the Army* (New York: Hill and Wang, 1978); Charles C. Moskos, Jr., "The American Combat Soldier in Vietnam," *Journal of Social Issues* 31 (1975); *Data on Vietnam Era Veterans* (Washington, D.C.: Reports and Statistics Service, Office of the Controller, Veterans Administration, June 1971); Lee N. Robbins, *The Vietnam Drug User Returns* (Washington, D.C.: Government Printing Office, 1974); Edward L. King, *The Death of the Army* (New York: Saturday Review Press, 1972); and *Comprehensive Report: Leadership for the 1970s, USAWC Study of Leadership for the Professional Soldier* (Carlisle Barracks, Pa.: Army War College [AWC], 1971).

[2] For summaries of the military balance, see Amos A. Jordan and William J. Taylor, *American National Security: Policy and Process* (Baltimore: Johns Hopkins University Press, 1981); and John M. Collins, *American and Soviet Military Trends Since the Cuban Missile Crisis* (Washington, D.C.: Center for Strategic and International Studies, 1978).

[3] Chaim Herzog, *The Arab-Israeli Wars: War and Peace in the Middle East* (New York: Random House, 1982), introduces the extensive literature on the war. Also see Herzog, *The War of Atonement: October 1973* (Boston: Little, Brown and Co., 1975).

[4] Jac Weller, "Infantry and the October War: Foot Soldiers in the Desert," *Army* 24 (August 1974).

[5] TRADOC Annual Rpt of Major Activities, FY 1974, pp. 14–19; and TRADOC Annual Rpt of Major Activities, FY 1975, ch. 1.

[6] Quote from John L. Romjue, *From Active Defense to AirLand Battle: The Development of Army Doctrine 1973–1982* (Fort Monroe, Va.: TRADOC, 1984), pp. 14–15. To survey the doctrine's evolution, see ibid., passim, and Donn A. Starry, "To Change an Army," *Military Review* (March 1983).

[7] Field Manual (FM) 100–5, *Operations* (May 1986); Robert A. Doughty, *The Evolution of U.S. Army Tactical Doctrine, 1946–1976*, Leavenworth Paper 1 (Fort Leavenworth, Kans.: Command and General Staff College [CGSC], 1979); Romjue, *From Active Defense to AirLand Battle*; Paul H. Herbert, *Deciding What Has to Be Done: General William E. DePuy and the 1976 Edition of FM 100–5, Operations*, Leavenworth Paper 16 (Fort Leavenworth, Kans.: CGSC, 1988); and Romie L. Brownlee and William J. Mullen III, *Changing An Army: An Oral History of General William E. DePuy, USA Retired* (Carlisle Barracks, Pa.: Military History Institute [MHI], 1985).

noted an increase of five Soviet armored divisions in Europe, the continued restationing of Soviet Army divisions farther to the west, and a major improvement in equipment, with T–62 and T–72 tanks replacing older models and with a corresponding modernization of other classes of weapons.[2] If general war had come to Europe during the 1970s, the U.S. Army and its NATO allies would have confronted Warsaw Pact armies that were both numerically and qualitatively superior.

The Arab-Israeli War that began on 6 October 1973 intensified concerns about the deadliness of modern weapons as well as the Army's Vietnam-era concentration on infantry-airmobile warfare at the expense of other forces.[3] American observers who toured those battlefields began to create a new tactical vocabulary when they reported on the "new lethality" of a Middle Eastern battlefield where, in one month of fighting, the Israeli, Syrian, and Egyptian armies lost more tanks and artillery than existed in the entire United States Army, Europe. Improved technology in the form of antitank guided missiles, much more sophisticated and accurate fire-control systems, and vastly improved tank cannons heralded a far more costly and deadly future for conventional war. Technology likewise brought changes to battlefield tactics. Egyptian infantry armed with missiles enjoyed significant successes against Israeli tank units, bolstering the importance of carefully coordinated combined arms units.[4] It seemed clear that in future wars American forces would fight powerful and well-equipped armies whose soldiers would be proficient in the use of extremely deadly weapons. Such fighting would consume large numbers of men and quantities of materiel. It became imperative for the Army to devise a way to win any future war quickly.[5]

A new operations field manual, the Army's specific response to new conditions that required new doctrine, was preeminently the work of General William E. DePuy, commander of the new U.S. Army Training and Doctrine Command (TRADOC). Surveying conditions of modern warfare that appeared to reconfirm the lessons of World War II, DePuy wrote in 1976 much of a new edition of Field Manual 100–5 and enlisted the help of the combat arms schools' commandants to revise and improve his ideas. Depuy's Field Manual 100–5 initially touted a concept known as the Active Defense, which once more focused on "the primacy of the defense." The handbook evolved from its first publication to become the keystone of a family of Army manuals that completely replaced the doctrine being practiced at the end of the Vietnam War.[6]

From these modest beginnings the Army's new doctrine, AirLand Battle, slowly emerged. In its final form AirLand doctrine was actually a clear articulation of fundamentals that American generals had understood and practiced as early as World War II, with an appropriate and explicit recognition of the role air power played in making decisive ground maneuver possible.[7] The U.S. Army Command and General Staff College at Fort Leavenworth, Kansas, acknowledged AirLand

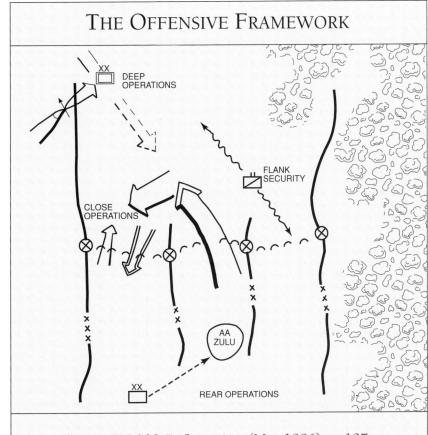

THE OFFENSIVE FRAMEWORK

DEEP OPERATIONS

FLANK SECURITY

CLOSE OPERATIONS

AA ZULU

REAR OPERATIONS

Source: FM 100-5, *Operations* (May 1986), p. 107.

Chart 1

Battle's basis in traditional concepts of maneuver warfare by teaching it and making frequent use of historical examples.[8]

In practical terms, the doctrine required commanders to supervise three types of operations simultaneously. In close operations, large tactical formations such as corps and divisions fought battles through maneuver, close combat, and indirect fire support. Deep operations helped to win the close battle by engaging enemy formations not in contact, chiefly through deception, deep surveillance, and ground and air interdiction of enemy reserves. Objectives of deep operations were to isolate the battlefield and influence when, where, and against whom later battles would be fought. Rear operations proceeded simultaneously with the other two and focused on assembling and moving reserves, redeploying fire support, continuing logistical efforts to sustain the battle, and providing continuity of command and control. Security operations, traffic control, and maintenance of lines of communications were critical to rear operations (*Chart 1*).

AirLand Battle generated an extended doctrinal and tactical discussion in the service journals after 1976 that helped to clarify and, occa-

[8] Field Manual 100–5 uses historical examples to illuminate the discussion of doctrine. The Command and General Staff College tactics instruction similarly uses examples of high-intensity World War II operations. The same was true of Leavenworth's battle analysis class. Christopher R. Gabel, *The 4th Armored Division in the Encirclement of Nancy* (Fort Leavenworth, Kans.: CGSC, 1986), p. 23.

[9] For a sample of the discussion, see "Army's Training and Doctrine Command: Getting Ready to Win the First Battle…and the Rest," *Armed Forces Journal International* 114 (May 1977); William E. DePuy, "FM 100–5 Revisited," *Army* 30 (November 1980); John S. Doerfel, "The Operational Art of the AirLand Battle," *Military Review* 62 (May 1982); Robert A. Doughty and L. D. Holder, "Images of the Future Battlefield," *Military Review* 58 (January 1978); Gregory Fontenot and Matthew D. Roberts, "Plugging Holes and Mending Fences," *Infantry* (May–June 1978); William S. Lind, "Some Doctrinal Questions for the United States Army," *Military Review* 57 (March 1977); Dan G. Loomis, "FM 100–5 Operations: A Review," *Military Review* 57 (March 1977); John M. Oseth, "FM 100–5 Revisited: A Need for Better Foundation Concepts?," *Military Review* 60 (March 1980); Donn A. Starry, "A Tactical Evolution—FM 100–5," *Military Review* 58 (August 1978); Robert E. Wagner, "Active Defense and All That," *Military Review* 60 (August 1980); and Huba Wass de Czege and L. D. Holder, "The New FM 100–5," *Military Review* 62 (July 1982).

sionally, to modify the manual.[9] General Donn A. Starry, who succeeded DePuy in 1977 at the Training and Doctrine Command, directed a substantial revision that concentrated on the offensive and added weight to the importance of deep operations by stressing the role of deep ground attack in disrupting the enemy's follow-on echelons of forces. Changes mainly dealt with ways to exploit what B. H. Liddell Hart described as the indirect approach in warfare by fighting the enemy along his line of least expectation in place or time.

The 1982 edition of Field Manual 100–5 stressed that the Army had to "fight outnumbered and win" the first battle of the next war, a concept that required a trained and ready peacetime force. The manual acknowledged the armored battle as the heart of warfare, with the tank as the single most important weapon in the Army's arsenal. Success, however, hinged on a deft manipulation of all of the arms, but especially infantry, engineers, artillery, and air power, to give free rein to the maneuver forces. Using that mechanized force, the doctrine required commanders to seize the initiative from the enemy; act faster than the enemy could react; exploit depth through operations extending in space, time, and resources to keep the enemy off balance; and synchronize the combat power of ground and air forces at the decisive point of battle.

AirLand Battle doctrine had additional utility because it helped to define both the proper equipment for its execution and the appropriate organization of military units for battle. Indeed, the doctrine explicitly acknowledged the growth of technology both as a threat and as a requirement. The U.S. Army and its NATO allies could not match large Soviet and Warsaw Pact forces either in masses of manpower or in masses of materiel. To that extent, AirLand Battle was both an organizational strategy and a procurement strategy. To fight outnumbered and survive, the Army needed to better employ the nation's qualitative edge in technology.

New Equipment

Military theorists generally agreed that a defending army could hope for success if the attacking enemy had no greater than a 3:1 advantage in combat power. The best intelligence estimates in the 1970s, however, concluded that the Warsaw Pact armies enjoyed a much larger advantage. Continuing budget constrictions made unlikely the possibility of increasing the size of the American military to match Soviet growth. To solve the problem of how to fight an enemy that would almost certainly be larger, the United States relied, in part, on technologically superior hardware that could defeat an enemy at ratios higher than 1:3. To achieve that end, the Army in the early 1970s began work on the "big five" equipment systems: a new tank, a new infantry combat vehicle, a new attack helicopter, a new transport helicopter, and a new antiaircraft missile.

Several factors affected new equipment design. Among the most important was the flourishing technology encouraged by the pure and applied research associated with space programs. Although the big five equipment originated in the years before AirLand Battle doctrine was first enunciated, that doctrine quickly had its effect on design criteria. Other factors were speed, survivability, and good communications, which were essential to economize on small forces and give them the advantages they required to defeat larger, but presumably more ponderous, enemies. Target acquisition and fire control were equally important, since the success of a numerically inferior force really depended on the ability to score first-round hits.

Such simply stated criteria were not easy to achieve, and all of the weapon programs suffered through years of mounting costs and production delays. A debate that was at once philosophical and fiscal raged around the new equipment, with some critics preferring simpler and cheaper machines, fielded in greater quantities.[10] The Department of Defense persevered, however, in its preference for technologically superior systems and managed to retain funding for most of the proposed new weapons. Weapon systems were expensive, but defense analysts recognized that personnel costs were even higher and pointed out that the services could not afford the manpower to operate increased numbers of simpler weapons. Nevertheless, spectacular procurement failures, such as the Sergeant York division air defense gun, kept the issue before the public, and such cases kept program funding for other equally complex weapons on the agenda for debate.[11]

The first of the big five systems, the M1 Abrams tank, weathered considerable criticism and, in fact, began from the failure of a preceding tank program. The standard tanks in the Army inventory had been various models of the M48 and M60, both surpassed in some respects by new Soviet equipment. The XM803 was the successor to an abortive joint American-German Main Battle Tank–70 project and was intended to modernize the armored force. Concerned about expense, Congress withdrew funding for the XM803 in December 1971, thereby canceling the program, but agreed to leave the remaining surplus of $20 million in Army hands to continue conceptual studies.

For a time, designers considered arming tanks with missiles for long-range engagements. This innovation worked only moderately well in the M60A2 main battle tank and the M551 Sheridan armored reconnaissance vehicle, both of which were armed with the MGM51 Shillelagh gun launcher system. In the late 1960s, however, tank guns were rejuvenated by new technical developments that included a fin-stabilized, very high velocity projectile that used long-rod kinetic energy penetrators. Attention centered on 105-mm. and 120-mm. guns as the main armament of any new tank.

Armored protection was also an issue of tank modernization. The proliferation of antitank missiles that could be launched by dismounted infantry and mounted on helicopters and on all classes of vehicles demonstrated the need for considerable improvement. At the same

[10] These themes were treated most thoroughly in the years after 1980 by the Military Reform Caucus, an informal group of members of Congress, military analysts, and journalists. On the caucus and its criticisms, see MS, Theresa Kraus, The Military Reform Caucus [Center of Military History (CMH), 1987]. Reformers focused on concrete issues of how to train, equip, and organize military forces, rather than on questions of strategy, and often used Dana Rasor's Project on Military Procurement to communicate with the press. Members held diverse views, but among those criticizing the complexity and costs of weapons were Walter Kross, *Military Reform: The High-Tech Debate in Tactical Air Forces* (Washington, D.C.: National Defense University [NDU] Press, 1985); and James Fallows, *National Defense* (New York: Random House, 1981). For a general survey, see Asa A. Clark et al., *The Defense Reform Debate: Issues and Analysis* (Baltimore: Johns Hopkins University Press, 1984).

[11] MS, Bruce R. Pirnie, Duster to DIVAD: The Army's Search for a Radar-Directed Gun [CMH, 1987].

time, weight was an important consideration because the speed and agility of the tank would be important determinants of its tactical utility. No less important was crew survivability; even if the tank were damaged in battle, it was important that a trained tank crew have a reasonable chance of surviving to man a new vehicle.

The Army made the decision for a new tank series in 1972 and awarded developmental contracts in 1973. The first prototypes of the M1, known as the XM1, reached the testing stage in 1976, and the tank began to arrive in battalions in February 1980. The M1 enjoyed a low silhouette and a very high speed, thanks to an unfortunately voracious gas turbine engine. Chobham spaced armor (ceramic blocks set in resin between layers of conventional armor) resolved the problem of protection versus mobility. A sophisticated fire control system provided main gun stabilization for shooting on the move and a precise laser range finder, thermal-imaging night sights, and a digital ballistic computer solved the gunnery problem, thus maximizing the utility of the 105-mm. main gun. Assembly plants had manufactured more than 2,300 of the 62-ton M1 tank by January 1985, when the new version, the M1A1, was approved for full production. The M1A1 had improved armor and a 120-mm. main gun that had increased range and kill probability. By the summer of 1990 several variations of the M1 had replaced the M60 in the active force and in a number of Army Reserve and National Guard battalions. Tankers had trained with the Abrams long enough to have confidence in it. In fact, many believed it was the first American tank since World War II that was qualitatively superior to Soviet models.[12]

The second of the big five systems was the companion vehicle to the Abrams tank: the M2 Bradley infantry fighting vehicle, also produced in a cavalry fighting version as the M3. Its predecessor, the M113 armored personnel carrier, dated back to the early 1960s and was really little more than a battle taxi. The 1973 Arab-Israeli War demonstrated that infantry should accompany tanks, but it was increasingly clear that the M113 could not perform that function because it was far slower than the M1, its obsolescence aside. European practice also influenced American plans for a new vehicle. German infantry used the well-armored Marder, a vehicle that carried seven infantrymen in addition to its crew of three, was armed with a 20-mm. gun and coaxial 7.62-mm. machine gun in a turret, and allowed the infantrymen to fight from within the vehicle. The French Army fielded a similar infantry vehicle in the AMX–10P in 1973. The Soviets had their BMP–1s, which had a 73-mm. smoothbore cannon and an antitank guided missile, as early as the late 1960s. Variations of the BMP were generally considered the best infantry fighting vehicles in the world during the 1980s. The United States had fallen at least a decade behind in the development of infantry vehicles. General DePuy and General Starry, who at that time commanded the U.S. Army Armor Center and School at Fort Knox, Kentucky, agreed the Army needed a new infantry vehicle and began studies in that direction.

[12] Orr Kelly, *King of the Killing Zone: The Story of the M1, America's Super Tank* (New York: W. W. Norton, 1989); Steve E. Dietrich and Bruce R. Pirnie, *Developing the Armored Force: Experiences and Visions. An Interview With MG Robert J. Sunell, USA Retired* (Washington, D.C.: CMH, 1989).

In 1980, when Congress restored funding to the Infantry Fighting Vehicle Program, the Army let contracts for prototypes, receiving the first production models the next year. Like the Abrams, the Bradley was a compromise among competing demands for mobility, armor protection, firepower, and dismounted infantry strength. As produced, the vehicle was thirty tons, but carried a 25-mm. cannon and 7.62-mm. coaxial machine gun to allow it to fight as a scout vehicle and a TOW (tube launched, optically tracked, wire command-link guided) missile launcher that enhanced the infantry battalion's antiarmor capability. The vehicle's interior was too small for the standard rifle squad of nine: it carried six or seven riflemen, depending on the model. That limitation led to discussions about using the vehicle as the "base of fire" element and to consequent revisions of tactical doctrine for maneuver. Critical to its usefulness in the combined arms team, however, the Bradley could keep up with the Abrams tank.

By 1990 forty-seven battalions and squadrons of the Regular Army and four Army National Guard battalions had M2 and M3 Bradleys. A continuing modernization program that began in 1987 gave the vehicles, redesignated the M2A1 and M3A1, the improved TOW 2 missile. Various redesigns to increase survivability of the Bradley began production in May 1988, with these most recent models designated the A2.[13]

The third of the big five systems was the AH–64A Apache attack helicopter. The experience of Vietnam showed that the existing attack helicopter, the AH–1 Cobra, was vulnerable even to light antiaircraft fire and lacked the agility to fly close to the ground for long periods of time. The AH–56A Cheyenne helicopter, canceled in 1969, had been intended to correct those deficiencies. The new attack helicopter program announced in August 1972 drew from the combat experience of the Cobra and the developmental experience of the Cheyenne to specify an aircraft that could absorb battle damage and had the power for rapid movement and heavy loads.[14] The helicopter would have to be able to fly nap of the earth and maneuver with great agility to succeed in a new antitank mission on a high-intensity battlefield.[15]

The first prototypes flew in September 1975, and in December 1976 the Army selected the Hughes YAH–64 for production. Sophisticated night vision and target-sensing devices allowed the pilot to fly nap of the earth even at night. The aircraft's main weapon was the HELLFIRE (helicopter launched fire and forget) missile, sixteen of which could be carried in four launchers. In place of the antitank missile the Apache could carry seventy-six 70-mm. (2.75-inch) Hydra 70 folding-fin rockets. It could also mount a combination of eight HELLFIRE missiles and thirty-eight rockets. In the nose, the aircraft mounted a Hughes 30-mm. single-barrel chain gun.

Full-scale production began in 1982, and the Army received the first aircraft in December 1983. As of the end of 1990 the McDonnell Douglas Helicopter Company (which purchased Hughes in 1984) had

[13] Department of the Army (DA), *Weapon Systems: United States Army, 1991* (Washington, D.C.: Government Printing Office, 1991), p. 17; Bruce R. Pirnie, *From Half-Track to Bradley: Evolution of the Infantry Fighting Vehicle* (Washington, D.C.: CMH, 1987); "M2A2/M3A2 Bradley Fighting Vehicles," *Army* 41:6 (June 1991).

[14] On the relationship between close air support issues, requirements for aircraft designed to participate in the direct ground battle, the competition for missions, and the design of the Cheyenne helicopter, see Charles E. Kirkpatrick, *The Army and the A–10: The Army's Role in Developing Close Air Support Aircraft, 1961–1971* (Washington, D.C.: CMH, 1987).

[15] As distinguished from simple low-level flight, nap of the earth is flight close to the earth's surface, following the contours of the ground as closely as possible. Airspeed and altitude vary according to terrain, weather, and the enemy situation.

delivered 629 Apaches, which equipped 19 active attack helicopter battalions. When production was completed, the Apaches were intended to equip 26 Regular Army, 2 Reserve, and 12 National Guard battalions, a total of 807 aircraft.[16]

The fourth of the big five systems, the fleet of utility helicopters, had already been modernized with the fielding of the UH–60A Black Hawk to replace the UH–1 Iroquois used during the Vietnam War. The Black Hawk could lift an entire infantry squad or a 105-mm. howitzer with its crew and some ammunition. The new utility helicopter was both faster and quieter than the UH–1.

The last of the big five equipment was the Patriot air defense missile, conceived in 1965 as a replacement for the HAWK (homing all the way killer) and the Nike-Hercules, both based on 1950s' technology. The Patriot benefited from lessons drawn from design of the antiballistic missile system, particularly the highly capable phased-array radar. The solid-fuel Patriot missile required no maintenance and had the speed and agility to match known threats. At the same time, its system design was more compact, more mobile, and demanded smaller crews than previous air defense missiles. Despite its many advantages, or perhaps because of the ambitious design that yielded those advantages, the development program of the missile, initially known as the SAM-D (surface-to-air missile-developmental), was extraordinarily long, virtually spanning the entire careers of officers commissioned at the end of the 1960s. The long gestation period and escalating costs incident to the Patriot's technical sophistication made it a continuing target of both press and congressional critics. Despite controversy, the missile went into production in the early 1980s, and the Army fielded the first fire units in 1984.

A single battalion with Patriot missiles had more firepower than several HAWK battalions, the mainstay of the 32d Army Air Defense Command in Germany. Initial fielding plans envisaged forty-two units, or batteries, in Europe and eighteen in the United States, but funding and various delays slowed the deployment. By 1991 only ten half-battalions, each with three batteries, were active.

Originally designed as an antiaircraft weapon guided by a computer and radar system that could cope with multiple targets, the Patriot also had the potential to defend against battlefield tactical missiles such as the Soviet FROG (free rocket over ground) and Scud. About the time the first units were fielded, the Army began to explore the possibility that the Patriot could also have an ATBM, or antitactical ballistic missile, mission. In 1988 testing authenticated the PAC–1 (Patriot antitactical ballistic missile capability, phase one) computer software, which was promptly installed in existing systems. The PAC–2 upgrade was still being tested in early 1991.

The Patriot missile, in the hands of the troops in the summer of 1990, was expected to be very effective against attacking aircraft and to have a limited capability to intercept rockets and missiles.[17] The Patriot was not, however, a divisional air defense weapon, although it could

[16] *Weapon Systems: United States Army, 1991*, p. 21; "The AH–64A Apache Attack Helicopter," *Army* 41:4 (April 1991).

[17] "Army's Patriot: High-Tech Superstar of Desert Storm," *Army* 41:3 (March 1991); "Modernization Program Systems Prove Themselves in the Desert," *Army* 41:5 (May 1991) For further information on the Patriot system, see Appendix A..

extend a certain amount of air defense protection over the battlefield from sites in a corps area. Air defense protection of the division still relied on the Vulcan gun and Chaparral missile, stopgap weapons more than twenty years old, and on the light Stinger missile. The failure of the Sergeant York gun project and the continuing difficulties involved in selecting its successor meant that the air defense modernization program essentially stopped forward of the division rear boundary.

The big five were by no means the only significant equipment modernization programs the Army pursued between 1970 and 1991. Other important Army purchases included the multiple launch rocket system (MLRS); a new generation of tube artillery to upgrade fire support; improved small arms; tactical-wheeled vehicles, such as a new 5-ton truck; and a family of new command, control, communications, and intelligence hardware. By the summer of 1990 this equipment had been tested and delivered to Army divisions.

While most of those developments began before the Training and Doctrine Command's first publication of AirLand Battle doctrine, a close relationship between doctrine and equipment swiftly developed. Weapons modernization encouraged doctrinal thinkers to consider more ambitious concepts that would exploit the capabilities new systems offered. A successful melding of the two, however, depended on the creation of tactical organizations that were properly designed to use the weapons in accordance with the doctrine. So, while doctrinal development and equipment modernization were under way, force designers also reexamined the structure of the field army.

New Organization

A basic issue in force design has always been how to configure units so as to direct the maximum firepower at the enemy. In the post–World War II era, conflicting influences complicated decisions about the correct size and organization of divisions and corps. The hazards of the nuclear and chemical battlefield deeply ingrained the notion that the concentration of large bodies of troops was dangerous.[18] Improved weapons technology further strengthened the imperative for dispersion, a trend facilitated by steadily improving communications systems. Despite that, the classic need to exert overwhelming force at the decisive point and time remained the basic prescription for winning battles.

America's isolated strategic position posed additional problems, particularly in view of the growth of Soviet conventional power in Europe and an evident Warsaw Pact intention to fight a quick ground war that would yield victory before the North Atlantic Treaty Organization (NATO) could mobilize and before the United States could send divisions across the Atlantic.[19] Time thus governed decisions that led to forward deployment of substantial ground forces in overseas theaters and the pre-positioning of military equipment in threatened areas. Issues of

[18] On the development of Army divisions between World War II and the early 1970s, see John C. Binkley, "A History of U.S. Army Force Structuring," *Military Review* 57 (February 1977): 67–82; A. J. Bacevich, *The Pentomic Era: The U.S. Army Between Korea and Vietnam* (Washington, D.C.: NDU Press, 1986); Robert P. Haffa, Jr., *Rational Methods, Prudent Choices: Planning U.S. Forces* (Washington, D.C.: NDU Press, 1988); William W. Kaufmann, *Planning Conventional Forces, 1950–1980* (Washington, D.C.: Brookings Institution, 1982); Virgil Ney, *Evolution of the U.S. Army Division 1939–1968* (Fort Belvoir, Va.: Combat Developments Command [CDC], 1969); John J. Tolson, *Airmobility, 1961–1971*, Vietnam Studies (Washington, D.C.: CMH, 1973); Maxwell D. Taylor, *Swords and Plowshares* (New York: W. W. Norton, 1972); and Glen Hawkins, *United States Army Force Structure and Force Design Initiatives, 1939–1989* (Washington, D.C.: CMH, 1991).

[19] For a discussion of this and related issues, see Haffa, *Rational Methods, Prudent Choices: Planning U.S. Forces*; and Kaufmann, *Planning Conventional Forces, 1950–1980.*

strategic force projection likewise influenced decisions about the types, numbers, and composition of divisions.

Fiscal and political considerations also loomed large. With the end of the Vietnam War, Congress abolished the vastly unpopular draft, created the all-volunteer force, and cut the Army's appropriation. The consequence was necessarily a much heavier reliance on reserve components, which was known as the Total Army concept (*Chart 2*).[20] Under this principle, the Army transferred many essential technical services and combat units to the Army Reserve and Army National Guard. As an economy measure, some Regular Army divisions were reconfigured with only two active-duty brigades instead of three. Upon mobilization, they were to be assigned a National Guard "roundout" brigade that trained with the division in peacetime.[21] Such plans ensured that equipment modernization would extend to the reserve components, with such equipment as M1 Abrams and Bradley fighting vehicles going to National Guard battalions at the same time they were issued to the Regular Army.

Such pragmatism had as much to do with Army organization as what might be called philosophical questions. Differing schools of thought within the Army tended to pull force designers in different directions. There were those, strongly influenced by the war in Vietnam, who believed that the future of warfare lay in similar wars, probably in the Third World. Accordingly, they emphasized counterinsurgency doctrine and light and airmobile infantry organization. Advocates of light divisions found justification for their ideas in the Soviet invasion of Afghanistan in 1979, when it appeared possible that the United States might have to confront Soviet forces outside the boundaries of Europe. That uncertainty encouraged ideas that called for the creation of light, quickly deployable infantry divisions.

Still, the emphasis within the Army throughout the decade of the 1970s remained on conventional war in Europe, where Chief of Staff General Creighton W. Abrams, General DePuy, and like-minded officers believed the greatest hazard, if not the greatest probability of war, existed. They conceived of an intense armored battle, reminiscent of World War II, to be fought in the European theater. If the Army could fight the most intense battle possible, some argued, it also had the ability to fight wars of lesser magnitude.

While contemplating the doctrinal issues that led to publication of Field Manual 100–5, General DePuy also questioned the appropriateness of existing tactical organization to meet the Warsaw Pact threat. DePuy suggested and General Frederick C. Weyand, who succeeded Abrams as chief of staff in 1974, agreed that the Army should study the problem more closely. Thus, in May 1976, DePuy organized the Division Restructuring Study Group to consider how the Army divisions might best use existing weapons of the 1970s and the planned weapons of the 1980s. DePuy's force structure planners, like those con-

[20] On the volunteer Army, see Willard Latham, *The Modern Volunteer Army Program: The Benning Experiment, 1970–1972* (Washington, D.C.: Government Printing Office, 1974); and Harold G. Moore and Jeff M. Tuten, *Building a Volunteer Army: The Fort Ord Contribution* (Washington, D.C.: Government Printing Office, 1975).

[21] In reaction to the failure to use the reserves in Vietnam, General Creighton Abrams, during his term as Army chief of staff, deliberately structured the Army Reserve and National Guard with respect to the Regular Army so that it would literally be impossible to go to war without calling up the citizen-soldiers. See Lewis Sorley, "Creighton Abrams and Active-Reserve Integration in Wartime," *Parameters* 21:2 (Summer 1991): 35–50.

cerned with phrasing the new doctrine, were also powerfully influenced by the 1973 Arab-Israeli War.[22]

The Division Restructuring Study Group investigated the optimum size of armored and mechanized divisions and the best mix of types of battalions within divisions. Weapons capabilities frankly influenced much of the work and had a powerful effect on force design. Planners noted a continuing trend toward an increasing number of technicians and combat support troops (the "tail") to keep a decreasing number of combat troops (the "teeth") in action. In general, the group concluded that the division should retain three brigades, each brigade having a mix of armored and mechanized infantry battalions and supported by the same artillery and combat service units. To simplify the task of the combat company commander, the group recommended grouping the same type of weapons together in the same organization, rather than mixing them in units, and transferring the task of coordinating fire support from the company commander to the more experienced battalion commander. Other recommendations suggested creating a combat aviation battalion to consolidate the employment of helicopters and adjusting the numbers of weapons in various units.[23]

General Starry, commander of the Training and Doctrine Command, had reservations about various details of the *Division Restructuring Study*. He was especially concerned that an emphasis on the division and tactics was too limiting. In his view, the operational level of war above the division demanded the focus of Army attention. After reviewing an evaluation of the Division Restructuring Plan, Starry ordered his planners to build on that work in a study he called Division 86.

The Division 86 proposal examined existing and proposed doctrine in designing organizations that could both exploit modern firepower and foster the introduction of new weapons and equipment. In outlining an armored division with six tank and four mechanized infantry battalions and a mechanized division with five tank and five mechanized infantry battalions, it also concentrated on heavy divisions specifically designed for combat in Europe, rather than on the generic division. Anticipating a faster pace of battle, planners also tried to give the divisions flexibility by increasing the number of junior leaders in troop units, thereby decreasing the span of control.

The Army adopted Division 86 before approving and publishing the new AirLand Battle doctrine, yet General Starry's planners assumed that the new doctrine would be accepted and therefore used it to state the tasks the new divisions would be called on to accomplish. Similar efforts, collectively known as the Army 86 studies, pondered the correct structure for the infantry division, the corps, and larger organizations.[24] Although Infantry Division 86 moved in the direction of a much lighter organization that would be easy to transport to other continents, such rapidly deployable contingency forces lacked the endurance and, frankly, the survivability, to fight alongside NATO divisions in open terrain. The

[22] See John L. Romjue, *A History of Army 86*, 2 vols. (Fort Monroe, Va.: TRADOC, 1982).

[23] Complete recommendations are in *Division Restructuring Study* (Fort Monroe, Va.: TRADOC, 1977).

[24] See Romjue, *A History of Army 86*, vol. 2, chs. II, III, IV.

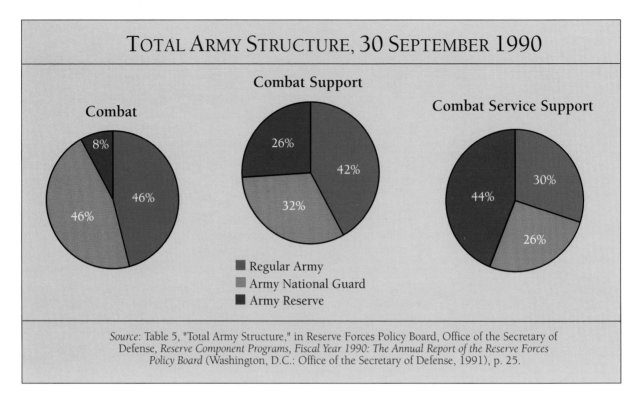

TOTAL ARMY STRUCTURE, 30 SEPTEMBER 1990

Combat

8%
46%
46%

Combat Support

26%
42%
32%

Combat Service Support

30%
44%
26%

■ Regular Army
■ Army National Guard
■ Army Reserve

Source: Table 5, "Total Army Structure," in Reserve Forces Policy Board, Office of the Secretary of Defense, *Reserve Component Programs, Fiscal Year 1990: The Annual Report of the Reserve Forces Policy Board* (Washington, D.C.: Office of the Secretary of Defense, 1991), p. 25.

Chart 2

search for a high-technology solution that would give light divisions such capacity led to a wide range of inconclusive experiments with the 9th Infantry Division, officially designated a test unit.

Under the "Army of Excellence" program, military leaders investigated further the plans for a heavier mechanized and armored force begun by Division 86 but reconsidered the role of light divisions. In August 1983 Chief of Staff General John A. Wickham, Jr., directed the Training and Doctrine Command to restudy the entire question of organization. The resulting Army of Excellence force design acknowledged the need for smaller, easily transportable light infantry divisions for the expressed purpose of fighting limited wars. At the same time, the plan kept the heavy divisions proposed by the Division 86 study, although with some modifications.[25]

Thus the new force structure—five corps with a total of twenty-eight divisions—available to the U.S. Army in the summer of 1990 was the product of almost twenty years of evolving design that had carefully evaluated the requirements of doctrine for battle and the capabilities of modern weapons. Army leaders now believed that they had found a satisfactory way to maximize the combat power of the division, enabling it confidently to fight a larger enemy force. The other vital task had been to devise a training system that imparted the necessary skills so that properly organized and equipped soldiers could carry out their combat and support functions, effectively accomplishing the goals specified by the new doctrine.

[25] See *The Army of Excellence Final Report*, 3 vols. (Fort Leavenworth, Kans.: U.S. Army Combined Arms Combat Development Activity Force Design Directorate, 1984).

New Training

The Renaissance infantryman who trailed a pike and followed the flag, like his successor in later wars who shouldered a musket and stood in the line of battle, needed stamina and courage, but required neither a particularly high order of intelligence nor sophisticated training. The modern infantryman, expected to master a wide range of skills and think for himself on an extended battlefield, faces a far more daunting challenge. To prepare such soldiers for contemporary battle, TRADOC planners in the 1970s and 1980s evolved a comprehensive and inter-connected training program that systematically developed individual and unit proficiency and then tested that competence in exercises intended to be tough and realistic.[26]

Individual training was the heart of the program, and the Training and Doctrine Command gradually developed a methodology for training, which clearly defined the desired skills and then trained the soldier to master those skills.[27] This technique cut away much of the superfluous and was an exceptional approach to the repetitive tasks that made up much of soldier training. Once the soldier mastered the skills appropriate to his grade, skill qualification tests continued to measure his grasp of his profession through a series of written and actual performance tests.

The training of leaders for those soldiers became increasingly important through the 1970s and 1980s.[28] By the summer of 1990 the Training and Doctrine Command had created a coherent series of schools that trained officers in their principal duties at each major turning point in their careers.[29] Lieutenants began with an officer basic course that introduced them to the duties of their branch of service and, after a leavening of experience as senior lieutenants or junior captains, returned for an officer advanced course designed to train them for the requirements of company, battery, and troop command. The new Combined Arms and Services Staff School (CAS³) at Fort Leavenworth instructed successful unit commanders in the art of battalion staff duty. The premier officer school remained the Command and General Staff College, which junior majors attended before serving as executive and operations officers of battalions and brigades. Although all Army schools taught the concepts and language of AirLand Battle, it was at Leavenworth that the professional officer attained real fluency in that doctrine. For the selected few, a second year at Fort Leavenworth in the School of Advanced Military Studies offered preparation as division operations officers and Army strategists. Finally, those lieutenant colonels with successful battalion commands behind them might be chosen to attend the services' prestigious senior schools: the Army War College, Carlisle Barracks, Pennsylvania; the Navy War College, Newport, Rhode Island; the Air War College, Maxwell Air Force Base, Alabama; and the National War College or Industrial College of the Armed Forces, Fort McNair, Washington, D.C. Beyond those major schools, officers might attend one

[26] Critiques from within the Army, such as Arthur S. Collins, Jr., *Common Sense Training: A Working Philosophy for Leaders* (San Rafael, Calif.: Presidio Press, 1978), spurred changes to training methods.

[27] TRADOC Regulation 350–7, *Systems Approach to Training* (1988), discusses the design of Army training; FM 25–100, *Training the Force* (1988), outlines the principles of all Army training. In 1990, FM 25–101, *Battle-Focused Training*, applied those principles to battalions and smaller organizations.

[28] Major studies include Officer Personnel Management System (OPMS) Task Group, *Review of Army Officer Educational System*, 3 vols. (Washington, D.C.: DA, 1971), known as the Norris Report; [TRADOC OPMS Task Group], *Education of Army Officers Under the Officer Personnel Management System*, 2 vols. (Fort Monroe, Va.: TRADOC, 1975); [Study Group for the Review of Education and Training for Officers], *Review of Education and Training For Officers (RETO)*, 5 vols. (Washington, D.C.: DA, 1978); and [Study Group for the Chief of Staff, Army], *Professional Development of Officers Study Final Report*, 6 vols. (Washington, D.C.: DA, 1985).

[29] The Army outlined the skills it expected an officer to develop at each grade in the Military Qualification Standards (MQS). Standard Testing Program (STP) 21–I–MQS, *Military Qualification Standards I: Manual of Common Tasks (Precommissioning Requirements)* (Washington, D.C.: DA, 1990); STP 21–II–MQS, *Military Qualification Standards II: Manual of Common Tasks for Lieutenants and Captains* (Washington, D.C.: DA, 1991).

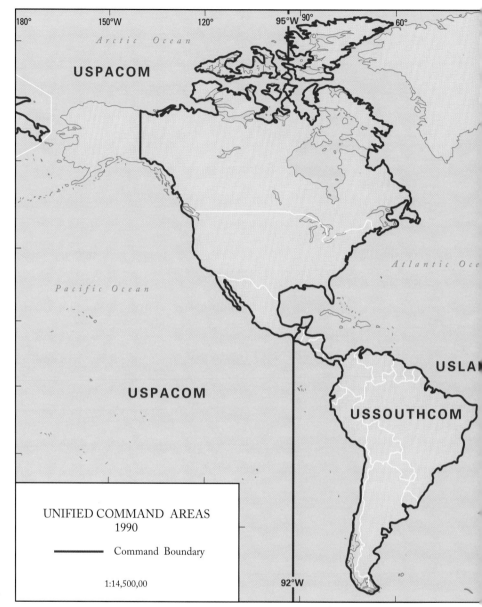

UNIFIED COMMAND AREAS
1990

——————— Command Boundary

1:14,500,00

Map 4

[30] Army Regulation (AR) 351–1, *Individual Military Education and Training* (1987), outlines the structure of the Army's formal schools; for the scope of resident training, see DA Pamphlet 351–4, *Army Formal Schools Catalog* (1990).

[31] DA Pamphlet 600–25, *U.S. Army Noncommissioned Officer Professional Development Guide* (Washington, D.C.: DA, 1987).

or more short courses in subjects ranging from foreign language to mess management.[30] The career officer thus expected to spend roughly one year of every four in some sort of school, either as student or as teacher.

The noncommissioned officer (NCO) corps also required a formal school structure, which ultimately paralleled that of the officer corps.[31] Initially, the young specialist or sergeant attended the primary leadership development course at his local NCO academy, a school designed to prepare him for sergeant's duties. The basic noncommissioned officer course trained sergeants to serve as staff sergeants (squad leaders) in their arm or service. Local commanders selected the soldiers who attended that course.

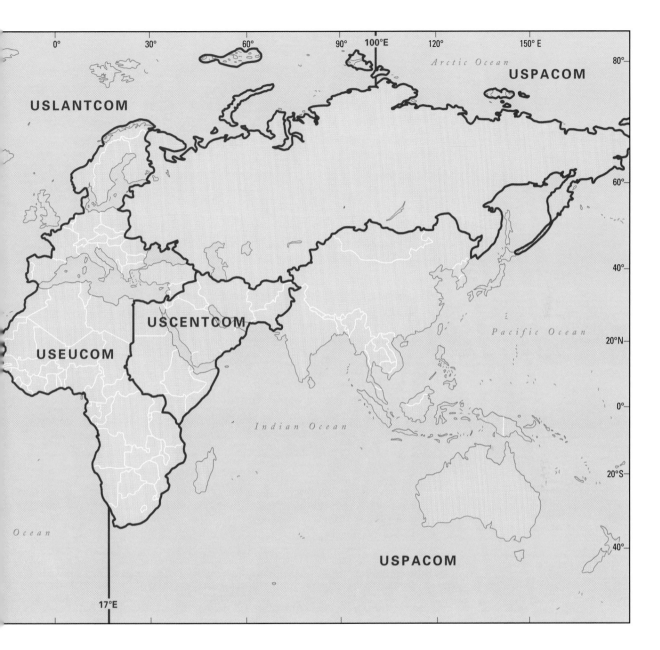

Staff sergeants and sergeants first class selected by a Department of the Army board attended the advanced noncommissioned officer course, where the curriculum prepared them to serve as platoon sergeants and in equivalent duties elsewhere in the Army. At the apex of the structure stood the U.S. Army Sergeants Major Academy at Fort Bliss, Texas, where a 22-week course qualified senior sergeants for the top noncommissioned officer jobs in the Army.

Professional development, of course, went hand in hand with both individual training and unit training programs. Progressively more sophisticated programs melded the individual's skills into those of the squad, platoon, company, and battalion. Just as the individual was tested, so were units, which underwent a regular cycle of evaluations, known at the lowest level as the Army Training and Evaluation Program. Periodically, both Regular Army and reserve-component units in the continental United States went to the National Training Center at Fort Irwin, California, where brigade-size forces fought realistic, unscripted maneuver battles against an Army unit specially trained and equipped to emulate Warsaw Pact forces.[32] Brigades assigned in Europe conducted similar exercises at the Combat Maneuver Training Center at Hohenfels, Germany, while light forces exercised at the Joint Readiness Training Center at Fort Chaffee, Arkansas.

Tactical units of the Army were subject to further tests and evaluations, the most important of which were exercises to reinforce units in Europe, generally known as REFORGER, the short form for "return of forces to Germany." Similarly, units went to the Middle East in BRIGHT STAR exercises, conducted in cooperation with the armed forces of the Republic of Egypt, and to Korea in TEAM SPIRIT exercises. Periodic readiness evaluations tested divisions' capacity for quick deployment, especially the 82d Airborne Division, long the Army's quick reaction force, and the new light divisions that had been designed for short-notice contingency operations.

As the Army entered the summer of 1990 it was probably better trained than at any time in its history and certainly better trained than it had been on the eves of World War I, World War II, and the Korean War. Sound training practices produced confident soldiers. Realistic exercises acquainted soldiers with the stress of battle as well as peacetime training could hope to manage. Force-on-force maneuvers, such as those at the National Training Center, tested the abilities of battalion and brigade commanders to make the combined arms doctrine work and confirmed commanders' confidence in their doctrine, their equipment, and their soldiers. But as thorough and professional as Army training was, the most important fact was that all training and exercises were specifically keyed to the doctrinal precepts laid down in Field Manual 100–5. Training brought the diverse strands of AirLand Battle together.

AirLand Battle would have been merely another academic exercise, however, had the Army not attended to the problems of morale, discipline, and professionalism that were obvious at the end of the Vietnam War. By confronting drug abuse, racism, and indiscipline directly, leaders gradually corrected the ills that beset the Army in 1972. Schools and progressive military education played a part, as did strict qualitative management procedures that discharged the worst offenders. More importantly, officer and NCO education stressed the basics of leadership and responsibility to correct the problems that existed at the end of the Vietnam War. Over time, in one of its most striking accomplishments, the Army cured itself.[33]

[32] Daniel P. Bolger, *Dragons at War: 2–34 Infantry in the Mojave* (Novato, Calif.: Presidio Press, 1986), depicts the realism of NTC training. The Army's goal was to send each active maneuver battalion to the National Training Center every two years, and each reserve-component roundout maneuver battalion every four years. *Army Focus* (Washington, D.C.: DA, 1990), p. 32. See also Anne E. Chapman, *The Origins and Development of the National Training Center, 1976–1984* (Fort Monroe, Va.: Office of the Command Historian, United States Army Training and Doctrine Command, 1992).

[33] For evidence of progress, see the *Department of the Army Historical Summary* (Washington, D.C.: CMH, annually) for fiscal years 1972–1986. They show a progressive decrease in the "indicators of indiscipline." At the same time, standards of recruitment and retention improved. Ninety percent of Army recruits graduated from high school in 1986, compared to 54.3 percent in fiscal year 1980.

The Army on the Eve of DESERT SHIELD

Army accomplishments over the years after the end of the Vietnam War were impressive. By 1990 the claim could reasonably be made that the service had arrived at a sound doctrine, the proper weapons, an appropriate organization, and a satisfactorily trained, high-quality force to fight the intense war for which General DePuy and his successors had planned. International developments in the first half of the year seemed, however, to have made the Army's modernization unnecessary. The apparent collapse of Soviet power and withdrawal of Soviet armies into the Soviet Union itself, the disintegration of the Warsaw Pact, and the pending unification of Germany removed the justification for maintaining a powerful U.S. Army in Europe. In view of all of these developments, the immediate political question was whether the nation needed to maintain such a large and expensive Army. In the interests of fiscal retrenchment, the Army projected budgets for the following five years that would decrease the total size of the active service from approximately 780,000 in 1989 to approximately 535,000 soldiers in 1995.[34]

Even after the Iraqi invasion of Kuwait and even while Army units were in the midst of frantic preparations for movement to Saudi Arabia, Army organizations concerned with "downsizing" the service to meet the long-range strength ceilings continued to work. Army QUICKSILVER and VANGUARD task forces had deliberated on the size of the Army's field and base force structure, recommending inactivations that now directly affected the forces preparing to deploy to the Middle East. The "Army 2000" study group at Headquarters, Department of the Army, considered the implications of such decreases in size and pondered the ways a smaller Army could continue to carry out its major missions. Among the major actions that the group managed in July and August 1990 was a scheduled command post exercise named HOMEWARD BOUND, designed to test a possible removal of Army units from Europe.[35] Army 2000 staff officers also weighed concerns voiced at the highest levels of the service that the drive to save defense dollars not produce another "hollow" force and thus reproduce the disaster of Task Force SMITH in July 1950 at the start of the Korean War.[36]

Department of the Army planners in operations and logistics found themselves in the anomalous situation of pulling together the combat and support units scheduled for deployment to the Middle East at the same time that their colleagues in personnel were proceeding with plans for a reduction in force. The latter plans were temporarily suspended when the Army's deployment to Saudi Arabia was announced, and orders went out likewise suspending retirements from active duty and routine separations from the Army. Still, uncertainty about the future, both for individuals and for major Army units, persisted as the Army prepared for overseas service and, possibly, for war.

[34] Various sections of *Army Focus* (September 1990) consider these questions. Especially see "National Security Environment," pp. 5–14.

[35] Memo, U.S. Army Concepts Analysis Agency (CAA) for Deputy Chief of Staff for Operations and Plans (DCSOPS), 6 Aug 90, sub: CPX HOMEWARD BOUND.

[36] Memo for Commander/Chief, CMH, 11 Jul 90, sub: Selcom Meeting, 10 July 1990. For details on the Task Force SMITH debacle, see Roy E. Appleman, *South to the Naktong, North to the Yalu (June–November 1950)*, United States Army in the Korean War (Washington, D.C.: CMH, 1961), ch. 6.

[37] CMH Fact Sheet, 9 Apr 91, sub: U.S. Army Operation URGENT FURY Statistics.

[38] The broadest survey of the era, although one that hews very much to orthodox judgments about Army performance in these skirmishes, is Daniel P. Bolger, *Americans at War: 1975–1986, An Era of Violent Peace* (Novato, Calif.: Presidio Press, 1988).

[39] For a summary, see MS, Theresa Kraus, DOD Reorganization and the Army Staff [CMH, 1990]. A discussion of earlier attempts at reorganization is Edgar F. Raines, Jr., and David R. Campbell, *The Army and the Joint Chiefs of Staff: Evolution of Army Ideas on the Command, Control, and Coordination of the U.S. Armed Forces, 1942–1985* (Washington, D.C.: CMH, 1986).

[40] *Army Focus* (September 1990), p. 23.

[41] The limited combat in Grenada and Panama did not rigorously test the systems used by Army units in those actions. In Panama, for example, eleven AH–64A aircraft flew a total of 246 combat hours, of which 138 were at night. Other weapon and communications systems were similarly unproven. A General Accounting Office analysis of hardware employment in Grenada (URGENT FURY), Lebanon, Libya (ELDORADO CANYON), and deployments to the Persian Gulf (EARNEST WILL) showed "significant problems" with joint communications equipment and several categories of precision-guided munitions. [United States General Accounting Office], Report to the Chairman, Committee on Government Operations, House of Representatives, *U.S. Weapons: The Low-Intensity Threat Is Not Necessarily a Low-Technology Threat*, USGAO/PEMD–90–13 (March 1990), app. II.

[42] Such discussions began as soon as the possibility of war arose. The best articulated warnings about the dangers of a ground war came from analyst Edward Luttwak in various television interviews as the virtually unopposed air campaign unfolded. Also see, for example, Gary Hart, "The Military's New Myths," *New York Times*, 30 Jan 91; "Intimations of a Long War," *Washington Post*, 25 Jan 91; "M1A1 will get stern test from T–72," *Washington Times*, 24 Jan 91.

Despite improvements in personnel, doctrine, and weapons, the Army that went to Saudi Arabia was largely inexperienced. The limited combat actions in Grenada and Panama, which were not real tests of AirLand Battle doctrine, gave very few soldiers experience under fire. The URGENT FURY operation in Grenada involved fewer than 8,000 Army soldiers, with actual Army combat being limited to the 1st and 2d Battalions of the 75th Ranger Regiment and certain units of the 82d Airborne Division. In fact, Army strength on the island during the period of combat probably did not exceed 2,500, and the heaviest combat, occurring during the first hours of the landing on 25 October 1983, was borne by Company A, 1st Battalion, 75th Rangers.[37] The fighting during Operation JUST CAUSE in Panama was similarly limited, although more Army units, totaling about 27,000 soldiers, participated.

In neither case was there serious opposition of the kind the Army had been training for decades to meet. Far and away the most important aspects of Operations URGENT FURY and JUST CAUSE were their utility in testing the effectiveness of U.S. joint forces command-and-control procedures, areas in which both operations, as well as subsequent joint deployments, revealed continuing problems.[38] Joint doctrine, a matter of concern since the Goldwater-Nichols Defense Reorganization Act of 1986 emphasized it, was far from complete.[39] Not until 1990 did the Army, acting for the Joint Chiefs of Staff, complete drafts of Joint Publication 3–0, *Doctrine for Unified and Joint Operations*, and prepare Joint Publication 3–07, *Joint Doctrine for Low-Intensity Conflict*, as a test manual to be issued late in the year. The two most important volumes, *Campaign Planning* and *Contingency Operations*, remained to be written.[40]

Still, the important questions that remained blunted the edge of pervasive official optimism as the Army deployed to the Middle East during the summer of 1990. Chief among them was how well new weapons would perform. The M1 series Abrams and M2 and M3 Bradleys had never faced combat. Neither had the multiple launch rocket system, the Patriot missile, the AH–64A Apache, or modern command, control, and communications mechanisms that were supposed to weld those sophisticated implements into a coherent fighting system.[41] Problems with weapons procurement over the preceding decade had conditioned many to doubt how well the new high-technology weapons would perform. As a result, media pundits and military commentators warned of a long and bloody war of attrition if the Middle East crisis could not be resolved through negotiation.[42]

The volunteer Army was a second source of concern. Overshadowed in the public eye by discussions about the efficacy of modern weapons and within the Army by the immediate concerns of preparing for war, the question of how to guarantee an adequate stream of trained replacements and a sufficient supply of new equipment loomed behind the possibility that the ground battle would be long and costly. The Army of July 1990, regulars and reservists, was the Army

THE JOINT COMMAND STRUCTURE, 1990	
UNIFIED	**SPECIFIED**
Geographic U.S. Pacific Command (USPACOM) U.S. Atlantic Command (USLANTCOM) U.S. European Command (USEUCOM) U.S. Southern Command (USSOUTHCOM) U.S. Central Command (USCENTCOM) *Specialized* U.S. Space Command (USSPACECOM) U.S. Special Operations Command (USSOCOM) U.S. Transportation Command (USTRANSCOM)	Strategic Air Command (SAC) Forces Command (FORSCOM)

Table 1

with which the nation would have to fight any war. Lacking the mechanism of an active draft, the Army had no way to assure replacements for extensive battle casualties. Similarly, without a mobilization of the industrial base, weapons production remained at a peacetime level.

The Army Within the Joint System

The Army of 1990 operated within unified and specified commands under the president of the United States through his agents: the secretary of defense and the chairman of the Joint Chiefs of Staff. Of eight unified commands, five were responsible for large geographic areas, while three controlled specialized functions (*Table 1*). Both unified and specified commands had broad, continuing missions, but specified commands were composed of only one service while unified commands contained forces drawn from two or more services (*see Map 4*).[43]

The United States Central Command, responsible for northeast Africa, Southwest Asia, and the surrounding waters, commanded U.S. forces during DESERT SHIELD and DESERT STORM. General H. Norman Schwarzkopf, Jr., commander of Central Command, controlled all of the Army, Navy, Marine, and Air Force elements assigned to the theater of operations. He reported to the Chairman of the Joint Chiefs of Staff, General Colin Powell. The Army component of Central Command (ARCENT) was the Third United States Army, colocated in peacetime with Forces Command at Fort McPherson, Georgia. At the beginning of

[43] Title 10, *United States Code (USC)*, secs. 161–67.

Gen. H. Norman Schwarzkopf

the operation, Central Command, which had no forces assigned to it during peacetime, requested troops from Forces Command, which allocated units stationed in the continental United States.

The Department of the Army performed its crisis role in accordance with service roles and missions as modified under the Goldwater-Nichols Act. In an attempt to streamline and create a more responsive and efficient Defense Department, Congress had altered the internal relations between the civilian secretariat and the Army Staff within the Department of the Army headquarters. While the secretariat acquired greater administrative and financial control, the Joint Chiefs of Staff gained increased responsibility in the operational area.[44] Under the new guidelines, the Joint Chiefs remained a corporate body with the service chiefs as members, but the chairman became the principal military adviser to the secretary of defense and the president. Reorganization gave the chairman of the Joint Chiefs the option of consulting with the service chiefs but did not require it. In addition, the joint chairman no longer had to forward to the secretary of defense, the National Security Council, or the president the dissenting and alternative views of the other members of the Joint Chiefs.[45] Congress also gave the operational unified and specified commanders greater authority over subordinate forces and provided them a greater role in acquisition of resources and materiel for specific military contingencies.

Throughout the crisis, the Army Staff supported ARCENT logistically and administratively. The staff had responsibility for ensuring that units identified to deploy into the theater were the best available for the mission; that they were adequately manned, equipped, and trained; that

[44] HQ, DA, *Report to Congress: Army Implementation of Title V, DOD Reorganization Act of 1986* (Washington, D.C.: DA, 1987), pp. i–3; Association of the United States Army (AUSA), *Fact Sheet: Department of Defense Reorganization Act of 1986, A Primer* (Arlington, Va.: AUSA, 1987), pp. 1–5.

[45] Draft Reorganization Bill, Talking Paper, DAMO-SSP, 3 Feb 87, included with Defense Organization: Meeting with Senators Goldwater and Nunn, filed with materials regarding Department of Defense Reorganization, 1985–1987, Historical Resources Branch, CMH.

United States Central Command, headquartered at MacDill Air Force Base, Tampa, Florida

other Army and Department of Defense assets were available to sustain and support the force; and, if not, that they were obtained and delivered for deployment in a timely manner. As a result, the staff was heavily involved in virtually every aspect of the force buildup and sustainment planning and execution. In addition, it had responsibility for coordination among the Army's major commands in the United States, with the Army component commands in the unified and specified commands, with the Joint Chiefs and the defense secretariat, and with civilian industry and agencies for procurement, contracting, and a broad spectrum of other areas related to the national industrial base. It also managed Department of Defense programs in support of the civil sector and other government agencies.

The Army's chief of staff, General Carl E. Vuono, took pride in his personal familiarity with virtually every major Army commander in the field and in the support base. In providing the Army resources necessary to support their plans and prepare for contingencies, General Vuono worked closely with these commanders, assuring that any disagreements over resources were resolved before they became issues that required intervention by the secretary of defense. In particular, he and General Schwarzkopf had known each other for more than three decades. This personal relationship created an atmosphere of mutual trust and confidence.[46]

From the Army Staff in the Pentagon to individual soldiers in rifle companies, many strands came together to make up the Army of DESERT STORM. Overall, the soldiers preparing for deployment to Saudi Arabia in the late summer of 1990 shared a pervasive confidence in their units, their weapons, and their own capabilities. Their leaders were equally sure that, in the doctrine they had so thoroughly rehearsed, they held the keys to battlefield success. The Iraqi invasion of Kuwait chanced to come at a moment when the United States Army was completing its twenty-year process of modernization and reform. The Army of 1990 was without a doubt the most proficient and professional military force the United States had ever fielded at the beginning of a foreign war.

[46] Interv, Brig Gen Harold W. Nelson with General Carl E. Vuono, USA (Ret.), 3 Aug 92, Washington, D.C. Also see Bob Woodward, *The Commanders* (New York: Simon and Schuster, 1991), pp. 303–04.

Chapter 3

CREATING THE SHIELD

Anticipating an Iraqi Threat

On 8 February 1990, the commanders in chief of three of the armed forces' unified commands appeared before the Senate Armed Services Committee to testify on the strategic and operational requirements of their commands. All were Army generals responsible for unified commands that focused on Third World defense and unconventional warfare. Two of them, Generals Maxwell R. Thurman, commander of the United States Southern Command, and James J. Lindsay, in command of the United States Special Operations Command, had recently been involved in the successful execution of Operation JUST CAUSE in Panama. The third, General H. Norman Schwarzkopf, Jr., was commander of the United States Central Command at MacDill Air Force Base outside Tampa, Florida.

Schwarzkopf's organization was unique within the unified command system. For political reasons Central Command headquarters was not in its assigned area of responsibility, and it had few units directly assigned to its command and control. The lack of a headquarters in the Middle East limited the command's familiarity with its potential area of operations as well as its relationships with friendly armed forces of the region. With a mission that demanded the flexibility to respond to contingencies and with long distances between its headquarters and its potential area of operations, Central Command had to be prepared to adapt quickly and on a very large scale.[1]

At the Senate committee hearings, General Schwarzkopf reviewed the situation in the Middle East, especially in light of the end of the Cold War. He also discussed the effect of the newly emerging world order on Central Command's operational strategy and needs. The committee chairman, Senator Sam Nunn of Georgia, was particularly interested in revising the Defense Department's planning guidance on the Middle East and in the resulting changes in force requirements.

Until shortly before the hearing, the command's planners had concentrated on a scenario involving a Soviet invasion of Iran. Although that assumption remained operative during the 1980s, changes in Eastern Europe and the continuing deterioration of conditions in the Soviet

[1] U.S. Congress, Senate, Committee on Armed Services, *Threat Assessment; Military Strategy; and Operational Requirements*, 101st Cong., 2d sess., 1990, p. 718.

Union made such a possibility less likely by 1990. From Schwarzkopf's perspective, a spillover "of some local conflict leading to a regional war which would threaten American lives and vital U.S. interests" was a more likely threat.[2] As he pointed out, there were then thirteen active conflicts in his area of responsibility, some of which had the potential of warranting the commitment of U.S. forces. Central Command had to be concerned with multiple contingency scenarios.

The change in the global situation called for a new look at the command. An amphibious assault on an Iranian beach created different problems than reinforcement of a friendly nation with secure airports and harbors. When asked by Senator Nunn about the type of forces and capabilities that Central Command required with that reorientation, General Schwarzkopf said that he "always had the requirement for the highly mobile contingency forces...that were based in the United States of America, but could rapidly deploy to [any] part of the world."[3] In the ensuing six months General Schwarzkopf's command planned on the basis of the concepts he articulated before the Senate committee.

During the spring of 1990 Central Command planners reassessed the threat in their area of responsibility. In light of President Saddam Hussein's increasing bellicosity, they identified Iraq as the most likely aggressor in the region. With Iraq as the potential threat, in March 1990 the command began preparing for a major joint command post exercise, INTERNAL LOOK 90, to test the assumptions of its developing contingency plan for the Middle East. During that computer exercise, Central Command simulated sending forces to the Middle East to deter an attack by "Country Red," to defend critical port and oil facilities, and to defeat enemy forces. The XVIII Airborne Corps had tactical command of the forces, and Army Central Command (ARCENT) had responsibility for sustaining the force.[4] Completed in July, the exercise confirmed the basic tenets of operation plan 1002–90.[5]

General Schwarzkopf and the Central Command staff also began preparing a response to a possible Iraqi invasion two days before Saddam Hussein's troops entered Kuwait. On 31 July and 1 August Schwarzkopf presented deployment options to Chairman of the Joint Chiefs of Staff General Colin Powell, Secretary of Defense Richard B. Cheney, President George H. Bush, and the National Security Council. On 4 August, two days after the invasion, the Central Command commander briefed the president on the availability of sea and air transport. Following that briefing, Schwarzkopf and Secretary Cheney flew to Saudi Arabia to negotiate the deployment of U.S. troops to that country.[6]

The Department of the Army had begun seriously monitoring intelligence reports coming out of the Middle East in July. Predicting that something was about to happen in Iraq, the Army Staff at the Pentagon began making preliminary assessments of specific Army actions if and when a crisis began. At the end of July, the staff principals met with Vice Chief of Staff General Gordon R. Sullivan to discuss possible Iraqi

[2] Ibid., p. 587.

[3] Ibid., p. 713.

[4] Draft MS, Col Richard M. Swain, Operational Narrative: Operations DESERT SHIELD–DESERT STORM, pp. 3–5.

[5] Draft MS, Capt Lawrence Douglas, U.S. Navy Reserve (USNR), CENTCOM History, pp. 1–2.

[6] Ibid., p. 10.

Lt. Gen. John J. Yeosock

intentions and military capabilities. At that meeting, each principal recommended a specific course of action should Iraqi troops cross the border into Kuwait. On 1 August the generals met again, this time with the commander of Army Central Command and Third United States Army, Lt. Gen. John J. Yeosock, to review the Army's portion of Central Command's draft operations plan for the Middle East. Realizing that the complications of logistics could create difficulties for any deployment to Southwest Asia, staff members discussed such questions in particular detail. Less than twenty-four hours after that meeting Saddam Hussein invaded Kuwait.[7]

From the beginning the Army Operations Center at the Pentagon had served as the DESERT SHIELD management center for the Department of the Army. A crisis action team, with representatives from each Army Staff element, manned the center on a 24-hour basis, compiling daily comprehensive briefings and updating them continuously. They monitored personnel, equipment, and maintenance requirements for the troops in the field and assisted in correcting shortcomings as they became evident. The center also coordinated the plans for Army support, the allocation of assets to meet worldwide demands, and the dissemination of information to and from the field.

To be able to respond to a variety of tasks and issues during the crisis, the Army Chief of Staff General Vuono and his deputy for operations, Lt. Gen. Dennis J. Reimer, created a strategic planning team. This group, which had six permanent members and added temporary specialists as needed, had responsibility for long-range planning and tried to anticipate Army needs during this time. The team studied such issues as unit rotation, replacement, reinforcement, and reemployment, as well as overall strategy, sustainment, and war termination.[8]

For this period General Vuono established three principal goals to focus the Army on his own integrated concept of the service's primary short-term and long-range objectives. The first of the goals, which he called vectors, was "to provide all the support necessary to accomplish U.S. national objectives in Operation Desert Storm." The other two, maintenance of a trained and ready force for other commitments and contingencies while reshaping the Army in light of declining post–Cold War resources, required constant attention to the overall state of affairs while prosecuting the war. Thus, throughout operations in Southwest Asia, Army leaders also shouldered the difficult job of preparing to respond to other contingencies in the world while planning to resume the reduction of the Army following the end of hostilities in the Middle East.[9]

Decision To Send Troops to Saudi Arabia

On 7 August 1990, Secretary of Defense Cheney, back in Washington after hurried consultations in Saudi Arabia, briefed President Bush on the Middle East situation. Cheney told the president that King Fahd had

[7] Interv, Richard Hunt and Theresa Kraus with Col Michael Harper, Chief, Army War Plans, 20 Mar 91, CMH transcript no. DSIT–C–017.

[8] Intervs, Theresa Kraus and Stephen Everett with HQDA staff, Mar and Jun 91; Vuono interview, 3 Aug 92. See Army Regulation (AR) 500–5, *The Army Mobilization and Operations Planning System* (1986).

[9] Michael P. W. Stone and Carl E. Vuono, *Maintaining a Trained and Ready Total Force for the 1990s and Beyond, A Statement on the Posture of the United States Army, Fiscal Years 1992 and 1993* (N.p.: 1991), p. 2.

agreed to permit the United States to send forces to defend the Kingdom of Saudi Arabia. After hearing Cheney's report, the president approved the deployment of combat forces to the kingdom. Shortly thereafter Cheney issued a directive assigning Central Command the mission to deter and counter any Iraqi aggression against Saudi Arabia.[10] A line had been drawn in the sand. The challenge for the U.S. Army and the other services was to turn that line into a substantial barrier through which Iraqi forces could not penetrate.

Shortly after Cheney released his directive, the Joint Chiefs of Staff issued the first Desert Shield deployment order to two F–15 squadrons, Maritime Prepositioned Squadrons 2 and 3, based on the islands of Diego Garcia and Guam; two carrier battle groups; the ready brigade of the 82d Airborne Division; and an airborne warning and control system (AWACS) unit. Cheney's directive unleashed what became the most concentrated and complex projection of American military power since World War II. Such a massive deployment, however, would not be easy. Several immediate issues required decisions before large-scale troop movements could be carried out, and Central Command had only recently begun to identify its detailed needs for deployment to the Middle East.

Fortunately, during the Internal Look exercise the command and its components had examined the requirements for responding to Iraqi aggression in the Middle East. That exercise provided the component commanders a chance to review their plans and requirements and to lay the foundation for subsequent planning. Among early problems confronting the Army and other services was the lack of an updated contingency plan. Although Central Command and its service-component commands worked on a unified campaign plan for the defense of Saudi Arabia during much of 1990, the plan was incomplete and had not yet been presented to the Joint Chiefs of Staff or the services for review. The lack of an approved plan was especially critical in the fluid situation of August. In peacetime once a unified campaign plan was approved, it provided the services with the force requirements that they would have to meet for execution of that plan. In the case of Southwest Asia, comprehensive force lists had to be developed. It took time to identify all the requirements and then match the requirements with specific units. The problem became particularly acute in identifying the many separate units needed to support a large force, among them water purification companies, tactical petroleum terminal units, engineer real estate detachments, and medium truck companies. Planners needed to develop ranges of deployment lists commensurate with service access to reserve capabilities. This process required a political decision by the president on mobilization of the reserves. During 10–28 August more than twenty messages changing the original deployment order passed between Central Command and the Pentagon, reflecting the complexity of the process of identifying specific units.[11]

[10] Memo for Secretary of the Army/Chief of Staff of the Army, 8 Aug 90, sub: Army Operations Update—Information Memorandum Number 1.

[11] Msg, Commander in Chief, Forces Command (CINCFOR), to Chairman, Joint Chiefs of Staff (CJCS), 28 Aug 90, sub: Sitrep Number 21.

Lt. Gen. Gary E. Luck

Theater Command Structure

A wartime command structure quickly developed to control the deploying Army units. ARCENT commander General Yeosock arrived in Saudi Arabia on 6 August. With the help of the handful of American officers who had been involved in the modernization of the Saudi Arabian National Guard, he set up an interim headquarters. On 16 August Yeosock set up ARCENT (Main) in Riyadh to oversee the arrival, sustainment, and overall combat planning for deploying Army units. Until General Schwarzkopf arrived in the theater on 25 August, Yeosock, who was commissioned in armor through the Reserve Officers Training Corps in 1959 after graduating from Pennsylvania State University, helped the acting deputy commander in chief, Lt. Gen. Charles A. Horner, U.S. Air Force, prepare for the arrival of the joint force. Yeosock already knew the terrain and climate and was familiar with his Saudi hosts. From 1981 to 1983 he had served in Riyadh as project manager for the modernization of the Saudi Arabian National Guard, and the experience would serve him well in the months ahead.

Once Yeosock went to Saudi Arabia, Maj. Gen. Horace G. "Pete" Taylor, chief of staff of Forces Command, took on the additional duty of ARCENT (Rear) headquarters. So in the early days of the crisis, ARCENT (Rear) helped to generate the requests for forces and filled them in conjunction with Forces Command. During that process General Taylor and General Edwin H. Burba, Jr., the FORSCOM commander, stayed in constant communication with General Yeosock in Saudi Arabia. As Yeosock established his operational headquarters in Saudi Arabia, Forces Command took over the task of building the force.

The First Deployments

The Army's first DESERT SHIELD priority was to develop its component force. General Yeosock wanted to deploy a force that could, if necessary, fight upon arrival. Because of insufficient air transport, limited host nation support, and a fluid Middle East situation, Yeosock hoped to deploy first aviation units, air defense systems, and antiarmor weapons.[12] Heavy forces would come in the second echelon.

The first Army units of the XVIII Airborne Corps began deploying to Saudi Arabia on 8 August. The rapid deployment of the ready brigade of the 82d Airborne Division signaled a clear U.S. national commitment to deter further Iraqi aggression. The brigade took its light antitank weapons and M551 Sheridans. Such lightly armed troops would be at risk should Iraq decide to invade Saudi Arabia before the United States completed its force buildup. Nevertheless, the decision made possible a rapid show of force and commitment.

The XVIII Airborne Corps, with its headquarters at Fort Bragg, North Carolina, served as the Army's contingency corps. Its mission required that it be ready to deploy on demand. Lt. Gen. Gary E. Luck had taken

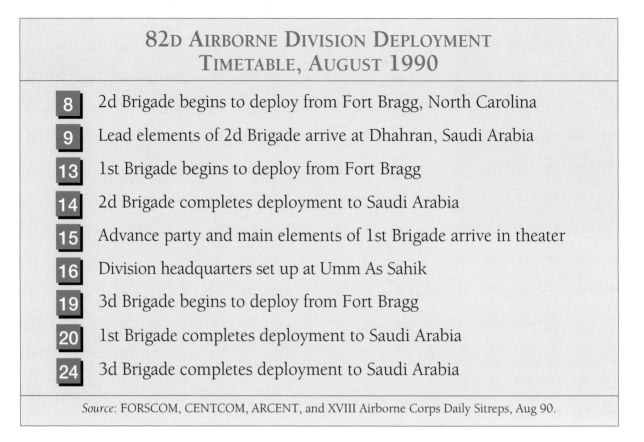

**82d AIRBORNE DIVISION DEPLOYMENT
TIMETABLE, AUGUST 1990**

8 2d Brigade begins to deploy from Fort Bragg, North Carolina

9 Lead elements of 2d Brigade arrive at Dhahran, Saudi Arabia

13 1st Brigade begins to deploy from Fort Bragg

14 2d Brigade completes deployment to Saudi Arabia

15 Advance party and main elements of 1st Brigade arrive in theater

16 Division headquarters set up at Umm As Sahik

19 3d Brigade begins to deploy from Fort Bragg

20 1st Brigade completes deployment to Saudi Arabia

24 3d Brigade completes deployment to Saudi Arabia

Source: FORSCOM, CENTCOM, ARCENT, and XVIII Airborne Corps Daily Sitreps, Aug 90.

Chart 3

over the corps in July 1990 after serving over three years as commander of the joint U.S. Special Operations Command and then the Army Special Operations Command. Like Yeosock, he entered the Army with a commission from the Reserve Officers Training Corps. In peacetime Luck had the 101st Airborne Division (Air Assault), the 24th Infantry Division (Mechanized), and the 82d Airborne Division under his command and control. The 101st Airborne Division stationed at Fort Campbell, Kentucky, was an infantry division whose primary means of movement was by helicopter. The 24th Infantry Division, located at Fort Stewart, Georgia, served as the XVIII Airborne Corps' heavy division. A heavy division such as the 24th was structured around, among other factors, the speed, flexibility, mobility, and firepower of its armored tracked vehicles. The 82d, the Army's premier tactical contingency force which routinely had one of its brigades designated as its ready brigade, prepared to begin deployment within eighteen hours of being alerted (*Chart 3*).

Placed on standby notice on 7 August, the 82d Airborne Division began deploying its ready brigade, the 2d Brigade commanded by Col. Ronald F. Rokosz, the next day. The first elements left Pope Air Force Base adjacent to Fort Bragg early in the afternoon of 8 August 1990 and began arriving in Dhahran, Saudi Arabia, the following day.[13] General Yeosock personally guided the first plane into its parking slot at the airfield.

[13] Msg, CINCFOR to CJCS, 8 Aug 90, sub: FORSCOM Sitrep.

Deployment of the 2d Brigade, 82d Airborne Division, Pope Air Force Base, North Carolina. After waiting in the passenger shed at Green Ramp, soldiers start to board a C–5B for the long flight to Saudi Arabia.

Rokosz's first troops established defenses around the airfield to provide security for the other arriving units. As additional troops came into the country, the perimeter expanded. By the afternoon of 13 August, when the ready brigade reported 100 percent of its troops deployed from Fort Bragg, with 88 percent of them already in Saudi Arabia, it had expanded its area of operations to provide security at Al Jubayl, the port through which the marines would enter the theater. On the fourteenth the 2d Brigade completed its deployment. One battalion of AH–64 attack helicopters from the Aviation Brigade, 82d Airborne Division, accompanied the 2d Brigade.[14]

The other two brigades of the 82d quickly followed the ready brigade. The 1st Brigade deployed an advance party on 13 August, which arrived in Saudi Arabia two days later, and completed its deployment on the twentieth. The 3d Brigade began its deployment on 19 August and completed it on the twenty-fourth. Around this time, selected elements of the XVIII Airborne Corps Support Command moved into Saudi Arabia.

While establishing defensive positions and conducting patrols, the soldiers began the long process of adapting to the environment. Their leaders carefully watched water consumption. The soldiers trained and worked only at night, in the early morning, and in late afternoon to limit exposure to the searing desert sun. The sand made its way into everything—weapons, vehicles, clothing, and food—and constant attention was required to make sure equipment and weapons would work when they were needed.

Although the corps' personnel flew to Saudi Arabia, most of their equipment moved by ship. The transshipment of materiel continued through August and September from five Atlantic and Gulf of Mexico ports. Corps support units were loaded at Wilmington, North Carolina.

Other Army units with more specialized missions quickly followed the 82d into Saudi Arabia. Special Forces planners who accompanied the 82d Airborne Division began preparing for the arrival of the 5th Special Forces Group (Airborne), 1st Special Forces. In addition, the lead elements of the 7th Transportation Group from Fort Eustis, Virginia, started their movement to the ports. That unit would control port operations and the unloading of equipment from ships once they docked in Saudi Arabia. On 14 August the commander of the 11th Signal Brigade arrived in theater and began establishing an Army communications network. The first elements

[14] Msg, Cdr, XVIII Airborne Corps, to CINCFOR, 14 Aug 90, sub: XVIII Abn Corps Sitrep No. 7; Msg, Commander, U.S. Army Central Command (COMUSARCENT), to Commander in Chief, Central Command (USCINCCENT), 13 Aug 90, sub: ARCENT Sitrep; FORSCOM, CENTCOM, ARCENT, and XVIII Airborne Corps Daily Sitreps, Aug 90.

Col. Ronald F. Rokosz (kneeling), commander of 2d Brigade, 82d Airborne Division, confers with liaison officers from the French 6th Light Armored Division the day before the attack.

A platoon of Bradleys in the Eastern Province of Saudi Arabia, positioned in a perimeter defense formation

of a Patriot missile battery of the 11th Air Defense Artillery Brigade also deployed in early August, and another battery from the 7th Air Defense Artillery arrived in Saudi Arabia on 16 August. The following day, the first aviation elements of the 101st Airborne Division and advance elements of the 24th Infantry Division arrived in theater.[15]

By the end of the first week of DESERT SHIELD, more than 4,000 Army soldiers had deployed to Saudi Arabia on 106 aircraft. Major weapon systems accompanying the soldiers included 15 AH–64 Apaches, 8 OH–58 Kiowa observation helicopters, 18 M551 Sheridans, 56 TOW antitank missile systems, 2 multiple launch rocket system launchers, and 12 105-mm. towed howitzers. In conjunction with Saudi Arabian forces in the Eastern Province and with deployed forces of the Air Force, Navy, and Marine Corps, Army units took position in the vicinity of Dhahran and Al Jubayl.

Although the DESERT SHIELD forces continued to deploy at a steady pace, General Schwarzkopf needed more firepower. In the early weeks of the deployment, he anxiously awaited the arrival of the 24th Infantry Division (Mechanized) with its 216 M1A1 tanks. Despite the rapid movement of the Army's first combat units into Saudi Arabia, time and the initiative still remained with Iraq, which had six divisions available in Kuwait to conduct operations with little or no advance warning.[16]

Support of the Deployed Forces

The flow of the XVIII Airborne Corps' combat forces into Southwest Asia as the initial elements of the DESERT SHIELD overshadowed the deployment of combat support forces. General Luck of XVIII Corps understood the need to move combat service support units to give his combat forces an adequate support structure, an imperative underscored by the austere environment of Southwest Asia. Army divisions had their own logistics organizations, capable of supporting operations for limited periods. With their defensive positions relatively near the ports, combat units could at least briefly use organic capabilities to transport and process supplies to locations in the field. Eventually, however, the sheer volume would overwhelm their ability to process, move, store, maintain, and account for materiel. Besides, such operations would detract from their main defensive mission. For sustained operations and a stay of over thirty days in Saudi Arabia, Army Central Command needed a mature logistics system. However, the need to counter possible large-scale surprise attacks by the Iraqis defined priorities and taxed the system. As XVIII Corps reported on the third day of its deployment, "the combination of moving combat forces as rapidly as possible as well as essential service support from the Corps has generated requirements which exceed limited resources immediately available to the corps."[17]

As General Yeosock and the ARCENT staff had rehearsed in INTERNAL LOOK 90, they planned on deploying initially only the minimum essential

[15] Msg, Cdr, Transportation Center (TRANSCEN), Fort Eustis, Va., to Cdr, Forces Command (FORSCOM), Fort McPherson, Ga., 14 Aug 90, sub: Installation Sitrep 002; Memo for the Secretary of the Army/Chief of Staff of the Army, 16 Aug 90, sub: Army Operations Update, Operation DESERT SHIELD—Information Memorandum Number 9; Draft MS, Swain, Operational Narrative, pp. 21–22.

[16] Information Paper, DAMO-AOC, 14 Aug 90, sub: Current Operations Situation, 141100 Aug 90; Msg, Cdr, XVIII Airborne Corps, to CINCFOR, 14 Aug 90, sub: XVIII Abn Corps Sitrep No. 7.

[17] Msg, Cdr, XVIII Airborne Corps, to CINCFOR, 9 Aug 90, sub: XVIII Abn Corps Sitrep No. 3.

Lt. Gen. William G. Pagonis
(Rank as of 7 February 1993)

support units and creating only a limited logistical base. Priority of deployment went to combat forces. Only later and if necessary would a mature logistics infrastructure be developed. Hence, when XVIII Airborne Corps units arrived in theater, logistical support was virtually nonexistent. Furthermore, the corps support units that were arriving quickly discovered they could not effectively handle the massive deployment of combat troops, who needed food, shelter, equipment, supplies, sanitation facilities, and transportation. General Yeosock quickly realized the need to expand the support system rapidly.

As early as 4 August Yeosock had suggested to Schwarzkopf that Maj. Gen. William G. Pagonis act as ARCENT's deputy commander for logistics. Yeosock had been impressed with Pagonis during a REFORGER exercise some years earlier, in which troops and equipment from the United States rehearsed deployment to Germany for a possible European war. At the time, Pagonis, a veteran logistician and another Reserve Officers Training Corps graduate of Pennsylvania State University, was serving as deputy chief of staff for logistics at Forces Command.

Burba readily agreed to the transfer, and by 7 August Pagonis was on his way to Saudi Arabia to set up a program for Saudi support of American forces. Four handpicked logisticians—Cols. Stephen J. Koons, John B. Tier, and Robert Klineman and Lt. Col. James Ireland—went with him, and the remainder of his personally selected 22-man team joined him within a few days. Pagonis landed in Riyadh on 8 August, scant hours before the first transport carrying the ready brigade of the 82d Airborne Division hit the tarmac at Dhahran, 250 miles away.

While en route to Saudi Arabia, Pagonis and his four staff officers had drafted a logistics plan for the theater. All had participated in REFORGER exercises, which provided the model for creating their DESERT SHIELD plan. The group outlined three major tasks necessary to create a sound logistics system in theater: the reception, onward movement, and sustainment of all soldiers, equipment, and supplies. Pagonis and his four subordinates took their proposal to Yeosock's headquarters in Riyadh. At that point, Yeosock formally designated Pagonis his deputy for logistics.

When Pagonis arrived at Dhahran the next day, he was appalled at what he found there. The initial combat troop arrivals had quickly overwhelmed the local resources. Colonel Ireland later recalled that as the soldiers poured in, "we just didn't have anything. We had…soldiers here with no place to put them, no way to get them out there if we did have a place to put them, and difficulty feeding them." Soldiers slept on the sand and on handball and tennis courts. Hundreds slept on the ground behind the quarters occupied by the United States Military Training Mission to Saudi Arabia and dug slit trenches for latrines.[18]

Three American officers from the training mission frantically tried to process the incoming soldiers from the XVIII Airborne Corps, who had started to arrive late in the morning of 9 August.[19] The training mission had no significant transportation resources of its own, so the

[18] Quote from Interv, Maj William W. Epley and Maj Glen R. Hawkins with Lt Col James Ireland, 25 Feb 91. Interv, Lt Col Wesley V. Manning and Maj Glen R. Hawkins with Col David A. Whaley, 13 Feb 91.

[19] Msg, CINCFOR (J3-CAT [Crisis Action Team]) to CJCS, 9 Aug 90, sub: CINCFOR Sitrep No. 3.

officers arranged for Saudi buses and trucks to take the troops to a vacated air defense facility 15 miles from the airport. With no personnel, no facilities, no resources, and very little information, those three officers made the best of a bad situation and provided whatever support they could, but the overwhelming demands quickly took a physical toll. His staff officers "looked like zombies," Pagonis later recalled. "They hadn't slept for…days."[20]

After the first night in Dhahran, Pagonis and his small staff took over two rooms in the training mission's building, one for bunks and another for an operations center. The staff quickly outgrew the two rooms and moved to the mission's recreation center, which they dubbed the "Hotel California." For the first three days, there was practically no rest.

The trickle of troops and equipment turned into a torrent with each passing day, and General Pagonis quickly decided that a full support command would be needed. His first priority was to find help to accomplish the myriad tasks involved in bringing units into the country and then supplying them because deploying units had placed their own organic support units at the end of the flow.[21] While waiting for the rest of his immediate staff to reach Saudi Arabia, Pagonis got assistance from units already on hand, putting together an ad hoc theater support organization. Newly arrived combat units routinely provided temporary help to round out the support command staff. When support units arrived, some of their people also joined the support command for an extended period. As General Pagonis put it, "anybody who had an Army uniform on, we just acquired them and said they worked for us."[22]

On 11 August the arrival of the 7th Transportation Group improved the situation. At that time, Pagonis had a staff of only ten, so he incorporated nearly one hundred members of Col. David A. Whaley's advance party into his own organization. In a short time, newly arriving members of the 7th Transportation Group and recalled reservists reconstituted the command, which was already at work operating the seaports. The evolving logistical command and control organization thus was a highly personalized, tailored headquarters that was shaped by the demands of a rapidly changing situation and the dire shortage of trained logisticians and their functional staffs.[23]

377th Theater Army Area Command and Capstone

Had the Army been able to deploy a key logistical command-and-control headquarters immediately into the theater, many of Pagonis' difficulties might have been avoided or at least greatly alleviated. Pre-crisis planning had designated a reserve unit, the 377th Theater Army Area Command, as the Third Army support command headquarters in the event of a Central Command contingency operation. This arrangement was part of what the Army called the Capstone program, which was intended to enhance the integration of reserve components into the active force.

[20] Quote from Pagonis interview, 3 Oct 90. Ireland interview, 25 Feb 91.

[21] Interv, Maj Larry Heystek with Maj Gen William G. Pagonis, 3 Oct 90; Msg, ARCENT (Forward) to FORSCOM, 9 Aug 90, sub: LogSitrep 1.

[22] Pagonis interview, 3 Oct 90.

[23] Whaley interview, 13 Feb 91.

Reserve components in this program planned and trained during peace-time with designated wartime commands, and development of a relation-ship hinged on associations built during training between Regular Army and reserve units. This relationship included links between active combat units and the reserve roundout organizations that had been designated by the Army to fill out and bring the combat units to full strength. Regulations specified that the roundout units would deploy with their active-duty sponsors based on the priorities of the theater commander to whom they would report.[24]

Maj. Gen. Alvin W. Jones, U.S. Army Reserve, commanded the 377th, a reserve unit from New Orleans, Louisiana, that had an autho-rized strength of 416. Under the Capstone program, the 377th's relation-ship with Third Army meant that it had concentrated its planning almost exclusively on Southwest Asia as a projected area of operations since Third Army was the designated Army component of Central Command. The 377th had helped draft the combat service support annexes of all the contingency operation plans for Southwest Asia and had geared all of its standing operating procedures to those operations. All of the 377th's training, including participation in three BRIGHT STAR exercises in 1985, 1987, and 1990, were built around Middle East scenarios. It had only one unit under its direct control, the 321st Support Center (Theater Army), which provided supply and materiel management at the corps support command level. In addition, the 377th had almost two hundred units in its Capstone trace, which was the specific support units that it was projected to control in the event of a national emergency.

When President Bush authorized the activation of the reserves on 22 August, Forces Command alerted the 377th. However, a division of opinion quickly developed over its possible deployment. The Army Staff and Forces Command generally supported activating the 377th, while Central Command and Army Central Command opposed it. The limited reserve call-up authority might well curtail the length of time the 377th would be available for active duty. Moreover, by the time the organization was alerted, General Pagonis had already handpicked his staff and assem-bled a functioning support organization. Installing a new headquarters, he believed, would disrupt the system at a critical juncture. General Vuono in Washington, working to provide the commanders in the the-ater of operations with what they wanted, felt that, rather than an addi-tional headquarters, the commanders wanted units to flesh out their existing logistics organization.[25] On 27 September Forces Command dropped the 377th Theater Army Area Command from the alert list.

Emergence of the Support Command

Pre-positioned stocks of equipment aboard ships stabilized most of the immediate crises in supplying and sustaining the new arrivals. Four ships that had been anchored off the coast of Diego Garcia brought rations, cots,

[24] AR 11–30, CAPSTONE Program (1983).

[25] Vuono interview, 3 Aug 92.

Unloading at a Saudi port

tents, blankets, and medical supplies, as well as refrigerated trailers, reverse osmosis water purification units, forklifts, and tactical petroleum terminals. Those ships, which had been stocked and positioned so that they could support an expeditionary force such as the one now deploying, arrived at Saudi Arabian ports on 17 August. They bought time for Pagonis to put into operation a more formal logistics system. "There was no doubt about it," Pagonis later said. "We would have never made it if we did not have those four Army pre-po ships."[26]

Within two weeks of General Pagonis' arrival in the theater, Army Central Command took steps to formalize the logistical operation. On 17 August Yeosock appointed Pagonis commander of ARCENT (Forward) to provide supervision for the increasing number of noncorps units assigned to the Dhahran area. Two days later the organization became an institutionalized ARCENT subordinate unit, the Provisional Support Command, using a standard theater army area command table of organization and equipment.

By the end of August the staff, slowly gaining control of the situation at the airport, began devoting more time to planning for anticipated long-term requirements. On 27 August General Pagonis created a conventional general staff and two days later moved to the training mission headquarters at the King Abdul Aziz Air Base.[27] By 31 August the support command's total strength, headquarters and subordinate units, stood at 2,291. Temporary personnel loans from the United States Army, Europe, staff and the reassignment of selected personnel from the ARCENT staff helped fill out the headquarters.

Pagonis and his staff built their logistics infrastructure while receiving and moving troops. Within fifteen days after assuming responsibility for the airport, they processed over 40,000 soldiers, formed an area support group and an area support battalion, and started unloading ships. By the end of September the Provisional Support Command moved over 100,000 people and discharged thirty-nine ships. In addition to serving its own elements, Pagonis' command supported the other Central Command component services—Navy, Air Force, and Marine Corps—once they were ashore in theater. The Army was also the point of contact for food, water, bulk fuel, ground munitions, port operations, inland cargo transportation, construction support, veterinary services, and graves registration for all U.S. forces, either providing the support directly or arranging for it through contracting or host nation support assets.

[26] Pagonis interview, 3 Oct 90.

[27] 22d Support Command (SupCom), DESERT SHIELD Command Rpt, 23 Mar 91, p. 2; Interv, Maj Glen R. Hawkins with Lt Col John J. Carr, 15 Feb 91; Ireland interview, 25 Feb 91.

Host Nation Support and Contracting

Satisfying as many supply requirements as possible from local sources promised to ease immediate logistical shortfalls and reduce the number of American support units ultimately deployed to the theater. Thus Provisional Support Command staffers quickly surveyed as many local contractors in the region as possible, and within a few short weeks had established the basis for an indigenous assistance and contracting program. Such measures became critical components of the overall logistical effort.

Saudi Arabia was not a backward, primitive state. Soaring oil revenues in the 1970s had enabled the kingdom to make major investments in public works. The telephone system ranked with the finest anywhere, although it ultimately proved too small to accommodate the demands of the coalition force, to which thirty-eight countries contributed.[28] The port of Ad Dammām may have been the best in the world. It and Al Jubayl had modern facilities, with immense capacities and staging areas. Airports, particularly Dhahran, were large and modern, and the primary road system was well built although inadequate for the high volume of traffic that a large military force would generate. Yet, with a total population of about seven million, the country just could not provide for the day-to-day needs of hundreds of thousands of soldiers.

The construction boom of the 1970s did at least present potential solutions to some of the problems involved in supporting the U.S. force. Huge public housing projects, designed initially for a growing population of expatriate workers and citizens migrating to the city, stood largely unoccupied. The U.S. Army did at least have a potential source for troop housing near ports of entry.

The establishment of a formal agreement for the use of resources available in Saudi Arabia proved critical to logistical success. Such an arrangement, known as host nation support, covered all assistance to allied forces

[28] U.S. Department of Defense, *Conduct of the Gulf War: Final Report to Congress* (Washington, D.C.: Government Printing Office, 1992), app. I.

The port of Ad Dammām

and organizations located in the host nation's territory. An agreement for peacetime and wartime help had long been in force between the United States and the Federal Republic of Germany, where the United States had thousands of soldiers, but none covered the American presence in Saudi Arabia. On 15 August General Pagonis had set up a staff section in his headquarters under Col. Roger W. Scearce to deal with host nation support matters. Scearce was succeeded from October to early January by Lt. Col. Donald L. Trautner and finally by Col. Robert H. Sholly.[29]

Because of the fluid situation in August, contracting activities were conducted in a very decentralized and informal manner. Initially there were no controls, and people at all levels did their own contracting. Many untrained individuals became involved in negotiations for critically needed resources and services. For example, second lieutenants in brigades were going out and buying brooms. Experienced contracting officers from the XVIII Airborne Corps, therefore, provided an invaluable service to the Provisional Support Command. By the end of the month Yeosock established a contracting office. In addition to initial billeting and transportation, contracting provided latrines, washbasins, and showers, as well as forklifts, food, water, fuel, and a variety of other supplies and services.[30]

Efforts to find billeting and to move troops from Dhahran revealed the unstructured nature of contracting activities in August and early September. In one case, Lt. Col. James Ireland, the acting support command headquarters commandant, heard about empty Saudi housing nearby. Desperate for more space, he dropped what he was doing, drove to the site, decided that the price was reasonable, and said he would take it. In another case, Lt. Col. Michael E. Velton cruised the streets of Dhahran looking for idle buses or trucks. Whenever he saw a group of vehicles, he tried to negotiate a deal. There was no time for the formal contracting process. "We were," Velton said, "literally out contracting for the buses while they [U.S. troops] were landing at the airport." He gave a Saudi entrepreneur a bag with $40,000 in cash, got a receipt, and waited for his trucks and buses. To his immense relief, the vehicles arrived as promised, and the soldiers moved off the airfield.[31]

The idiosyncrasies of the Saudi Arabian bureaucracy added to the challenge of contracting. Often the Saudis would deal only with officers, preferably high-ranking officers. They refused to negotiate with an Arabic-speaking chief warrant officer in the Provisional Support Command's contracting office, so he wore a major's gold leaves when he did business with them. The practice of temporarily "commissioning" or "promoting" people occasionally smoothed business dealings.[32]

The Saudi Arabian government never intended to let the United States shoulder all of the expenses of the deployment. As early as 18 August the logistics operations center developed a list of the command's basic needs for host nation support for the next forty-five days. The Saudis reacted energetically and cooperatively, providing tents, food, transportation, real estate, and civilian labor support (*Table 2*).[33]

[29] Richard F. Nyrop, ed., *Saudi Arabia, A Country Study*, 4th ed. (Washington, D.C.: Government Printing Office, 1984), ch. 3; Field Manual (FM) 55–2, *Division Transportation Operations* (1985), p. glossary-4.

[30] 22d SupCom, DESERT SHIELD Command Rpt, 23 Mar 91, p. 9 and tab J; Memo, ARCENT Contracting Command, 10 Mar 91, sub: Command Report for Operation DESERT SHIELD; Interv, Maj Glen R. Hawkins with Lt Col Don Trautner, 12 Apr 91.

[31] Ireland interview, 25 Feb 91. Quote from Interv, Lt Col Wesley V. Manning and Maj Glen R. Hawkins with Lt Col Michael Velton, 2 Feb 91.

[32] Whaley interview, 13 Feb 91.

[33] Memo, SupCom Assistant Chief of Staff, Host Nation Activities, 2 Oct 90, sub: Historical File, dtd 2 October 1990, pp. 3–5 and attachment 5; 22d SupCom, DESERT SHIELD Command Rpt, 23 Mar 91, p. 9; Draft MS, John J. McGrath and Michael D. Krause, Theater Logistics and the Gulf War [1992], p. 151.

HOST NATION SUPPORT REQUIREMENTS[a]	
Products/Services	Quantity
Water	1.5 million gallons/day
Ice	95 short tons/day
Subsistence (A-rations)	270,000 meals/day
Tents	8,416
Fuel	
Gasoline	181,000 gallons/day
Diesel	120,000 gallons/day
Jet	52,000 gallons/day
Vehicles	
Buses	700 each
Trucks	12,150 (various sizes)
POL tankers	380 (various types)
Water tankers	300 (various types)
Hygiene	
Latrines	2,700 units
Showers	2,250 units
Laundry	40,000 bundles/day
Refuse collection	145,000 short tons/day

[a] For period C+12 (19 Aug 90) to C+56 (2 Oct 90) based on a force of 135,000.

Source: Draft MS, John J. McGrath and Michael D. Krause, *Theater Logistics and the Gulf War* [1992], p. 151.

Table 2

On 10 September King Fahd verbally committed his nation to provide comprehensive support, although the details remained unclarified until mid-October, when the Department of Defense sent a negotiating team to Saudi Arabia. Instead of concluding a contract or international agreement with the Saudis, the team reached an understanding which became a de facto agreement. That was done to prevent bureaucratic delays and to make giving a gift from Saudi Arabia to the United States as easy as possible, while addressing the kingdom's continuing desire to avoid formal ties. Saudi Arabia agreed to pay the costs of all contracts entered into by U.S. forces as of 30 October 1990 and backed up its promise with a check for $760 million that a very nervous American officer carried back to New York for deposit. Saudi Arabia agreed to pay for all freshly prepared meals—known as Class A meals or A-rations in the Army—water, fuel, transportation within Saudi Arabia, and facilities, including construction. By December that assistance was valued at about $2.5 billion projected over one year. American forces still could negotiate for themselves if the Saudis did not meet their needs, but the United States would pay for those contracts.[34]

In time the system of Saudi support and contracting matured and helped sustain American forces in theater, but the need to move the troops and their equipment from the ports still presented tremendous challenges. Both sat waiting for transportation, as it became apparent that unloading equipment at the ports was easier than delivering it to cantonments. The port of Ad Dammām, which before the crisis had averaged only six ships a week, handled that many every day after the crisis began.[35] Ground transportation provided the key link between the ports and assembly areas.

Transportation

Many of the improved roads in Saudi Arabia became main supply routes for the Army. The Army used two routes north from Dhahran to prepare for and execute the war. The northern route had two segments. The first, designated main supply route AUDI, was a very good multi-lane road running from Dhahran, along the coast, to just north of Al Jubayl. The second, named DODGE, was a paved two-lane road running generally northwest from AUDI to Ḥafar al Bāṭin and then onward to Rafha. Old hands also called DODGE the Tapline Road, because it paralleled the Trans-Arabian Pipeline, but the vehicular code names were appropriate for roads that ran through and near some of the largest oil fields in the world.

[34] Interv, Maj Glen R. Hawkins with Robert Gorman, senior attorney, Office of the Assistant General Council (Logistics), Department of Defense (DOD), 12 Apr 91.

[35] Interv, Maj Glen R. Hawkins with Col Daniel G. Brown, 15 Jan 91.

Tapline Road passing through logistical base CHARLIE

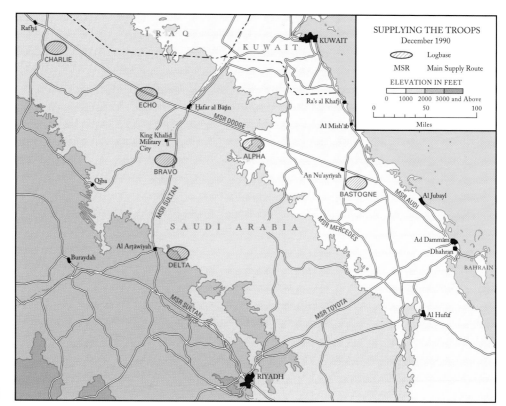

Map 5

The southern route also consisted of two main supply routes. An excellent multilane road running between Dhahran and Riyadh was named TOYOTA. The last segment, SULTAN or NASH, ran north from Riyadh to Ḥafar al Bāṭin, where it intersected DODGE. SULTAN was a multilane road for about one-third of the distance north from Riyadh before narrowing to two lanes. Some of these roads were well surfaced and in good repair, but there were not enough of them for the high volume of traffic.

The distances were great, 334 miles from Dhahran to the theater logistical base at King Khalid Military City near Ḥafar al Bāṭin along the northern main supply route and 528 miles via Riyadh. The XVIII Airborne Corps' forward tactical assembly area was over 500 miles from Ad Dammām by the northern route and 696 by the southern road. The highways thus became high-speed avenues for combat units and supplies moving to their destinations. Because large stretches were multilane roads they allowed heavy volumes of traffic to move fast, both as individual vehicles and as convoys. Even those roads that were not multilane were paved and in generally good condition (*Map 5*).

To increase the efficiency of the road network, General Pagonis established a series of convoy support centers. Those truck stops operated twenty-four hours a day and had fuel, latrines, food, tents for sleeping, and limited repair facilities. They added to the comfort, safety, and morale of allies traveling in the theater and greatly enhanced the ability of the transporters. Because of the long distances, the primitive rest areas quickly became favorite landmarks to those who drove the main supply routes.

With excellent ports and durable roads, all the Army needed was the means to move equipment and supplies. The oil industry had traditionally needed large vehicles to transport heavy equipment to various well sites, so there were many heavy equipment transporters as well as tractor-trailer cargo trucks in the country. The growing wealth of the kingdom with an increased urban population and an expanding pool of expatriate workers meant a large fleet of buses. Likewise, expanding interaction with the West had prepared the business community with how to deal with Americans and had provided a relatively sophisticated core of bureaucrats and decision makers to deal with the overwhelming demands placed on their economy.

Feeding the Troops

CWO4 Wesley C. Wolf, handpicked by General Pagonis to be food service adviser for the theater, improvised from the beginning. The first troops had landed without their basic load of rations, and an enterprising XVIII Airborne Corps mess sergeant had met their immediate needs with bags of hamburgers from the American-style fast-food restaurant—a Hardee's—near the airport. Wolf continued this practice while he considered the Army's plan for feeding its soldiers through a combination of three daily prepackaged meals: either two meals-ready-to-eat (MREs), called meals refused by Ethiopians by the soldiers, and one T-ration—a tray pack meal that could be heated by cooks to provide more palatable food, or one MRE and two T-rations.

Rations for the troops

Wolf thought that it was foolish to feed soldiers from prepackaged meals when A-rations could be used. He contended that the Army had done poorly by its soldiers, taking away cooks and refrigerated vans and substituting T-rations for fresh food. A-rations improved troop morale and preserved the valuable limited supply of MREs for potential combat operations.

Before he managed to put his ideas into practice,

the influx of soldiers severely strained the ability of the system to supply MREs. During the early days of the deployment, the stock dwindled to one-half day's worth. When the XVIII Airborne Corps arrived, Wolf distributed a "horrendous amount of MRE's" because he had no caterers. As Wolf put it, "if it wouldn't have been for the A-rations that we were receiving from the host nation, we would have run out of food."[36]

Wolf worked with the Saudi's to set up dining halls operated by local contractors. When Army units landed without their cooks and field mess equipment, they would use a contract mess hall. If units did not have cooks, they would use the contract mess hall on a permanent basis. The kingdom did not have any large caterers, so at first only one contract mess operated in the Dhahran area, at the XVIII Airborne Corps' "Dragon City." That first effort served unfamiliar Saudi cuisine, which the troops did not appreciate. As the American presence increased, so too did the local kitchen expertise. Soon contract mess halls fed American troops in Riyadh, Dhahran, Al Jubayl, King Khalid Military City, and other locations. While indigenous contractors learned to operate from the Army's ten-day feeding menu and to prepare American meals, Army veterinarians inspected locally purchased food to ensure that it met American standards.

In another effort to conserve MREs, Wolf implemented a program of supplements. He wanted to serve fruit, juice or soft drinks, pastries, and bread with jelly or some other sandwich filler with an MRE at noon. Wolf hoped the soldiers would eat only part of their MRE and save the other part, cutting consumption of the critical operational meals. The program succeeded, and with time, especially when the MREs were critically short, the supplement became the only issue for the noon meal. General Pagonis christened it the "fruitbasket in every foxhole" program.[37]

From Tents to Luxury Apartments

To fix the existing situation in which soldiers slept in warehouses, airplane hangars, and on the sand itself, more tents were needed. A large number of Army-issue tents on the pre-positioned ships provided the first real relief, and eventually every tent in U.S. Army, Europe, reserves found its way to Saudi Arabia. The Provisional Support Command poured cement slabs and erected tent cities. Later, huge German festival tents provided protected storage sites and served as post exchanges.

Empty public housing projects ultimately provided the solution to many transient billeting problems. Those projects were large complexes of duplex-style villas and high-rise apartments. Ultimately, most of the Americans assigned to Riyadh lived in Eskan Village, a massive complex with modern duplexes featuring marble floors, four and five bedrooms, and two or three baths. These had been originally built for Western workers. They housed the American troops and provided ample office space as well.

[36] Interv, Lt Col Wesley V. Manning and Maj Glen R. Hawkins with CWO4 Wesley C. Wolf, 16–17 Feb 91.

[37] Ibid.

Temporary quarters in a warehouse, used by 24th Infantry Division soldiers after their arrival in Saudi Arabia

In Dhahran the Saudis turned over a similar high-rise complex to the Americans. Al Khubar Village consisted of 219 multistory apartment buildings with over 4,100 apartments. Here also the floors were marble, even in the stairwells, and each apartment was very spacious. At times, as the American buildup continued, over 23,000 soldiers would be crammed in the apartments. As many as eight or ten to a room, they waited for their equipment to arrive so their unit could move to its tactical assembly area in the desert. In the early days facilities were procured primarily by imaginative officers who hunted them out and arranged leases through the host nation support office. Nevertheless, transient units still relied heavily on tents and warehouses.[38]

Despite the confusion suggested by the extemporaneous solutions to feeding, housing, and moving the incoming soldiers, Army Central Command could point to great progress during the first month in Saudi Arabia. By early September the entire 82d Airborne Division and the first elements of the 24th Infantry Division had arrived. The rest of the 24th and the 101st Airborne Division were on the way. The partnership with the Saudi government was evolving well, and a logistical support organization was emerging. The SHIELD was in place.

[38] Memo, SupCom Assistant Chief of Staff, Host Nation Activities, 1 Jan 91, sub: Historical File, p. 4; Ireland interview, 25 Feb 91.

Chapter 4
EXPANDING THE SHIELD

To fight the large well-armed Iraqi military, Central Command needed mechanized and armored units. The Army's heavy forces, which emphasized the power of tanks, armored personnel carriers, and self-propelled artillery, were located in the United States and Europe. In the United States the Army had the 1st, 4th, 5th, and 24th Infantry Divisions (Mechanized), the 1st Cavalry Division (Armored), a brigade of the 2d Armored Division, and the 3d Armored Cavalry. The 3d and 8th Infantry Divisions (Mechanized), the 1st and 3d Armored Divisions, the 2d and 11th Armored Cavalry, and forward-deployed brigades of the 1st Infantry Division and the 2d Armored Division were in Germany. Those units formed the pool from which heavy forces would be drawn for Central Command.

In response to a request by General Schwarzkopf, General Colin Powell, Chairman of the Joint Chiefs of Staff, asked the services to begin identifying additional units for deployment. On 10 August 1990, Forces Command issued a deployment order for follow-on forces to Southwest Asia. The message provided an intelligence summary from which to plan and identify deployment requirements and shortages. The summary identified at least six Iraqi divisions in Kuwait with an additional five near Al Baṣrah. The summary concluded by positing courses of action that the Iraqis might take in response to the initial deployment: invading Saudi Arabia to occupy possible American entry points and seize oil production facilities; interdicting the air- and seaports of debarkation by conventionally or chemically armed aircraft and missiles; or attacking U.S. ships as they passed through the Persian Gulf with aircraft, mines, and missiles.

The message also outlined the force deployment objective. By 16 September Forces Command intended to deploy to Southwest Asia the two remaining ground maneuver brigades of the 82d Airborne Division, the 101st Airborne Division (Air Assault), and the 24th Infantry Division (Mechanized). Added to the troop list to give the XVIII Airborne Corps more punch were the 3d Armored Cavalry and the 1st Cavalry Division. Thus, by mid-September Forces Command wanted to move into Saudi Arabia about 50,000 soldiers, over 700 tanks, 564 M113s, 572 M2 and M3 Bradleys, 145 AH–64 Apaches, 294 155-mm. self-propelled howitzers, 48 Patriot missile launchers, and thousands of other items of equipment ranging from generators to computer vans.[1] The soldiers would travel by air and their equipment by sea.

Commanders of the installations where the units were located and of the units themselves were instructed to deploy according to a series of staggered dates. For example, General Edwin H. Burba, Jr., of Forces Command told the commander of Fort Bliss to send one Patriot air defense missile battalion to Southwest Asia no later than 18 August. He also directed the commander of III Corps, at Fort Hood, Texas, to move the 1st Cavalry Division and the 1st Brigade, 2d Armored Division, out by 16 September.

In identifying combat units to meet Central Command's needs, General Burba had an important decision to make. Both the 24th Infantry Division and the 1st Cavalry Division had only two active-duty brigades. The others were designated as roundout brigades of the Army National Guard, which were designed to bring the divisions up to full strength when mobilized. However, as of 8 August the reserve components had not been called, so the National Guard brigades were not available to augment the deploying divisions.

The Roundout Brigade Program

The roundout system had been created for two purposes. The first was economic: reserve-component units were less expensive than active-component units to maintain during peacetime. The second was a more subtle imperative. At the time the Total Army policy was adopted in 1973, many believed that the Vietnam disaster had resulted from a failure of both a clearly articulated policy and will. The great debate on goals had come late in the war. If American military forces could not be committed without mobilization of the reserves, then the public debate would have to take place at the outset. The Total Army thus served as a political trip-wire.[2]

Despite the misgivings of many, the Department of Defense was firmly committed to the roundout system. From 1973 to 1989 the Army had grown from thirteen to eighteen divisions while maintaining a post-Vietnam personnel strength of around 785,000. That was accomplished partly by manning some continental United States active-duty divisions with only two maneuver brigades; the third divisional, or roundout, brigade would come from the reserve component. By mid-1990 six active Army divisions contained roundout brigades, all but one from the National Guard (*Table 3*).

The 24th Infantry Division stationed at Fort Stewart, Georgia, was the first heavy division slated for deployment. The 48th Infantry Brigade of the Georgia National Guard served as its roundout brigade. When the 24th received deployment notification, no political decision had been made on the issue of reserve mobilization. This and other factors led Forces Command to select the Regular Army's nondivisional 197th Infantry Brigade at Fort Benning, Georgia, to deploy instead of the 48th.

[1] Equipment numbers from Chart, DESERT SHIELD Combat System Deployment, filed in Army Operations Daybook no. 3, 11–17 Sep 90.

[2] Lewis Sorley, "Creighton Abrams and Active-Reserve Integration in Wartime," *Parameters* 21:2 (Summer 1991): 43–50.

THE ROUNDOUT BRIGADE PROGRAM	
Active Component	Reserve Component
	Army National Guard
1st Cavalry Division (Armored)...................	155th Armored Brigade (Miss.)
4th Infantry Division (Mechanized).....	116th Cavalry Brigade (Idaho/Oreg./Nev.)
5th Infantry Division (Mechanized)..................	256th Infantry Brigade (La.)
9th Infantry Division (Motorized)	81st Infantry Brigade (Wash.)
10th Mountain Division (Light)	27th Infantry Brigade (N.Y.)
24th Infantry Division (Mechanized)................	48th Infantry Brigade (Ga.)
	Army Reserve
6th Infantry Division (Light).............................	205th Infantry Brigade

Table 3

Burba regarded the 197th as the best-qualified, readily available force to bring the 24th Division to full strength.

Breaking the roundout connection between the 48th Brigade and its parent 24th Division touched off some debate. The nature of the dispute seemed surprising because everyone had been bracing for a hostile reaction to the calling of the reserve components. The outcry, however, came not from the public, but from reservists aggrieved because they were not called.

The roundout program had been designed to bring to full strength seven divisions stationed in the United States to stop a full-scale Warsaw Pact attack in central Europe or to meet a major contingency outside of Europe while maintaining strength along the Iron Curtain. Those scenarios presumed a full or even total mobilization. Despite public discussion to the contrary, it had never been assumed by the Army Staff that any of the roundout units would deploy with their parent organizations in a short-term scenario that did not involve the Soviet Union. The United States had enough combat forces to deal with the immediate crisis in August 1990. Retired Lt. Gen. John W. Woodmansee, Jr., former V Corps commander, summed up the feeling of many in the active components when he said, "it's patently absurd to take relatively untrained troops when you have trained troops available."[3] Had the 48th deployed, it would have left behind in the United States ten highly trained heavy divisional brigades of the active component, an unhappy prospect for many in the Army leadership. Given the Capstone program, however, many reservists and the congressional delegations that represented them had assumed that in all circumstances the roundout unit would deploy with the parent division.

There was a second crucial reason for not calling the roundout brigades into active service. The call-up authorization granted on 22

[3] *New York Times*, 29 Sep 90, p. 4.

August was limited in number and function. The Army's share of that 48,800-soldier increment, 25,000 combat support and combat service support personnel, was based directly on the number requested by Chief of Staff General Carl E. Vuono.[4] The active components had adequate combat forces available and needed support personnel. The early mobilization of the Army National Guard combat brigades would have eaten into the initial call-up authorization without providing the support forces that the Regular Army needed most.

Other issues affected the call-up of the reserves. The most obvious was congressional support in terms of appropriations that had been dedicated to strengthening combat elements of the reserve components. Another concern centered on the question of Total Army viability. The total force policy was much on the minds of congressional leaders because the Persian Gulf crisis coincided with force reduction planning following the end of the Cold War. Implicit was their assumption that the reserve components would play an even larger role.

Congressman G. V. "Sonny" Montgomery of Mississippi raised those points in letters on 15 August to President Bush and on 24 and 28 August to Secretary of Defense Cheney.[5] Those letters became part of a public debate that intensified in September. On the congressional side, in addition to Montgomery, the issue was joined most vocally by Congressman Les Aspin of Wisconsin, Chairman of the House Committee on Armed Services; Congresswoman Beverly B. Byron of Maryland; and Congressman Dave McCurdy of Oklahoma. They directed their observations to Secretary Cheney in a joint letter on 6 September 1990.[6] In particular they stressed the need to test the Total Army policy, which by inference was associated with the roundout units. They tied the need for that test to the forthcoming force restructuring and reductions debate.

In reply, Secretary Cheney cited two reasons for not authorizing the call of the roundout brigades. First, he said, the military had not asked for them. Second, "the statutory time limits on the use of Selected Reserve units imposes artificial constraints on their employment." He was referring to the restrictions in Section 673b of Title 10, *United States Code*, that limited the call-up to ninety days renewable for ninety days. Too much of that time, he explained, would be spent on mobilization, training, and movement to make the remaining time in the Middle East worthwhile. He concluded that point by saying that "Congress has within its power the ability to lengthen the period of maximum service under Section 673b, to permit more effective use [of] Selected Reserve units."[7] Those observations clearly implied that the failure to call the roundout units revolved around the time available to the units to be actively used. The difficulty lay with congressionally imposed limitations.

That issue, as old as the Constitution, involved the executive powers of the commander in chief and the legislative war-making powers. The operative sections of Title 10 had been deliberately crafted to require

[4] Memo, Secretary of Defense Richard Cheney for Secretaries of the Military Departments and Chairman of the Joint Chiefs of Staff, 23 Aug 90; Vuono interview, 3 Aug 92.

[5] Ltr, Congressman G. V. Montgomery to Secretary of Defense Richard Cheney, 24 Aug 90; Ltr, Montgomery to Cheney, 28 Aug 90.

[6] Ltr, Congressmen Aspin, Montgomery, and McCurdy and Congresswoman Byron, to Secretary of Defense Cheney, 6 Sep 90.

[7] Ltr, Secretary of Defense Cheney to Congressman Aspin, 18 Sep 90.

close consultation between the executive branch and Congress if the president wanted to use extensive force. The president had the power to use as many as 1 million reservists for two years simply by declaring a national emergency. That was a step the administration did not want to take in early September. Even within the 200,000 troops available under presidential authority, Secretary Cheney only authorized the call-up of the minimum needed for the short run.

The debate continued into October. By that time, the House Armed Services Committee characterized the failure to call combat reservists as "anti-reserve bias."[8] Led by those critics, Congress took up Secretary Cheney's challenge and crafted an exception to Section 673b. Signed into law on 5 November, the amendment extended the period for which the president could activate reserve-component combat units from a total of 180 days to 360 days for fiscal year 1991. The provision weakened any argument that a lack of time to mobilize, train, deploy, serve, and redeploy prevented call-up of the roundout units.

Additional Deployments of Active Units

While the debate over the roundout concept continued in Washington, the Regular Army units alerted for deployment began preparations to go to Saudi Arabia. The 101st Airborne Division, alerted on 12 August, began shortly thereafter to move its helicopters and other equipment from Fort Campbell by air, land, and water to Jacksonville, Florida, for loading aboard ships. The advance element of the 101st, consisting of seventy-three soldiers and six Apaches, arrived in Saudi Arabia on 17 August.[9]

At Forts Hood and Bliss the pace was as intense as it was at Bragg, Campbell, and Stewart. Although the 1st Cavalry Division and 3d Armored Cavalry were to be the last major Army combat elements to deploy, that fact did not lessen the sense of urgency. Early in the movement, both sent liaison officers to the XVIII Airborne Corps headquarters to study the experiences of units that had already gone. On 22 August the 3d Armored Cavalry began moving its equipment to Beaumont, Texas. Over the next five days twelve trains delivered the regiment's heavy equipment to the port. Its aircraft flew to Beaumont, where they were disassembled and packed for shipment.

The 1st Cavalry Division at Fort Hood, with the 1st Brigade of the 2d Armored Division attached, began moving to the Port of Houston on 4 September and started loading ships two days later.[10] The division's first ships, of an eventual fifteen, were on their way by 9 September and arrived in Saudi Arabia on 3–4 October. By the first week in November the division was in the desert setting up its defensive positions and training for combat (*Maps 6 and 7*).

Deployment activities were not limited to the United States. On 15 August the Joint Chiefs of Staff ordered the United States European Command to send an attack helicopter brigade from the United States

[8] House Armed Services Committee, News Release, Anti-Reserve Bias Behind Combat Unit Absence, 16 Oct 90.

[9] Msg, COMUSARCENT, 8 Oct 90, sub: ARCENT MAIN G3 Sitrep.

[10] Memo for Secretary of the Army/Chief of Staff of the Army, 2 Sep 90, sub: Army Operations Update Operation DESERT SHIELD—Information Memorandum Number 26.

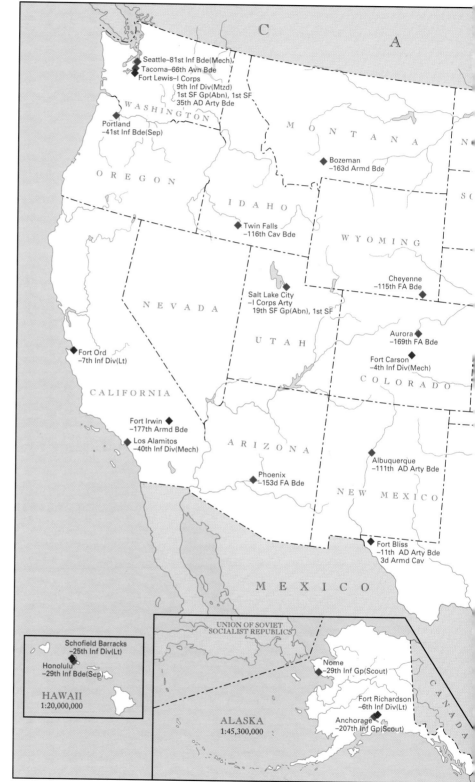

Seattle–81st Inf Bde(Mech)
Tacoma–66th Avn Bde
Fort Lewis–I Corps
  9th Inf Div(Mtzd)
  1st SF Gp(Abn), 1st SF
  35th AD Arty Bde

Portland
–41st Inf Bde(Sep)

Bozeman
–163d Armd Bde

Twin Falls
–116th Cav Bde

Cheyenne
–115th FA Bde

Salt Lake City
–I Corps Arty
  19th SF Gp(Abn), 1st SF

Aurora
–169th FA Bde

Fort Carson
–4th Inf Div(Mech)

Fort Ord
–7th Inf Div(Lt)

Fort Irwin
–177th Armd Bde

Los Alamitos
–40th Inf Div(Mech)

Albuquerque
–111th AD Arty Bde

Phoenix
–153d FA Bde

Fort Bliss
–11th AD Arty Bde
  3d Armd Cav

UNION OF SOVIET
SOCIALIST REPUBLICS

Nome
–29th Inf Gp(Scout)

Fort Richardson
–6th Inf Div(Lt)

Anchorage
–207th Inf Gp(Scout)

ALASKA
1:45,300,000

Schofield Barracks
–25th Inf Div(Lt)

Honolulu
–29th Inf Bde(Sep)

HAWAII
1:20,000,000

Map 6

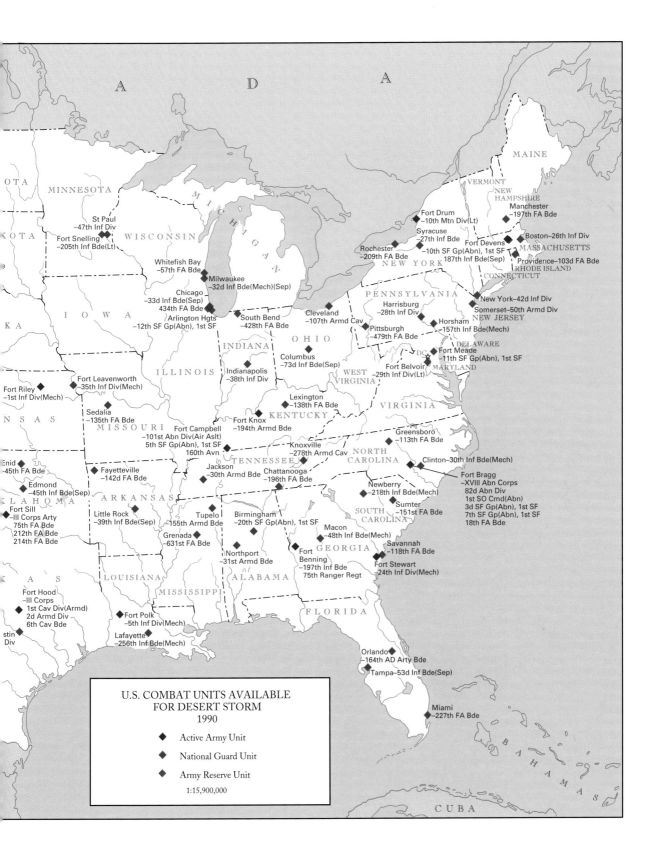

U.S. COMBAT UNITS AVAILABLE
FOR DESERT STORM
1990

◆ Active Army Unit

◆ National Guard Unit

◆ Army Reserve Unit

1:15,900,000

St Paul
–47th Inf Div

Fort Snelling
–205th Inf Bde(Lt)

Whitefish Bay
–57th FA Bde

Milwaukee
–32d Inf Bde(Mech)(Sep)

Chicago
–33d Inf Bde(Sep)
434th FA Bde

Arlington Hgts
–12th SF Gp(Abn), 1st SF

South Bend
–428th FA Bde

Cleveland
–107th Armd Cav

Columbus
–73d Inf Bde(Sep)

Indianapolis
–38th Inf Div

Lexington
–138th FA Bde

Fort Knox
–194th Armd Bde

Fort Leavenworth
–35th Inf Div(Mech)

Fort Riley
–1st Inf Div(Mech)

Sedalia
–135th FA Bde

Fort Campbell
–101st Abn Div(Air Aslt)
5th SF Gp(Abn), 1st SF
160th Avn

Jackson
–30th Armd Bde

Chattanooga
–196th FA Bde

Knoxville
–278th Armd Cav

Fayetteville
–142d FA Bde

Enid
–45th FA Bde

Edmond
–45th Inf Bde(Sep)

Fort Sill
–III Corps Arty
75th FA Bde
212th FA Bde
214th FA Bde

Little Rock
–39th Inf Bde(Sep)

Tupelo
–155th Armd Bde

Birmingham
–20th SF Gp(Abn), 1st SF

Grenada
–631st FA Bde

Northport
–31st Armd Bde

Fort Benning
–197th Inf Bde
75th Ranger Regt

Macon
–48th Inf Bde(Mech)

Savannah
–118th FA Bde

Fort Stewart
–24th Inf Div(Mech)

Newberry
–218th Inf Bde(Mech)

Sumter
–151st FA Bde

Fort Hood
–III Corps
1st Cav Div(Armd)
2d Armd Div
6th Cav Bde

Fort Polk
–5th Inf Div(Mech)

Lafayette
–256th Inf Bde(Mech)

stin
Div

Orlando
–164th AD Arty Bde

Tampa–53d Inf Bde(Sep)

Miami
–227th FA Bde

Fort Drum
–10th Mtn Div(Lt)

Manchester
–197th FA Bde

Syracuse
–27th Inf Bde

Fort Devens
–10th SF Gp(Abn), 1st SF
187th Inf Bde(Sep)

Boston–26th Inf Div

Rochester
–209th FA Bde

Providence–103d FA Bde

Harrisburg
–28th Inf Div

New York–42d Inf Div

Somerset–50th Armd Div

Horsham
–157th Inf Bde(Mech)

Pittsburgh
–479th FA Bde

Fort Meade
–11th SF Gp(Abn), 1st SF

DC

Fort Belvoir
–29th Inf Div(Lt)

Greensboro
–113th FA Bde

Clinton–30th Inf Bde(Mech)

Fort Bragg
–XVIII Abn Corps
82d Abn Div
1st SO Cmd(Abn)
3d SF Gp(Abn), 1st SF
7th SF Gp(Abn), 1st SF
18th FA Bde

U.S. COMBAT UNITS
AVAILABLE FOR DESERT STORM
1990
◆   Active Army Unit
◆   National Guard Unit

GERMANY
1:5,100,000

Garlstedt
–2d Armd Div(Fwd)

Berlin
–Berlin Bde

Giessen
–42d FA Bde
Fulda
–11th Armd Cav
Frankfurt
–V Corps
V Corps Arty
3d Armd Div
Weisbaden
–12th Avn Bde
Wertheim
–72d FA Bde
Wuerzberg
–3d Inf Div(Mech)
Bad Kreuznach
–8th Inf Div(Mech)
Herzogenaurach
–210th FA Bde
Darmstadt
–32d AD Cmd
Babenhausen
–41st FA Bde
Illesheim
–11th Avn Bde
Nuremberg
–2d Armd Cav
Ansbach
–1st Armd Div
Stuttgart
–VII Corps
Schwäbisch-Gmünd
–56th FA Cmd
Goeppingen
–1st Inf Div(Fwd)
Augsburg
–17th FA Bde
VII Corps Arty

DENMARK

POLAND

NETHERLANDS

BELGIUM

LUXEMBOURG

CZECHOSLOVAKIA

FRANCE

AUSTRIA

SWITZERLAND

San Juan
–92d Inf Bde(Sep)

PUERTO RICO
1:6,200,000

Fort Clayton
–193d Inf Bde

PANAMA
1:4,100,000

CHINA

USSR

NORTH
KOREA

Tongduchon
–2d Inf Div
Uijongbu
–Cmb Fld Army
(ROK/US)

SOUTH KOREA
1:19,500,000

JAPAN

Map 7

Army, Europe, to Saudi Arabia. The 12th Aviation Brigade, assigned to the V Corps in Germany, met the requirement. The brigade's deployment started a steady stream of troops and materiel that flowed from Europe to the Middle East to support Operation DESERT SHIELD. It also set the precedent for transfer of American troops from their NATO roles in Europe to service in Southwest Asia. Through the remainder of August, in addition to the 12th Aviation Brigade, an air ambulance company and four chemical reconnaissance platoons deployed. By the end of the month the 12th began moving by land and air to the port of Livorno, Italy, to meet its ships. By 13 September the brigade had loaded three vessels bound for Saudi Arabia. The 12th arrived on 2 October and was in its assembly area by early October.

Supporting the Movement

Although a large-scale reserve call-up had not yet been authorized, reservists participated in the rapid deployment of the active-duty units. Army Reserve deployment specialists played a decisive premobilization role in moving equipment from home stations through the ports of embarkation. Those reservists worked in the Army's Military Traffic Management Command (MTMC), a component of the unified United States Transportation Command. The Army component command managed the distribution of all Army supplies and played a major role from the beginning of mobilization.[11]

[11] MS, John R. Brinkerhoff, Loading the Ships for DESERT STORM: The Total Army in Action in the Military Traffic Management Command [Washington, D.C.: Office, Chief of the Army Reserve, 1991].

Military Traffic Management Command Terminal, Rota, Spain, the site of transshipment operations during DESERT SHIELD

The MTMC headquarters in Falls Church, Virginia, managed its far-flung activities through four subordinate commands. The Eastern Area ran U.S. Atlantic and Gulf of Mexico ports from Bayonne, New Jersey. The Western Area operated U.S. Pacific ports in addition to Japanese and Korean operations from San Francisco, California. The European Division handled western European facilities from near Rotterdam, the Netherlands. The Transportation Engineering Activity in Newport News, Virginia, provided technical support.

The command's 5,900-member worldwide staff included 2,154 civilians who were Army reservists and 22 who were Navy reservists. These people, who served as individual mobilization augmentees or in a few highly specialized units, provided the surge capacity needed to operate the ports during the deployment. Their units, among the least well known of Army organizations, did jobs that were vital to the movement of troops. Deployment control units, each of which had an authorized strength of 39 officers and 44 enlisted people, broke down into twelve teams that helped units at their home stations prepare equipment for movement to a port of embarkation and served as a liaison with the port. Transportation terminal units of 28 officers and 47 soldiers managed the traffic operations of military ports. They prepared loading plans and manifests, received equipment, supervised the overall operation, and contracted labor to load the ships. The unit commander also usually commanded the port. Another type, port security detachments of 3 officers and 64 enlisted personnel, managed overall port security in conjunction with police, Coast Guard, and other security forces. Cargo documentation detachments of 8 enlisted personnel documented the loading, unloading, and transferring of cargo from one form of transportation to another. They worked at all types of terminals and could document the movement of 500 short tons of cargo or 480 containers per day. Railway support units of 5 officers and 142 enlisted people provided railway equipment operating specialists. The scope of support this organization offered was vast: in the first sixty days, 520,000 tons of cargo and 107,000 passengers deployed.

Opening the Ports

Between 8 and 27 August the job of opening and operating the military ports thus fell to a mixed group of regulars, mobilization augmentees, individual volunteers, and units serving their annual periods of active-duty training. Col. Robert H. McInvale, an individual mobilization augmentee assigned to the Military Traffic Management Command's Eastern Area as its deputy commander for mobilization, was called on 8 August and asked to open and operate the Port of Jacksonville so as to load the equipment of the 101st Airborne Division. After organizational meetings that night in Bayonne and coordination with the 101st at Fort Campbell on 9 August, he arrived in Jacksonville on 10 August. He began work with a trailer, a telephone, and an ad hoc group of less than a dozen soldiers and civilians.

Port operations at Beaumont, Texas (top), and Sunny Point, North Carolina (bottom)

Thirty more reservists volunteered to help on 11 August, and the equipment from the 101st Division began arriving the next day. It was only on 13 August that his command got permission to accept the volunteers who had offered their services and started work. In twenty days that ad hoc unit directed the loading of all ten ships of 101st Airborne Division equipment.

The tempo could not be maintained without whole units operating within a normal structure. On 27 August, during the first reserve call-up, five terminal units were activated. Col. Richard Simmons, commander of the 1181st U.S. Army Transportation Terminal Unit, who had already been working at the port with twenty-four other volunteer members of his unit, took command of the Port of Jacksonville.

The same process unfolded at Savannah, the port of embarkation for the 24th Infantry Division and the 197th Infantry Brigade. Volunteers from the 1182d and 1189th U.S. Army Transportation Terminal Units from Charleston, South Carolina, began the process. The 1185th U.S. Army Transportation Terminal Unit from Lancaster, Pennsylvania, diverted to Savannah, Georgia, from Wilmington, North Carolina, where it was to have begun its annual two-week training exercise on 13 August, soon joined them. When the two-week tour ended, the 1185th went on extended active duty with the other terminal units. The first ship with 24th Division equipment left Savannah on 13 August. The 1185th, commanded by Col. Donald R. Detterline, stayed on and worked at Savannah, proceeding to Wilmington and Sunny Point, North Carolina; Bayonne; Newport News; and Rotterdam. The unit ended its long tour of duty on 24 July 1991.

The use of volunteers, mobilization augmentees, and units on annual training in addition to Regular Army forces was a makeshift, but workable, approach to opening and operating military ports throughout the United States. Once the decision to activate the reserves was made, a more permanent structure developed. On 27 August the Army activated five terminal units, two port security units, and a deployment control unit in addition to other movement control units. These units supported the entire East Coast deployment from home installation to port operations at Bayonne, Wilmington, Savannah, Jacksonville, Houston and Beaumont, Texas, and the Military Ocean Terminal at Sunny Point, a specialized facility for handling munitions. When the reinforcement of VII

Corps forces began in November, the 1181st, 1182d, 1185th, and 1189th terminal units deployed to Amsterdam and Rotterdam in the Netherlands; to Antwerp, Belgium; and to Bremerhaven, Germany. The 1190th U.S. Army Deployment Control Unit set up headquarters in Stuttgart, Germany, to support deployment of VII Corps to Saudi Arabia.

Moving the Force

The number of vessels and aircraft available to move those alerted units affected the pace of deployment. The transportation requirements of heavy forces were more complex than those of light forces. Tanks, armored fighting vehicles and personnel carriers, and self-propelled artillery had to be transported by ship and took longer to arrive in an area of operations than the equipment of lighter forces.

The Transportation Command, responsible for moving the joint force and its equipment, had other priorities and, at times, requirements simply exceeded availability of resources. On 11 August, for example, XVIII Airborne Corps needed the equivalent of 40 C–141 aircraft to move 4,000 passengers and a portion of the vehicles that belonged to the 82d Division's ready brigade. It expected only thirty-one.[12] The number of aircraft increased only when the Civil Reserve Air Fleet, a program for the emergency use of the nation's civil air carriers, was activated on 17 August for the first time in its forty-year existence.[13]

Shipping was scarcer than aircraft. Four ready reserve fleet ships expected to be available by 17 August were delayed for almost a week. Mechanical problems beset other vessels.[14] Moreover, some ships were not designed to expedite the loading of equipment. The majority were break-bulk carriers onto which cranes lifted individual pieces of equipment through deck hatches. Once under way, those ships were also slower than the fast sealift ships.

On 11 August the first of the fast sealift ships, the USNS *Capella* and USNS *Altair*, steamed into the Port of Savannah to begin loading the 24th Infantry Division's equipment. The reservists and regulars of the ready brigade of the 24th Infantry Division and the 1185th U.S. Army Transportation Terminal Unit of the Army Reserve began loading the brigade's equipment on the *Capella* in midafternoon and finished in less than forty-eight hours. The vessel sailed for Saudi Arabia on 13 August, loaded with 88 M1 tanks, 26 M2 infantry fighting vehicles, 12 M3 cavalry fighting vehicles, 9 multiple launch rocket system launchers, 6 AH–1S Cobras, 4 OH–58 Kiowas, and 3 self-propelled 20-mm. Vulcan air defense guns. The Vulcans were carried on deck, along with Stinger anti-aircraft missiles, to provide air defense for the ship in case of attack after it passed through the Strait of Hormuz and crossed the Persian Gulf heading for the Saudi ports. Also on board were one hundred soldiers of the 24th Infantry Division who accompanied the unit's equipment and would help unload the ship at the end of the two-week voyage.

[12] Information Paper, Army Operations Center, 11 Aug 90, sub: Current Operations Situation, 11 Aug 90.

[13] Memo, DCSOPS for Secretary of the Army/Chief of Staff of the Army, 18 Aug 90, sub: Army Operations Update Operation DESERT SHIELD—Information Memorandum Number 11.

[14] Ibid.; Memo, DCSOPS for Secretary of the Army/Chief of Staff of the Army, 27 Aug 90, sub: Army Operations Update Operation DESERT SHIELD—Information Memorandum Number 20.

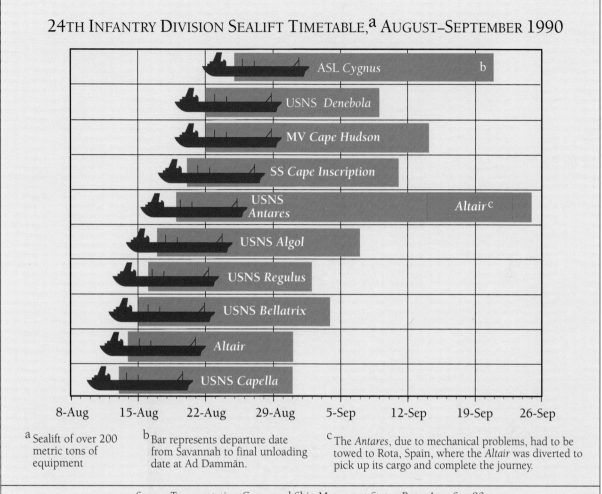

24TH INFANTRY DIVISION SEALIFT TIMETABLE,[a] AUGUST–SEPTEMBER 1990

[a] Sealift of over 200 metric tons of equipment

[b] Bar represents departure date from Savannah to final unloading date at Ad Dammān.

[c] The *Antares*, due to mechanical problems, had to be towed to Rota, Spain, where the *Altair* was diverted to pick up its cargo and complete the journey.

Source: Transportation Command Ship Movement Status Rpts, Aug–Sep 90.

Chart 4

[15] Msg, Cdr, XVIII Airborne Corps, to CINCFOR, 22 Aug 90, sub: XVIII Abn Corps Sitrep No. 15; Msg, COMUSARCENT to USCINCCENT, 20 Aug 90, sub: ARCENT AFRD-DTO Sitrep; Msg, CINCFOR to CJCS, 16 Sep 90, sub: FORSCOM FCJ3-CAT Sitrep No. 40; Memo for Secretary of the Army/Chief of Staff of the Army, 25 Sep 90, sub: Army Operations Update Operation DESERT SHIELD—Information Memorandum Number 49; TRANSCOM Ship Movement Status Rpts, Aug–Sep 90.

Problems with the USNS *Antares* delayed completion of the 24th Division's movement. The vessel departed Savannah on 19 August with elements of the 24th's support command and Aviation Brigade on board. While en route the ship had serious boiler problems and had to be towed to Spain for repairs. With the *Antares* unable to complete the trip, the USNS *Altair* was diverted from its return voyage to the United States to take on the cargo of the *Antares*. The *Altair* sailed from Rota, Spain, on 14 September. The breakdown of the *Antares* delayed completion of the 24th Division's deployment by over two weeks. The division finished its move to Saudi Arabia on 25 September with the unloading of the *Altair*. The ten-ship sealift took forty-six days to move over 200 metric tons of equipment (*Chart 4*).[15]

The first ship carrying 101st equipment, the MV *American Eagle*, left Jacksonville on 19 August with 9 105-mm. towed howitzers, 3 Cobras, 3 Kiowas, and 20 Chinook transportation helicopters. The ship began unloading in Saudi Arabia on 9 September. The division finished its movement to Saudi Arabia thirty days later.[16]

The 3d Armored Cavalry started loading its first ship on 27 August at Beaumont. Four days later it set sail. During its first day at sea the ship suffered mechanical problems and returned to port for quick repair. The problem was less serious than the trouble that beset the *Antares*, and the vessel returned to sea within several days. From 26 August to 10 September the 3d loaded five ships. Another of its transports suffered mechanical problems and was towed to Jacksonville for repair.[17] Although the regiment's original schedule called for arrival in Saudi Arabia before the end of September, it did not finish unloading its equipment until 17 October.[18]

The Reserve Call-Up

When the decision was made to send combat troops to Saudi Arabia, Army planners recognized that the force could be sustained over an extended period only with a large reserve call-up.[19] Staff work to meet that requirement began immediately, and by 11 August the Joint Chiefs were coordinating for General Powell's signature a memorandum to Secretary Cheney requesting presidential authority to call up the Selected Reserve. Supporting documentation foresaw the immediate need for 135,781 reservists of all services, including 88,000 Army troops to be called beginning in August through October.[20] Though allowances had been made for volunteers and host nation support, those numbers were needed to build a strong and stable support structure in the event of hostilities.

The request contained 63,400 combat support and combat service support personnel in 614 units and 11,000 medical personnel. The 48th Infantry Brigade of the Georgia National Guard and the 155th Armored Brigade of the Mississippi National Guard, each containing 2,750 troops, were also included in the initial package although it was projected that they would not deploy. In draft letters prepared on 14 August for the president's signature to notify Speaker of the House of Representatives Thomas S. Foley (Washington) and President Pro Tempore of the Senate Robert C. Byrd (West Virginia) of the call-up, General Powell added a paragraph indicating that reserve combat troops might be needed in the Middle East. However, he later agreed with a Joint Chiefs recommendation that only those units actually requested by the service components of Central Command should be activated for deployment and that the units to be mobilized for U.S. service should be justified on a case-by-case basis by the service secretaries.[21]

The first three weeks of August were filled with long hours of difficult analysis, coordination, and negotiation. Faced with a formidable task, the staff planners tended toward large numbers within a projected 200,000 limit. The Bush administration, though prepared to authorize

[16] Msg, COMUSARCENT, 8 Oct 90, sub: ARCENT MAIN G3 Sitrep.

[17] Msg, FORSCOM Sitrep, 13 Sep 90.

[18] Msg, COMUSARCENT to AIG 11743, 17 Oct 90, sub: ARCENT MAIN G3 Sitrep.

[19] Msg, CINCFOR to CJCS, 8 Aug 90, sub: FORSCOM Situation Report.

[20] Joint Staff (JS) Action Processing Form, Crisis Action Team (CAT) 0067, 11 Aug 90.

[21] JS Form 136L, 17 Aug 90, initialed "CP."

as many reserves as necessary to support operations, wanted no more than the minimum required. Every unit called had to serve an essential mission and be seen by the public as being absolutely necessary for the task.[22] The administration and the Army wanted to avoid the perception that the lives of reservists, their families, and their communities were being disrupted for no good reason. The results of those considerations could be seen in the declining numbers of required troops in each revision of the proposed force list.

On 15 August Secretary Cheney asked President Bush to execute his authority to call up the Selected Reserve, while the final numbers were still being worked out.[23] Several days later, Bush decided to activate reserve forces. On 22 August he promulgated the decision in Executive Order 12727. In letters to Congressman Foley and Senator Byrd informing them of his decision, the president did not mention reserve combat units.[24]

Having received presidential authorization, Secretary Cheney directed the Army to call up Selected Reserve units, but many fewer than had originally been discussed. In the last briefing Cheney received on the day the decision was announced, General Powell asked for a total of 46,703 reservists from all services. That number included 4,912 Army reservists for call-up in August and an additional 19,822 by 1 October. Secretary Cheney authorized the call-up of 48,800 people for all services. Of those, the Army was authorized to activate 25,000 reservists drawn exclusively from combat support and combat service support units, thus eliminating the combat brigades from immediate call-up.[25]

The first reserve call-up triggered a major debate that lasted throughout the crisis and remains unresolved. Despite the Total Army policy in place since 1973, major currents worked against it. One was a fear within the administration that a large reserve call-up would generate a hostile backlash against the Persian Gulf policy and ruin efforts to build a domestic and international consensus. Policy makers were aware of the antiwar sentiment of the Vietnam War years, and there remained a lingering institutional memory of the negative response in 1961 during the Berlin crisis when the 49th Armored Division of the Texas National Guard and Wisconsin's 32d Infantry Division were called but not actively used. The public had little understanding of or patience with the concept of activating those divisions to reconstitute the forces in the United States to prepare for further emergencies. There was also an underlying fear among some government officials that a reserve call-up would trigger a public reaction against the use of "civilians," now reservists rather than draftees, in anything less than a total effort of the World War II variety. Those considerations seem to have played a role in limiting the number of reservists called in the first three months of the crisis.

Skepticism over the use of roundout maneuver brigades in the combat divisions also fueled the controversy. Long before the crisis, civilian military analysts had raised questions about the ability of National Guard

[22] CAT Tasking Form 8302, 17 Aug 90.

[23] CAT Tasking Form 8241, 16 Aug 90.

[24] Ltr, President Bush to Speaker of the House of Representatives and President Pro Tempore of the Senate, 22 Aug 90.

[25] Memo, Secretary of Defense Richard Cheney for Secretaries of the Military Departments and Chairman of the Joint Chiefs of Staff, 23 Aug 90.

maneuver units to reach the proficiency of their Capstone partners.[26] That skepticism also existed in the Regular Army. Maj. Gen. Robert E. Wagner, commander of the Army Reserve Officers Training Corps Command, said publicly in 1986 what many believed. "Our service is literally choking on our reserve components....Our reserve components are not combat-ready, particularly National Guard combat units. Roundout is not working. Those units will not be prepared to go to war in synchronization with their affiliated active-duty formations."[27]

As the public debate continued, Forces Command worked to create a reserve force list. Once Secretary Cheney gave his approval, units were alerted on 24 August, and fifty-seven units containing almost four thousand reservists were activated on 27 and 28 August. In addition to troop-unit personnel, by the end of August 2,500 Army National Guard and Army Reserve volunteers and over 1,000 individual mobilization augmentees were on active duty.

Although the units were typical of the hundreds that followed in later months, they reflected the needs of the early days of the crisis. They varied in size from the 142d Military Intelligence Battalion's five-member prisoner-interrogation teams of the Utah National Guard to the 295-soldier 5064th U.S. Army Reserve Garrison from Detroit, Michigan. Functionally those units in the August call-up fell into four distinct areas: support for the continental United States, movement support, support of the deployed force, and medical support.

The first two categories consisted of relatively small numbers. Within the United States, the 3320th, 3397th, and 5064th U.S. Army Reserve Garrisons provided administrative support at mobilization stations, and a U.S. Army Reserve Intelligence Support Element was assigned to Forces Command. Those involved in assisting the movement of troops, equipment, and supplies to the ports of embarkation and from ports of debarkation in Saudi Arabia did a wide array of jobs. Twenty-six transportation units, including cargo documentation, movement control, freight consolidation and distribution, transportation terminals, and port security detachments, were activated. The terminal units were those that had already been serving under two-week orders. The six-member 1158th Transportation Detachment (Movement Control) of the Colorado National Guard was alerted on 24 August and activated on the twenty-seventh. It arrived at Fort Carson, Colorado, on the thirtieth, and became the first guard unit to deploy to Southwest Asia on 9 September.

Medical Personnel

Between August 1990 and January 1991, forty-four Army hospitals deployed to Saudi Arabia, Bahrain, the United Arab Emirates, and Oman. Those included station hospitals, evacuation hospitals, combat support hospitals, and the traditional mobile Army surgical hospitals (MASH). Regulars and reservists from six Army Medical Department corps served

[26] See, for example, Martin Binkin and William W. Kaufmann, *U.S. Army Guard and Reserve: Rhetoric, Realities, and Risks* (Washington, D.C.: Brookings Institution, 1989).

[27] Ltr, Maj Gen Wagner to Gen Vuono, 25 Aug 86, quoted in Binkin and Kaufmann, *U.S. Army Guard and Reserve*, p. 96.

Desert evacuation exercise by 44th Medical Brigade medics

during the conflict—the Medical Specialist Corps, Dental Corps, Medical Service Corps, Veterinary Corps, Nurse Corps, and Medical Corps. The process of medical mobilization and the transition to wartime presented some unique problems.

The Health Services Command provided both peacetime and wartime care for service members and their families. Those duties required the simultaneous existence of two types of medical organizations. The peacetime organization provided a complete range of medical care in permanent U.S. and overseas facilities. After Iraq's invasion of Kuwait, the system continued to provide normal medical care but took on new duties. The Health Services Command provided medical and dental support for the mobilization stations; expanded the hospital beds available in the continental United States by 4,000; provided personnel to Central Command, Europe; and deployed reserve-component units. It also certified that all the deploying reserve medical units met the personnel, equipment, and training criteria.

Medical operations in support of Operation DESERT SHIELD began the second week of August when the Army Medical Department received the dual mission of deployment to Southwest Asia and the continuous care of soldiers and their families in the United States and overseas. By the end of the month the 44th Medical Brigade, the 47th Field Hospital, the 28th Combat Support Hospital, and the 5th Surgical Hospital (Mobile Army) were on their way. At first the deployment created a shortage of trained medical personnel. More than 1,700 volunteers—from the Retired Reserve, from the Individual Ready Reserve, and from the Selected Reserve's Individual Mobilization Augmentees and Troop Program Units—responded to the request for help and were placed in health care facilities from which the active-duty people were deploying.

The Army Medical Department prepared to meet the intense needs of combat operations by providing care ranging from combat medics at the forward line to field hospitals in the communications zone. With the onset of Operation DESERT SHIELD, medical assets began to shift to support the field units. The key to this transition was the Professional Officer Filler System (PROFIS). This system matched Regular Army medical professionals with vacancies in deploying medical units. As the medical staff shifted to deploying units, Army leadership looked to the reserve components for the remaining manpower necessary to accomplish the mission.

During previous mobilizations, increased demands had been matched by a declining need to provide dependent and retired health care. In August, however, General Vuono instructed The Surgeon General, Lt. Gen. Frank F. Ledford, Jr., to continue medical service to all beneficiaries. That verbal instruction was followed early in September by a strongly worded letter from Congressman John P. Murtha of Pennsylvania, Chairman of the Defense Subcommittee of the House Committee on Appropriations, to Secretary Cheney. Murtha said that the failure to replace deploying medical personnel on a one-to-one basis with reservists degraded patient care and increased expenses by raising the costs of CHAMPUS, the Civilian Health and Medical Program of the Uniformed Services that used civilian providers reimbursed by the government to treat dependents and retirees when uniformed military care was not available. "This," Murtha stated, was "totally unacceptable and must be remedied."[28]

General Powell disagreed with some specific points of Congressman Murtha's letter.[29] The patient load at many U.S. facilities, such as Fort Stewart, the home of the 24th Division, had gone down dramatically, precluding the need for one-on-one replacement. General Powell also noted that while CHAMPUS was expensive, so was calling up additional reservists. Finally, he pointed out that calling too many reservists could have a detrimental impact on the civilian health care system.

[28] Ltr, Congressman John P. Murtha to Secretary of Defense Richard B. Cheney, 11 Sep 90.

[29] Memo, Gen Colin Powell for the Secretary of Defense, 19 Oct 90.

Secretary of Defense Cheney, balancing Congressman Murtha's concerns and General Powell's appraisal, communicated to the service secretaries the mandate to support DESERT SHIELD, to continue all peacetime care, and to maintain the same level of CHAMPUS expenditures. Beginning in August, the Health Services Command moved quickly within that framework to activate more medical reservists to support its mission.

Fifteen hundred Army Medical Department reservists from eleven units were activated on 28 August 1990. A problem immediately became apparent as mobilization progressed. The stateside hospitals needed replacements for health care professionals who had gone into deploying units under PROFIS. Planners had always assumed that individual ready reservists would fill that need during mobilization. The reserve activation of August 1990, however, was taking place under terms of Title 10, *United States Code*, Section 673b, which limited the call-up to members of the Selected Reserve. This included only specifically assigned individual mobilization augmentees and members of units that were designed to remain intact.

The Health Services Command used 800 of the medical personnel who had volunteered in the first days of the crisis, but they were not sufficient to fill the need.[30] It appeared that entire hospitals and dental detachments would have to be activated to get enough health care providers, including physicians, dentists, nurses, physician assistants, and Army Medical Service Corps officers. Such unit call-ups would activate many unneeded reservists, who in turn would use many of the limited spaces that Cheney had authorized. In addition, the medical personnel were not needed in large numbers at any one hospital.

A solution was devised that met legal requirements and limited the original call-up to the professional care givers who were needed. Each Army unit had a unique unit identification code, a combination of letters and numbers. From the 3297th U.S. Army Hospital, a 1,000-bed U.S. Army Reserve hospital stationed in Chamblee, Georgia, the Health Services Command created five "derivative" or modified units, each with a similar code number but distinct in the last digit. They contained only professional health care providers and no administrative personnel. Those new units, the 3297th U.S. Army Hospital sections 2, 3, and 4 plus the 3297th U.S. Army Hospital Augmentation, were activated on 28 August with only the health care professionals from the parent unit. The new units did not serve as teams, however, because the personnel were not needed in large numbers at any one hospital. Individuals were dispersed to hospitals across the country as needed.

In that way, eighteen of the twenty-four U.S. Army hospitals in the contiguous United States were eventually called to active duty in two phases. In phase one, beginning in August, nine derivative hospitals and two derivative dental units were activated. Then, in phase two, the remainder of the hospitals were alerted on 14 December and called to active duty on 8 January 1991. That process was used for other types of

[30] Information Paper, DASG-PTM, 28 Dec 90, sub: Deployment/Activation of AMEDD Personnel for Operation DESERT SHIELD.

Combat service support by quartermaster personnel, overseeing the storage and delivery of water

units including the training divisions, schools, and intelligence units among others.

On 6 December 1990, the U.S. Army Forces Central Command Medical Group (Echelons Above Corps) (Provisional) was established. The Central Command Medical Group was the higher headquarters for four medical groups and several direct reporting units in the Southwest Asia theater of operations. The VII Corps and the XVIII Airborne Corps provided additional hospitals and medical resources tailored to meet the mission. More than 24,000 health care personnel deployed to Southwest Asia. Theater-wide, the forty-four hospitals provided 13,580 beds in four countries. After the liberation of Kuwait, a combat support hospital was located in Kuwait City.

Additional Reserve Mobilization

A second surge of reserve mobilization took place in September with the activation of 138 National Guard and Army Reserve units, containing 6,300 guardsmen and 6,700 reservists. This levy contained a much larger percentage of combat support and combat service support troops slated to deploy to Saudi Arabia than the earlier list. In August twenty-five of the forty-six units called served in the United States. Of the units called in September, all but three deployed to Southwest Asia.

Combat support elements contained 1,900 military policemen, including the headquarters of the 112th and 160th Military Police Battalions and twelve military police companies. Given the history of Iraq's use of chemical weapons against the Iranians and Kurds, the threat of chemical warfare was taken seriously throughout the crisis, and of the seven chemical units activated, six were nuclear, biological, and chemical defense and decontamination units.

Combat service support units formed the largest segment of the September call-up. Although the medical contingent of that phase was small, it included the first operational units—four helicopter ambulance detachments—deployed. Twenty-three quartermaster units included fifteen water purification and distribution elements and six petroleum supply units. Five ordnance conventional ammunition companies added another one thousand troopers to the list. The largest single element of the September call-up was provided by the Transportation Corps. Twenty-one truck companies and twenty-three movement and transportation management units were included in the 4,100 soldiers that constituted over 30 percent of the total.

Vehicles were a major part of the equipment supply problem that had always plagued the reserve components and were of particular concern during DESERT SHIELD. Although Congress had made large appropriations for the reserves in recent years, at the time of the call-up many units did not meet the Army's deployment standard. The issue involved the serviceability of equipment and its compatibility with the newest equipment issued to the Regular Army. The National Guard alone at the end of September was short 10,000 5-ton trucks nationwide.[31] In the case of the guard, units were brought to adequate readiness by sharing equipment among the units within individual states. During the crisis almost 3,300 pieces of equipment were redistributed between units in Alabama alone.[32] When shortages persisted the Department of the Army assigned vehicles right off the assembly line. The 1461st Transportation Company (Light Truck) of the Michigan National Guard sent its drivers from Fort Indiantown Gap, Pennsylvania, to Marysville, Ohio, to pick up 50 M939A2 5-ton trucks as they rolled out of the factory. The 253d Transportation Company (Light/Medium Truck) of the New Jersey National Guard got its on-the-road training the same way, convoying 46 new M923A2 trucks from the Ohio factory to Fort Dix, New Jersey.

By October the units called in August and September had been integrated into the Regular Army and were serving in every phase of the operation except as infantry, armor, and artillery units. They were joined then by thirty-eight additional units containing 4,700 troops. These were called up in three increments, the largest on 11 October, with two additional units activated on both 15 and 19 October. As in September the bulk of these reserve forces supported the combat force defending Saudi Arabia. As part of this call-up thirteen truck companies and a transportation battalion headquarters were activated. The Quartermaster Corps provided eight petroleum, water, and heavy material supply units. Five combat support maintenance companies, a supply company, two postal units, and a personnel services company rounded out the combat service support elements. Combat support troops included an aviation company and three combat engineer companies. In addition to these companies, a derivative unit headquarters of the 416th Engineer Command was activated. The 416th Engineer Command Headquarters (minus), commanded by Maj. Gen. Terrence D. Mulcahy, became the command element of ARCENT's 416th Engineer Group. Those turned out to be the last units called up during the initial deterrent or defensive phase of Operation DESERT SHIELD.

Unit Mobilization Process

Both active and reserve units followed similar procedures when alerted for mobilization. A unit first received an "alert" or "warning" order which helped the unit and its personnel begin premobilization preparations. Normally only a few days passed between the alert and activations, but during the early days of the crisis a month or more sometimes went by. In fact, not all units alerted were mobilized. Those that received mobilization orders reported to home stations and, after initial processing, moved to one of the mobilization stations.

At the mobilization stations, units made final preparations for movement. They completed all the administrative tasks involved in prepara-

[31] National Guard Bureau, Operation DESERT STORM Briefing Book 4, tab 28.

[32] Draft MS, National Guard Bureau, ARNG After Action Report, Part II: Lessons Learned [3 June 1991], p. 39, citing JULLS No. 43028–76914 (00014).

tion for overseas movement, were brought to full personnel and equipment strength, and undertook further training as time allowed. There, arriving units fell under the command of the garrison commander, who was supported by the installation garrison and a readiness group.[33]

Installation garrisons and jointly located active troop units, also often in the process of deployment, provided administrative support. In addition, many reserve-component units were called up specifically to support the mobilization effort. The 3397th U.S. Army Reserve Garrison from Chattanooga, Tennessee, for example, was one of four such units that provided installation support. It was mobilized on 27 August and served at Fort Campbell, Kentucky. Although it maintained its unit status, it was completely integrated into the active garrison already in place. That support included medical screening and care, bringing units to full strength, issuing equipment, and training within the limited time and facilities available.

As in all previous mobilizations, administrative processing was complex and time consuming. Although requirements and guidelines had been in place for years, many units and individual reservists lacked such basic necessities as wills, checking accounts and the accompanying "Sure-Pay"—direct pay deposit—paperwork, and panographic X-rays.

Dental and other medical conditions caused some serious delays but did not hinder deployment of many individuals. In some reserve units as many as 50 percent of the soldiers lacked dental X-rays and many needed extensive dental work, although that did not affect deployability. In addition, many reserve officers over forty years old had not received cardiovascular screening. That also did not affect deployability unless serious problems were discovered during routine screening, but it slowed the mobilization process somewhat. In one unit screening delays affected half of the officers.[34] Requirements for eyeglasses and hearing aids caused similar delays.

Army readiness groups of the Regular Army played major roles in mobilization of reserve units. Thirty readiness groups operated in the continental armies, eight each in the First and Second United States Armies, five in the Fourth and Sixth United States Armies, and four in the Fifth United States Army. In peacetime they helped reserve-component units reach and maintain high levels of readiness and during wartime assisted them to mobilize and deploy. The readiness groups were organized into combat arms, combat support, and administrative branches, and each branch was further subdivided into small teams. When alert orders were issued, readiness groups dispatched liaison teams to home stations to facilitate administrative preparation. Once mobilization was ordered, each readiness group formed mobilization assistance teams that joined the units at their home station, helped them move to the mobilization station, supervised postmobilization training, and ultimately provided the garrison commander with the information needed for a decision on unit validation.

---

[33] Andrulis Research Corporation, *Preliminary Report: Phase I— Operation Desert Shield* (Bethesda, Md.: Andrulis Research Corporation, 1990), p. 13.

[34] Ibid., p. 13.

At the mobilization stations the mobilization assistance teams helped plan and supervise predeployment training and advised the commander about the status of units at the station. Ultimately, it was the responsibility of the garrison commander to validate each unit, that is, to certify that each unit met the personnel, equipment, and training criteria for deployment. The readiness group, however, actually supervised the validation process.

Throughout that process the headquarters of the continental armies were key coordinators. They ensured that units in their respective geographical areas were brought to full equipment and personnel strength. They achieved that primarily through a distribution process. At home and mobilization stations, personnel were balanced between units, leaving some units understrength and unavailable for activation. If the mobilization stations did not have the necessary resources to accomplish the task, then the continental army took over and redistributed troops and equipment between installations within its geographical boundaries. The continental armies referred personnel problems they could not resolve to Forces Command. Forces Command in turn worked with the Army Personnel Command, which distributed personnel at the national level.

Equipment

During peacetime the Army's equipment did not sit in rows in motor pools awaiting the call to arms. In the course of training vehicles were driven, helicopters were flown, tanks and artillery pieces fired rounds down range, and trucks hauled supplies and equipment. Transmissions broke down, gun tubes became worn, and engines required overhaul. Fully outfitting a unit before it deployed to Southwest Asia was critical. If a unit was not filled prior to departure, the materiel and supplies would have to catch up to the unit overseas. That was a minor problem for units going to Europe or Korea where fully developed theater logistics systems already existed. In Southwest Asia no such infrastructure existed, and until it did, units depended on what they took with them. Furthermore, equipment and supplies sent to catch up with deployed units took up valuable space on ships and airplanes and stressed the weak theater logistics system.

Forces deploying from the United States therefore faced serious equipment shortages. Given sufficient time, they could take equipment from other units not deploying. For example, the 5th Infantry Division at Fort Polk, Louisiana, filled radio shortages in the 197th Infantry Brigade. When sharing did not work, deploying units identified shortages and submitted requisitions through the supply system, hoping those requisitions would be expedited for delivery before deployment. In the days after notification of deployment the 24th Infantry Division placed requisitions valued at $50 million for vehicles, ammunition, flak jackets, uniforms, and other requirements.[35]

[35] *Soldiers* 45:11 (November 1990): 10.

Basically units deployed with what they had, not necessarily the best the Army owned. Modern equipment generally went first to units that were deployed in forward areas. Units in the United States waited their turn. For example, armor units in Europe had M1A1 tanks equipped with 120-mm. cannons and chemical protection, while the 24th Infantry Division had M1 tanks with the less powerful 105-mm. guns and outdated chemical protection. The 197th Infantry Brigade had some even older M60A3s from the previous generation of tanks. The Army reassessed its modernization plans while concentrating on getting a credible deterrent force into the Saudi Arabian desert.

Ammunition was of paramount importance. There were critical shortages of artillery antitank ammunition, ball and tracer ammunition for M16A2 rifles, dual-purpose artillery munitions, and others.[36] As of 8 August the 24th Infantry Division had only enough stock at its local ammunition supply point to provision a single brigade-size task force. Other units faced similar situations, and Army depots worked overtime during August. At Letterkenny Army Depot in Pennsylvania, for example, workers pulled ammunition from storage in over 900 ammunition storage igloos and loaded as many as fifteen trucks a day for shipment to deploying units.[37]

Once alerted, soldiers at Forts Bragg, Benning, Stewart, Campbell, Hood, Bliss, Huachuca (Arizona), and elsewhere, found themselves in the throes of preparing for deployment. Not only did they prepare themselves, but they also repaired and packed equipment. One battalion of the 1st Brigade, 2d Armored Division, had to replace the gun tubes on 21 of its 58 tanks, put new sets of track on 24 others, and changed 430 roadwheels before it could finish loading its materiel.[38] Ammunition accompanying the troops was issued and stored on vehicles. Medical sets were checked, stocked, and packed.

Some critical equipment such as communications gear and attack helicopters went with the soldiers by air, but the bulk of the equipment that went by sea had to be railroaded, driven, or flown to the ports to be loaded for the two-week voyage to Saudi Arabia. Once the ships were loaded, the soldiers returned to their home stations to train on individual and unit skills and to enjoy their last days at home before they had to begin processing for overseas movement. Their air movement overseas would be geared to the expected arrival date of their equipment.

Every component of the Army supported the deployment effort. The Army Materiel Command provided the equipment and supplies that the Army needed to fight. It also took on the added task of providing equipment, vehicles, and parts to allied countries in accordance with guidance and priorities from the Department of Defense. Depots, supply facilities, and shops throughout the country produced the equipment, parts, ammunition, meals, and other items essential to the maintenance and sustainment of the force.

[36] Msg, Cdr, 24th Infantry Division, to Cdr, FORSCOM (Personal for Maj Gen Pagonis, J4, FORSCOM), 8 Aug 90, sub: Key Ammunition Short Falls—24th Infantry Division (Mech).

[37] *Soldiers* 45:11 (November 1990): 10.

[38] *Army Times*, 10 Jun 91, p. 16.

Despite heroic efforts on the part of agencies such as the Army Materiel Command, deploying units faced critical shortages of supplies and equipment. Scarcely one week after the initial deployment order, the XVIII Airborne Corps reported shortages in desert camouflage uniforms and chemical protective overgarments at Fort Bragg.[39] Other installations also reported shortages of uniforms and overgarments.[40]

On 18 August additional chemical protective overgarments were released for issue from U.S. Army, Europe, stocks. U.S. stocks of desert camouflage uniforms were also released as the logistics system increased production. On 19 August Secretary Cheney and General Vuono learned that the Army had enough desert uniforms to support the deploying forces at two sets per soldier. Meanwhile, the Defense Personnel Support Center, which had enough cloth on hand to make 200,000 more, redirected two contractors to produce the uniforms and expedited the procurement of an additional 1 million.[41] While efforts continued to increase production, the vast stores of equipment and supplies in Europe helped ease immediate needs. On 21 August a shipment of chemical suits went from Europe to Fort Bragg. Later a direct supply line between Europe and Saudi Arabia met needs for clothing, tents, radios, and other scarce items of supply.[42]

The largest and most significant shipment of items from European stocks during the first phase of DESERT SHIELD involved tanks. In October Secretary Cheney's office approved a request to replace the Army's older models in Saudi Arabia. Over 600 newer M1A1 tanks with 120-mm. guns and chemical overpressure protection were shipped from pre-positioned stocks in Germany.

Although the shipment of tanks from Germany was by far the largest force modernization activity during DESERT SHIELD, there were others. From the beginning of the deployment, modernization efforts enhanced ARCENT capabilities. These efforts were managed centrally from Army headquarters at the Pentagon. As General Vuono had promised, they proceeded without disrupting readiness. Modernization ranged from the shipment of improved kitchen trailers to off-the-shelf purchases of tactical locating devices and, in other areas, took the form of incremental improvements to current models of equipment. Overall, the changes had a positive effect on troop morale.[43]

Incremental improvements were particularly important in the case of helicopters. Operations in the Saudi desert gave Army aviation units some rare challenges. The pilots had some desert flying experience from training at the National Training Center at Fort Irwin and during Central Command's biennial exercise BRIGHT STAR in Egypt conducted with Egyptian forces, but flying and maintaining aircraft in Saudi Arabia was unique. The fine desert sand eroded the leading edges of rotor blades, clogged fuel lines and particle separators, and pitted windscreens. The Army's aviation community studied each problem, looking for solutions with the least effect on operations and readiness. To protect rotor blades

[39] Msg, CINCFOR to CJCS, 16 Aug 90, sub: Sitrep, 15 Aug 90.

[40] Msg, Cdr, TRANSCEN, to Cdr, FORSCOM, 19 Aug 90, sub: Installation Sitrep Number 7.

[41] Memo, Deputy Chief of Staff for Operations and Plans for Secretary of the Army and the Chief of Staff, 19 Aug 90, sub: Army Operations Update Operation DESERT SHIELD—Information Memorandum Number 12.

[42] Msg, Cdr, XVIII Airborne Corps, to CINCFOR, 22 Aug 90, sub: Sitrep No. 15, 22 Aug 90.

[43] Vuono interview, 3 Aug 92.

from erosion caused by airborne sand, a special paint, and later a special tape, was applied to the blades' leading edge. Improved particle separators were developed and shipped to the area of operations for installation. Windscreen covers were tested and purchased. They were particularly important because pitted windscreens affected the ability of the pilots to fly at night.

The erosion caused by the blowing sand distorted images in the pilots' night vision goggles and increased the chances of accidents. Resolving problems associated with flying and fighting at night was crucial. The Army's ability to do so would provide it a clear-cut advantage over Iraqi forces.

Morale

Once in theater, the soldiers had to prepare for their military mission and become accustomed to the Middle East environment and culture. Learning to cope with the stress, discomfort, and boredom, as well as the Saudi culture, became their main challenges. They knew very little about Saudi culture and society. Liquor was banned, Mecca beckoned five times a day, women could not show their faces in public, and religious police patrolled the streets.[44]

Maintaining the morale of soldiers, the bedrock of an Army's efficiency, became one of the commander's most important tasks. In the austere physical, cultural, and social environment of Saudi Arabia the soldier's morale took on an added significance, and commanders found and

[44] *Soldiers* 45:11 (November 1990): 13–14.

Life in the desert. VII Corps soldiers make the best of their austere field conditions, getting haircuts, disposing of waste, and washing their clothes.

Maintaining the soldiers' morale with mail service and roving hamburger stands

applied field expedient solutions to the problems. Recreation specialists from the United States established programs and recreation centers. "Care packages" from relatives and even strangers in the United States also helped. Nevertheless, as Col. Theodore W. Reid of the 197th Infantry Brigade observed, keeping up the morale of the troops as they adapted to life in their primitive camps, operating bases, and firing positions in the desert was "darned tough."[45]

The Army went to great lengths to grapple with this situation. Within a week of the beginning of the deployment, the XVIII Airborne Corps' forward command post in Saudi Arabia asked for mobile field post exchanges, and the dispatch of health and comfort items for deployed troops. Mail service started soon after the first deployments. At first a trickle, the flow quickly turned into a torrent. A microwave system went into Dhahran on 15 August for Armed Forces Radio and Television Service's broadcasters and technicians.[46] Army field rations, including the infamous MREs, were supplemented by fruits, vegetables, and other products from the local economy. Roving hamburger stands, dubbed Wolfmobiles after the ARCENT food service officer who set them up, soon made their rounds.

The Clash of Cultures

Maintaining morale while respecting the sensibilities of the host nation required compromises on the part of the U.S. forces as well as the Saudi Arabian government. Questions and observations regarding an expected serious clash of cultures between U.S. troops and the Saudi Arabian people received much press attention in the United States. The U.S. military in Saudi Arabia, however, made extraordinary efforts to reduce tensions and to avoid offending the Saudis. The Saudis in turn made some cultural con-

[45] *Soldiers* 45:10 (October 1990): 36.

[46] Msg, Cdr, XVIII Airborne Corps, to CINCFOR, 14 Aug 90, sub: Sitrep No. 7, 14 Aug 90.

cessions to the armies protecting them, especially within the military bases shared by U.S. and Saudi troops.

Particularly stressful to the Saudis was the role of female soldiers during the crisis. The Saudis found uniformed female soldiers, who lived in the same billets as male soldiers and frequently gave orders to men, disconcerting and almost incomprehensible. Concessions had to be made by all to protect host nation sensibilities while giving the soldiers enough latitude to accomplish their jobs.

Although women are forbidden to drive in Saudi Arabia, U.S. servicewomen could discreetly drive vehicles while on duty. Women who ventured off base, however, were sometimes required to wear black robes and veils, depending on the location of the base and the policies of the military district in which it was located. Generally, female troops were most restricted in urban areas, where their chances for contact with host nationals were greatest. If shopping off-base, women were required to have a male escort, and men and women were discouraged from engaging in public physical contact.[47] The restrictions on dress and activities placed on women angered many male and female soldiers, as well as Congresswoman Patricia Schroeder of Colorado. "Can you imagine," she asked, "if we sent black soldiers to South Africa and asked them to go along with apartheid rules?"[48]

Since alcoholic beverages were forbidden in Saudi Arabia, Army leadership enforced that prohibition. Soldiers turned to other methods of relaxation and entertainment, one of which was an increased use of tobacco.[49]

Another potential problem centered on religion and the overt practice of religious beliefs. Saudi Arabia forbade the practice of any religion except Islam. Although the Army leadership realized that they could not ask soldiers to refrain from practicing their religion without precipitating a severe morale problem, they asked Army chaplains to be discreet in their activities, to the point of limiting Christmas celebrations. The chaplains tried to comply with these restraints, while many soldiers, isolated from their families and attempting to deal with the harsh desert environment, were in the process of discovering an increased interest in religion.[50] Soldiers were asked to refrain from displaying religious symbols outside and indoors in areas frequented by the Saudis, and the Army chaplains were asked to remove their insignia when outside of U.S.-controlled areas.

Initially, the Saudis requested that such terms as "church services" and "chaplains" not be used and that the phrases "morale services" and "morale officers" be substituted.[51] The ban on the terms "chaplain" and "church service" was lifted in January. As a general rule, those troops located near major urban areas experienced more restrictions than did those in areas of infrequent contact with host nationals.

Saudi customs officials closely inspected all incoming mail for the U.S. troops and strictly enforced the ban on mailing religious materials to private individuals. In December the Saudis lifted that prohibition.[52]

[47] Molly Moore, "For Female Soldiers, Different Rules," *Washington Post*, 23 Aug 90, p. D1; James LeMoyne, "Army Women and the Saudis: The Encounter Shocks Both," *New York Times*, 25 Sep 90, p. 1.

[48] "Our Women in the Desert," *Newsweek* (10 September 1990): 22.

[49] Information Paper, Stanley Prepscius, DAPE-HR-PR, 19 Mar 91.

[50] Interv, Henry O. Malone and Susan Canedy with Chaplain (Col) Gaylord E. Hatler, 14 Jun 91.

[51] Ibid.

[52] Information Paper, Chaplain (Lt Col) Jack Anderson, DAPE-HR-S, Religious Support For Deployed Personnel During Operation DESERT SHIELD/STORM (All Services), n.d.

Regardless of the prohibitions, chaplains in Southwest Asia conducted 17,394 Protestant services attended by 649,281 soldiers. In addition, 9,421 Catholic services attracted 425,772 attendees, and 390 Jewish services drew an attendance of 9,803. Almost 900 other types of religious services were held for 22,539 interested troops. A special Passover Seder was organized for 350 Jewish soldiers on board the Cunard *Princess*, a rest and recreation ship leased by the U.S. government. Working with the Saudi government, the chaplains also organized a small haj, or pilgrimage, to Mecca for U.S. Muslim soldiers.[53]

The 681 chaplains included 560 Protestants, 115 Catholics, and 6 Jews. Between them they distributed a variety of religious literature and objects, among them over 300,000 books and pamphlets, 150,000 audio tapes, and 700 menorahs. That material had been shipped to Southwest Asia by the Military Airlift Command and was not subject to the mailing prohibitions.[54]

The chaplains managed to finesse their way around the delicate issue of communion wine. Roman Catholics, Episcopalians, and some Lutherans required wine for the sacrament. As wine was forbidden in Saudi Arabia, the chaplains came up with the idea of a "chaplain consumable resupply kit," a box containing enough wine, grape juice, crosses, scriptures, communion wafers, and rosaries to last two weeks.[55]

Rotation and Reinforcement

Once deployed, the soldier's basic question quickly became "when am I going home?" In August the Army was already studying that question as the first units arrived in Saudi Arabia. Tentative assumptions and scenarios addressed long-range force requirements for Southwest Asia. Many significant variables clouded the analysis. Would Iraq attack? Would the president commit U.S. ground forces for an extended period of time? Would a diplomatic solution be arranged? Other unclear aspects involved the troop commitments of coalition partners and mobilization of the reserves. If the reserves were mobilized would the Army receive the number of reserve units and soldiers requested? It became increasingly clear from these early assessments that sustainment of even a short-term presence of a sizable contingent of Army forces required involvement of the entire Army.[56]

By 18 August action officers had prepared a briefing discussing various strategies for supporting long-term force commitments in Southwest Asia for presentation to General Vuono. Among the matters requiring immediate attention of the chief of staff was the establishment of individual or unit rotations. A decision to conduct such rotation raised questions regarding whether units should deploy with their own equipment or should assume responsibility for equipment already in the theater and whether unit equipment would be modernized. The length of a tour of duty also remained a serious issue.[57]

[53] Ibid.; Hatler interview.

[54] Information Paper, Chaplain Anderson, Religious Support For Deployed Personnel; Geraldine Baum, "Baptism of Fire," *Los Angeles Times*, 2 Jan 91.

[55] Hatler interview.

[56] Discussion Paper, Strategic Planning Team, Office of the Deputy Chief of Staff for Operations, Department of the Army, 29 Aug 90, sub: DESERT SHIELD—Why We Are There: A Discussion of Strategy and Policy.

[57] Briefing Slides, Sustaining the SWA Force, in the Army Operations Center Daybook no. 3, 11–17 Sep 90.

On 15 October Central Command presented its recommendations for a DESERT SHIELD rotation policy to the Joint Chiefs of Staff. Central Command suggested two different schemes. For combat and support units at operating bases and defensive positions in the desert, Central Command wanted a six- to eight-month cycle. For other units and personnel in less demanding environments the command recommended a twelve-month tour of duty. General Schwarzkopf and his planners were to maintain the existing combat capability indefinitely; to preserve the continuity of planning, operations, coalition relationships, and the understanding of the culture and environment; to establish and maintain equity among services; to provide tactical reliefs of units; and, when possible, to have incoming units take over major weapon systems and equipment. The assumptions that influenced the development of the policy and its objectives included the expectation that Central Command's force structure and mission would stay the same, that DESERT SHIELD would last at least one year, and that rotation would be phased so all units would not be replaced all at once. The plan also assumed that force modernization activities would not adversely affect rotations, that the first priority was preserving combat capability, and that if the mission changed the rotation policy too would be changed or terminated.[58]

The Army Staff and the Army's subordinate headquarters evaluated and adjusted the Army's deployment procedures to support that proposal and possible revisions. On 13 October Army Central Command, anticipating the announcement of a rotation policy, asked for the assignment of specially trained noncommissioned officers to help formulate the redeployment troop list.[59] Three days later Forces Command hosted a two-day workshop to create a data base for the redeployment of units. The goal was to identify active and reserve units that could exchange with units deployed to Saudi Arabia. Forces Command wanted to develop and distribute the data base to its subordinate headquarters by 1 November, but reminded its subordinates that "the decision on rotation and timing are currently unknown." Indeed, final choices on rotation awaited more basic decisions. If coalition forces were about to become involved in ejecting the Iraqis from Kuwait, reinforcement, not rotation, would become the focus of planning.[60]

By the time that these discussions took place, the SHIELD had expanded dramatically. Three complete combat divisions of the XVIII Airborne Corps had reached Saudi Arabia from the United States. So had advance elements of the 1st Cavalry Division, the entire 3d Armored Cavalry, and the first of a steady flow of reserve-component units. Six Patriot batteries and the 12th Aviation Brigade had come from Germany. The soldiers in Operation DESERT SHIELD were acclimating themselves to the physical and cultural environment, and, as their numbers grew, their vulnerability to an Iraqi attack was diminishing.

[58] Msg, USCINCCENT to Joint Chiefs of Staff (JCS), 15 Oct 90, sub: DESERT SHIELD Theater Rotation Policy.

[59] Msg, COMUSARCENT, 13 Oct 90, sub: USARCENT MAIN G3 Sitrep.

[60] Msg, CINCFOR to Cdr, First U.S. Army, 20 Oct 90, sub: Operation DESERT SHIELD Rotational Units; Vuono interview, 3 Aug 92.

Chapter 5
REINFORCEMENT FOR AN OFFENSIVE

On 8 November 1990 President George H. Bush announced that the United States would send additional armed forces to Southwest Asia to provide the coalition with a ground offensive option. Until that point the United States and its coalition partners had concentrated on the deployment of enough troops and materiel to safeguard Saudi Arabia from attack by Iraq. Now, if economic sanctions proved insufficient to dislodge President Saddam Hussein's occupying forces from Kuwait, Bush wanted the capability to launch an attack. To this end, U.S. Army planners now began preparing for one of the most impressive offensive operations of modern times.

Ground Offensive Option

As early as the Camp David meeting on 4–5 August, two days after the invasion, General Schwarzkopf had raised the possibility of an attack on the Iraqis. At that time he estimated that he would need eight to twelve months to assemble the necessary forces. Already, the plans section at the United States Central Command (CENTCOM) was investigating specific courses of action for such an offensive. At this early date, however, Central Command was so involved with the deployment to Saudi Arabia that it could not devote much time or thought to an offensive movement.[1]

Real planning for the offensive started in mid-September. To focus the process and ensure secrecy at a time when leaks might have touched off a preemptive Iraqi strike or disrupted the fragile coalition, General Schwarzkopf decided to form a special planning cell within Central Command. He asked Army Chief of Staff General Carl E. Vuono to send four graduates of the Army's School of Advanced Military Studies. This element of the Command and General Staff College at Fort Leavenworth, Kansas, was, according to Col. Richard M. Swain, the U.S. Army Central Command (ARCENT) historian, "the Army's premier school of the operational art." Lt. Col. Joseph H. Purvis, Maj. Gregory M. Eckhart, Maj. William S. Pennypacker, and Maj. Daniel J. Roh arrived in Saudi Arabia on 16 September. They met two days later with Schwarzkopf, who sketched his rough concept of a campaign to oust the Iraqis from Kuwait.

[1] Draft MS, Capt Douglas, CENTCOM History, p. 7; Interv, David Frost with General H. Norman Schwarzkopf, 20 Mar 91, Riyadh, Saudi Arabia; Thomas L. Friedman and Patrick E. Tyler, "From the First, U.S. Resolve to Fight," *New York Times*, 3 Mar 91; Interv, Maj Larry Heystek with CENTCOM Planning Cell, Operation DESERT STORM, 7 Mar 91, Riyadh, Saudi Arabia (hereafter cited as CENTCOM Planning Cell interview), p. 2.

He envisioned a thrust across the Kuwaiti frontier toward the Ar Rawḍatayn oil fields, cutting the main north-south route from Kuwait City to the Iraqi border. He placed almost no constraints on the group, beyond limiting their consideration to available forces in the theater, but asked that they look at the problem and report back to him.[2]

The four officers agreed that the environment posed enormous obstacles. West of the coastal flats, the terrain along the Saudi border consisted largely of a vast stony plain, cut by infrequent wadies, streambeds that were dry for most of the year but occasionally filled with the runoff from torrential rains. Farther west, beyond the triborder area of Kuwait, Iraq, and Saudi Arabia, that plain gave way to wide sandy stretches of almost featureless desert, sparsely inhabited except by pastoral nomads. Temperatures during the summer reached as high as 130 degrees Fahrenheit, although they dropped to the 50's and 60's in January and February.

During the winter the occasional rains could turn desert sand into a quagmire for men and vehicles. Annual rainfall followed the dry pattern of desert regions—only three to seven inches—with about 90 percent coming in the November–April period, the season of DESERT SHIELD and DESERT STORM. Brief periods of concentrated rainfall produced the wadies. Several large ones extended across the Iraqi-Saudi border on a northeast-southwest axis. These long straight depressions had long raised concerns about invasion among peoples of the region, especially among the Saudis since the development of their oil resources. One in particular, the Wādī al Bāṭin, formed the western border of Kuwait and extended 150 miles on a straight line to the southwest into Saudi Arabia.

Winds whipped the talcum-fine sand at almost hurricane force for hours at a time, cutting visibility and rendering life almost intolerable. The southern and southeasterly *sharqi*, a dry wind that occurred from April to early June and again from late September through November, gusted to over 50 miles an hour and raised dust storms several thousand feet high. The northern and northwesterly *shamal* brought a more continuous wind of lower velocity from mid-June to mid-September.

If the climate could make desert operations uncomfortable, the vast distances and lack of transport could make them practically impossible. From the port city of Ad Dammām, the key base of King Khalid Military City lay 334 to 528 miles away, depending on whether one used the northern or southern route, and the village of Rafḥā, from which flank units of XVIII Airborne Corps would launch their attack, lay 502 to 696 miles away. In contrast, the famed Red Ball Express of World War II covered a round trip of 746 miles.[3]

Assuming American troops could overcome such environmental conditions, they still would need to defeat an enemy force of more than one million soldiers. In the last two years of the Iran-Iraq war the Iraqi Army had impressed observers with its flexibility, centralized command structure, and ability to coordinate large-unit operations over great distances. Its General Headquarters supervised up to ten corps headquarters, which

[2] CENTCOM Planning Cell interview; Chronology, Special Planning Cell, J–5, CENTCOM (hereafter cited as Special Planning Cell chronology), p. 1; Quote from Draft MS, Swain, Operational Narrative, pp. 34, 36.

[3] Draft MS, Swain, Operational Narrative, pp. 9, 60; Nyrop, ed., *Saudi Arabia, A Country Study*, pp. 66–67, 70; Nyrop, ed., *Iraq: A Country Study*, p. 71; U.S. Army Center for Army Lessons Learned, *Winning in the Desert* (Fort Leavenworth, Kans.: Army Center for Lessons Learned, 1990), pp. 1, 5; Dan Janutolo, "101st on the Front Lines," *Soldiers* 46 (January 1991): 19; W. F. Gabella, "Formidable Natural Hazards Await U.S. Coalition Forces," *Armed Forces Journal International* (March 1991): 36.

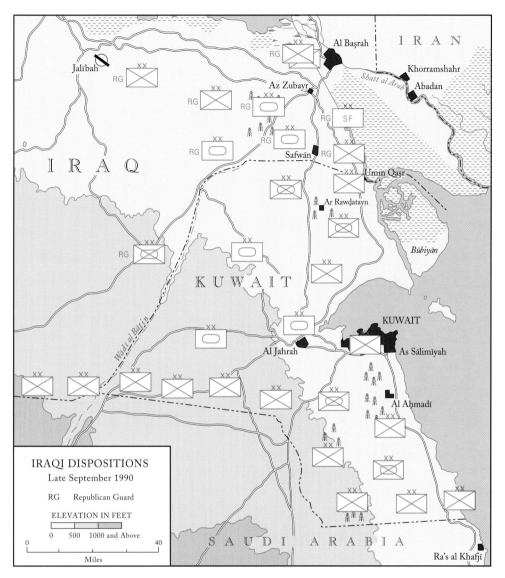

IRAQI DISPOSITIONS

Late September 1990

RG   Republican Guard

ELEVATION IN FEET

0   500   1000 and Above

0   40

Miles

Map 8

not only performed administrative and logistical tasks but also fought the battles. Each corps directed as many as ten armored, mechanized, or infantry divisions, depending on the tactical situation. The brigade was normally the smallest unit to operate independently. Also subordinate to the General Headquarters but separate from the regulars was the corps-size *Republican Guard Forces Command*, the shock troops of Iraq's military. Originally created to protect the government, its tanks, mechanized infantry, infantry, and special forces had done well in the Iran-Iraq war as a theater reserve for counterattacking Iranian breakthroughs. The Iraqi Army's 4,500 main battle tanks included about 500 Soviet T–72s. Its artillery of 3,200 guns included the massive South African 155-mm. G–5s that far outranged any comparable weapon in the U.S. inventory. With time, Iraqi weaknesses in morale, equipment, training, and initia-

Iraqi fortifications around
Kuwait City. A front-line communications trench connected
tank firing positions along the
beach to defend against an
amphibious assault that never
materialized.

tive at lower levels would become evident. But in September 1990 the Iraqi Army enjoyed a reputation as one of the best equipped, most combat-hardened forces in the world (*see Map 8*).[4]

While the Iraqis had developed some offensive skills by the end of the Iran-Iraq war and Iraqi doctrine paid lip service to the primacy of the offensive, the Iraqi Army remained essentially a defensive force that thought in linear terms. Iraqi defensive tactics demonstrated the influence of Soviet doctrine, with its emphasis on obstacles, mutual fire support, and preplanned kill zones. Generally, the Iraqis prepared defenses in depth, positioning two units forward and one back to create a triangular kill zone in which artillery and armor could hammer any unit that broke through the front lines. Occasionally, the artillery would use chemical weapons, especially mustard and nerve agents, but these weapons remained under tight presidential control and were not an integral part of corps or lower-level plans. Interestingly, in view of later events, the Iraqi logistical organization had earned a fair amount of respect from Western observers for its ability to supply units over long distances. In keeping with the centralized command structure, higher headquarters "pushed down" supplies to corps depots, from which the corps distributed them to the divisions.[5]

Saddam Hussein's August offensive into Kuwait with *Republican Guard*, mechanized, and special forces had caused grave concern in Washington and Riyadh over whether the Iraqis would continue their drive south into Saudi Arabia. Some of the initial apprehension abated in the ensuing weeks. According to U.S. intelligence information for mid- to late September, the Iraqis were repositioning their troops and constructing fortifications for a defense of Kuwait. The reports noted infantry units taking the place of mechanized formations along the border, with mechanized troops moving into immediate reserve, and the *Republican Guard* redeploying into theater reserve, just north of the Iraq-Kuwait border. Iraqi engineers were building roads to support the new deployment and developing a front-line system of triangular strongpoints fronted by wire, minefields, six- to fifteen-foot sand berms, and forty-foot tank ditches.

[4] U.S. Army Intelligence and Threat Analysis Center, How They Fight: DESERT SHIELD Order of Battle Handbook, AIA–DS–2–90, Sep 90 (hereafter cited as Order of Battle Handbook), pp. 5, 43–44; U.S. Army Intelligence Agency, Identifying the Iraqi Threat and How They Fight, AIA–DS–1–90, Sep 90 update, p. 2; National Training Center Handbook 100–91, The Iraqi Army; Organization and Tactics [3 Jan 91], pp. 1–2; MS, Col Robert A. Doughty, War in the Persian Gulf [United States Military Academy (USMA), Apr 91], pp. 5–6.

[5] Order of Battle Handbook, pp. 43, 60, 64; David Eshel, "Obstacle Breaching Techniques," *Armor* 100 (January–February 1991): 11; Southwest Asia (SWA) Military Operations Opposing Forces, Tactics and Doctrine, pp. 14, 27–30.

The coalition tidal wave. This psychological operations leaflet, printed for distribution among Iraqi forces in Kuwait, reinforced the impression that coalition forces would attempt a massive amphibious assault.

This defensive system extended west of the triborder area. Any attack on these works promised to be a bloody venture.[6]

Inadequate Capabilities

Such was the task facing Colonel Purvis' special planning cell as it started its deliberations. The planners began with the objectives of the operation: ousting the Iraqis from Kuwait and reinstating Kuwait's legitimate government, destroying the Iraqi ground forces' offensive capability, and restoring the regional balance of power. To achieve these goals, they assumed that they would have the support of coalition forces, as well as all of the forces of XVIII Airborne Corps—the 82d Airborne Division, the 101st Airborne Division (Air Assault), the 24th Infantry Division (Mechanized), the 1st Cavalry Division (Armored), and the 3d Armored Cavalry. Even with coalition backing, however, the planners realized that allied forces lacked the clear superiority traditionally required by an attacking force, and they were well aware of the need to minimize friendly losses. So they concluded that any plan with a fair chance of success had to bypass centers of Iraqi resistance and use air power to cut in half

[6] Tamir Eshel, "Drawing (Defensive) Lines in the Sand," *Armed Forces Journal International* (February 1991): 18; Office of the Deputy Chief of Staff for Intelligence (ODCSINT) Intelligence Summaries for mid- to late September.

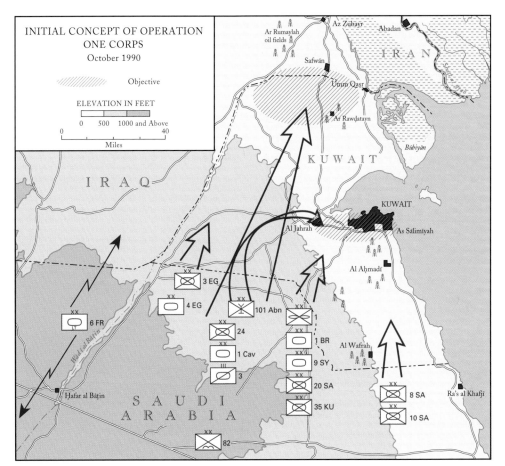

Map 9

the enemy's strength before the start of the ground war. Already, they were attracted by the open Iraqi western flank; but, given the limited available forces and great distances, they felt that a wide swing around the flank would leave XVIII Airborne Corps isolated at the end of a long uncertain line of communications.

The initial plan presented to General Schwarzkopf on 6 October had all the appearances of a bloody frontal assault. The one that he approved called for a shallow envelopment between the triborder area and the elbow of Kuwait, driving north and east to the main north-south highway in the area of Al Jahrah with an option to continue on to the Ar Rawḍatayn oil fields and the northern Kuwait-Iraq border. Although bypassing Iraqi strongpoints, the proposed attack would still encounter key Iraqi ground units. No one seemed to have been comfortable with the plan, and Schwarzkopf indicated this to his superiors in Washington. When CENTCOM chief of staff Marine Maj. Gen. Robert B. Johnston and his team presented the concept to President Bush, Secretary of Defense Richard B. Cheney, and the Joint Chiefs of Staff on 10–11 October, they were told to develop it further, requesting more resources if necessary (*Map 9*).[7]

The Flanking Movement

Directed by General Schwarzkopf to work on both a two-corps and a one-corps concept, Colonel Purvis' special planning cell looked hard at options for much wider flanking movements. Assuming availability of a second corps, the biggest hurdle was logistical, especially the distances involved, transportation, storage, and the ability of the desert floor to support the mass movement of heavy vehicles. Maps and other data on the area of operations were scarce, and efforts to gather information faced the twin obstacles of secrecy and the embryonic status of the Army's intelligence-gathering apparatus in the theater. The planners compensated for the lack of information with their own examinations of the terrain. Purvis, Pennypacker, Eckhart, and Roh, joined by CENTCOM staff members and Saudis, flew over, drove, or walked portions of the area of operations. More information came from photographic analyses and conversations with Bedouins. Meanwhile, XVIII Airborne Corps tested the ability of heavy vehicles to maneuver northwest of Ḥafar al Bāṭin. From the intelligence community, notably the 513th Military Intelligence Brigade, which had just arrived in Saudi Arabia, the planners got detailed terrain analyses and data on the Iraqi order of battle. Fortunately for the secrecy of their own work, they found that fellow graduates of the School of Advanced Military Studies at many CENTCOM levels were willing to share information without asking too many probing questions.[8]

By late October the plan for the envelopment was taking shape. General Schwarzkopf took an active role in the planning process. Through frequent conferences with Purvis, Pennypacker, Eckhart, and

[7] Draft MS, Swain, Operational Narrative, pp. 12, 36–39; Special Planning Cell chronology, pp. 1–2; CENTCOM Planning Cell interview, pp. 9–12, 48. General Schwarzkopf later declared that he had only prepared this plan in response to queries from Washington on his course of action should he be ordered to attack with the forces available. He indicated that his main purpose was to show the difficulty of an offensive by one corps to strengthen his case for another corps. See Interv, Frost with Schwarzkopf.

[8] Draft MS, Swain, Operational Narrative, pp. 36, 39; CENTCOM Planning Cell interview; Special Planning Cell chronology, pp. 2–3; Gabella, "Formidable Natural Hazards Await U.S. Coalition Forces," p. 38.

Roh, he heard their ideas and provided his own thoughts and direction for development of the concept. As a result of his influence, the plan focused on destruction of the *Republican Guard* as the main operational objective of the ground attack. To do this, the planners had discarded as too costly an amphibious assault on the heavily fortified Kuwaiti coast. Instead, two corps would drive across southern Iraq, west of Kuwait, to cut Iraqi communications at the key transportation center of An Nāṣirīyah on the Euphrates River. Trapped within the pocket created by this envelopment, the *Republican Guard* could then be destroyed at leisure by air and artillery fire. While several logistical problems remained to be solved, the plan appeared feasible.[9]

On 22 October, during General Colin Powell's visit to Central Command, the planners presented the concept to the Joint Chiefs chairman, who agreed to back the command's request for a second corps. Shortly thereafter in Washington, both Powell and Cheney decided that, in addition to a European-based corps, other forces should also be deployed. These included the 1st Infantry Division (Mechanized), three additional aircraft carrier battle groups, a battleship, the corps-size I Marine Expeditionary Force, and the 5th Marine Expeditionary Brigade.

Decision on Reinforcements

Four days after General Powell had met with General Schwarzkopf, Secretary Cheney held a special news briefing to announce the administration's decision to augment U.S forces in the Persian Gulf. Neither the exact number of additional troops nor the date for the completion of the buildup had been selected. These determinations, the secretary made clear, would also be made by President Bush.

On 30 October Cheney and Powell briefed the president on the reinforcements option, but told him that the new buildup could not be completed until 15 January 1991. The following day, at a meeting attended by Cheney, Powell, National Security Adviser Brent Scowcroft, and White House Chief of Staff John H. Sununu, Bush formally approved the idea. Concerned about adverse public reaction, he delayed making the decision public until after the 6 November congressional elections.[10] At a news briefing on the afternoon of 8 November President Bush publicly announced his decision to increase troop strength in Southwest Asia to ensure "an adequate offensive military option."[11]

Secretary Cheney signed the deployment orders that day. The augmentation required a major call-up of Army Reserve and Army National Guard units in all fifty states. Among the National Guard units eventually federalized were the 48th Infantry Brigade from Georgia; the 155th Armored Brigade from Mississippi; the 256th Infantry Brigade (Mechanized) from Louisiana; the 142d Field Artillery Brigade from Arkansas and Oklahoma; and the 196th Field Artillery Brigade from Tennessee, Kentucky, and West Virginia. The reinforcements package also cut in half the U.S. Army's divi-

[9] Special Planning Cell chronology, pp. 4–5; CENTCOM Planning Cell interview; Interv, Frank N. Schubert with Col Richard M. Swain, 20 Jun 91, Fort McPherson, Ga.

[10] Woodward, *The Commanders*, pp. 309–21; "The Path to War," *Newsweek*, Commemorative Edition (Spring/Summer 1991): 45–46.

[11] U.S. Congress, Senate, *Crisis in the Persian Gulf Region: U.S. Policy Options and Implications, Hearings Before the Committee on Armed Services*, 101st Cong., 2d sess., 1990, p. 109.

sional strength in Europe by ordering the redeployment of one of the two Army corps stationed there. Those units selected to deploy from Germany included the VII Corps headquarters, stationed in Stuttgart; the 1st Armored Division in Ansbach; the 3d Brigade, 2d Armored Division (Forward) in Garlstedt; the 3d Armored Division in Frankfurt; the 2d Armored Cavalry in Nuremberg; the 11th Aviation Brigade in Illesheim; and the 2d Support Command (Corps) in Stuttgart. In addition, the 1st Division at Fort Riley, Kansas, also received deployment orders.[12] The decision to send two additional armored divisions eventually raised the level of U.S. forces in the Persian Gulf region to over 400,000 (*see Table 6*).

About a week later Lt. Gen. Jimmy D. Ross, the Army's deputy chief of staff for logistics, raised again the issue of activating the 377th Theater Army Area Command. In his message of 14 November to Lt. Gen. John J. Yeosock, the ARCENT commander, he suggested that activation was the doctrinally sound approach. Ross acknowledged that the new headquarters would cause some immediate disruption, but he contended that the robust organization had been designed, staffed, and trained to support the larger operational force being built and would pay dividends in the long run. By this time the Provisional Support Command in Saudi Arabia had been in operation for three months, and the theater commanders remained uninterested in utilizing the 377th. Although the headquarters was never activated, Forces Command (FORSCOM) drew heavily on the units in its Capstone trace. By the middle of November fifty-five of the 377th's subordinate units were mobilized, with more to come.[13]

DEFORGER 90

Discussions of the possible use of units based in Europe for DESERT SHIELD dated from early August, when Department of the Army planners had asked for redeployment of combat support and combat service support units from Germany to Saudi Arabia. With the precedent for deployment of American forces from duty with the North Atlantic Treaty Organization (NATO) already established, the Army could consider using not only its I and III Corps from the United States but also its V and VII Corps from Germany.

Deployment from Europe offered numerous advantages. The corps were nearer to the theater of operations and had greater combat power, based on their readiness, size, and possession of the most modern equipment in the Army's inventory, such as the Abrams tank, the Bradley fighting vehicle, and the Apache helicopter. In addition, the deployment afforded General Vuono the opportunity to accelerate the inevitable reduction of American forces in Europe. General Crosbie E. Saint, who commanded U.S. Army, Europe (USAREUR), and Seventh Army, supported participation of USAREUR units in any possible crisis.[14]

But the move presented problems. A forward-deployed corps had never carried out a deployment of the kind and magnitude contemplat-

[12] Ibid., p. 676; Department of Defense Public Affairs Release, no. 540–90, More Heavy Divisions, Marines, and Ships Headed for the Persian Gulf, 8 Nov 90.

[13] Msg, Lt Gen Ross to Lt Gen Yeosock, 14 Nov 90, sub: Recall/Deployment of 377th Theater Army Area Command; Draft MS, John Brinkerhoff, The Case of the Unit that Wasn't Called, 15 Jan 92.

[14] Interv, Theresa L. Kraus with Headquarters, U.S. Army, Europe (HQ, USAREUR), staff, 22 May 91, Heidelberg, Germany (hereafter cited as HQ, USAREUR, staff interview); Vuono interview, 3 Aug 92.

ed by General Saint. Furthermore, VII Corps was neither structured for nor assigned a role in major out-of-theater contingencies. By deployment standards set by troops based in the United States, the movement from Germany would be unique. Unlike other transfers, in which units tended to be located on a single installation, USAREUR units came from several posts and numerous small communities. Such dispersion would complicate any relocation.[15]

Anchored by dependence on host nation support and fixed facilities for logistics, the corps also had responsibility for a network of military communities across southern Germany, supporting more than 92,000 soldiers and their families. Any deployment involved major challenges. The deploying corps would have to leave behind adequate means to take care of families and communities. They also had to move the soldiers and equipment to the Middle East as quickly as possible, allowing them time to assemble at arrival ports, collect equipment, deploy into the tactical assembly areas, equip and organize themselves for combat operations, and prepare and train for battle.[16]

While the U.S. Army, Europe, prepared for a possible deployment, ongoing developments affected the troops in Germany. General Saint and his staff were planning to close about 100 installations, to return facilities and other properties to the German government, and to restructure the residual force into a single combat-ready corps able to operate under NATO agreements. Accordingly, about twenty-one battalions were preparing to stand down, to turn in their equipment and property, and to return to the United States as a result of an arms reduction agreement between NATO and Warsaw Pact nations. In September 1990 the Department of Defense had announced the first units scheduled to leave Europe; some of those departures were set for as early as 1 March 1991 and others for 1 May. In anticipation of the reduction, U.S. Army, Europe, already had plans to withdraw the remaining contingents. Considerations for selecting units for deployment included plans for withdrawing selected units as well as capabilities, recent training, and the status of equipment modernization.[17]

In early September General Saint began planning for the possible deployment of his forces, either on rotation or as reinforcements, for units in the Persian Gulf. While the United States Transportation Command, alerted by the Army Staff that a European corps might later go to Southwest Asia, began considering how to position its vessels to carry out such a deployment, Saint entrusted early planning to his deputy chief of staff for operations, Maj. Gen. John C. Heldstab, and to USAREUR's Conventional Forces, Europe, Division. Because the division had responsibility for planning the drawdown of forces from Europe, the staff maintained a detailed computer data base on all U.S. Army units in Europe and knew which units were well trained, as well as the types and quantities of equipment each had. Since any deployment planning had to consider which units to leave in Europe, which to send home for drawdown, and the status of training and equipment of those units that might

[15] "Deploying the 'Keepers of the Faith,'" *Army Logistician* (May–June 1991): 26.

[16] Draft MS, HQ, VII Corps, Historical Narrative of VII Corps' Participation in Operations DESERT SHIELD and DESERT STORM, 22 Mar 91; Msg, Commander in Chief, U.S. Army, Europe (CINCUSAREUR), to V Corps, VII Corps, et al., 14 Nov 90.

[17] HQ, USAREUR, staff interview; "Deploying the 'Keepers of the Faith,'" p. 26.

Gen. Frederick M. Franks, Jr.
(Rank as of 23 August 1993)

be deployed, the planners closely scrutinized the selection of those units that eventually deployed.[18] By late October, with the concurrence of General John R. Galvin, Supreme Allied Commander Europe and Commander in Chief, United States European Command, Generals Saint and Heldstab developed the preliminary force package for an anticipated announcement on 2 November.[19]

On 2 and 3 November Secretary of the Army Michael P. W. Stone visited the U.S. Army, Europe, on his way to Saudi Arabia. He met with General Saint and the VII Corps commanding general, Lt. Gen. Frederick M. Franks, Jr., a taciturn, highly decorated tanker who had lost a leg in Vietnam. Presumably, at that meeting, the secretary discussed the completed draft of the force package. Also, at a luncheon attended only by a few officers, he probably alerted the two commanders of the president's upcoming announcement on the eighth.[20]

The day after Secretary Stone left, Generals Franks and Saint discussed the final organization of the corps units selected to deploy. Saint asked Franks to convene a small planning cell to determine the final force package and to begin deployment planning. USAREUR and VII Corps planners eventually settled on a force package with an atypical corps structure. They developed a heavy corps, organized around two heavy divisions of V and VII Corps units and other theater assets, that provided the types of units lacking in XVIII Airborne Corps. In particular, the inclusion of the 3d Armored Division, a V Corps unit with M1A1 Abrams tanks in its inventory, provided more armor than currently existed in other VII Corps units.[21] Its deployment rather than the VII Corps' 3d Infantry Division (Mechanized) also left an infantry unit in the Wuerzberg area so that southern Germany was not stripped totally of combat troops.

Because of time differences, President Bush's 8 November evening address to the nation was heard in Europe during the early morning hours of 9 November. Upon official notification, General Saint immediately issued a warning order. Within two days Deployment Order 22 was issued to participating units.

On 9 November General Franks held a commanders conference to give training guidance to the deploying units, as well as to begin planning for the base organization that would stay behind. The day after the conference, key VII Corps commanders departed for a reconnaissance trip to Saudi Arabia. Franks went to the Persian Gulf a few days later to talk with Schwarzkopf. At a 13 November strategy meeting of the CENTCOM staff Schwarzkopf told Franks his mission would be to attack the *Republican Guard*, an assignment that did not change once the ground war began. While in Riyadh Franks also discussed potential deployment problems with General Yeosock and Maj. Gen. William G. Pagonis, commander of the Provisional Support Command. After returning to Germany, the VII Corps commander formed a small tactical planning cell to outline the plan for the attack on the *Republican Guard*. On 5 December Yeosock and Franks reviewed the proposed draft. A CENTCOM briefing

[18] HQ, USAREUR, staff interview; Vuono interview, 3 Aug 92.

[19] Briefing Slides, USAREUR DCSOPS Conventional Forces, Europe (CFE), Division, Deployment of USAREUR Units to Saudi Arabia, n.d.

[20] Interv, Theresa L. Kraus with Russell Parkinson, 1 Jul 91, Washington, D.C.

[21] HQ, USAREUR, staff interview.

3d Armored Division troops combat the ubiquitous desert dust by performing daily maintenance on their M1A1s

on the tactical plans was scheduled for Cheney and Powell on 15 December, and General Franks, together with his primary staff, returned to Saudi Arabia on the fourteenth.[22]

Meanwhile, a VII Corps liaison team met with General Yeosock's staff in Riyadh about planning and controlling the identification and movement of the deploying force.[23] Thereafter, an ARCENT briefing team went to Germany to look into deployment priorities. The ARCENT team suggested that VII Corps adopt a movement sequence that began with a VII Corps tactical advance party. Next would come combat support and combat service support units, the 2d Armored Cavalry, the 7th Engineer Brigade, additional combat support and combat service support units, the 1st Armored Division, the 11th Aviation Brigade, VII Corps Headquarters and Headquarters Company, VII Corps Artillery, the 2d Armored Division (Forward), and, finally, the V Corps' 3d Armored Division.[24] In the only change made to the recommended priority list, General Saint decided to send the 2d Armored Cavalry to Saudi Arabia first. The regiment, a self-contained unit, could deploy immediately to set up assembly areas and prepare to receive the rest of the corps.[25]

With the movement sequence in place, USAREUR and VII Corps planners arranged for the deployments. Preparing for the large movement was not a new experience for U.S. Army, Europe. Beginning in 1967, soldiers from combat divisions in the United States had flown into European airports for twenty-one REFORGER exercises, conducted in response to the threat of a Warsaw Pact attack against NATO forces

[22] Interv, Theresa L. Kraus with Lt Col Peter Kindsvatter, 22 May 91, Moehringen, Germany.

[23] CINCUSAREUR Deployment Order 22, 10 Nov 90.

[24] Briefing Slides, USARCENT Briefing to VII Corps, c. Nov 91.

[25] Interv, Theresa L. Kraus with Maj Stephen Howard, Office of the Deputy Chief of Staff for Logistics (ODCSLOG), USAREUR, 24 May 91, Heidelberg, Germany.

in what was then West Germany. Subsequently, they picked up unit equipment that had been shipped into the Antwerp, Rotterdam, and Bremerhaven seaports, as well as unit gear—Pre-positioned Organizational Materiel Configured in Unit Sets (POMCUS)—that had been stored in Europe. For deployment to Southwest Asia the process would be reversed, with some changes. Yet the similarity to REFORGER exercises was so apparent that the soldiers and allies dubbed the movement DEFORGER 90.[26] Phase I commenced in August with the deployment of USAREUR units to Saudi Arabia.[27] Although modest in scale, it provided practical experience for Phase II in November–December with the deployment of VII Corps.

The 1st Transportation Agency (Movement Control) supervised the Phase II movement. The agency staff decided the mode of transportation to be used and served as the USAREUR manager for competing demands on the transportation system. The Military Traffic Management Command, Europe, chose ports and ordered and loaded the ships. The 21st Theater Army Area Command (TAACOM) operated the support areas at the ports and staging areas and provided the link in host nation support matters. To do this job, the 21st joined forces with its old REFORGER partners, the Military Sealift Command and the Military Traffic Management Command.[28] Since VII Corps deployed its corps movement control center, most of its logistical staff, and its 2d Support Command to Southwest Asia early, USAREUR deputy chief of staff for logistics, Maj. Gen. Joseph S. Laposata, along with the 1st Transportation Agency commander and other key staff officers, went to VII Corps headquarters to coordinate the movement of equipment. General Heldstab also went to Stuttgart to establish and oversee an air movement control center, which helped arrange the transfer of soldiers from Germany to Saudi Arabia.[29]

In about seven weeks the U.S. Army, Europe, moved more than 122,000 soldiers and civilians and 50,500 pieces of equipment from Germany to Saudi Arabia. The tight schedule, coupled with the unpredictable German winter weather conditions, made it essential to use all available modes of transportation. Thousands of tracked and wheeled vehicles, hundreds of aircraft, and tons of equipment and supplies deployed every way possible—421 barge loads from the primary loading sites at Mannheim and Aschaffenburg; 407 trains, with 12,210 railcars; and 204 road convoys, totaling 5,100 vehicles. In a deliberate effort to reduce the burden of increased traffic on the autobahns and to expedite the move, the large majority of vehicles, both tracked and wheeled, traveled by rail or barge.[30]

Once at the three ports,[31] the equipment was assembled in staging areas and subsequently sent in 154 shiploads to Saudi Arabia. The soldiers flew out of Ramstein, Rhein Main, Nuremberg, and Stuttgart. It took 1,772 buses to move the troops to the airports, 1,008 vehicles and drivers from the 37th Transportation Group to carry the baggage, and

[26] "Deploying the 'Keepers of the Faith,'" pp. 26–27; M. Sgt. Adolph C. Mallory, "TAACOM Moves the Equipment to Calm Desert Storms," *21st TAACOM Support Sentinel*, Jan/Feb 91, p. 4.

[27] During Phase I of Operation DESERT SHIELD, USAREUR deployed the following units (with over 1,900 personnel) and equipment: the 12th Aviation Brigade, with 100 aircraft (of which were 37 AH–64s); the 421st Medical Battalion, with 12 UH–60 medevac aircraft; VII and V Corps nuclear-biological-chemical platoons, with 30 Fox vehicles; the 655th Medical Company (Blood), with its organic equipment; the 483d Medical Detachment (Veterinary), with its organic equipment; and the 207th Medical Company, with 2 C–12 aircraft.

[28] Briefing Slides, USAREUR ODC-SLOG, Operation DESERT SHIELD/STORM, n.d.

[29] Howard interview.

[30] Briefing Slides, USAREUR ODC-SLOG, Contribution to the Victory in the Gulf, Operation DESERT SHIELD.DESERT STORM, n.d.; Draft MS, Charles E. White, First in Support: The 21st Theater Army Area Command in Operation DESERT SHIELD, n.d., History Office, 21st TAACOM; Steve Wesbrook, VII Corps Debarkation and Onward Movement, in Chief of Staff's Assessment and Initiatives Group, Issues Book, 14 Jun 91; HQ, VII Corps, Public Affairs Office (PAO), From Germany to Kuwait: VII Corps in Action During DESERT STORM, n.d.; Draft MS, HQ, VII Corps, Draft Historical Narrative on VII Corps' Participation in Operations DESERT SHIELD and DESERT STORM, 22 Mar 91.

[31] The port at Bremerhaven opened on 3 November for VII Corps' deployment operation, Antwerp on 17 November, and Rotterdam on 21 November.

578 aircraft to fly them all to Southwest Asia.[32] As VII Corps neared completion of the process, Lt. Gen. William S. Flynn, the 21st TAACOM commander, noted how much more complex the move was than REFORGER. "We usually plan all year long to unload two or three ships in one port," he said. "For Desert Shield we planned for a week and loaded some 115 ships through three ports and moved more than a corps worth of equipment through the lines of communication."[33]

Partnerships forged with Belgian, Dutch, and German allies through the REFORGER exercises proved invaluable to commanders rushing to Southwest Asia. On Saturday, 17 November, General Galvin asked the citizens of Germany, Belgium, and the Netherlands for help. The deployment quickly became a combined effort of four nations. On that day, for the first time since the end of World War II, German and Dutch railroad officials exchanged liaison officers to ease rail movement of American equipment.[34]

In Belgium, in Operation SANDY COCKTAIL, representatives of the 21st Theater Army Area Command, the Military Traffic Management Command, the Belgian Ministry of Defense, and the Belgian firm Noord Natie worked together around the clock to load ships at Antwerp. Belgian military forces coordinated the arrival of railcars, barges, and convoys from Germany with American transportation officials. U.S. military vehicles arriving in Antwerp first went to the Delwaid Dock staging area, where they were inspected for safety and counted. Then all equipment was arranged in groups by type, size, and weight for loading. Belgian soldiers patrolled the areas around the ports, and Belgian Navy divers jumped into dockside waters to patrol the waters surrounding the ships.[35]

Movement of the materiel from posts in Germany would not have been possible without the help of the German government. For example, shipping ammunition to Saudi Arabia became a theater team effort with handling units from the *Bundeswehr* and the *Bundesbahn* helping USAREUR personnel. American soldiers and German workers loaded munitions onto 1,276 trucks and 2,300 railcars at four railheads and three ports. During the peak of this operation more tons of ammunition were moved in one day than the theater normally shipped in one year.[36]

While waiting their turn to leave, the heavy divisions continued training and readied their equipment and themselves for war. The VII Corps units, collectively considering themselves to be the U.S. Army's most flexible corps, readjusted their training to concentrate on a more active defense and on offensive operations. Tankers and Bradley fighting vehicle crewmen fired crew-level gunnery at the Seventh Army Training Center at Grafenwoehr and the Hohenfels Combat Maneuver Training Center; used computer simulators at their home bases; and trained extensively with chemical protection equipment.[37]

Many soldiers had to learn to work with new faces. Because of the force reductions in Europe and other factors, Army planners and commanders assembled complete divisions using battalions and brigades borrowed from other divisions and support components that consisted, in part, of

[32] Briefing Slides, USAREUR ODC-SLOG, Operation DESERT SHIELD/STORM; Briefing Slides, USAREUR, Contribution to the Victory in the Gulf, Operation DESERT SHIELD.DESERT STORM, n.d.; Draft MS, White, First in Support; Wesbrook, VII Corps Debarkation and Onward Movement; HQ, VII Corps, PAO, From Germany to Kuwait: VII Corps in Action During DESERT STORM, n.d.; Draft MS, HQ, VII Corps, Draft Historical Narrative on VII Corps' Participation in Operations DESERT SHIELD and DESERT STORM, 22 Mar 91.

[33] Lt. Gen. William Flynn, "Operation DESERT SHIELD," *21st TAACOM Support Sentinel*, Jan/Feb 91, p. 2.

[34] Draft MS, White, First in Support, p. 18.

[35] Briefing Slides, 80th Area Support Group, Operation SANDY COCKTAIL, n.d.; M. Sgt. Adolph C. Mallory, "Operation Sandy Cocktail," *21st TAACOM Support Sentinel*, Jan/Feb 91, p. 5; Mallory, "TAACOM Moves the Equipment to Calm Desert Storms," p. 4.

[36] Briefing Slides, USAREUR ODC-SLOG, Operation DESERT SHIELD/STORM.

[37] "We're Going to Saudi," *Army Times*, 26 Nov 90, pp. 12–13.

Reserve and National Guard units from the United States and Germany. Corps-level combat support and combat service support organizations also mixed regular and reserve units under a single headquarters. For example, military police from three regular brigades and two reserve battalions deployed under the VII Corps' 14th Military Police Brigade headquarters. The 2d Support Command swelled from its peacetime strength of nearly 8,000 to 25,000 through reserve augmentation.[38]

The 2d Armored Cavalry deployed to Southwest Asia first. Within days of President Bush's 8 November announcement, the regiment, which had patrolled West Germany's border with the East for more than forty-five years, had its equipment loaded and was under way. After reaching Saudi Arabia in early December, it began preparations for the arrival of the remaining VII Corps units at the tactical assembly area.[39]

The movement from Germany proved agonizingly slow. Most VII Corps field commanders expected eventually to go to the Middle East, but security requirements delayed official notification until 9 November. With little advance warning, unit commanders assembled troops for the move to the designated ports. Ordered to take all necessary organizational property and equipment with them, they struggled to prepare. Inter-unit transfers of equipment became necessary as deploying soldiers obtained the best available gear from units staying in Germany. To facilitate movement, V Corps deployed its own units, which were reassigned to VII Corps after they had reached Al Jubayl, Ad Dammām, or Dhahran in the Persian Gulf. Overall, the deployments from Germany showed that rapidly dispatching forward-deployed units into another theater as a contingency force was a major challenge.

With no formal doctrine for such massive inter-theater movements, and hampered by bad weather, dock strikes, and the problems inherent with loading hundreds of tanks and wheeled vehicles onto railcars and ships, the remaining VII Corps units did not share the 2d Armored Cavalry's success. Although all corps equipment quickly reached the European ports for transshipment, ships did not put all of VII Corps in Southwest Asia by the target date of 15 January. At this time, only 91 percent of the corps' soldiers, with 67 percent of the tracked vehicles and 66 percent of the wheeled vehicles, had made it.[40]

Once in the theater of operations, the distribution of unit equipment delayed movement to the tactical assembly areas in the desert. Commanders had hoped to deploy in tactical formation, but the property of individual units frequently became dispersed among a number of ships. Equipment did not arrive in unit sets, complicating the buildup at the Saudi ports and delaying forward movement of VII Corps. Lack of coordination between sea and air traffic had major effects on port overcrowding, preparation for combat, and force protection. For example, on 9 January, over 35,000 VII Corps soldiers were in staging areas at Saudi ports waiting for their equipment or for ground transportation to move to the field.[41]

[38] HQ, VII Corps, PAO, From Germany to Kuwait.

[39] Steve Vogel, "On the Way," *Army Times*, 17 Dec 90, p. 14; Vogel, "Ever-ready Armored Unit Struts Its Stuff," *Army Times*, 10 Dec 90, pp. 20, 68.

[40] Wesbrook, VII Corps Debarkation and Onward Movement, 14 Jun 91.

[41] Ibid.

VII Corps elements in Saudi Arabia. Some troops await transportation to their assembly areas, while others unload their gear from an aircraft.

Soldiers flew into airports near Al Jubayl and Ad Dammām. From there they moved to the ports, where they stayed in warehouses or tent cities and waited for their equipment. Once their equipment arrived, the soldiers oversaw the loading of their tanks, artillery, and other tracked vehicles onto heavy equipment transporters. Buses carried the officers, soldiers, and baggage.[42] Between the arrival of the first ship on 5 December 1990 and 18 February 1991, when the last equipment departed the Saudi ports for the VII Corps' tactical assembly areas, the corps launched 900 convoys; moved over 6,000 armored vehicles and thousands of other pieces of equipment over 340 miles into the desert; and sent 3,500 containers with critical unit equipment, repair parts, and supplies forward.[43]

VII Corps Rear Base Operations

After the VII Corps deployed, a single corps remained in Germany. It consisted of the 8th Infantry Division (Mechanized), the 3d Infantry Division, the 11th Armored Cavalry, and assorted combat support and combat service support units.[44] Consequently, on 5 December General Saint redefined the command-and-control arrangements in Europe. He attached those VII Corps tactical units still in Germany to V Corps, under the command of Lt. Gen. David M. Maddox. Maj. Gen. Roger K. Bean, commander of the 56th Field Artillery Command, took over VII Corps residual staff and all VII Corps units not attached to V Corps. General Bean also assumed responsibility for protecting U.S. lives, property, and installations in southern Germany.[45]

The duties of those units staying in Germany did not diminish. The uncertainty of the situation, as well as the nearness of Europe to the Persian Gulf, meant that those troops still in Germany would become a major supplier of equipment to Central Command. Personnel from both European Command and U.S. Army, Europe, became responsible for the logistical sustainment of units already in Saudi Arabia.

USAREUR logistical support began in August 1990 as soon as the first support elements arrived in Southwest Asia and peaked in January 1991 as General Schwarzkopf made final preparations for war. The American forces remaining in Germany sent ammunition as well as large numbers of Abrams tanks, Bradley fighting vehicles, and hospital sets, which General Yeosock and his ARCENT staff used to equip and modernize their forces and to set up a theater reserve for what many anticipated to be a longer war. The Army also used equipment from the European theater reserves and pre-positioned stocks to fill the large number of security assistance requests received from coalition partners.[46] Although Generals Galvin and Saint tried to keep enough materiel in Europe to deter a possible crisis, European Command ran short of HELLFIRE and Copperhead missiles. Virtually all tents were sent out of the theater, and stocks of fighting vehicles were drawn down significantly.[47]

[42] HQ, VII Corps, PAO, From Germany to Kuwait.

[43] Wesbrook, VII Corps Debarkation and Onward Movement, 14 Jun 91.

[44] Msg, Public Affairs Guidance for Deployment of Additional Forces to Operation DESERT SHIELD, 9 Nov 90.

[45] Msgs, CINCUSAREUR to VII Corps/V Corps/21st Theater Army Area Command (TAACOM) et al., 18 and 19 Nov 90, and to Cdr, Berlin Brigade, 20 Nov 90.

[46] Briefing Slides, USAREUR ODC-SLOG, Operation DESERT SHIELD/ STORM; Briefing Slides, USAREUR, Contribution to the Victory in the Gulf, Operation DESERT SHIELD.DESERT STORM.

[47] Howard interview.

USAREUR also had responsibility for sending initial crew replacements to the Gulf. During the crisis it sent 116 M1 crews, 108 M2 crews, 24 M3 crews, 24 155-mm. artillery crews, 8 203-mm. artillery crews, and 10 OH–58 crews, totaling 1,900 soldiers, to Saudi Arabia. The headquarters also deployed 4,780 troops in a follow-on force package.[48]

To assist those who stayed, forty-one Army Reserve units and fourteen Army National Guard units from the United States and Europe helped provide force protection, medical care, and transportation support. For example, 44 chaplains and 3,460 medical personnel deployed to Germany to replace those recently sent to Saudi Arabia.[49]

In a unique development in U.S. military history, nearly all 300,000 U.S. dependents remained in Europe. Since the deploying units would return to Germany after the Persian Gulf crisis, the families remained in familiar surroundings, among friends, and within a functioning family support structure. In addition to his other responsibilities, General Bean took command of the newly established major command support area directly under General Saint. Bean became responsible for a community structure encompassing the cities of Ansbach, Aschaffenburg, Augsburg, Bad Toelz, Bamberg, Goeppingen, Heilbronn, Munich, Neu Ulm, Nuremberg, Schweinfurt, Stuttgart, and Wuerzburg.[50] Those military communities bonded together more closely. To ease the disruptions caused by the deployment, local German communities offered their assistance to those left behind. As General Saint later explained, "There is an advantage to staying with people you've been with, because you're all in it together and you can support each other....This is home." The movement from Germany marked the first time a large forward-deployed force had been sent to another country while family and support structures stayed behind.[51]

1st Infantry Division Deployment

Like VII Corps in Europe, the 1st Infantry Division in the United States prepared for its deployment to Southwest Asia. The division commander, Maj. Gen. Thomas G. Rhame, had judged from the start of the Persian Gulf crisis that his unit would be mobilized and, in early August, had instructed unit commanders to take reasonable and prudent measures to begin preparing for a possible deployment. Readying for such an eventuality was not uncommon for 1st Division soldiers, who had for years rehearsed for a large-scale deployment. Also, the unit's emergency deployment plan, although geared toward a crisis in Europe, could be adapted easily to almost any locale. Once trouble began in the Persian Gulf, division planners tailored the deployment concepts to fit a move to the Middle East.[52]

Meanwhile, the soldiers began preparing for combat. Several months before the Persian Gulf crisis began, the 1st Division had completed extensive desert training at the National Training Center at Fort Irwin, California. In late August the 1st underwent more training at Fort Hood, Texas, rehearsing a Middle East scenario against III Corps soldiers. Assuming that they

[48] Briefing Slides, USAREUR, Contributions to the Victory in the Gulf, Operation DESERT SHIELD.DESERT STORM; Memo, USAREUR for Surgeon General, 11 Dec 90, sub: General from USAREUR, Reception and Onward Movement of Reserve Component Medical Augmentation.

[49] Ibid.

[50] Msg, CINCUSAREUR to VII Corps/V Corps/21st TAACOM et al., 19 Nov 91; S. Sgt. William H. McMichael, "Deforger: Europe to Saudi," *Soldiers* (February 1991): 22.

[51] McMichael, "Deforger: Europe to Saudi," p. 22.

[52] "From the Plains to the Desert: 1st Inf. Div. Deploys," *Soldiers* (March 1991): 13; Interv (telephone), Theresa L. Kraus with Lt Col Gregory Fontenot, 16 Jul 91.

1st Infantry Division soldier securing a vehicle to a railcar

[53] Leslie Garven, "Rhame: Big Red One Trained and Ready," *Daily Union* (Junction City, Kans.), 11 Nov 90, p. 11; Fontenot interview.

[54] "From the Plains to the Desert," pp. 14–15.

[55] Ibid.

[56] Ibid., p. 15; Fontenot interview; 1st Infantry Division Daily Sitreps, Nov–Dec 90.

[57] Leslie Garven, "Big Red One's Mission Covered in Day-by-Day Detail," *Daily Union*, 24 May 91, p. 11; Fontenot interview; 1st Infantry Division Daily Sitreps, Dec 90–Jan 91.

would deploy, unit commanders expended the resources allocated for the year's readiness training. For example, during September and October, individual units fired all of their training ammunition in preparation for combat operations. Predeployment activities culminated in late November with refresher training in combat skills.[53]

The soldiers also used the immediate predeployment period to learn about new equipment, like the M1A1 Abrams tank. Just before the division deployed, forty-three members of the New Equipment Transition Team from Fort Knox, Kentucky, visited Fort Riley with fifteen M1A1s and provided tank crews with sixteen hours of intensive transition training. Once in Saudi Arabia, the division's M1s were replaced with M1A1s.[54]

The entire Fort Riley community helped prepare for the deployment. Between 1 October and 20 November, as 1st Division soldiers readied themselves and their equipment for the movement overseas, Fort Riley's Force Modernization Office worked to ensure that the unit had all it needed for its mission. The office staff worked around the clock to coordinate receipt of almost 600 new five-ton trucks, over 500 high mobility multipurpose wheeled vehicles, 3,000 9-mm. pistols, and 50 AN/AVS–6 aviation night vision imaging systems. In addition, the division acquired a reverse osmosis water purification unit before departing for Saudi Arabia.[55]

Equipment loading began in late November, after which time the troops continued training without their gear while awaiting their deployment dates. Reservists from the 1179th Deployment Control Unit at Fort Hamilton, New York, monitored Fort Riley's railheads to ensure that the 1st Division's equipment was properly loaded for shipment to the Port of Houston in Texas. The unit loaded 650 vehicles on the first day and altogether shipped about 7,000 vehicles and trailers to Texas. During the period 1 to 24 December fourteen ships were filled with the division's equipment. The first, the *Merzario Italia*, departed Houston on the sixth and the last, the USNS *Algol*, on the twenty-eighth. As was the case for the deployments from Germany, materiel was not shipped in unit sets, later causing some confusion at the Saudi ports.[56]

On 12 December Brig. Gen. William G. Carter III, the assistant division commander for maneuver, went to Southwest Asia with a 200-man advance party. Seven days later the group set up a tactical assembly area, code-named ROOSEVELT, in the north Saudi Arabian desert. Beginning on the fifteenth, the nearly 11,900 soldiers of the 1st Division departed, incrementally, from Forbes Field in Topeka, Kansas (*Table 4*). The majority of the troops reached Saudi Arabia on the thirty-first, and the last equipment ship docked in late January.[57]

As in Germany, family support groups sprang up at Fort Riley. The post set up a 24-hour hotline; established family support centers; and scheduled daily activities for children, teens, and adults. In addition, the staff used a facsimile machine, donated by AT&T, to send newsletters from the home front to the troops in the Middle East.

Mobilizing the Army National Guard

The all-volunteer force depended very much on the Army Reserve and Army National Guard. More than 1,040 reserve and guard units, totaling about 140,000 soldiers from every state and territory, supported the Persian Gulf operation. During the Phase II deployments, regular, reserve, and guard units began to move by mid-November and reached full combat readiness in Saudi Arabia by early February.

After President Bush's 8 November order to increase troop levels in Southwest Asia, Secretary Cheney not only announced the deployment of the VII Corps and the 1st Division but also, after months of public debate and congressional pressure, the federalization of three combat roundout brigades—the 48th Infantry from Georgia, the 155th Armored from Mississippi, and the 256th Infantry (Mechanized) from Louisiana—and two field artillery brigades—the 142d from Arkansas and Oklahoma and the 196th from Tennessee, Kentucky, and West Virginia.

The announcement actually came as no surprise for the three combat roundout brigades. Four days earlier the Department of Defense had disclosed that Congress had extended the call-up authority to 360 days for combat units, permitting the reserve combat units to be called to active duty in the event General Schwarzkopf needed either reinforcements in a prolonged conflict or rotational units in a lengthy deployment.

1ST INFANTRY DIVISION AIRLIFT, 15 DECEMBER 1990–17 JANUARY 1991

Aircraft[a]	Number of Flights	Personnel
C–5	6	273
C–141	14	226
DC–10	5	1,192
L–1011	9	1,753
747	23	8,404
Total	57	11,848

[a]Along with division personnel, 1,600 short tons of equipment were moved.

Source: 1st Infantry Division Daily Sitreps, Dec 90–Jan 91.

Table 4

The three combat brigades received official alert notices on 15 November. Fifteen days later the approximately 4,200 officers and men of the 48th and 5,500 soldiers of the 256th reported to active duty; the 3,700 men of the 155th reported on 7 December. The delay in the 155th's call-up provided the local commanders at Fort Hood and the National Training Center at Fort Irwin some flexibility in scheduling training. Army planners estimated at that time that it would cost about $120 million to activate all three units.[58]

The Army set the same deployment criteria for reserve combat units as for regular component units at its highest C–1 standard. A unit could have no deficiencies in the prescribed levels of wartime resources and training and had to have 90 percent of its personnel and equipment. Occasionally a unit at a C–2 readiness level, with minor deficiencies and 80–90 percent of its personnel and equipment, also deployed. For the three roundout brigades, a detailed training program and personnel plan was established to upgrade the units, when necessary, to C–1.

Predeployment training followed call-up. Once alerted, each brigade had thirty days to report to a mobilization station and used the time to assess training, to prepare leaders, to hone individual and small-unit skills, and conduct maintenance and logistics training. At the mobilization station, the reservists prepared for overseas movement and underwent more individual and crew training. Finally, each brigade separately attended the Army's unique recertification training course at the National Training Center.[59] Secretary Cheney claimed that the decision to send the brigades through predeployment training at the center did not reflect a lack of confidence in their combat readiness: "I'm not eager to send units that are not fully ready....They need to go to the National Training Center to get into shape as if they were an active duty division."[60]

Upon federalization, soldiers of Brig. Gen. William A. Holland's 48th Infantry Brigade gathered at Fort Stewart, Georgia, their mobilization station. Between 5 and 8 December they prepared for overseas movement. Like the regulars, they underwent physical, psychological, and dental evaluations; received new dog tags and identification cards, if necessary; and completed wills and financial forms. While at Fort Stewart the soldiers also worked on common training tasks, generally referred to as basic survivability skills, such as weapons qualification, tank systems familiarization, and training in chemical warfare.[61]

On 17 December the soldiers began loading their equipment on railroad cars for the cross-country trip to the National Training Center. Personnel movement by air to Fort Irwin began ten days later. The final flight of soldiers arrived in California on 3 January. Movement into the desert training area commenced the following day.[62]

The arrival of the 48th Infantry Brigade posed a major challenge to Brig. Gen. Wesley K, Clark, commander of the National Training Center (NTC). Previously, the mission of the desert exercise post was to

[58] Memo, SAPA-PP for Principal Officials of Headquarters, Department of the Army, 21 Nov 90, sub: Public Affairs Guidance for Call-Up of Reserve Component Combat Units in Support of Operation DESERT SHIELD.

[59] Decision Briefing, ODCSOPS, 48th Infantry Brigade-Mechanized, n.d.

[60] "President Bush Orders Call-Up of Three Guard Roundout Brigades," National Guard, Dec 90, p. 4.

[61] Draft MS, National Guard Bureau (NGB), ARNG After Action Report, Operation DESERT SHIELD and DESERT STORM, Part III, Chronology of Events: 2 August 1990–28 February 1991, 2 Jun 91 (hereafter cited as NGB Chron); Maj. Jean Marie Beall, "48th Infantry Brigade: Ready, Willing, and Able for Combat," *National Guard*, Apr 91, p. 18.

[62] Ibid.

rigorously test and evaluate the performance of active Army armor and mechanized battalions that rotated through the center every thirty days or so. Now Clark had to address the training needs of an entire brigade, determine its ability to accomplish what the Army termed its Mission Essential Task List (METL—or, in Army jargon, its "Metal"), and then use his NTC cadre to train the components of the 48th to meet Regular Army standards in each mission area. Ultimately, the job took some fifty-five days and included squad-, platoon-, and company-level training in both live fire and opposing force environments, culminating in a twelve-day continuous exercise for the full brigade. On the advice of Army leaders like General Vuono and General Burba, the FORSCOM commander, Clark designed a training sequence that also incorporated lessons already learned in the Middle East, such as breaching the kinds of defense obstacles that Iraq had erected in Kuwait and defending against Iraqi tactics used in the eight-year war against Iran.[63] The 48th completed its postmobilization training on 28 February.

Although Forces Command certified the 48th Infantry Brigade's readiness after its stint at Fort Irwin, the overall roundout program remained plagued with controversy. Contined scrutiny by the press led many to question the validity of the entire concept, especially in the midst of these comparatively long predeployment training programs. Criticism increased on 14 February, when the Second United States Army commander, Lt. Gen. James W. Crysel, with the consent of General Burba, released General Holland from active duty; assigned him to another general officer position in the Georgia guard; and replaced him with the 48th's deputy commander, Col. James R. Davis.[64]

While waiting for the 48th to finish at Fort Irwin, the 155th Armored Brigade trained at Fort Hood. The tank crews of the 155th had serious difficulties on the gunnery ranges. Col. Fletcher C. Coker, commander of the 155th, claimed that training at Fort Hood "was an eye opener." The ranges were up to 1.8 miles wider and 2.5 miles deeper than the unit's normal training range at Camp Shelby, Mississippi. After intensive training at Fort Hood, the brigade spent three weeks at the National Training Center.[65]

The training of the 256th Infantry Brigade, under the command of Brig. Gen. Gary J. Whipple, created new rounds of controversy regarding the competence and use of the roundout brigades in combat. The brigade had received M1 Abrams in 1989 and was still in the new equipment training process when federalized. The soldiers had only recently learned to drive the tanks, and maneuver, gunnery, and maintenance training had not yet been scheduled. In addition, the 256th, like the 155th, had arrived at its mobilization station, Fort Polk, Louisiana, with insufficient chemical protection and communications equipment, partially because of extensive redistribution of equipment to other National Guard units called up earlier.[66]

[63] Beall, "48th Infantry Brigade," pp. 18–19.

[64] "Infantry Brigade Gets New Leader as Training for Gulf Role Drags On," *Washington Post*, 15 Feb 91, p. 34; HQ, Second U.S. Army, PAO, Press Release, 48th Brigade Gets New Commander, 15 Feb 91.

[65] Briefing Slides, DCSOPS, 155th Armored Brigade—Training and Readiness, n.d.; Memorandum for the Record (MFR), Capt John R. Minihan, Office of the Chief of Staff, Army (OCSA), 11 Mar 91, sub: House Armed Services Committee—8 Mar 91, CINCFOR/Director of the National Guard Bureau/Cdrs of Three Roundout Brigades, Reserve Component Roundout Issues (hereafter cited as Minihan MFR); Information Paper, National Guard Bureau, 7 Dec 90, sub: Roundout Units to the 5th Infantry Division (Mech).

[66] Memo, Lt Col Glenn O. Cassidy for Lt Col Carlson, 11 Mar 91, sub: Congressional Hearing, 8 Mar 91.

While training at its mobilization station, the 256th lost eight company commanders, who were released from active duty. Although not relieved for cause, those officers, according to General Burba, had "never had the opportunity to go through sustained stress." The training at Fort Polk "provided an opportunity to evaluate and correctly replace inadequate commanders with better commanders."[67]

Perhaps the most serious problem the 256th faced came when sixty-seven soldiers from the 1st Battalion, 156th Armor, were absent without leave. Shortly after arriving at Fort Hood on 21 January, the 1st Battalion commenced field training. Before the unit returned to the fort on 4 February, some of the soldiers apparently had obtained a draft copy of a training schedule that indicated a two-day break between field exercises. They assumed, without being told by the battalion commander, that they would get passes for the entire two days. After the exercise, however, the commander informed the unit that, because of duty requirements, half of the battalion would go on pass the first day and the other half would go the following day. The soldiers complained that the one-day pass would prevent them from visiting their families.[68]

On 5 February some of the soldiers left without authorization for Shreveport, Louisiana. Once there, they met with the media and described the "deplorable conditions" at Fort Hood. Complaints included stressful training, homesickness, poor food, substandard living conditions, and a lack of time off. The incident involved only 1 percent of the brigade's members—twenty-seven had passes but had exceeded their limit, and forty were absent without leave. Legal cases resulting from the incident were handled on an individual basis. By the fifteenth, forty-four had been discharged and the remaining cases either were still pending or had been dismissed.[69]

On 7 February the command discovered another potential absence problem within the 256th Brigade. Soldiers of the 3d Battalion, 156th Armor, apparently held several meetings to discuss leaving Fort Hood without authorization. About eighty attended the initial meeting, although fewer and fewer soldiers went to later ones. The command intervened before any of the soldiers were absent without leave.[70]

In March, just as the 48th Brigade finished at Fort Irwin and redeployed to Fort Stewart, the House Armed Services Committee began hearings on the roundout program.[71] Disagreements over the readiness levels of the three roundout brigades surfaced as General Burba and Lt. Gen. John B. Conaway, chief of the National Guard Bureau, debated how much training the brigades required for certification. Burba argued that they needed a full ninety days of training. Conaway disputed the necessity of such a long training period, claiming that the units should be given training credit for the work done before arriving at the mobilization centers.[72]

Despite the controversy over the readiness of the roundout brigades, General Conaway explained that some postmobilization training was always planned to bring National Guard units to a full ready

[67] Minihan MFR.

[68] Information Paper, National Guard Bureau, 6 Feb 91, sub: Unauthorized Absence of 1st Bn., 156th Armor Personnel; Information Paper, DAPE-MO-PCC, 15 Feb 91, sub: AWOL Incident, 256th Infantry Brigade, Fort Hood.

[69] Ibid.

[70] Information Paper, DAPE-MO-PCC, 15 Feb 91, sub: AWOL Incident, 256th Infantry Brigade, Fort Hood.

[71] The 48th Brigade completed its demobilization on 10 April, the 256th Brigade on 7 May, and the 155th on 14 May 1991.

[72] Minihan MFR.

status. Furthermore, training time differed depending on the training plan and the unit mission. Conaway pointed out that the three brigades were trained and resourced for deployment within forty-five to sixty days of federalization. Training time was extended because the mission-essential task lists changed to adjust to lessons being learned in Saudi Arabia by the troops already there. All three brigades, Conaway claimed, had already met the readiness standards and task-list requirement for which they were originally designed before mobilization.[73]

The two field artillery brigades, the 142d and the 196th, were federalized at about the same time as their maneuver counterparts. At this time, both artillery brigades were nearly fully trained in gunnery. Unlike the maneuver brigades, the artillery units did not need the movement and synchronization skills taught at the National Training Center. On 21 November the 142d Field Artillery Brigade and its three subordinate units—the 1st and 2d Battalions, 142d Field Artillery, from Arkansas and the 1st Battalion, 158th Field Artillery, from Oklahoma—reported to active duty. The brigade arrived at its mobilization station, Fort Sill, Oklahoma, between 23 and 25 November.[74] On arriving at Fort Sill, the commander of the 2d Battalion, Lt. Col. William D. Wofford, said his postmobilization training would focus on "last minute" training exercises in chemical warfare, communications procedures, and survival skills.[75]

The 1st Battalion, 158th Field Artillery, was the only multiple launch rocket battalion in the reserves. It had twenty-seven launchers, which were among the Army's newest field artillery weapons. At the time of the 1st's mobilization the commander, Lt. Col. Larry D. Haub, echoed Wofford's training assessment. Haub indicated his unit would focus on chemical warfare defense and individual marksmanship, rather than artillery firing exercises during postmobilization training.[76]

By 15 December, only twenty-four days after federalization, the 142d Brigade had its equipment at the Port of Galveston in Texas, awaiting transshipment to Southwest Asia. Consequently, borrowed equipment was used to refresh skills while at Fort Sill. On 16 January the brigade deployed to Saudi Arabia, with the 1st and 2d Battalions, 142d Field Artillery, leaving three days later and the 1st Battalion, 158th Field Artillery, on 2 February.[77]

On 15 December the 196th Field Artillery Brigade was federalized with three subordinate battalions. On 2 February the 196th deployed to Saudi Arabia with one of its subordinate units, the 1st Battalion, 201st Field Artillery, from West Virginia. The two other units—the 1st Battalion, 623d Field Artillery, from Kentucky and the 1st Battalion, 181st Field Artillery, from Tennessee—joined the brigade several days later.

The success of both field artillery brigades during Operation DESERT STORM showed that reserve combat units could serve effectively as part of the total force. The 142d and 196th Brigades, the first reserve units to fight a major action since the Vietnam War, performed with distinction.[78]

[73] Statement by Lt Gen John B. Conaway, Chief, National Guard Bureau, Before the Defense Policy Panel, Committee on Armed Services, House of Representatives, 102d Cong., 1st sess., 8 March 1991, Record Version.

[74] NGB Chron, pp. 36–37.

[75] J. Paul Scicchitano, "National Guard Combat Troops Mobilized," *Army Times*, 3 Dec 90.

[76] Ibid.

[77] NGB Chron, pp. 42, 52, 58.

[78] Ibid., pp. 52, 58.

Mobilizing the Individual Ready Reserve

In addition to federalizing the five Army National Guard brigades, Secretary Cheney on 14 November authorized the call-up of another 72,500 Army National Guard and Army Reserve troops. The new authority, which did not require the approval of Congress, more than doubled the number of citizen-soldiers called.

Reserve mobilization reached a new level on 18 January 1991, when President Bush authorized the activation of the Individual Ready Reserve. That decision to call up reservists who were not already assigned to units gave the Department of Defense greater authority and flexibility as the Persian Gulf crisis approached its critical stage. The president's action permitted the activation of up to 1 million ready reservists for twenty-four months, ending the 200,000-person and 180-day limitations. The new declaration also permitted the involuntary call-up of individuals.[79] With the authority delegated by the president, Secretary Cheney increased the overall reserve-component call-up from 189,000 to 316,000. The Army's share rose from 115,000 to 220,000.[80]

With the possibility of ground combat becoming more likely, the Army Staff was most concerned that follow-on units be at full strength and qualified individual replacements be readily available. To accomplish this, mailgrams ordered 20,000 reservists to report to designated reception centers by 1 February. As the date approached, no one was certain of whether the ready reservists could be located or would even report. Concern turned to mild panic when, by 30 January, only 300 had reported for duty. The Pentagon staffers, all of field rank, had either forgotten such factors as youth or the GI mentality. In a scene that probably had parallels at other posts, just before midnight on 31 January a stretch limousine pulled into Fort Jackson, South Carolina, with four enlisted reservists reporting for duty. Their compatriots were not far behind.

Those selected were in occupational specialties where replacements would most likely be needed. Infantry, artillery, armor, and engineer skills accounted for 42 percent of the individuals activated, while mechanics and vehicle operators added an additional 20 percent. Screening at the reception centers provided medical, compassionate, and administrative releases. With less than two weeks available, their formal preparation was often limited to donning gas masks, zeroing in individual weapons, and performing physical training to harden muscles and increase endurance. As many were experienced soldiers who had recently participated in Operation JUST CAUSE, further retraining could best be accomplished by their assigned units. Some 13,000 ready reservists completed this process, of whom 5,800 were assigned in the United States; 4,500 to Europe; 2,700 to Southwest Asia; and 120 to the Pacific.

To assist mobilization of the Individual Ready Reserve, the Training and Doctrine Command provided additional reception and training support. Beginning in January, elements of the 70th, 78th, 80th, 84th, 85th,

[79] Title 10, *USC*, Sec. 673.

[80] Memo, Secretary of Defense Richard Cheney for Secretaries of the Military Departments and Chairman of the Joint Chiefs of Staff, 19 Jan 90; Fact Sheet, Department of the Army, OSD-RA-PS, 18 Jan 91, sub: President Approves Ready Reserve Call-Up Authority.

98th, 100th, and 108th Divisions (Training) were mobilized in each of the continental army areas and supported eight mobilization stations.[81] The 4159th U.S. Army Reserve Forces School had been mobilized in December to assist in the training of guardsmen at Fort Hood. In January the 2077th U.S. Army Reserve Forces School, the Sixth U.S. Army Intelligence Training Army Area School, and parts of five additional schools, one from each continental army area, were mobilized.[82] The training divisions and schools provided the basic skills refresher and military occupational specialty training for roundout units and ready reservists.

By the middle of March many of the ready reservists had completed their whirlwind mobilization and returned to civilian life. The evidence suggests that many had found the brief experience irritating, disruptive, and without purpose. Nevertheless, they had come forward when called and provided crucial backup for the Army.

The late mobilization and deployment of some reserve units and the decision not to activate others whose training and organization had earmarked them for Southwest Asia, although frustrating to those involved, were based on sound and calculated decisions of the Army leadership. The evolving situation in the theater of operations combined with transportation shortages and statutory restrictions to limit the employment of reserve components. The fluidity of the situation led to significant changes in contingency plans and made flexibility in mobilization and subsequent deployments vital.

Initially, the Army delayed the decision for the overseas movement of National Guard and reserve organizations until additional training could be accomplished. Although ultimately many units remained in the United States, they provided the Army with a strategic reserve. Had further reinforcements to Central Command been necessary for rotational or replacement purposes, or had unforeseen contingencies occurred elsewhere, those units could have been committed by the beginning of 1991. And, had they deployed to a combat zone, additional reserve and guard units of similar size and capability were ready to be activated and take their place.

Overall, the creation of a major expeditionary force of regular, reserve, and guard units was a remarkable accomplishment. The groundwork for this achievement had been carried out during the previous two decades, which witnessed the steady improvement in the quality and responsiveness of the Army's reserve components. Never before had the nation mobilized and deployed such an effective and diverse force so quickly. A flexible approach proved critical to that success. As in the Regular Army, not every reservist or guardsman reached the combat zone. Thousands of reservists filled positions vacated by regulars in the United States and overseas, ensuring that the Army's training and sustainment base remained intact and that commitments elsewhere in the world would not be neglected. Every reserve and guard unit, whether mobilized or not, constituted a part of the total strategic reserve and, in that role, was as significant as those regular forces that remained in Europe, in Korea, and at other stations.

[81] Information Paper, Lt Col Fritz, DAAR-FMF, 9 Feb 91, sub: USAR Training Units Activated for DESERT STORM.

[82] Information Paper, Lt Col Fritz, DAAR-FMF, 18 Dec 90, sub: Tasking of 4159th USAR School (-).

Chapter 6
THE OFFENSIVE TAKES SHAPE

With sufficient troops now assured and the overall concept of a flanking movement in place, work on a full-fledged plan for the ground offensive began in earnest in January 1991. The center of planning shifted to Army Central Command. The ARCENT commander, Lt. Gen. John J. Yeosock, his operations officer, Brig. Gen. Steven L. Arnold, and his staff logistician, Brig. Gen. James W. Monroe, had followed the process since mid-October, but the shift in responsibilities caught the component command in an awkward position. Most of the plans section, including its chief, Col. Harold E. Holloway, had been detailed to ARCENT's Coalition Coordination Communication Integration Center, set up in August to coordinate between American and allied forces. Responsibility for ARCENT planning fell to General Arnold. To assist Colonel Purvis' CENTCOM planners, Arnold formed a special planning cell with personnel from the ARCENT staff, the 513th Military Intelligence Brigade, and the XVIII Airborne Corps. Eventually, this combined planning team received additional support with the return of some of Holloway's section personnel and the arrival of a few Army Staff planners from the United States.

Inevitably, the plan that emerged from Army Central Command reflected the personality of its commander. Quiet and self-effacing, General Yeosock saw himself as not only a provider and allocator of resources but also a buffer between the corps commanders in the field and the flamboyant, often impatient Schwarzkopf. He set only general objectives for his subordinate commanders, allowing them to respond to the changing imperatives of the battlefield at discretion.[1]

To carry out the flanking movement, Army Central Command would have, in effect, both the light XVIII Airborne Corps and the heavy VII Corps. For a time, XVIII Corps included the 1st Cavalry Division (Armored), but in early January General Yeosock put this unit in theater reserve and moved the French 6th Light Armored Division out to XVIII Corps' left flank. The VII Corps, which arrived wearing the dark green woodland uniforms designed for combat in Europe, had perhaps the greatest concentration of armor and firepower ever assembled under a corps headquarters. By the time of the ground offensive

[1] Interv, David W. Hogan with Col Harold E. Holloway, 14 Jun 91, Fort McPherson, Ga.; Interv, Hogan with Maj Steve Holley, 21 Jun 91, Fort McPherson, Ga.; Swain interview; Draft MS, Swain, Operational Narrative, pp. 40, 43, 48, 55; Special Planning Cell chronology, p. 6.

its collective strength became even more imposing with the addition of the British 1st Armored Division to its forces.[2]

Coalition Forces

Because the VII and XVIII Corps were only two elements of the coalition forces organizing for the ground offensive, questions of command and control surfaced during the decisive weeks of planning. Army Central Command would function as the higher headquarters for all U.S. ground forces, except the U.S. Marines, and would have no authority over the coalition forces. For political reasons, the creation of an overall ground command that included the Arab troops among the nearly 700,000 soldiers from twenty-eight countries was virtually impossible. General Schwarzkopf planned to be his own ground commander, dismissing arguments similar to those advanced by the British about General Dwight D. Eisenhower in World War II that he lacked the time and resources to supervise the battle while dealing with strategic and politico-military issues at the CENTCOM level. Indeed, in practice, Central Command left several matters for the Army component and the Marines to resolve among themselves, resulting in friction over boundaries and the transfer of the 1st (or Tiger) Brigade, 2d Armored Division, to the Marines to increase their firepower.[3]

Internal command and control problems were fairly straightforward compared to the confusing lines of authority between Central Command and other coalition partners. During the first months of DESERT SHIELD the coalition worked under an informal arrangement, whereby General Schwarzkopf led the Americans; General Mohammed Saleh Al Hammad, chief of the Royal Saudi General Staff, directed the Saudis, Egyptians, and Moroccans; and the leaders of the other national forces reported directly to their respective governments. When it came to issues of common interest, the coalition commanders conferred with each other. Such an amorphous relationship led to calls for a more formal command structure, perhaps a political committee and a council of military commanders, but no formal combined organization ever emerged. In accord with NATO practice, the British government placed its force under Schwarzkopf, except in matters of grand strategy and policy, and the French later followed suit. By the time of the ground offensive the coalition had effectively evolved into two combined commands—the Western allies under General Schwarzkopf, and the Arab members now under His Royal Highness Lt. Gen. Prince Khalid ibn Sultan, commander of the Joint Forces. In practice, the Arabs followed CENTCOM's lead, but without formally ceding authority to Schwarzkopf. Although inconsistent with the unity-of-command principle, the structure was probably the best available given the linguistic, cultural, and doctrinal differences between Westerners and Arabs.

Considerable coordination and the professional dedication of the senior officers who were involved made the coalition arrangement work.

[2] Draft MS, Swain, Operational Narrative, pp. 65, 90–91; "Ground Planner Franks Knows War Horrors Well," *Army Times*, 4 Feb 91, p. 20; Jim Tice, "Seasoned Group Poised to Lead at Border," *Army Times*, 4 Feb 91, p. 39; Draft MS, Maj Alan T. Carver, How VII Corps Won the War, p. 8.

[3] CENTCOM Planning Cell interview, pp. 38–39; Holley interview; Holloway interview.

At the top of the hierarchy Schwarzkopf, General Khalid, and the commanders of the British and French contingents, Air Chief Marshal Sir Patrick Hine and Lt. Gen. Michel Roquejeoffre, met regularly each day. In addition, Saudis under Khalid and Americans under Maj. Gen. Paul R. Schwartz addressed issues of mutual interest in the Coalition Coordination Communication Integration Center. Schwartz, who had previously served in Saudi Arabia and was Yeosock's deputy, ran the center, which provided a model for inexperienced Saudi staff officers, gave American planners easier access to the Saudi command system, and permitted combined staffing on such matters as acquisition of training areas and the host nation support program. With CENTCOM and Saudi General Staff headquarters located in adjacent facilities in Riyadh, substantial coordination also took place between American and Saudi staff officers on a daily basis. In the field the Army Central Command, the VII and XVIII Airborne Corps, and the 5th Special Forces Group (Airborne), 1st Special Forces, stationed liaison teams with Arab units, reaching down in some cases below the brigade level. Other ARCENT and corps liaison officers served with the British and French allies.[4]

Not surprisingly, the Americans found it easier to work with the British and French, with whom they shared a European defense tradition. Normally part of the British Army of the Rhine, the British 1st Armored Division drew on its own history in desert warfare operations, carried out in North Africa by the famed "Desert Rats" of World War II. The French 6th Light Armored Division, which resembled a large armored cavalry regiment more than a truly integrated division, likewise had substantial desert expertise. Among its 10,000 men were elements of the renowned Foreign Legion, perhaps the best desert-trained troops on the allied side, and several formations that had seen combat against Libyan forces in Chad. Despite differences in equipment, organization, and doctrine, the French division worked well with the XVIII Airborne Corps, with which it shared the role of a highly mobile rapid deployment force.[5]

The Arab forces varied in size and quality. The 40,000-man Egyptian contingent looked the best. The Egyptian 4th Armored and 3d Mechanized Divisions had experienced, well-trained, disciplined troops under senior officers, many of whom had served as battalion commanders in the 1973 war with Israel; were equipped with American materiel; and had participated with Americans in multinational exercises. The Saudis also used American equipment, but any similarity to the Egyptians ended there. The Saudi army, consisting of the relatively well-financed Saudi Arabian National Guard and the Royal Saudi Land Forces, lacked manpower, experienced leadership, training, logistical support, and expertise in large-unit operations. What remained of the Kuwaiti Army also lacked training and, as a consequence of the invasion, equipment. The 10,000 troops from Bahrain, Qatar, Oman, and the United Arab Emirates were in need of equipment too. On the other hand, their level of training surpassed that of the Saudis and Kuwaitis.

[4] Department of the Army, Crisis Planning Team, Combined Command and Control Arrangements, 29 Oct 90, with Encls; Combined Operations Command Relations, 18 Aug 90, in JCS Policy Folder 1; Holley interview; Holloway interview; Eric Schmitt and Michael R. Gordon, "A Lot of Hurdles on the Way to Winning the War," *New York Times*, 24 Mar 91, p. 18; Memo, ARCENT G–3 Plans for DESERT STORM Study Group, 4 Jun 91, sub: OPLAN 1002, DESERT SHIELD and DESERT STORM Planning (hereafter cited as Memo for DESERT STORM Study Group); Draft MS, Swain, Operational Narrative, pp. 28, 87; MS, Doughty, War in the Persian Gulf, p. 3; Interv, Maj Robert K. Wright with Maj John S. Turner, XVIII Airborne Corps Liaison Officer to Eastern Province Area Command, 22 May 91, Fort Bragg, N.C.; Special Planning Cell chronology, p. 13.

[5] Sean D. Naylor, "New 'Desert Rats,'" *Army Times*, 22 Oct 90, p. 15; Holloway interview; Suzanne Lowry, "British Barbs Upset France's Soldiers," *Daily Telegraph*, 14 Dec 90, p. 10.

Coalition partners. American and Saudi (top), British (above), and French (right) allies work and train as members of the multinational coalition.

Of the other coalition partners, Morocco, Pakistan, and Bangladesh provided relatively small but well-trained forces, each with experience in counterinsurgency; Afghanistan, 300 Mujahadeen to serve as military police; and Senegal, 500 soldiers, who impressed American observers with their daily 90-minute sessions of physical conditioning. Syria's force of 15,000 represented the least-known quantity. No one knew how the Syrians would perform, but the memory of their defeat by the Israelis in the Bika Valley in 1982 was not encouraging.[6]

With such a mosaic of national forces, misunderstandings did occur. Schwarzkopf and Yeosock needed all of their considerable skills as diplomats to resolve conflicts. As a former project manager for the effort to modernize the Saudi Arabian National Guard, Yeosock was sensitive to Arab pride and the slow, complex ways of the Saudi bureaucracy—especially the fact that the royal family made all of the important decisions. Saudi staff officers wanted to be part of the planning process, yet the need to turn to higher authority often left them out of the chain. Not all problems were overcome. At the end of December Syria declined to take part in any offensive, and ARCENT planners had to promise more breaching equipment and the support of the 1st Cavalry Division to the anxious Egyptians. On the eve of the ground war Syria changed its mind, but its units were assigned only rear-echelon duty, in part because their Soviet-made equipment too closely resembled that of the Iraqis.

Even with the British and French, problems arose. Eager to be part of the main drive, the British pushed for and received a transfer from the U.S. Marines to VII Corps, thus causing CENTCOM planners to reassign the Tiger Brigade to provide better armor support for the Marines. Coordination with the French was sometimes strained since they, like the Saudis, needed to refer any matter of consequence to their political leaders for decision. Considering the coalition command structure and the potential for disagreement, however, serious conflicts were few in number.[7]

Considering the Enemy

In early 1991 Iraq's military reflected the influence of both the British Army and the Soviet Army. The British influence remained in staff organization and in reliance on the corps as the largest independent operational unit. Soviet influence, dating from the 1960s, was clearest in the heavy reliance on artillery and in a broad range of Warsaw Pact equipment and weapons. But in replacing losses and upgrading capability since the war with Iran, Baghdad had incorporated weapons and other technology from many countries, including Italy, Yugoslavia, Austria, Romania, Switzerland, the Netherlands, South Africa, and the People's Republic of China. Iraq also flew French helicopters and used a variety of American equipment.

By February Iraq had an army of more than 1 million men—about 950,000 regulars, of which some 480,000 were reserve and new conscripts, and about 90,000 volunteers. The regulars were organized into

[6] Sean D. Naylor, "Allies Under the Shield," *Army Times*, 22 Oct 90, p. 14; Holloway interview; Turner interview; MS, Doughty, War in the Persian Gulf, p. 4; Schmitt and Gordon, "A Lot of Hurdles on the Way to Winning the War," p. 18.

[7] Schmitt and Gordon, "A Lot of Hurdles on the Way to Winning the War," p. 18; Margaret Roth, "Yeosock: Back in Familiar Territory with Shield," *Army Times*, 24 Sep 90, p. 9; Draft MS, Swain, Operational Narrative, pp. 25–26, 78, 88; Holloway interview; Turner interview; Steve Vogel, "U.S.-Egyptian Raid Silences Iraqi Artillery," *Army Times*, 25 Feb 91, p. 6; Interv, Maj Dennis P. Levin with Lt Col John R. Vines, 4th Battalion, 325th Airborne Infantry (2d/82d), 25 Jan 91, Rafha Airfield, Saudi Arabia; Special Planning Cell chronology, pp. 13, 15.

seven corps and the volunteers into the corps-size *Republican Guard Forces Command*, the offensive component of Iraq's military. Three corps were deployed northward, partly facing the borders of Turkey, Syria, and Iran. The remaining four corps and the *Republican Guard Forces Command* were in southern Iraq, in Kuwait, and along the eastern part of the Iraqi–Saudi Arabian border and thus were of immediate interest to Central Command.

The corps was the principal controlling headquarters in the Iraqi field forces. Each corps commander controlled a variety of combat support and combat service support units: air defense, reconnaissance, engineer, chemical defense, medical, aviation, antitank, signal, electronic warfare, and special forces battalions. Of these elements, coalition commanders paid the most attention to artillery, air defense artillery, and rocket brigades. Each artillery brigade nominally had seventy-two weapons, and in some sectors brigades had twice that many. These mortars, howitzers, and guns generally reflected the Soviet inventory and included at least six sizes, ranging from 100 mm. to 160 mm. One type of Iraqi towed artillery, the South African G–5, with a range of 25 miles, particularly concerned allied ground commanders.

Each rocket brigade probably had eighteen transporter-erector-launchers able to launch one of two major weapon systems: Soviet-made FROG (free rocket over ground) rockets, and three types of Scud intermediate-range ballistic missiles. The designation Scud was the NATO code name for the Soviet-designed SS–1 missile and its variants, which the Iraqis had bought from the Soviets and North Koreans during the war with Iran and modified to extend the range. With clearance from the General Headquarters, corps commanders could use the Soviet Scud-B or either of the two Iraqi-modified Scuds, the *Al-Hussein* and the *Al-Abbas*, with ranges between 200 and 400 miles.

Iraq's missile inventory represented a two-pronged threat to the effort to liberate Kuwait. On the strategic level the Scuds menaced the integrity of the allied coalition. Capable of reaching Israel, the Scuds could provoke a counterattack by the Jewish state, the archenemy of many of the Muslim countries that had deployed military contingents against Iraq. Such a development would almost certainly fragment the coalition. On the tactical level the missiles, as well as a variety of artillery pieces and aircraft, could be used to unleash a threat of great concern to coalition field commanders and governments alike: chemical attack.

During the seven months of the crisis, the Iraqi Army had between fifty-five and sixty divisions, the number fluctuating with draft calls, training cycles, and attrition rates. The Iraqis fielded several types of divisions: armored, mechanized, and motorized infantry. Each was nominally organized into three maneuver brigades, divisional artillery, and various combat support and combat service support units. A typical armored division had two armored brigades and one mechanized brigade; a mechanized division had two mechanized brigades and one armored brigade; and a motorized infantry division had three infantry brigades and one tank battalion. After extended deployment, however, many divisions evolved to meet specific situations, expanding to include as many as eight maneuver brigades of any type, depending on the perceived threat in a particular sector. The large numbers of tracked and armored vehicles in Iraqi divisions—4,500 main battle tanks and 2,880 armored personnel carriers all told—indicated impressive battlefield mobility and offensive potential. This armored capability was strengthened by the direct support of some 3,300 artillery pieces in the Kuwaiti theater of operations.[8]

The *Republican Guard* was the best of the Iraqi ground forces. During the Iran-Iraq war this organization had been expanded from a Palace Guard of one brigade into a separate force—the *Republican Guard Forces Command*—of thirty to thirty-three brigades in seven divisions and had been the key to the victory over Iran in the final battles. The *Republican Guard Forces Command* possessed advantages of personnel and equipment over the larger Regular Army. All *Republican Guard* troops were highly motivated volunteers rather than conscripts; all had more training than the regulars; and all had the most modern equipment in the Iraqi inventory, including the Soviet T–72 M1 tank with night vision capability. This elite corps included infantry, mechanized and motorized infantry, and armored divisions.[9]

The *Republican Guard Forces Command* was divided into two sub-corps groups, an independent division, twenty special forces (commando) brigades, and one naval infantry brigade. The heroic names of some of the subordinate elements underscored their elite character. The *1st Subcorps Group*, deployed in southern Iraq and northern Kuwait, consisted of two armored units, the *Hammurabi* and *Madina Divisions*; one mechanized infantry unit, the *Tawakalna Division*; and a motorized infantry unit, the *Al-Faw Division. The 2d Subcorps Group*, deployed south of Baghdad, consisted of two motorized infantry units, the *Nebuchadnezzar* and the *Adnan Divisions*. The independent mechanized infantry unit was the *Baghdad Division*, stationed in and around the Iraqi capital. In January 1991 the formation of five more *Republican Guard* divisions was announced, all motorized infantry. The names of only three of them were known to Central Command: the *Al-Abed*, *Al-Mustafa*, and *Al-Nidala Divisions*.[10]

By mid-February the Iraqis had forty-three divisions along their southeastern border and in Kuwait. These divisions were organized in the *II, III, IV,* and *VII Corps* of the Regular Army and in the *Republican Guard*. The Iraqi order of battle in the triborder area included thirty-one infantry, four mechanized infantry, and eight armored divisions arranged in distinct lines and masses. A nearly solid line of infantry divisions, stretching from the Persian Gulf across southern Kuwait and extending about 100 miles farther west into southern Iraq, faced coalition forces and the Saudi Arabian border. Behind the east end of this infantry line, in a defensive arc south and west of Kuwait City, stood two mechanized infantry and two armored divisions; behind the west end, another armored

[8] National Training Center Handbook 100–91, The Iraqi Army; Organization and Tactics [3 Jan 91], pp. 2–25; MS, Doughty, War in the Persian Gulf, p. 5.

[9] National Training Center Handbook 100–91, The Iraqi Army; Organization and Tactics [3 Jan 91], pp. 25–32.

[10] Richard Jupa and James Dingeman, "The Republican Guards: Loyal, Aggressive, Able," *Army* (March 1991): 54–62.

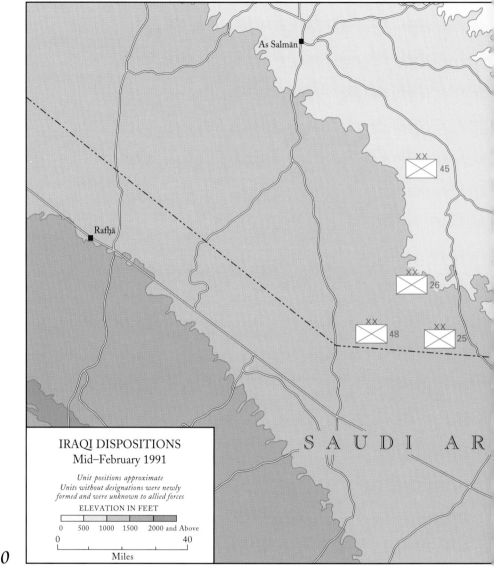

Map 10

IRAQI DISPOSITIONS
Mid–February 1991

*Unit positions approximate
Units without designations were newly
formed and were unknown to allied forces*

ELEVATION IN FEET

0   500   1000   1500   2000 and Above

0   40
              Miles

division. This front line of Iraqi units totaled twenty-eight divisions, all
Regular Army. A second tier of fifteen divisions, including the remaining
armored and mechanized infantry divisions, deployed in a more dispersed
pattern across northern Kuwait and southeastern Iraq. Twelve of those divisions, five of them armored, were *Republican Guard* units (*Map 10*).[11]

Identifying the Variables

While coordinating with the coalition, Army Central Command worked
almost around the clock on the plan for the two-corps flanking attack, to
include identifying the significant variables with tactical implications. In a
schoolhouse at Eskan Village, ARCENT planners pondered the strength of the

[11] ODCSINT Intelligence Summary
400, 23 Feb 91.

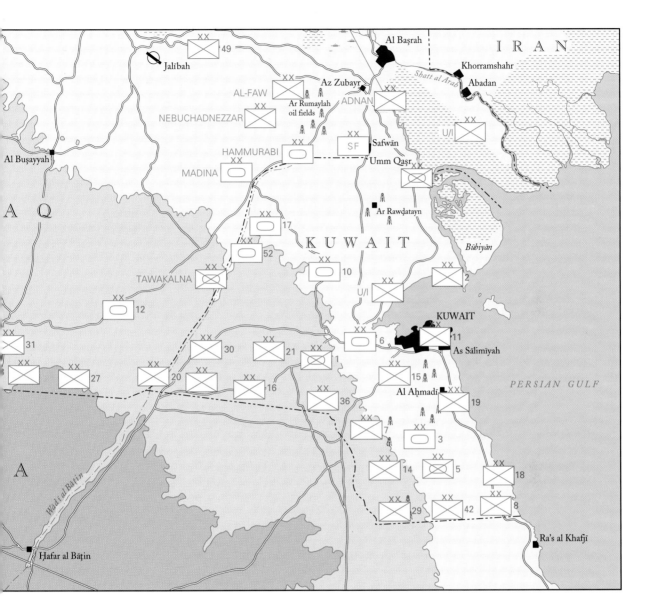

Iraqi defenses, the logistical feasibility of the proposed move, and the roles of the two corps. They were concerned that allied forces might bog down trying to break through the obstacles, leaving them vulnerable to artillery and chemical weapons, which few seemed to doubt the Iraqis would use.

Factored into ARCENT planning were the environmental variables of weather and terrain. In Iraq, a large desert zone sprawled west and southwest of the Euphrates River. It was part of the Syrian Desert, which covered parts of Syria, Jordan, and Saudi Arabia as well. The alluvial plain, created by the Euphrates and Tigris Rivers, extended from north of Baghdad to the Persian Gulf. Intermittent lakes and marshlands, the sizes of which varied from year to year and season to season, dotted the plain, as did the wadies, which were sometimes obstacles but mostly good avenues of approach.

A tactical operations center flooded by torrential rains

The terrain and climatic features of the theater of operations present-ed tactical challenges that ground commanders and ARCENT planners could not ignore. The land surface of the desert zone was generally stony, with rare sandy stretches, and unusually level for great distances. While these conditions made cover and concealment very difficult, they invited rapid mechanized assaults, including armored strikes, and appeared to ease ground logistical support, since wheeled vehicles could apparently make their own roads in most places. In Kuwait itself, a gravelly and undulating land surface with intermittent sand dunes made defensive preparations easier and rapid assaults harder. The alluvial plain, with its many lakes and channels as well as the Euphrates and Tigris Rivers, offered barriers to mechanized movement. Marshlands would slow or prohibit ground operations if CENTCOM forces had to maneuver close to the Iranian border. The seasonal rain and *sharqi-shamal* phenomena threatened to slow, if not stop, ground operations by reducing vision and degrading base construction. And the wadies had to be taken into account to prevent their use as avenues of Iraqi attack.[12]

With so much of the terrain essentially featureless, ARCENT planners had to create objectives and draw phase lines that were not tied to promi-nent natural and man-made features. Although phase lines represented in graphic form a tactical concept rather than geometric purity, the lines for the offensive would show an unusually uniform ladder-like appearance as a result of the flat sameness of the desert. Corps and division commanders could establish supplemental phase lines within corps sectors as needed.

Logistics was probably the biggest problem. To preserve secrecy, Army Central Command could not move its troops and the required sixty days of supplies west of the triborder area until the start of the air war. Yet, once the air war began, the ARCENT staff estimated that it

[12] Nyrop, ed., *Iraq: A Country Study*, pp. 69, 72, 75–76; Nyrop, ed., *Area Handbook for the Persian Gulf States* (Washington, D.C.: Government Printing Office, 1977), pp. 123–24; Safran, *Saudi Arabia*, pp. 206–07.

would have only two weeks to deploy the vast numbers of soldiers and quantities of materiel before the start of the ground offensive, a formidable task in view of the limited number of roads and lack of vehicles to transport heavy equipment. To complicate matters, VII Corps would still be arriving in Saudi Arabia well after the start of the air war and would want time to acclimate and train its troops for their specific missions before moving them into position for the attack.

Theater Logistics

As General Arnold's ARCENT planning team shaped the details of the ground offensive, a responsive logistics system developed apace. Under Maj. Gen. William G. Pagonis, the Provisional Support Command at Dhahran accelerated efforts to draft an operational logistics plan, to select suitable sites for depots, and to manage the flow of supplies.

In October the Provisional Support Command established two forward logistical bases to provide critical medical, maintenance, fuel, and ammunition resupply services. The bases were huge, with perimeters as long as 80 miles. Within their boundaries, various units set up storage areas hundreds of yards apart. At an ammunition supply depot, numerous clusters of several dozen boxes were spaced far apart over many thousands of square yards. Combat service and combat service support units at those bases, such as hospitals, set up their operations and built low earthen hills around their borders. The first bases, code-named BASTOGNE and PULASKI, allowed the logisticians to clear the ports, stockpile vast quantities of materiel, and better plan their support of the spread-out XVIII Airborne Corps. Since it was becoming increasingly difficult to manage theater support operations from Dhahran, General Pagonis created the Northern Logistics Operations Center at King Khalid Military City in

Mock logistical installation. As part of DESERT SHIELD deception, this refueling point was created using a simulated helicopter, fake fuel blivets, and a simulated HMMWV under a camouflage net. In the background is an artificial brigade tactical operations center.

Ammunition supply depot near Dhahran, which was known as "The Quarry"

[13] Interv, Maj William W. Epley with Col James W. Ireland, 1 Apr 91, Dhahran, Saudi Arabia; Draft MS, John J. McGrath and Michael D. Krause, Theater Logistics and the Gulf War [1992], p. 27.

[14] Operations Plan 91–1, 12 November 1990, was the theater logistical plan for receiving VII Corps. Plan 91–2, 4 November 1990, was the logistical support plan for the reception, onward movement, and sustainment of U.S. forces. Plan 91–3 was for support of the Kuwaiti Task Force. Plan 91–4, 5 March 1991, concerned redeployment support. The dates and the numbering of the operations plans are out of sequence because the first two were published and then numbered later.

[15] Maj William W. Epley, Notes of Lt Gen Pagonis' Briefing, 6 Mar 91, Dhahran, Saudi Arabia; Pagonis Briefing to Secretary of the Army Michael Stone, Apr 91, Dhahran, Saudi Arabia (videotape); Draft MS, McGrath and Krause, Theater Logistics, p. 158.

[16] Pagonis Briefing to Secretary of the Army Stone, Apr 91.

[17] 22d Support Command (SupCom), Operations Plan 91–4, 4 Mar 91.

November. The move put him nearer to the action and facilitated support as more of the coalition forces moved forward. At the end of the month Pagonis established three more logistical bases—ALPHA, BRAVO, and DELTA—to support VII Corps and to provide a theater reserve.[13]

Also in November the Provisional Support Command began work on a comprehensive logistics plan. The objective was to support the arrival of VII Corps, to sustain the scheme of maneuver once hostilities started, and to provide for the redeployment of Army troops after the shooting stopped. General Pagonis and his staff contemplated a five-stage process, which they published in four command operations plans.[14] To rehearse those plans, the staff and select subordinate elements participated in a two-day logistics exercise on 1–2 January 1991.

The first plan, Phase Alpha, involved the repositioning of Support Command units and theater-level stockage of supplies while receiving and moving the VII Corps to its tactical assembly area (*Table 5*).[15] The second plan consisted of two stages: Phase Bravo, the movement of the VII and XVIII Airborne Corps from their tactical assembly areas to their attack positions; and Phase Charlie, the support of the ground offensive into Kuwait and Iraq. All classes of supplies, but especially fuel, ammunition, food, and water, would be transported, based on the "90-mile rule"—delivering supplies up to 90 miles into Iraq for transfer to the corps-level support organizations. Two new logistical bases, designated OSCAR and NELLINGEN, would also be constructed deep inside Iraq to sustain the offensive if necessary.[16] The last two plans focused on postwar operations. Phase Delta involved logistical support of civil-military efforts to restore services inside Kuwait once the coalition liberated that country. Phase Echo, designated Operation DESERT FAREWELL, envisioned the use of theater-wide assets to redeploy all U.S. Army units.[17]

As the theater matured, units from the United States continued to augment the logistical organization, which shed its provisional status and became the 22d Support Command as of 16 December. During the

Theater Stockage Objectives	
Class	Days of Supply
I (Rations)	20
II (Individual equipment)................	23
IIIB (POL bulk)	26 [a]
IIIP (POL package)	23
IV (Construction).........................	23
V (Ammunition)	45
VI (Sundry items)........................	20
VII (Major end items)............	As needed
VII (Medical)	0
IX (Repair parts) [b]	As needed

[a] Eighteen days host nation storage

[b] Selected major assemblies only

Source: Draft MS, John J. McGrath and Michael D. Krause, Theater Logistics and the Gulf War (1992), p. 158.

Table 5

month the 21st Theater Army Area Command, Augmentation, an Indiana reserve unit trained to reinforce a regular theater-level logistics unit in Europe, arrived and further reinforced the 22d's headquarters staff. A number of other reserve units, for example, the 800th Military Police Brigade and the 318th Transportation Agency (Movement Control), also deployed to the theater. Eventually, almost 60 percent of the 22d's personnel were reservists. In addition to the reserve units, such active-duty units as the 593d Support Group (Area) and the 89th Military Police Brigade served as subordinate components of the Support Command.[18]

With logistical operations spread over eastern Saudi Arabia, timely communications was critical to the coordinated delivery of supplies and equipment to the forward units. The 22d Support Command was fully aware that combat units could not move if fuel did not arrive on time. Many of its subordinate logistical units found that they were not authorized enough radios, which exacerbated the problem for the logisticians. Col. Daniel G. Brown, who replaced Col. David A. Whaley as commander of the 7th Transportation Group, had only three radios with which to coordinate the work of his command, which included 9,100 troops. One of his truck battalions had none.[19] Col. Michael T. Gaw, commander of the 32d Transportation Group, fared no better. His headquarters deployed only the communications gear that was organic to his headquarters company.

The 22d's own logistical units faced similar communications equipment problems, but they were able to develop creative solutions. They took advantage of the modern civilian infrastructure of Saudi Arabia and used the telephone network extensively. Pagonis' staff also contracted for cellular, vehicle-mounted phones to distribute to unit commanders. In addition, units used U.S. Air Force AM radios, mobile subscriber equipment, and satellite hookup phones to talk and send data over the long distances.[20]

The 22d Support Command also had responsibility for the weapon system replacement program, a theater-wide effort to prepare fully trained replacement crews for Abrams tanks, Bradley fighting vehicles, artillery pieces, helicopters, and light infantry squads. Those crews and their equipment would go to the forward combat elements as replacements for battle casualties. Although the 22d exercised command

[18] 22d SupCom, Desert Shield Command Rpt, 23 Mar 91, p. 8.

[19] Epley Notes taken at 22d SupCom AAR, 1 Apr 91, Dhahran.

[20] 22d SupCom, Desert Storm Command Rpt, 5 Apr 91.

Signal troop adjusts a tactical satellite dish at a desert installation, consisting of the dish, two generators, and a shelter

responsibility for the program, the Seventh Army Training Center provided mobile training team support.[21] General Pagonis considered that training among the most urgent aspects of his mission, and he closely monitored the effort.[22] Hence, as the combat troops prepared for their move into the desert, the training teams readied a total of 116 tank crews, another 108 for Bradleys, 57 for a variety of artillery, and 27 light infantry squads to serve as battle replacements. Because the ground war was brief and casualties very light, the system was barely utilized and after the cease-fire the crews were among the first to return to their home stations.

The high operational readiness of the various pieces of combat equipment resulted from effective preventive maintenance by operators as well as materiel management. Leaders ensured that crews meticulously performed routine maintenance to keep their equipment combat ready. Infusions of new equipment throughout the entire campaign also helped keep the operational rates for Army equipment in theater remarkably high. In fact, the rates were better in most cases than for other Army units stationed in the United States. For example, those for key equipment, such as the M1A1 and the M2, during DESERT STORM were always above 90 percent, usually between 92 and 98 percent.[23]

Overseeing materiel management for General Pagonis' command was the 321st Support Center (Theater Army), a reserve unit, which arrived in Saudi Arabia in October. Its primary mission was to manage all classes of supply, especially Class IX, the spare parts for Army equipment. Yet prior to the 321st's arrival XVIII Airborne Corps already had its own centers working on materiel management, and thus several weeks passed before the 321st officially took over. Until then, the corps had to deal directly with Stateside agencies for spare parts. Eventually, theater-level control over repair parts was established. So long as the operational readiness rates of equipment remained high, Pagonis was reluctant to tamper with the arrangement.[24] Overall, by January 1991, the 22d Support Command was well on its way to being able to support offensive ground operations.

ARCENT and the Corps

While theater logisticians strove to provide necessary personnel, supplies, and equipment to the forward units, the roles of the corps became the subject of animated discussion among the ARCENT and corps planners. Each corps was supposed to work out the details of its place in the overall planning concept and submit them to Army Central Command for approval. The XVIII Airborne Corps, in particular, repeatedly pro-

[21] Msg, ARCENT to SupCom, 17 Feb 91, sub: WSRO Operations.

[22] SupCom Daily "sit down" Briefing Charts, Jan–Feb 91.

[23] 22d SupCom LogSitreps, 25 and 31 Jan, and 7, 20, and 25 Feb 91.

[24] 22d SupCom MMC AAR, 6 Apr 91; Epley Notes and Videotape of 22d SupCom AAR, 1 Apr 91.

posed plans that would enhance its role, such as a drive down the Euphrates River valley to cut Iraqi communications. It asked the addition of an armored division, preferably the return of the 1st Cavalry Division from theater reserve, to make such a maneuver possible.

From the start, however, CENTCOM and ARCENT planners intended to give the heavier VII Corps the primary task of destroying the *Republican Guard*. The main question regarding the XVIII Airborne Corps appeared to have been how that corps could support the VII Corps' mission. The planners were concerned that two corps operating in the same area would constrain each other's movements, and the VII Corps' desire that the XVIII Corps cover its right flank was rejected by ARCENT because it might leave the XVIII Corps in the kind of breaching role for which it was ill suited. So ARCENT planners put XVIII Corps in a screening role west of VII Corps and in position to support the latter (*Map 11*).

From 27 to 30 December Army Central Command hosted a map exercise to review the draft plan and resolve differences between the VII and XVIII Corps. Through situational briefings, discussions within working groups, and general sessions to review those discussions, General Yeosock and his planners sought to anticipate every contingency. The exercise confirmed having the VII Corps in the lead role and keeping the 1st Cavalry Division in its capacity as theater reserve, but especially revealed the inherent problems in deploying the corps to their attack positions within two weeks of the start of the air war.

Refining the Plan

Through January CENTCOM, ARCENT, and corps planners, together with 22d Support Command logisticians, refined the details of the offensive. The ARCENT team concentrated its effort on developing responses for contingencies, including a counterattack by the *Republican Guard* and a failure to breach the defensive works along the Kuwaiti border. With Syria's decision at the end of December to stay out of the offensive, concern about the ability of the Egyptians to do their job deepened. This concern, along with nagging doubts about being able to support adequately XVIII Airborne Corps' advance to the Euphrates, caused General Schwarzkopf to direct a review of the entire concept.

In response, ARCENT planners modified some of the riskier features. They moved the base of XVIII Airborne Corps' projected northward drive to the east, nearer to the VII Corps, and arranged to cut Highway 8, the key Iraqi line of retreat, with air power rather than ground forces. Although staffs revised details up to the eve of the ground offensive, the main elements were clear by February. A Marine amphibious force would demonstrate off the coast of Kuwait to divert Iraqi attention from the western flank. Near first light on G-day, Arab forces along the coast and Marines farther inland would attack the main Iraqi fortifications and fix the enemy's tactical and operational reserves. Meanwhile, the French 6th

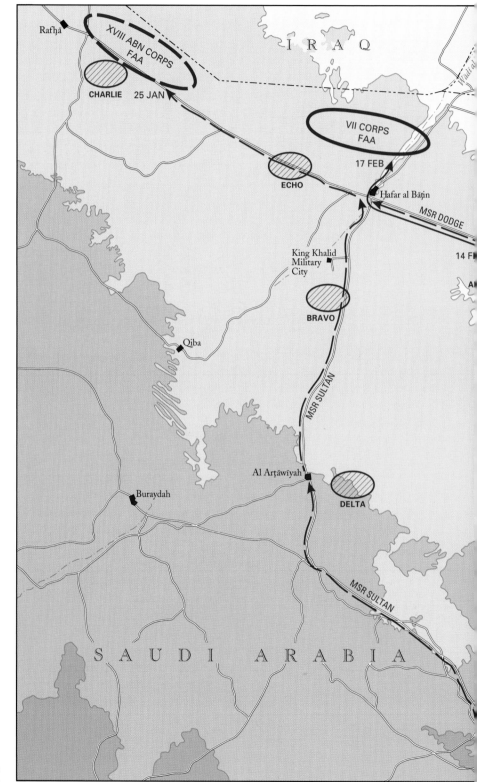

Map 11

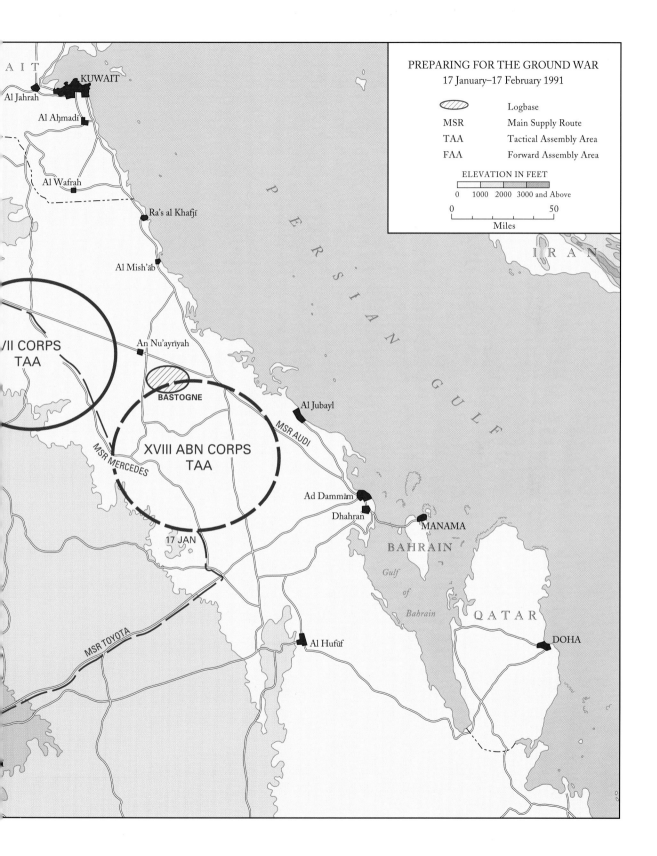

PREPARING FOR THE GROUND WAR
17 January–17 February 1991

Logbase	
MSR	Main Supply Route
TAA	Tactical Assembly Area
FAA	Forward Assembly Area

ELEVATION IN FEET

0 1000 2000 3000 and Above

0   50

Miles

KUWAIT

Al Jahrah

Al Aḥmadī

Al Wafrah

Ra's al Khafjī

Al Mish'āb

P E R S I A N

VII CORPS
TAA

An Nu'ayrīyah

BASTOGNE

Al Jubayl

G U L F

XVIII ABN CORPS
TAA

MSR AUDI

MSR MERCEDES

Ad Dammām

Dhahran

MANAMA

17 JAN

BAHRAIN

Gulf

of

Bahrain

QATAR

MSR TOYOTA

Al Hufūf

DOHA

I R A N

25 Memo for DESERT STORM Study Group; Holloway interview; Holley interview; Special Planning Cell chronology, pp. 9–17; Draft MS, Swain, Operational Narrative, pp. 56–60, 71–74, 78–80, 90–91; CENTCOM Planning Cell interview, pp. 49–50, 56–61; Memo for COMUSARCENT, Attn: History Office, 25 Feb 91, sub: Training, Command Report Operation DESERT SHIELD; Swain interview; ARCENT Planning Slides, 8 Feb 91.

26 ARCENT Exercises and Training Command Rpt, 25 Feb 91; Memo for COMUSARCENT G–3, 12 Feb 91, sub: Training, Significant Historical Events, Operation DESERT SHIELD; Interv, David W. Hogan with Exercises and Training Section, ARCENT G–3, 14 Jun 91, Fort McPherson (hereafter cited as Exercises and Training Section interview); Vines interview; Interv, Maj Dennis P. Levin with Maj Walter Wilson, S–3, 1st Battalion, 504th Infantry (1st Brigade, 82d Airborne Division), 14 Jan 91, 82d Airborne Division Range Complex in Eastern Saudi Arabia; Dan Janutolo, "101st on the Front Lines," *Soldiers* 46 (January 1991): 16–19.

27 *Washington Post*, 13 Sep 91.

Soldiers review MICLIC manual prior to firing

Light Armored Division and the 82d and 101st Airborne Divisions on the far left would attack north toward Baghdad and the Euphrates Valley, securing the coalition's left flank.

The main attack would come on the next day. The VII Corps' enormous armored force, with the XVIII Corps' 24th Infantry Division (Mechanized) and the 3d Armored Cavalry on the left, would break through the enemy's fortifications, drive deep into the rear, and destroy the enemy's theater reserve, the *Republican Guard*. One hour after VII Corps' attack, the Egyptians and other Arab forces on the right would attack into southwestern Kuwait to cover VII Corps' right flank. Between the Arabs and the VII Corps, in position to support the former, the 1st Cavalry Division would feint up the Wādī al Bāṭin. Following Yeosock's leadership style, the plan only sketched the initial stages of the attack, leaving later moves to be determined by his corps commanders in response to events.[25]

Training for the Attack

Meanwhile, both corps trained for the attack. While still focusing on maneuver warfare, XVIII Airborne Corps, as early as October, had begun training on breaching techniques and attacks on strongpoints. Army Central Command was only beginning to receive training supplies, including targets and laser devices for combat simulation, and the bulk of the training ammunition did not show up for more than two months. The XVIII Corps improvised with tin cans, car bodies, flares, and other available materials. Using intelligence gained from satellite photographs, its subordinate units replicated Iraqi fortifications, tank ditches, minefields, and wire entanglements. The 82d Airborne Division built its own model of an Iraqi triangular work based on observer reports of the Iran-Iraq war, and the 101st Division used an abandoned village to practice street fighting.[26]

Similar activities occupied VII Corps. The 1st Infantry Division's engineer, Lt. Col. Stephen C. Hawkins, created two life-size models of Iraqi trenches for training in breaching techniques. The division experimented against these mock-ups and came up with a tactic that took advantage of the shifting desert sands and eliminated the need for troops to leave their armored vehicles to eject an entrenched enemy. The technique required plow-equipped tanks and armored combat earthmovers (ACEs) to turn along the trench lines after breaking through them. Then, while Bradley crews alongside poured cannon and machine-gun fire into the trenches, one tank or ACE moving along the front lip and the other along the rear filled in the trenches with their plows. If ever employed, this tactic could be expected to cause panic among the enemy while neutralizing his defensive works.[27]

Much of the training focused on the unique problems of desert warfare. Almost all of the Army's units had benefited from training at the Fort

A soldier in full chemical protective gear drinks from a canteen

Irwin National Training Center in California, and certain units, like the 24th Division, had stressed desert warfare in their own training programs. Still, the Saudi Arabian desert, with its lack of landmarks and its fine, abrasive sand, presented unique challenges. By November XVIII Airborne Corps soldiers had learned much about survival there, developing skills in land navigation, drinking copious amounts of water, working at night, and driving their vehicles abreast to avoid bogging down in each other's tracks. Using desert operations in World War II and the Arab-Israeli wars as case studies, they also learned to cope with the wide frontages, lack of concealment, dispersion, and emphasis on speed and maneuverability inherent in desert warfare.[28]

As American television viewers well knew, XVIII Airborne Corps spent a lot of training time on breaching operations. To create paths through minefields, tank ditches, and barbed wire, the corps worked with bulldozers, mine-rollers pushed by tanks, and portable bridges. They also practiced with the mine clearing line charge (MICLIC), a rocket-launched cable carrying a line of charges that, when fired across a minefield, exploded mines in its path. Training against the 82d Division's model of an Iraqi defensive system, one battalion matched each of its two assault companies with a bulldozer, MICLIC, and antitank platoon. The companies crossed the path created by these devices and attacked a triangular position at about the same time that friendly air and artillery fire shifted to supporting triangles.

After engineers opened holes in the sand berm wall with dynamite and plastic explosives, the two companies burst through the breach and fanned out into the trenches. Meanwhile, the battalion's third company maneuvered by the flank to block reinforcements from adjacent positions. In the end, these well-publicized exercises probably proved more valuable as decoys for the Iraqis than as preparation for the actual mission, but at the time no one could be sure of the 82d's eventual role.

Underlying much of the training was the concern that the Iraqis might use chemical weapons. They were known to possess mustard and nerve gas and had not hesitated to use chemicals against Iranian troops or rebellious Kurds. Outwardly, American military spokesmen minimized the threat, calling chemical weapons indecisive and relatively harmless with proper countermeasures. But the Army's logistical agencies rushed to meet the demand for protective gear and antidotes. The specter of American troops, unable to breach Iraqi lines and caught in a rain of chemical-laced artillery shells, haunted American generals.

[28] Trainers later acknowledged the value of literature from the Center for Army Lessons Learned in preparations for desert warfare. See Exercises and Training Section interview. See also Interv, Maj Dennis P. Levin with members of 2d Battalion, 319th Field Artillery (82d Airborne Division), 2 Feb 91, near Rafha, Saudi Arabia; Lee Ewing, "Tricks of the Trade," *Army Times*, 10 Dec 90, p. 30; Center for Army Lessons Learned, Winning in the Desert, pp. 7–12; Sean D. Naylor, "No Place to Hide," *Army Times*, 5 Nov 90, p. 14; Wallace Franz, "Army's Ability to Move Could Mean Desert Success," *Army Times*, 5 Nov 90, p. 29; Sean D. Naylor, "Sand Draws the Lines for Artillery in the Desert," *Army Times*, 26 Nov 90, p. 18.

Troops training in trench warfare at Tire City, a simulated Iraqi defense complex in the Eastern Province of Saudi Arabia

Even if losses could be minimized by prompt counteraction, it would be extremely difficult to operate in the hot, cumbersome protective suits, masks, gloves, and overshoes. To prepare for such an eventuality, XVIII Airborne Corps placed considerable emphasis on chemical warfare instruction, including detection, quick changes into protective suits, and use of antidotes. Like breaching training, the sight of American soldiers rushing to don gas masks became common on American television screens.[29]

The XVIII Corps' training priorities shifted to maneuver warfare and force modernization during December and early January. As modernization picked up speed, the corps devoted considerable time to live fire exercises to become familiar with new equipment. Shortages of training ammunition complicated such exercises, but by the start of the offensive practically every unit, except the air defense battalions, had tested its weapon systems. Often using live ammunition, corps troops worked on maneuver techniques, stressing the use of helicopters, concealment, and responses to different situations. Through exercises with the artillery and the Air Force, they improved coordination of fire support. At higher levels the corps used the Battle Command Training Program, designed at Fort Leavenworth, to hold seminars and exercises for instruction of staffs in command and control, a major concern of Lt. Gen. Gary E. Luck, the corps commander.[30]

The number of live fire exercises, along with concern in the United States over casualties among troops in the Persian Gulf, made safety a major concern for XVIII Airborne Corps. When the corps first arrived in the theater, it had had problems with helicopter crashes due to the pilots' inability to distinguish terrain features at night. In response, the Army had banned night flights below 150 feet for crews new to the desert, required every night helicopter mission to carry at least a three-soldier crew, and accelerated plans to put audio warning systems on altimeters. The problem had largely been solved by December, and other safety measures, such as careful marking of live fire ranges and surveillance of those ranges by helicopters, were implemented. By 22 February the death toll among American troops from noncombat causes had reached thirty, the majority from traffic accidents and freak gunshot incidents that occurred outside of training exercises.[31]

From the start of the campaign, training of allied forces had a high priority in Central Command. Although the Army had worked with Egyptians and Jordanians in past exercises, it had never trained with the Saudis or other Arabs in the coalition. Elements of the 5th Special Forces Group had deployed with the first American troops to arrive in Southwest Asia. By 1 December they had already instructed 13,000 allied troops in forty-three different subjects. Since the allied troops would rely on a largely American air force, communications and close air support received special emphasis, but the Green Berets also stressed weapons training and basic small-unit tactics, chemical countermeasures, and land navigation. As allied offensive plans developed, breaching operations came to dominate the training program.

[29] Wilson interview; Vines interview; Caleb Baker, "Against the Wall," *Army Times*, 28 Jan 91, p. 24; Steve Vogel, "Burden of Breaching Iraqi Line Falls to Engineers," *Army Times*, 4 Feb 91, p. 15; Exercises and Training Section interview; Guy Gugliotta, "U.S. Experts Doubt Power of Poison Gas," *Washington Post*, 14 Dec 90, p. 45; "Chemical Weapons Not a Trump Card, Experts Say," *Army Times*, 1 Oct 90, p. 29; Philip Shenon, "Troops Who'll Counter Gas Attack: Ready or Not?," *New York Times*, 13 Dec 90, p. 20; J. Paul Scicchitano, "Pentagon Says Iraqi Chemical Threat Is Real," *Army Times*, 20 Aug 90, p. 16; Holley interview.

[30] See XVIII Airborne Corps Sitreps for December and early January; Exercises and Training Section interview; Janutolo, "101st on the Front Lines," pp. 16–19; Vines interview; ARCENT Exercises and Training Section Command Rpt, 25 Feb 91; Interv, Maj Dennis P. Levin with 2d Battalion, 159th Aviation (18th Aviation Brigade), 30 Dec 90, 18th Aviation Brigade Heliport near King Abdul Aziz Air Base.

[31] J. Paul Scicchitano, "Clipped Wings: Army Hopes Copter Flight Restrictions Will Cut Accidents," *Army Times*, 22 Oct 90, p. 20; Exercises and Training Section interview; 2d Battalion, 159th Aviation, interview; "Two Soldiers Die in Accidents," *Army Times*, 14 Jan 91, p. 16.

Soldiers playing cards in their tent

The XVIII Airborne Corps also became involved in combined training, instituting a partnership program that paired its units with Saudi formations from the Eastern Province Area Command. The 3d Armored Cavalry, for example, conducted live fire exercises with the Saudi 8th Brigade, and American engineers taught their Saudi counterparts breaching techniques. Since many Arabs spoke English and some Americans Arabic, language did not prove a major barrier, but at times cultural sensitivities made combined training a challenge for both sides.[32]

When not training, the troops of XVIII Airborne Corps made their life in the desert as comfortable as possible. Through December the corps stayed in practically the same position it had occupied since its arrival, backing up the Arabs along the Saudi Arabia–Kuwait border. The 3d Armored Cavalry held an advanced position near An Nu'ayrīyah, with the 24th Division directly behind it at assembly areas HINESVILLE, MIDWAY, and COLUMBUS, and the 101st Division on its flanks at assembly areas CARENTON and EAGLE. Behind this line the 1st Cavalry Division had assembled at HORSE, and the 82d Division had deployed from CHAMPION MAIN, north of Dhahran, to FALCON BASE, near Abq Aiq. The troops also constructed living quarters from whatever lay handy, building houses and furniture from scrap lumber and cardboard. In the heat and dust, accompanied by clouds of flies, a cold drink of water, a fly swatter, and mail were a soldier's most valued commodities. The troops read, wrote letters, and played cards, volleyball, and football as they waited for whatever the future might bring. Looming over everything was the United Nations' 15 January deadline for Iraq to withdraw from Kuwait.[33]

[32] See CENTCOM Sitrep for 6 Dec 90; see also CENTCOM and ARCENT Sitreps for Dec 90 and Jan 91; ARCENT Exercises and Training Command Rpts; Exercises and Training Section interview; "Armies Coordinate During Exercises," *Army Times*, 17 Dec 90, p. 60; Caleb Baker, "Saudi Soldiers Sense Urgency in Training," *Army Times*, 21 Jan 91, p. 20; Turner interview; Draft MS, Richard Stewart, Army Special Operations Forces in Operation DESERT STORM, pp. 2–5.

[33] ARCENT Sitreps for Dec 90; William H. McMichael, "Playing the Waiting Game in Saudi," *Soldiers* 45 (December 1990): 13–17; Phil Prater, "First Team in the Desert," *Soldiers* 46 (February 1991): 13–16; Janutolo, "101st on the Front Lines," p. 16; Phil Prater, "Guarding Saudi Skies," *Soldiers* 46 (February 1991): 17; "Tanks and Men: Desert Storm from the Hatches," *Army* 41 (June 1991): 31; Vines interview.

Chapter 7

READYING FOR THE STORM

As 15 January 1991 approached, the last hopes for peace evaporated in an atmosphere of mutual recriminations. On 30 November 1990 President George H. Bush had invited Iraqi Foreign Minister Tariq Aziz to Washington and had offered to send Secretary of State James H. Baker to Baghdad in an effort "to go the extra mile for peace." Iraq accepted but sought again to include Palestine and the Israeli-occupied territories in the discussion. As before, this was unacceptable to the Bush administration, which had categorically rejected any linkage between the Persian Gulf crisis and the Palestinian problem.

Further discussions finally led to a dramatic meeting in Geneva on 9 January between Baker and Aziz. After over six hours of talks, a somber Baker informed reporters that he saw no signs of Iraqi flexibility or intention to comply with the United Nations resolutions. Three days later both houses of Congress passed resolutions authorizing the president to use military action to enforce the United Nations demand for an Iraqi withdrawal from Kuwait. As neutral diplomats worked frantically to reach a last-minute settlement, all eyes turned toward the Gulf in grim expectation of the outbreak of war.

Hostilities were not long in coming. At 2300 local time on 16 January, the crews of nine Apaches and one Black Hawk of the 101st Airborne Division (Air Assault) boarded their helicopters after a final intelligence update. They joined a squadron of Air Force search-and-rescue helicopters and flew into western Iraq, using night vision goggles and infrared radar to navigate and keeping low to avoid detection. About 0200, 17 January, the Apaches locked on to their targets, two early warning intercept stations, and fired HELLFIRE missiles at them. Within minutes, the missiles knocked out every piece of radar equipment in the stations, crumbling buildings and vehicles. As the Apaches turned away from the destruction, the crews heard over one hundred Air Force jets overhead, passing through the gap in the radar bound for Baghdad. One hour later, television networks broke into their scheduled news broadcasts to report the bombing of the Iraqi capital. With well-synchronized destruction of early warning sites by raids and Navy-launched cruise missiles, the coalition air forces caught the Iraqis completely by surprise.[1]

[1] William H. McMichael, "First Shots Fired in Anger," *Soldiers* 46 (April 1991): 21–24; CENTCOM Sitrep, 17 Jan 91; William Matthews, "Thunder and Lightning of Desert Storm," *Army Times*, 28 Jan 91, p. 12.

Apaches and the air war. One of the Apache helicopters returns from striking a blow against Iraqi radar sites.

Scuds and Patriots

The Iraqis soon recovered enough to retaliate with Scud missile attacks against Saudi Arabia and Israel. At distances beyond 175 miles the Scud was highly inaccurate and prone to breakup in flight, making its military value negligible. As an instrument of terror against densely populated areas, however, the Scud posed a significant threat, especially if the Iraqis, as rumored, had been able to mount a chemical warhead on the missile.

For months, President Saddam Hussein, hoping to rally Arab support, had warned that he would attack Israel in the event of a conflict. He now moved to carry out his threat. Within twenty-four hours of the allied air attack, the Iraqis launched the first of seven Scuds at Israel, injuring twelve in the Tel Aviv area. By 25 January the Iraqis had fired twenty Scuds at Israel and twenty-four at allied bases and cities in Saudi Arabia. Israelis called for revenge, but their government, at the request of the United States, agreed to forego immediate retaliation.

The Scud attacks brought to center stage the Army's Patriot antimissile system. By the start of DESERT STORM Army Central Command had deployed about sixty Patriot systems to defend American military facilities, Saudi population centers, and industrial sites. Each battery consisted of a radar set, a computer-directed engagement control station, a power plant, antennae, and up to eight launchers, each with four ready-to-fire missiles in canisters. Originally designed as an antiaircraft device, the system had been modified by Raytheon, practically on the eve of the war, to shoot down missiles. Its antimissile capability had never been tested in combat and only rarely on the range.

Nevertheless, the system seemed to perform well in its first combat trial. The apparent success of the Patriot sent a wave of relief through the

Patriot launcher near King Abdul Aziz Air Base. This launcher engaged the first Iraqi Scud fired during the war.

[2] MS, Doughty, War in the Persian Gulf, p. 8; "Weekly Briefing," *Army Times*, 4 Feb 91, p. 40; Matthews, "Thunder and Lightning of Desert Storm," p. 12; J. Paul Scicchitano, "Patriot: New Kind of War Hero," *Army Times*, 4 Feb 91, p. 34; Holley interview; Anthony H. Cordesman, "Rushing to Judgment on the Gulf War," *Armed Forces Journal International* (June 1991): 72; Heike Hasenauer, "Theater Missile Defense: Improved Patriot," *Soldiers* 46 (June 1991): 25; Interv, Maj Robert B. Honec and S Sgt LoDona S. Kirkland with Maj Stephen B. Finch, Air Defense Element, XVIII Airborne Corps, 2 Feb 91, XVIII Airborne Main Command Post, Rafha, Saudi Arabia; Steve Vogel and Julie Bird, "First Combat Patriot Hit Scores Big," *Army Times*, 28 Jan 91, p. 28A; William H. McMichael, "Patriot Passes the Combat Test," *Soldiers* 46 (April 1991): 18; Donna Miles, "Desert Storm Rises," *Soldiers* 46 (March 1991): 6–11.

[3] Department of the Army, Classification of SWA Army Weapons Systems Performance, 8 Mar 91; MS, Doughty, War in the Persian Gulf, p. 8; Draft MS, Swain, Operational Narrative, p. 86; Cordesman, "Rushing to Judgment on the Gulf War," p. 72; Finch interview.

coalition and the international community, troubled by the prospect of chemical attacks by missiles targeted at defenseless cities. In response to an Israeli request, the United States, on 19 January, sent two batteries and their American crews to Israel to guard against further Scud attacks.[2]

Later evaluations showed that the Patriot, while it seemed to perform beyond expectations, was not infallible. As of early March 1991 the Army estimated that the Iraqis had fired eighty-six Scuds, eleven of which were aimed at Israel prior to the deployment of Patriots. Of the remaining seventy-five, forty-seven were considered threatening and Patriots engaged forty-five of them. Other studies gave different success rates, one estimating that Patriots destroyed 89 percent of the missiles aimed at Saudi Arabia and 44 percent of the Scuds targeted on Israel.

Occasionally, the Patriot did fail, largely because it was not designed to intercept the modified Scud, with its smaller warhead. Often, the Scud disintegrated in flight, and the Patriot went after the largest fragment, rather than the warhead. The missile which killed twenty-eight Pennsylvania reservists in their Dhahran barracks on 25 February seemed to have fallen into that category. Still, considering the relatively untested status of the Patriot system before the Persian Gulf operation, it performed well.[3]

Whatever the success rate, the Patriot took a major psychological weapon from the Iraqis in a war that, by any measure, was going badly for them. Thanks largely to the surprise achieved on the first night, U.S. and allied air forces quickly established dominance of the skies, destroying Iraqi planes on the ground and driving the rest into hiding or internment in Iran. Flying 2,000 sorties a day, coalition jets hit airstrips, command centers, air defense facilities, and nuclear and chemical plants. After the first week of DESERT STORM only five Iraqi air bases were still in operation, and allied jets had bombed 75 percent of Iraq's command centers. Having established air supremacy, the allies concentrated on the lines of communications of Iraqi forces in the Kuwaiti theater of operations. In three weeks they knocked out thirty-three of the thirty-six bridges along Iraqi supply lines and cut shipments of food, spare parts, and medical supplies to the Kuwaiti theater from 20,000 to 2,000 tons per week. By the fourth week the air phase of the offensive, intended to shape the battlefield for successful ground operations, entered its final stage, as the allies attacked troop concentrations and other targets in Kuwait. The air war went like clockwork, its only major digression being the effort to find and knock out the mobile Scud missile launchers.[4]

Engine overhaul at Ad Dammām

Moving Into Position

While the aviators continued to rain destruction on Iraqi forces, the Army moved 270,000 troops with supplies into position for the attack (*Table 6*). Through December Maj. Gen. William G. Pagonis' newly redesignated 22d Support Command had shifted supplies from the ports to depots near King Khalid Military City, where engineers were building three enormous supply bases. With the start of the air war on 16 January, the supply experts moved west of the Wādī al Bāṭin to set up a forward logistical base for each corps. The Army Central Command sought to fill those bases with sixty days of supplies by G-day, a formidable task given the shortage of heavy trucks and drivers, the lack of railroads, and the heavy civilian traffic on the roads. For five weeks supply vehicles rolled northwest on the main supply route DODGE, or Tapline Road, the highway alongside the pipeline from the ports to Jordan.[5]

The massive westward shift of the XVIII Airborne Corps and VII Corps to their attack positions began on 20 January, and the movement continued unabated for about three weeks.[6] Both corps traveled long distances, over 500 miles for XVIII Corps and over 330 miles for VII Corps. The movement of massive amounts of military equipment and supplies over the expanses of the Arabian desert strained theater transportation units. To save tracked combat vehicles from wear and tear, the 22d Support Command acquired almost 4,000 heavy trucks and distributed them to the corps in direct and general support. Among those vehicles were about 1,300 heavy equipment transporters, 450 lowboys, and 2,200 flatbeds. General Pagonis took trucks from internal U.S. military assets, European donations, loans that included an entire Egyptian battalion of heavy equipment transporters, and commercial, locally contracted sources. Many of the drivers were civilians from the Indian subcontinent.[7]

[4] Matthews, "Thunder and Lightning of Desert Storm," pp. 12, 14; Miles, "Desert Storm Rises," pp. 6–11; William Matthews, "The Best Is Yet to Come," *Army Times*, 11 Feb 91, pp. 3–4; Matthews, "Assessing the Damage," *Army Times*, 18 Feb 91, p. 3; CENTCOM Sitreps, Jan–Feb 91; Vuono interview.

[5] Draft MS, Swain, Operational Narrative, pp. 60–61; CENTCOM Daily Sitreps, Sep 90–Feb 91.

[6] Msg, Cdr, ARCENT, to Cdr, ARCENT SupCom, 15 Jan 91, sub: Corps Movement.

[7] 22d SupCom, DESERT STORM Command Rpt, 5 Apr 91, p. 3.

| U.S. Forces in the Persian Gulf |||
Date	Army	Total
1 September1990	31,337	95,965
7 November 1990	124,704	266,096
15 January 1991	245,290	422,041
22 February 1991	296,965	533,608
Source: CENTCOM Daily Sitreps, Sep 90–Feb 91.		

Table 6

The Support Command's 318th Transportation Agency (Movement Control) coordinated the movement by allocating blocks of time for each corps to use designated main supply routes. The 89th Military Police Brigade provided checkpoint and traffic control on all lines.[8] During the height of the movement, about eighteen vehicles per minute passed along any given stretch of road on the main supply route DODGE.[9]

During the last half of January the roads northwest of the ports were choked with vehicles taking the two corps to the front. Moving in the combat formation intended for the attack, most of VII Corps arrived at its designated assembly areas by 3 February. The 2d Armored Cavalry held an advanced position west of the Wādī al Bāṭin at forward assembly area RICHARDSON, while the 1st Infantry Division (Mechanized), 1st Armored Division, British 1st Armored Division, elements of the 3d Armored Division, and the 11th Aviation Brigade stayed at tactical assembly areas astride the Tapline Road east of Wādī al Bāṭin.

[8] Ibid.

[9] Pagonis Briefing to Secretary of the Army Stone, Apr 91, Dhahran.

Securing supplies on a flatbed for movement forward

Unloading the versatile Chinook helicopter. The Special Forces used the pictured fast assault vehicle for reconnaissance behind enemy lines.

Meanwhile, XVIII Airborne Corps began its 500-mile deployment to Rafḥā by air and truck along the Tapline Road and a more southern route. Essentially, the entire corps had to leapfrog around the newly deployed VII Corps to reach its destination on the left flank of the CENTCOM line, where its mobility would be a key asset in the flanking movement. When the great shift west was completed in the third week of February, XVIII Corps occupied the western portion of the Army line and VII Corps the eastern. The XVIII Corps presented a front of three divisions and one separate regiment, with another division just behind the line. From left to right (west to east) stood the French 6th Light Armored Division, the 101st Airborne Division, the 24th Infantry Division (Mechanized), and the 3d Armored Cavalry. The 82d Airborne Division held a position behind the French. The VII Corps presented a front of five divisions and one separate regiment. From left to right stood the 1st and 3d Armored Divisions, the 1st Infantry Division, the British 1st Armored Division, and the 1st Cavalry Division (Armored). The 2d Armored Cavalry screened the boundary with XVIII Corps on the left.[10]

If an Iraqi pilot had managed to penetrate the air space over the border area during the great shift west, he would have been stunned by the panorama below. It was "mile after mile of tank transporters, gasoline tankers, troop and ammunition carriers," while "overhead was the continuous clatter of C–130 transport planes and cargo helicopters." Occasionally, a truck pulled into one of the rest stops along the twelve- to fourteen-hour ride from the ports to the assembly areas. If any proof of allied air supremacy were necessary, this was it: "I shudder to think," an American observer wrote, "what a couple of Iraqi planes could have done

[10] Ibid.

to that column on a strafing and bombing run." Fortunately, Saddam Hussein had been, as the phrase went, "de-aired." Nor did the terrain prove too soft to support the vehicles, a concern of ARCENT planners in the early stages. Indeed, drivers found the ground along the road firmer than the coastal sands.[11]

More Forward Logistical Bases

As the two corps moved to their attack positions in January, the 22d Support Command set up forward logistical bases CHARLIE and ECHO. The shift of supplies forward, coupled with the movements of VII and XVIII Airborne Corps, put a premium on central management of transportation assets and further strained the supply routes. General Pagonis had wanted to establish these bases earlier, but General Schwarzkopf thought that early positioning of supply bases might signal his intention to shift forces to the west and that an Iraqi preemptive strike could overrun the theater supply stocks. As Schwarzkopf told Pagonis, "How many lives are worth one truck?"[12]

Bases CHARLIE and ECHO each measured about 3 by 5 miles. CHARLIE supported the XVIII Airborne Corps and ECHO the VII Corps during the ground offensive. Each contained enough food, fuel, and ammunition to supply its designated corps. Before the ground offensive the two corps support commands drew their supplies directly from these bases. Once the land war started, the theater support command transported these commodities forward to trailer transfer points, where the respective corps took over responsibility.

The theater stockage in food, fuel, and ammunition was critical to the success of the ground offensive. Stock levels were expressed as "days of supply." General Pagonis set the theater stockage goal at sixty days by the start of the ground offensive, although he anticipated probable shortages in each of the commodity areas.[13] By G-day, which was on 24 February, the available supply levels were nearly 29 days in food, 5.2 in fuel, and 45 days of ammunition.[14]

Fuel reserves gave the most cause for concern. POL (petroleum, oil, lubricants) arrived in the depots every day, but was consumed in vast quantities. To expedite the movement of these products forward, General Pagonis ordered the building of a pipeline from Ad Dammām to Al Bāṭin. The project was only partially completed by 28 February, when offensive operations were halted. At that point Pagonis, a lieutenant general as of 7 February, canceled the pipeline. Meanwhile, the 475th Quartermaster Group used 1,200 civilian POL trucks to haul the fuel forward from the ports as quickly as possible. However, because of the swift closure of operations and lower-than-expected consumption levels, fuel did not become a major problem at the theater level. At the end of February 22d Support Command records indicated 5.6 days of supply on hand, an overall increase.[15]

[11] Quotes from David H. Hackworth, "Light Near the End of the Tunnel," *Newsweek* (4 February 1991): 35.

[12] Pagonis Briefing to Secretary of the Army Stone, Apr 91, Dhahran.

[13] Theater Logistics Concept Briefing Charts for Secretary of Defense Cheney, 27 Dec 90.

[14] 22d SupCom Daily "sit down" Briefing Charts, 24 Feb 91.

[15] Ibid., 28 Feb 91.

General Pagonis also worried about food and ammunition supplies. Like fuel, however, the 22d Support Command maintained adequate quantities throughout DESERT STORM. When the shooting stopped, theater supplies of food were sufficient for twenty-five days and of ammunition for sixty-six days. Ammunition stores rose because of lower-than-expected expenditures and the arrival of several ammunition ships during the war.

Moving Supplies Forward

Once the troops were in place, the 22d Support Command had to provide materiel and stores to the forward units. Until the arrival of the 32d Transportation Group in January, the 7th Transportation Group served as the Support Command's long-distance trucker as well as manager of the ports. The 32d Group took over most heavy lift and some trucking missions just before DESERT STORM started. Sorely taxed by the demands of its mission, the 7th was pleased to have help. The group commander, Col. Daniel G. Brown, estimated that his drivers logged about 1.2 million miles per week, and "that," he emphasized, "is a lot of miles." Brown had about 1,200 vehicles on the road every day and still did not have enough. He signed a contract for 500 commercial vehicles on 15 January and sent a group of military drivers to Riyadh to try to pick up an additional 100 commercial flatbed trucks. Yet he still hoped to get more. The Army's appetite for vehicles seemed insatiable.[16]

In addition to managing the thousands of heavy trucks, the 7th and 32d Groups employed over 2,000 civilian drivers. The civilian drivers and commercial vehicles were organized into battalions with cadres of American soldiers, such as the 1103d Transportation Battalion of the 32d Group and the 702d Transportation Battalion (Provisional) of the 7th Group.[17] Concern over the reliability of civilian drivers once offensive operations commenced prompted the 22d Support Command to acquire over 3,000 U.S. soldiers as backup drivers. During DESERT STORM daily absentee rates of civilian drivers fluctuated between 10 and 55 percent.[18] By the end of the war, as the Iraqi threat decreased, attendance improved. Nevertheless, soldiers stood by to fill vacancies when civilians failed to report for work.

Heavy equipment transportation assets were the single most critical type of equipment in support of DESERT STORM. Just one of the five heavy divisions, the 24th Division, needed 1,277 heavy vehicles—323 heavy equipment transporters, 445 lowboys, and 509 flatbeds—to move its heavy equipment from its forward assembly area to its attack positions.[19]

Approximately 1,000 Support Command cargo trucks also moved supplies for the two corps throughout DESERT STORM. But the number of military trucks on hand to haul supplies and heavy equipment simultaneously was never enough. The Army's heavy transporter units could move only about one-fourth of the total U.S. tanks at any one time.[20]

[16] Interv, Maj Glen R. Hawkins with Col Daniel G. Brown, 15 Jan 91, Dhahran.

[17] 32d Transportation Group Command Rpt, 28 Feb 91; Interv, Maj William W. Epley with Maj Richard S. Gula, 20 Mar 91, Dhahran.

[18] 22d SupCom Daily "sit down" Briefing Charts, 29 Jan 91.

[19] 32d Transportation Group Command Rpt, 28 Feb 91.

[20] Interv, Lt Col Wesley V. Manning and Maj Glen R. Hawkins with Col David A. Whaley, 13 Feb 91, King Khalid Military City, Saudi Arabia.

Contracting and host nation support provided much of the solution to the transportation problem. Over half of the heavy transportation assets were either contracted commercial trucks or donated trucks from Europe. The 32d Transportation Group commander, Col. Michael T. Gaw, credited the Saudis with providing enough commercial trucks to keep the Army moving on schedule.[21] The operations officer of the 7th Transportation Group, Maj. Richard S. Gula, agreed. "If it were not for the Saudi HETs [heavy equipment transporters] and lowboys," he observed, "we could have never moved XVIII Airborne Corps."[22]

America's allies donated additional transportation assets. Such programs as the so-called Gifts of Japan contributed almost 2,000 four-wheel-drive sport utility vehicles, water trucks, refrigerator vans, and fuel vehicles.[23] The small commercial four-wheel-drive trucks enhanced the flexibility and command and control capability of many units. It was commonplace in Saudi Arabia to see commanders traveling in brightly painted Japanese sport utility vehicles.

Donated and contracted commercial vehicles helped the theater logistical organizations make up for the lack of assigned military vehicles. Although fully equipped with authorized assets, many still lacked the mobility to meet the great demand for transportation in Saudi Arabia. Virtually every logistical unit commander faced a shortage of organic military transportation. All of the area support groups, which were major subordinate elements of the 22d Support Command that sustained units in specific geographic areas from fixed locations, reported they were only about 25-percent mobile. Those groups were not expected to be fully self-mobile because of the limited scope of their missions, but the long distances and frequent moves involved in DESERT STORM continually forced them to seek more vehicles.

[21] 32d Transportation Group Command Rpt, 28 Feb 91.

[22] Gula interview.

[23] 22d SupCom, DESERT STORM Command Rpt, 5 Apr 91, tab J, sub: Japanese (GOJ) and German Contributions.

A Nissan sport utility vehicle, one of the Gifts of Japan, receiving gas from a 5,000-gallon tank truck

Prisoners of War

The 22d Support Command also had overall responsibility for the confinement and treatment of prisoners of war (POW), which included building and operating POW facilities; processing prisoners from the line to the camps; and providing food, medical care, and transportation. Actual day-to-day operations fell to the 800th Military Police Brigade, a major subordinate element of the Support Command. This brigade, with over 7,000 soldiers, was a composite Army National Guard and Army Reserve unit from the northeastern United States that specialized in POW operations.

With engineer assistance, the 800th built two large POW compounds BROOKLYN and BRONX in the north along the main supply route DODGE. Completed in early February, each could hold about 28,000 prisoners of war at any one time. The brigade had intended to process Iraqi prisoners in accordance with the Geneva Conventions and eventually turn them over to Saudi authorities for final disposition. However, shortly after the start of the air war, POW operations took on their own dynamic because prisoners began to accumulate before the facilities were fully manned or finished. The Support Command diverted resources to ensure more rapid completion of the camps. The first Iraqi prisoners were received on 21 January; by G-day, a little over a month later, their number totaled 518.[24]

Preparing for Battle

Once in their assembly areas, units rushed to complete last-minute training before moving to jump-off points. The VII Corps, having just arrived, faced a major task of acclimatization in addition to other necessary preparations. Fortunately, the longer-than-expected air campaign allowed enough time for the corps to learn something of desert warfare; to test new tanks and other equipment acquired in the force modernization program; to train for breaching; and to carry out regimental, brigade, and division exercises. The 1st Infantry Division, which would spearhead the attack, concentrated on training for breaching operations, often with the British 1st Armored Division.

In contrast to VII Corps, XVIII Airborne Corps had enjoyed plenty of time to prepare. Except for combined training with the French 6th Light Armored Division in close air support and recognition of each other's equipment, most of the corps' training near Rafḥā consisted of rehearsals, sand table exercises, and measures to sustain existing skills. Farther south, at King Khalid Military City, the 22d Support Command was equipping squads and crews from Army units outside the theater and training them to serve as replacements for the coming offensive.[25]

At the border, fighting had already started. The 1st Cavalry Division and the 2d Armored Cavalry patrolled the area west of the Wādī al Bāṭin to screen the VII Corps' buildup from enemy reconnaissance scouts. The flat, open plain gave little concealment except for the wadies, in which an

[24] 22d SupCom, DESERT STORM Command Rpt, 5 Apr 91.

[25] ARCENT, VII Corps, and XVIII Airborne Corps Sitreps, 16 Jan–15 Feb 91; Swain interview; Exercises and Training Section interview; Draft MS, Carver, How VII Corps Won the War, passim; ARCENT Exercises and Training Section Command Rpts.

unwary Bradley fighting vehicle could be surprised in the dark. To the north, cavalry patrols could see flashes and hear rumbling along the border as the Air Force pounded Iraqi positions. Occasionally, they picked up Iraqi deserters or destroyed enemy observation posts. More frequently with time, they clashed with Iraqi scouts seeking to penetrate the screen and learn the meaning of the activity to the south.

On 22 January, in XVIII Corps' sector near the boundary with VII Corps, the 3d Armored Cavalry took part in the first ground encounter of the campaign. A squad exchanged fire with an Iraqi force of undetermined size, possibly from the border police. Two Iraqis were killed and six captured at the cost of two American wounded. On the extreme left, patrols of the French 6th Light Armored, the 82d Airborne, and the 101st Airborne Divisions screened XVIII Corps' front near Rafḥā, manning listening posts and driving vehicles into the barren wastes. They encountered fewer Iraqi scouts this far west, but similar clashes nevertheless occurred.[26]

To discover what lay behind the border berms to the north, Central Command relied partly on Army special operations forces. During the early days of the crisis troops of the 5th Special Forces Group (Airborne), 1st Special Forces, in cooperation with Saudi paratroopers, had manned observation posts and driven vehicles along the Kuwaiti border to provide early warning of an Iraqi attack. Since September, almost the entire 5th Group had become involved in liaison work and combined training, and Central Command obtained a battalion of the 3d Special Forces Group (Airborne), 1st Special Forces, to carry out long-range patrols north of the border. The risky nature of the task guaranteed that each mission was reviewed carefully at the highest levels, and, in the end, the Green Berets carried out twelve such operations. Many of the missions failed because of poor prior intelligence, as in the case of a team that landed in the middle of an Iraqi armored division, but some performed valuable work. One team used low-light cameras and soil-probing equipment to determine if the terrain north of the border would support the heavy vehicles of VII Corps, while others watched suspected Iraqi reinforcement routes and hunted Scud launchers.

Psychological operations (PSYOPS) also made a major contribution. Radio and TV broadcasts, leaflets, and loudspeakers used the themes of Arab brotherhood, allied air power, and Iraqi isolation to induce large numbers of enemy soldiers to desert. One of the most effective tactics involved the dropping of leaflets on a particular unit, informing it that it would be bombed within twenty-four hours and had to surrender to avoid destruction. In other special operations, Army helicopters cooperated with those of the Air Force to rescue downed pilots, and civil affairs officers worked closely with the Kuwaiti government in its reconstruction planning. Although DESERT STORM proved to be primarily a campaign of mass units, special operations played an important part in the final victory.[27]

[26] ARCENT, VII Corps, and XVIII Airborne Corps Sitreps, 16 Jan–15 Feb 91; Steve Vogel, "Border Defined by Bomb Flashes," *Army Times*, 25 Feb 91, p. 6; "Cavalry, Patrol Exchange Gunfire in First Ground Encounter," *Army Times*, 4 Feb 91, p. 16; Vogel, "Stand Ready: 1st Cavalry Division Scouts the Border for Iraqi Movements," *Army Times*, 25 Feb 91, p. 4; William H. McMichael, "Looking for Clues," *Soldiers* 46 (April 1991): 25–27.

[27] General H. Norman Schwarzkopf, Briefing to the Press, 27 Feb 91 (hereafter cited as Schwarzkopf briefing); CENTCOM Sitreps; Draft MS, Stewart, Army Special Operations Forces in Operation DESERT STORM, pp. 1–11.

PSYOPS leaflets, showing the prevalent themes of Arab brotherhood (top), coalition air superiority (middle), and Iraqi isolation (bottom).

28 Phil Prater, "Night Moves in the Gulf," *Soldiers* 46 (May 1991): 14; Interv, Maj Robert K. Wright with Lt Col Bruce Simpson, 13 Feb 91, Manama, Bahrain; Miles, "Desert Storm Rises," p. 10.

29 ARCENT and VII Corps Sitreps, 11–15 Feb 91; Draft MS, Swain, Operational Narrative, p. 94; Draft MS, Carver, How VII Corps Won the War, passim.

While not a special operations unit, the 4th Squadron, 17th Cavalry, carved its own niche during the opening weeks of DESERT STORM. The Army had originally formed the unit to help the Navy monitor American-flagged tankers in the Persian Gulf during the Iran-Iraq war. It had returned to the region to help enforce United Nations sanctions before DESERT STORM. With the outbreak of war, the squadron patrolled, watched for Iraqi vessels, and raided offshore oil platforms used by the Iraqis to observe allied ship and plane movements. Technically part of the 18th Aviation Brigade, the unit operated from U.S. Navy frigates and received its missions from the Navy. On 18 January squadron helicopters from the frigate USS *Nicholas* cooperated with a Kuwaiti patrol boat to subdue Iraqi detachments on nine oil platforms in the northern Persian Gulf, capturing twenty-three prisoners in the process. The nine platforms represented the first Kuwaiti territory to be liberated in the war.[28]

To the west, as the air war entered its fifth week, VII Corps in battle formation moved to jump-off areas near the Iraqi border. The 1st Cavalry Division had already shifted to the corps' right flank to cover the Wādī al Bāṭin. Once the last units of the 3d Armored Division filed into tactical assembly area HENRY on 11 February, VII Corps sped up preparations for the drive north. On the fifteenth the 1st Infantry Division and 2d Armored Cavalry moved to forward positions north of logistical base ECHO just short of the border, and the 1st Armored Division began its long march to forward assembly area GARCIA, on the left of VII Corps. The next day the 3d Armored Division drove to forward assembly area BUTTS, in the center and behind the 1st Infantry Division, while the British 1st Armored Division took position on the right at forward assembly area RAY and the 11th Aviation Brigade deployed to logistical base ECHO. By 17 February VII Corps had assembled over 1,500 tanks, 1,500 armored fighting vehicles, and 650 artillery pieces at the border.[29]

During the next week the VII and XVIII Airborne Corps completed their preparations while stepping up artillery bombardments and patrols. Because of the great range of the Iraqi artillery and its deployment 7 to 12 miles behind the border, allied gunners initially confined themselves to "shoot and scoot" artillery raids, penetrating well within the Iraqi

*The multiple launch
rocket system*

range to unleash a few salvos and changing their position. When it became clear that the Iraqis could not find them, allied batteries stayed in position and even closed the range to deliver a killing fire against enemy forward positions. Gunners from the 1st Infantry, the 1st Cavalry, and the British 1st Armored Divisions hit command posts, artillery emplacements, air defense facilities, and supply depots. Rockets from the multiple launch rocket system, dubbed "steel rain" by the Iraqis, shattered materiel and morale. One Iraqi division lost 97 of its 100 guns to a bombardment by 300 rocket pods and two battalions of 203-mm. howitzers. The Iraqi response to this fire was negligible. At times, allied gunners even tried to bait Iraqi artillery to pinpoint positions for counterbattery fire.[30]

As allied artillery and air power systematically eliminated the Iraqi artillery threat, allied cross-border patrols were winning the battle for no-man's-land. On VII Corps' front, long-range surveillance units with the 2d Armored Cavalry observed Iraqi dispositions and fortifications. Using holes cut by engineers in the border berm, other patrols ventured into Iraqi territory to reconnoiter positions, to set ambushes, to capture prisoners, and to call in air and artillery fire against tanks, armored personnel carriers, command posts, and radar stations.

On the left flank XVIII Airborne Corps conducted mounted and aerial raids deep into Iraqi territory to hit armor, artillery, bunkers, and observation posts. In one armed reconnaissance mission by the Aviation Brigade of the 101st Airborne Division on 20 February, a helicopter with a loudspeaker induced 476 frightened Iraqis to surrender after fifteen of their bunkers were destroyed by air and TOW missile fire. The cross-border operations were not without cost, but Iraqi resistance was generally so weak that by the twenty-second helicopters of the 82d Airborne Division were penetrating deep into enemy territory in broad daylight.[31]

[30] ARCENT and VII Corps Sitreps, 15–23 Feb 91; "'Steel Rain' Shut Down Iraqi Artillery," *Armed Forces Journal International* (May 1991): 37.

[31] ARCENT, VII Corps, and XVIII Airborne Corps Sitreps, 15–23 Feb 91; William Matthews, "Final Round," *Army Times*, 4 Mar 91, p. 6; Interv, Maj Dennis P. Levin with Maj Gen James H. Johnson, Jr., 20 May 91, Fort Bragg, N.C.

*Loading HELLFIRE missiles
on an Apache helicopter*

With so many allied patrols into disputed areas, fratricide was inevitable. Eight marines were killed by friendly fire in the first week of February. Then, on the seventeenth, two soldiers of the 2d Armored Division were killed and six wounded when a HELLFIRE missile, launched by an Apache to suppress Iraqi fire, crashed into their Bradley. The mixing of friend and foe in the enemy's rear, characteristic of American battle doctrine, as well as the deadliness of modern weapons beyond the range of easy identification, had created a situation in which friendly fire could be expected without proper countermeasures. To correct the situation, VII Corps experimented with glint and thermal tape, strobe and chemical lights, illuminated paint, and panels in an attempt to find a material that could easily identify a friendly vehicle at night without giving its position away to the enemy. Considering the number of friendly units in disputed areas, the number of incidents remained remarkably low, but the problem clearly would demand attention in the future.[32]

However menacing allied air power occasionally could be to friendly troops, it inflicted infinitely more punishment on the Iraqis. By G-day, intelligence indicated that the Iraqis had lost 53 percent of their artillery and 42 percent of their tanks in ARCENT's sector. Air attacks had reduced frontline units to less than 50 percent and reserves to 50 to 75 percent of their strength. Nearly 1,000 Iraqis, hungry and tired of the incessant bombing, had already given up to American troops. Unknown to the coalition at the time, thousands more apparently had deserted north. When an Iraqi reconnaissance in force to R'as al Khafjī in late January was repulsed by Arab and Marine forces, American commanders interpreted the foray as a desperate Iraqi attempt to boost morale.

[32] "Weekly Briefing," *Army Times*, 18 Feb 91, p. 10; Margaret Roth, "Officer Relieved After Fire Kills Two," *Army Times*, 4 Mar 91, p. 12; ARCENT Sitreps, 10, 18, and 22 Feb 91; Memo for DESERT STORM Study Group.

American generals had other reasons to be optimistic. Intelligence indicated that the Iraqis did not have many troops or defenses west of the triborder area. Although Iraqi strength in the Kuwaiti theater had risen from twenty-seven to forty-three divisions since November, most of the new troops had joined the forces inside Kuwait. Only seven weak Iraqi infantry divisions, backed by an armored division, manned improvised works on VII Corps' front, while three widely dispersed infantry divisions faced XVIII Corps.[33]

After DESERT STORM General Schwarzkopf and some of his officers criticized the quality of the intelligence they had received. The coalition, they believed, had greatly overestimated enemy strength and capabilities. In retrospect, the intelligence effort reflected strengths and weaknesses that had long characterized Western information-gathering and analysis. Eavesdropping devices, satellite photography, and reconnaissance aircraft, frequently using new technology, produced high-quality raw data on Iraqi movements and positions. On the other hand, the number of agencies involved resulted in duplication of effort, and security compartmentalization prevented timely dissemination of information to the field. Commanders complained that they received reconnaissance photographs that were at least one day old and that estimates were often too vague to be meaningful. For all the aerial reconnaissance, Army Central Command apparently was never able to piece together an accurate picture of the defenses west of the triborder area, perhaps because the secrecy surrounding the flanking move had left responsible agencies unaware of the need. Finally, as in past crises, the lack of agents on the ground left American leaders in the dark regarding Iraqi intentions.[34]

The Army and the Air War

For the most part, the Army played a minor role in the air war, but, since the timing of the ground offensive depended on reduction of Iraqi forces to a certain level, the Army had a major voice in the assessment of bomb damage. ARCENT planners assumed that the proper level of attrition was roughly 50 percent of the Iraqi armor and artillery, including 90 percent of the tanks and guns at the breach sites. The Army Central Command was supposed to keep track of bomb damage assessments and decide on the proper timing of the ground offensive. Unfortunately for the planners, damage assessments, by their nature, were subjective and imprecise, particularly since the Iraqis tried to mislead the coalition regarding the damage done by the air strikes. The process was also hampered by diversion of surveillance planes and other resources to the hunt for Scud launchers. The stakes in bomb damage assessment were high. An incorrect evaluation could result in high casualties in the ground war, with far-reaching political consequences. Fortunately, the Air Force was inflicting more damage to Iraqi morale and materiel than the assessments indicated.

[33] ARCENT Sitreps, 16 Jan–24 Feb 91; ODCSINT, Iraq-Kuwait Situation Updates, Dec 90–24 Feb 91; VII Corps and XVIII Airborne Corps Sitreps, 16 Jan–23 Feb 91; Draft MS, Swain, Operational Narrative, pp. 64, 87, 97; Holley interview; Julie Bird and Steve Vogel, "First Contact: Battle of Khafji," *Army Times*, 11 Feb 91, p. 12; Schwarzkopf briefing; MS, Doughty, War in the Persian Gulf, p. 11.

[34] *New York Times*, 13 Jun 91; William Matthews, "U.S. Intelligence Not Geared to Read an Enemy's Motive," *Army Times*, 27 May 91, p. 18; Exercises and Training Section interview; Holley interview; Draft MS, Swain, Operational Narrative, pp. 82–84.

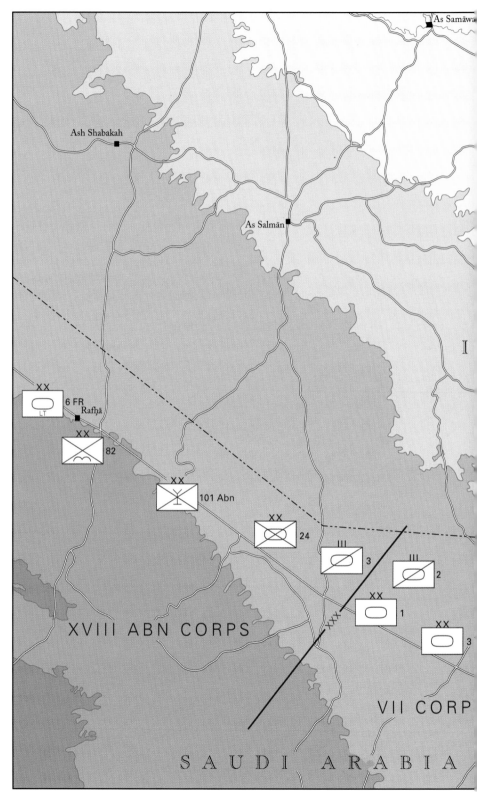

As Samāwa

Ash Shabakah

As Salmān

XX
6 FR
LT
Rafḥā

XX
82

XX
101 Abn

XX
24

III
3

III
2

XX
1

XX
3

XVIII ABN CORPS

VII CORP

I

SAUDI ARABIA

Map 12

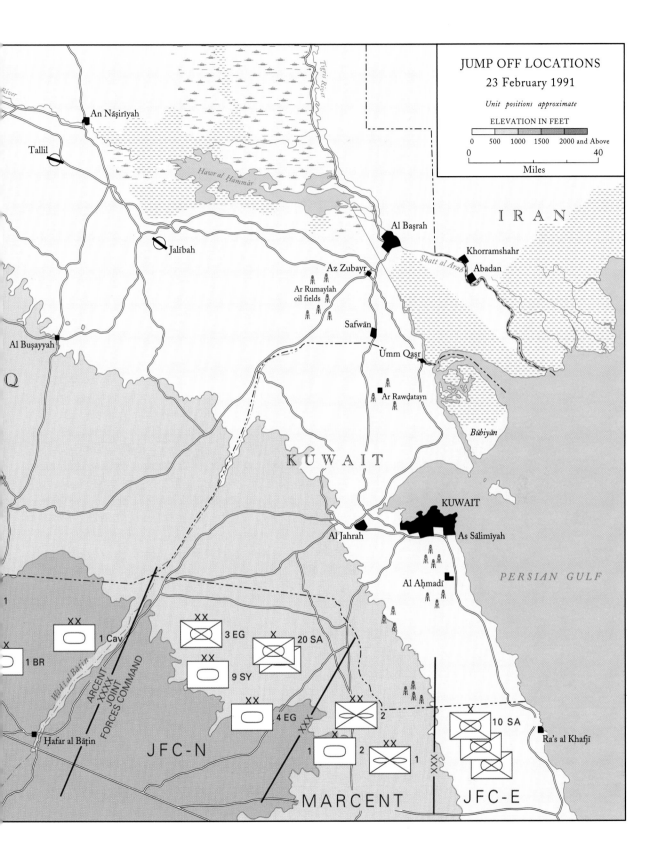

JUMP OFF LOCATIONS
23 February 1991

Unit positions approximate

ELEVATION IN FEET

| 0 | 500 | 1000 | 1500 | 2000 and Above |

0 _____ 40

Miles

River

An Nāṣirīyah

Tallil

Jalībah

Al Buṣayyah

Q

Ḥawr al Ḥammār

Tigris River

Al Baṣrah

Az Zubayr

Ar Rumaylah oil fields

Safwān

Umm Qaṣr

Ar Rawḍatayn

I R A N

Khorramshahr

Shaṭṭ al Arab

Abadan

Būbiyān

K U W A I T

KUWAIT

Al Jahrah

As Sālimīyah

Al Aḥmadī

PERSIAN GULF

Ra's al Khafjī

Ḥafar al Bāṭin

Wādī al Bāṭin

ARCENT
XXXX
JOINT
FORCES COMMAND

XX 1 Cav

X 1 BR

XX 3 EG

X 20 SA

XX 9 SY

XX 4 EG

XX 2

XXX

XX 2

XX 1

X 10 SA

JFC-N

M A R C E N T

JFC-E

The high stakes contributed to friction between the Air Force and the Army over targeting. Although the two components had developed their plans separately, the respective planners had coordinated with each other during the process. Still, the Army believed that it lacked enough influence on the air plan's Phase III, the destruction of Iraqi units and defenses in Kuwait. Matters came to a head in early February, when the corps commanders and some on the ARCENT staff bitterly complained that the Air Force was not hitting the targets they had chosen. In part, the friction arose from misunderstandings, but the rigid planning cycle contributed to the problem. ARCENT's targets, drawn from the two corps and based on intelligence already several hours old, would not make the Air Force's daily list of targets until a day after they were submitted. Too often, the targets had moved by the time the bombers arrived. In the end, lower levels worked out their own arrangements, as Air Force wings talked directly with ARCENT headquarters and bypassed the cumbersome targeting process.[35]

Accurate bomb damage assessment would prove critical to the setting of the date for the ground offensive. On 27 January Lt. Col. Joseph H. Purvis' special planning cell, which had returned to Central Command, received orders to gauge the progress of the air war and project a date for the start of the ground campaign. Given the controversy surrounding the assessments and their preparation, the task proved difficult. Pentagon and Central Intelligence Agency analysts estimated the attrition of Iraqi forces at lower levels than Central Command, which put greater credence in the more optimistic reports of pilots. On 9 February CENTCOM and ARCENT planners reported that they were planning on fourteen more days to "shape the battlefield," but they did not specify a date to open the ground offensive. Another two weeks passed, as staffs kept a close watch over bomb damage assessments. On the twenty-first Army Central Command notified its commanders to be ready to move at any time. Later that day, G-day and H-hour were set for 24 February, at 3:00 AM Saudi time.[36]

Final Preparations

One final flurry of diplomatic activity remained as Iraq sought to salvage something from a rapidly deteriorating situation. Baghdad's offer on 15 February to leave Kuwait carried numerous conditions. Its demands that the allies also withdraw, pay Iraq's war debts, and induce the Israelis to pull out of the West Bank drew a scornful response from the coalition. At this point the Soviets stepped into the picture. Perhaps discomfited at the prospect of a humiliating defeat for their longtime client, they invited Foreign Minister Aziz to Moscow. After five days of talks the Iraqis, on the twenty-second, finally agreed to leave Kuwait within twenty-one days of a cease-fire. President Bush immediately rejected the Soviet-Iraqi proposal and warned Baghdad to begin an unconditional withdrawal from

[35] Holley interview; Holloway interview; CENTCOM Planning Cell interview, pp. 20–27; Draft MS, Swain, Operational Narrative, pp. 68–70; Interv, Col Richard M. Swain with Lt Col Bart J. Engram, ARCENT G–3, Deep Operations, 27 Mar 91.

[36] Special Planning Cell chronology, pp. 18–19; Vines interview; Draft MS, Swain, Operational Narrative, pp. 92, 95; Holloway interview; Holley interview.

Kuwait by noon, 23 February, or face the consequences. The ultimatum came amid unmistakable signs that the Iraqis were setting fire to oil wells and otherwise inflicting as much damage as possible on Kuwait. When noon, 23 February, passed without an Iraqi response to the president's message, a ground war seemed inevitable (*see Map 12*).[37]

Tariq Aziz was still in Moscow when the Iraqis responded to the increasing tempo of CENTCOM attacks by igniting 145 oil wells throughout Kuwait. Their action, apparently intended to hide their defensive positions in Kuwait and southern Iraq from allied aerial observation, came too late to matter. In the end, the act became a liability to Iraqi field operations in ensuing days and to Iraq's longer term interests as well.[38]

From R'as al Khafjī to Rafḥā American troops braced for what the experts predicted would be a bloody confrontation. In Riyadh the ARCENT commander, Lt. Gen. John J. Yeosock, who had just returned from surgery in Germany, outlined his vision of the coming battle. The 1st Cavalry Division, back in theater reserve, prepared for its feint up the Wādī al Bāṭin. To the left a patrol of the 1st Infantry Division engaged twenty Iraqi tanks, knocking out fourteen. Two squadrons of the 2d Armored Cavalry penetrated almost 10 miles into Iraq to protect engineers cutting a passage through the border berm. As day passed into evening on 23 February, XVIII Corps put long-range surveillance detachments into enemy territory. In a battalion of the 24th Infantry Division a sergeant major reminded his men, "The only way home is through Iraq." Rumors had already spread among the troops that 500 fillers were waiting to take the places of those who were killed and wounded. As the main forces waited, artillery bombardments and helicopter raids continued along the line.[39] At 0100 on the morning of 24 February, the word came from Central Command: "EXECUTE ORDER FOR GROUND OFFENSIVE OPERATIONS (PHASE IV)."[40]

[37] Margaret Roth and Sean D. Naylor, "This Is the Culminating Point of the Battle," *Army Times*, 4 Mar 91, p. 4; Matthews, "Final Round," pp. 3, 6.

[38] ODCSINT Intelligence Summary 400, 23 Feb 91; Yergin, *The Prize*, pp. 180–81.

[39] "Tanks and Men: Desert Storm from the Hatches," *Army* 41 (June 1991): 30; Michael Donnelly, "Groping Through G-Day in a Dust Storm," *Army Times*, 15 Apr 91, p. 16; ARCENT and XVIII Airborne Corps Sitreps, 23–24 Feb 91.

[40] Draft MS, Swain, Operational Narrative, pp. 96–98.

Chapter 8

ONE HUNDRED HOURS

On 24 February, when ground operations started in earnest, coalition forces were poised along a line that stretched from the Persian Gulf westward 300 miles into the desert. The XVIII Airborne Corps, under Lt. Gen. Gary E. Luck, held the left, or western, flank and consisted of the 82d Airborne Division, the 101st Airborne Division (Air Assault), the 24th Infantry Division (Mechanized), the French 6th Light Armored Division, the 3d Armored Cavalry, and the 12th and 18th Aviation Brigades. The VII Corps, under Lt. Gen. Frederick M. Franks, Jr., was deployed to the right of the XVIII Airborne Corps and consisted of the 1st Infantry Division (Mechanized), the 1st Cavalry Division (Armored), the 1st and 3d Armored Divisions, the British 1st Armored Division, the 2d Armored Cavalry, and the 11th Aviation Brigade. Between them these two corps covered about two-thirds of the line occupied by the huge multinational force.

Three commands held the eastern one-third of the front. Joint Forces Command North, made up of formations from Egypt, Syria, and Saudi Arabia and led by His Royal Highness Lt. Gen. Prince Khalid ibn Sultan, held the portion of the line east of VII Corps. To the right of these allied forces stood Lt. Gen. Walter E. Boomer's I Marine Expeditionary Force, which had the 1st (or Tiger) Brigade of the Army's 2d Armored Division as well as the 1st and 2d Marine Divisions. Joint Forces Command East on the extreme right, or eastern, flank anchored the line at the Persian Gulf. This organization consisted of units from all six member states of the Gulf Cooperation Council. Like Joint Forces Command North, it was under General Khalid's command.[1]

After thirty-eight days of continuous air attacks on targets in Iraq and Kuwait, President George H. Bush directed Central Command to proceed with the ground offensive. General Schwarzkopf unleashed all-out attacks against Iraqi forces very early on 24 February at three points along the allied line. In the far west the French 6th Light Armored and the 101st Airborne Divisions started the massive western envelopment with a ground assault to secure the allied left flank and an air assault to establish forward support bases deep in Iraqi territory. In the approximate center of the allied line, along the Wādī al Bāṭin, Maj. Gen. John H.

[1] Unless otherwise noted, material in this chapter is based on U.S. Department of Defense, *Conduct of the Persian Gulf War, An Interim Report to Congress* (Washington, D.C.: Government Printing Office, 1991), p. 4-6; Third U.S. Army, After Action Review, 12 Mar 91; Draft MS, Swain, Operational Narrative; and Robert H. Scales, Jr., *Certain Victory: The United States Army in the Gulf War* (Washington, D.C.: Office of the Chief of Staff, United States Army, 1993).

Tilelli, Jr.'s 1st Cavalry Division attacked north into a concentration of Iraqi divisions, whose commanders remained convinced that the coalition would use that and several other wadies as avenues of attack. In the east two Marine divisions, with the Army's Tiger Brigade, and coalition forces under Saudi command attacked north into Kuwait. Faced with major attacks from three widely separated points, the Iraqi command had to begin its ground defense of Kuwait and the homeland by dispersing its combat power and logistical capability.[2]

Day One: 24 February 1991

The attack began from the XVIII Airborne Corps sector along the left flank. At 0100 Brig. Gen. Bernard Janvier sent scouts from his French 6th Light Armored Division into Iraq on the extreme western end of General Luck's line. Three hours later the French main body attacked in a light rain. Their objective was As Salmān, little more than a crossroads with an airfield about 90 miles inside Iraq. Reinforced by the 2d Brigade, 82d Airborne Division, the French crossed the border unopposed and raced north into the darkness.

But before they reached As Salmān, the French found some very surprised outposts of the Iraqi *45th Infantry Division*. General Janvier immediately sent his missile-armed Gazelle attack helicopters against the dug-in enemy tanks and bunkers. Late intelligence reports had assessed the *45th* as only about 50-percent effective after weeks of intensive coalition air attacks and psychological operations, an assessment soon confirmed by feeble resistance. After a brief battle that cost them two dead and twenty-five wounded, the French held 2,500 prisoners and controlled the enemy division area, now renamed ROCHAMBEAU. Janvier pushed his troops on to As Salman, which they took without opposition and designated Objective WHITE. The French consolidated WHITE and waited for an Iraqi counterattack that never came. The allied left flank was secure.[3]

[2] *Army Focus*, Jun 91, p. 22.

[3] XVIII Airborne Corps Sitrep, 24 Feb 91; Peter David, *Triumph in the Desert* (New York: Random House, 1991), p. 78; Interv (telephone), Charles R. Anderson with Maj Robert K. Wright, command historian, XVIII Airborne Corps, May 91.

American howitzers supporting the French attack on Objective ROCHAMBEAU

Maj. Gen. James H. Johnson, Jr.'s 82d Airborne Division carried out a mission that belied its "airborne" designation. While the division's 2d Brigade moved with the French, its two remaining brigades, the 1st and 3d, trailed the advance and cleared a two-lane highway into southern Iraq—main supply route TEXAS—for the troops, equipment, and supplies supporting the advance north.

The XVIII Airborne Corps' main attack, led by Maj. Gen. J. H. Binford Peay III's 101st Airborne Division, was scheduled for 0500, but fog over the objective forced a delay. While the weather posed problems for aviation and ground units, it did not abate direct support fire missions. Corps artillery and rocket launchers poured fire on objectives and approach routes. At 0705 Peay received the word to attack. Screened by Apache and Cobra attack helicopters, 60 Black Hawk and 40 Chinook choppers of XVIII Airborne Corps' 18th Aviation Brigade began lifting the 1st Brigade into Iraq. The initial objective was the forward operating base COBRA, a point some 110 miles into Iraq. A total of 300 helicopters ferried the 101st's troops and equipment into the objective area in one of the largest helicopter-borne operations in military history.[4]

Wherever they went in those initial attacks, Peay's troops achieved tactical surprise over the scattered and disorganized foe. By midafternoon they had a fast-growing group of stunned prisoners in custody and were expanding COBRA into a major refueling point 20 miles across to support subsequent operations. Heavy Chinook helicopters lifted artillery pieces and other weapons into COBRA, as well as fueling equipment and building materials to create a major base. From the Saudi border, XVIII Corps support command units drove 700 high-speed support vehicles north with the fuel, ammunition, and supplies to support a drive to the Euphrates River.[5]

As soon as the 101st secured COBRA and refueled the choppers, it continued its jump north. By the evening of the twenty-fourth its units had cut Highway 8, about 170 miles into Iraq. Peay's troops had now closed the first of several roads connecting Iraqi forces in Kuwait with Baghdad.[6]

[4] *Army Times*, 11 Mar 91, p. 15; Wright interview.

[5] Ibid.

[6] Wright interview.

Prisoner-of-war cage at forward operating base COBRA

Spearhead units were advancing much faster than expected. To keep the momentum of the corps intact, General Luck gave subordinate commanders wider freedom of movement. He became their logistics manager, adding assets at key times and places to maintain the advance. But speed caused problems for combat support elements. Tanks that could move up to 50 miles per hour were moving outside the support fans of artillery batteries that could displace at only 25 to 30 miles per hour. Luck responded by leapfrogging his artillery battalions and supply elements, a solution which cut down on fire support, since only half the pieces could fire while the other half raced forward. As long as Iraqi opposition remained weak, the risk was acceptable.[7]

In XVIII Corps' mission of envelopment, the 24th Infantry Division had the central role of blocking the Euphrates River valley to prevent the escape north of Iraqi forces in Kuwait and then attacking east in coordination with VII Corps to defeat the armor-heavy divisions of the *Republican Guard Forces Command.* Maj. Gen. Barry R. McCaffrey's division had come to the theater better prepared for combat in the desert than any other in Army Central Command. Designated a Rapid Deployment Force division a decade earlier, the 24th combined the usual mechanized infantry division components—an aviation brigade and three ground maneuver brigades, plus combat support units—with extensive desert training and desert-oriented medical and water purification equipment.

When the attack began, the 24th was as large as a World War I division, with 25,000 soldiers in thirty-four battalions. Its 241 Abrams tanks and 221 Bradley fighting vehicles provided the necessary armor punch to penetrate *Republican Guard* divisions. But with 94 helicopters, and over 6,500 wheeled and 1,300 other tracked vehicles—including 72 self-propelled artillery pieces and 9 multiple rocket launchers—the division had given away nothing in mobility and firepower.[8]

General McCaffrey began his division attack at 1500 with three subordinate units on line, the 197th Infantry Brigade on the left, the 1st Brigade in the center, and the 2d Brigade on the right. Six hours before the main attack the 2d Squadron, 4th Cavalry, had pushed across the border and scouted north along the two combat trails that the division would use, X-RAY on the left and YANKEE on the right. The reconnaissance turned up little evidence of the enemy, and the rapid progress of the division verified the scouts' reports. McCaffrey's brigades pushed about 50 miles into Iraq, virtually at will, and reached a position roughly adjacent to Objective WHITE in the French sector and a little short of forward operating base COBRA in the 101st's sector.

In their movement across the line of departure, and whenever not engaging enemy forces, battalions of the 24th Division generally moved in "battle box" formation. With a cavalry troop screening 5 to 10 miles to the front, four companies, or multi-platoon task forces, dispersed to form corner positions. Heavier units of the battalion—whether tanks or Bradleys—occupied one or both of the front corners. One company, or

[7] Ibid.

[8] Desert Shield and Desert Storm Operations Overview, 9 May 1991, prepared for United States Senate Armed Services Committee, Document no. 77 in HQ, 24th Infantry Division (Mech), *Historical Reference Book* (Fort Stewart, Ga., 1992), copy in CMH.

smaller units, advanced outside the box to provide flank security. The battalion commander placed inside the box the vehicles carrying ammunition, fuel, and water needed to continue the advance in jumps of about 40 miles. The box covered a front of about 4 to 5 miles and extended about 15 to 20 miles front to rear.[9]

Following a screen of cavalry and a spearhead of the 1st and 4th Battalions, 64th Armor, McCaffrey's division continued north, maintaining a speed of 25 to 30 miles per hour. In the flat terrain the 24th kept on course with the aid of long-range electronic navigation, a satellite-reading triangulation system in use for years before DESERT STORM. Night did not stop the division, thanks to more recently developed navigation technology. Unit commanders and vehicle drivers used image-enhancement scopes and goggles, and searched for targets with infrared- and thermal-imaging systems sensitive to personnel and vehicle heat signatures. Small units used hand-held Trimpack and Magellan global positioning systems. Around midnight McCaffrey stopped his brigades on a line about 75 miles inside Iraq. Like the rest of XVIII Airborne Corps, the 24th Division had established positions deep inside Iraq against surprisingly light opposition.

Command and control, as well as protection against fratricide, were accomplished with the transmitting device Budd Light, named for its inventor, Henry C. "Budd" Croley of the Army Materiel Command. Consisting of infrared light-emitting diodes snapped onto the tops of commercial batteries, Budd Lights were placed on vehicle antennas in varying numbers to distinguish command or guide vehicles from others. Easily visible up to 1.2 miles through night vision goggles, the purplish glow of 10,000 Budd Lights enabled the 24th Division and other units to move safely at night. Other safety measures included marking all coalition vehicles with inverted V's, rather than the insignia of each participating country, in a reflective infrared paint.[10]

The VII Corps had the mission of finding, attacking, and destroying the heart of President Saddam Hussein's ground forces, the armor-heavy *Republican Guard* divisions. In preparation for that, Central Command had built up General Franks' organization until it resembled a mini-army more than a traditional corps. The "Jayhawk" corps of World War II fame had a 3d Infantry Division (Mechanized) brigade attached to the 1st Armored Division and four field artillery brigades, the 42d, 75th, 142d, and 210th. To make deep attacks, to ferry infantry units into trouble spots, and to help armor crews kill tanks, the corps also had the 11th Aviation Brigade. Franks' command numbered more than 142,000 soldiers, compared with Luck's 116,000. To keep his troops moving and fighting, Franks used more than 48,500 vehicles and aircraft, including 1,587 tanks, 1,502 Bradleys and armored personnel carriers, 669 artillery pieces, and 223 attack helicopters. For every day of offensive operations, the corps needed 5.6 million gallons of fuel, 3.3 million gallons of water, and 6,075 tons of ammunition.[11]

[9] Interv, Maj William H. Thomas III with Lt Col Edwin W. Chamberlain III, commander, 1/18th Infantry, 197th Infantry Brigade, 24th Infantry Division (Mech), 16 May 91.

[10] Interv, Charles R. Anderson with Walter B. Morrow, Center for Night Vision and Electro-Optics, U.S. Army Communications-Electronics Command, Fort Belvoir, Va., 2 Jul 91.

[11] MS, Doughty, War in the Persian Gulf, p. 15; Draft MS, Carver, Narrative of VII Corps in Operation DESERT STORM, pp. 3–4.

Refueling an armored personnel carrier during the attack

The plan of advance for VII Corps paralleled that of Luck's corps to the west: a thrust north into Iraq, a massive turn to the right, and then an assault to the east into Kuwait. Because Franks' sector lay east of Luck's—in effect, closer to the hub of the envelopment wheel—VII Corps had to cover less distance than XVIII Airborne Corps. But intelligence reports and probing attacks into Iraqi territory in mid-February had shown that VII Corps faced a denser concentration of enemy units than did XVIII Corps farther west.

Once the turn to the right was complete, both corps would coordinate their attacks east so as to trap *Republican Guard* divisions between them and then press the offensive along their wide path of advance until Iraq's elite units either surrendered or were destroyed.

General Schwarzkopf originally had planned the VII Corps attack for 25 February. But XVIII Corps advanced so fast against such weak opposition that he moved up his armor attack by fourteen hours. Within his own sector Franks planned a feint and envelopment much like the larger overall strategy. On VII Corps' right, along the Wādī al Bāṭin, the 1st Cavalry Division would make a strong, but limited, attack directly to its front. While Iraqi units reinforced against the 1st, Franks would send two divisions through berms and mines on the corps' right and two more divisions on an "end around" into Iraq on the corps' left.

On 24 February the 1st Cavalry Division crossed the line of departure and hit the Iraqi *27th Infantry Division*. That was not their first meeting. General Tilelli's division had actually been probing the Iraqi defenses for some time. As these limited thrusts continued in the area that became known as the Ruqī Pocket, Tilelli's men found and destroyed elements of five Iraqi divisions, evidence that the 1st succeeded in its theater reserve mission of drawing and holding enemy units.

The main VII Corps attack, coming from farther west, caught the defenders by surprise. At 0538 Franks sent Maj. Gen. Thomas G. Rhame's 1st Infantry Division forward. The division plowed through the berms and hit trenches full of enemy soldiers. Once astride the trench lines, it turned the plow blades of its tanks and combat earthmovers along the Iraqi defenses and, covered by fire from Bradley crews, began to fill them in. The 1st neutralized 10 miles of Iraqi lines this way, killing or capturing all of the defenders without losing one soldier, and proceeded to cut twenty-four safe lanes through the minefields in preparation for passage of the British 1st Armored Division. On the far left of the corps sector, and at the same time, the 2d Armored Cavalry swept around the Iraqi obstacles and led 1st and 3d Armored Divisions into enemy territory.[12]

The two armored units moved rapidly toward their objective, the town of Al Buṣayyah, site of a major logistical base about 80 miles into Iraq. The 1st Armored Division on the left along XVIII Corps' boundary and the 3d Armored Division on the right moved in compressed wedges 15 miles wide and 30 miles deep. Screened by cavalry squadrons, the divisions deployed tank brigades in huge triangles, with artillery battalions between flank brigades and support elements in nearly 1,000 vehicles trailing the artillery.

Badly mauled by air attacks before the ground operation and surprised by Franks' envelopment, Iraqi forces offered little resistance. The 1st Infantry Division destroyed two T–55 tanks and five armored personnel carriers in the first hour and began taking prisoners immediately. Farther west, the 1st and 3d Armored Divisions quickly overran several small infantry and armored outposts. Concerned that his two armored units were too dispersed from the 1st Infantry Division for mutual reinforcement, Franks halted the advance with both armored elements on the left only 20 miles into Iraq. For the day, VII Corps rounded up about 1,300 of the enemy.[13]

In the east Marine Central Command (MARCENT) began its attack at 0400. General Boomer's I Marine Expeditionary Force aimed directly at its ultimate objective, Kuwait City. The Army's Tiger Brigade, 2d Armored Division, and the 1st and 2d Marine Divisions did not have as far to go to reach their objective as did Army units to the west—Kuwait City lay between 35 and 50 miles to the northeast, depending on the border crossing point—but they faced more elaborate defense lines and a tighter concentration of the enemy. The 1st Marine Division led from a position in the vicinity of the elbow of the southern Kuwait border, and immediately began breaching berms and rows of antitank and antipersonnel mines and several lines of concertina wire. The unit did not have Abrams tanks, but its M60A3 tanks and TOW-equipped high mobility multipurpose wheeled vehicles, supported by heavy artillery, proved sufficient against Iraqi T–55 and T–62 tanks. After the marines destroyed two tanks in only a few minutes, 3,000 Iraqis surrendered.[14]

At 0530 the 2d Marine Division, with Col. John B. Sylvester's Tiger Brigade on its west flank, attacked in the western part of the Marine Central Command sector. The Army armored brigade, equipped with M1A1 Abrams tanks, gave the marines enough firepower to defeat any armored units the Iraqis put between Boomer's force and Kuwait City. The first opposition came from a berm line and two mine belts. Marine M60A1 tanks with bulldozer blades quickly breached the berm, but the mine belts required more time and sophisticated equipment. Marine engineers used mine clearing line charges and M60A1 tanks with forked

[12] *Army Focus*, Jun 91, p. 22; *Washington Post*, 12 and 13 Sep 91; 1st Infantry Division (Mech), Operations DESERT SHIELD and DESERT STORM Command Rpt, 19 Apr 91, p. 4; VII Corps Commander's Sitrep (Combat) 38, 24 Feb 91.

[13] VII Corps Sitrep, 24 Feb 91; MS, Maj Guy C. Swan, 1st Armored Division in Combat, 21–28 February 1991, p. 1; Draft MS, Carver, Narrative of VII Corps in Operation DESERT STORM, p. 4.

[14] *Army Times*, 11 Mar 91, pp. 14–15; Lt Gen Walter E. Boomer, Command Brief: Persian Gulf Campaign; U.S. Marine Corps Operations, n.d.; Intervs, Charles R. Anderson with Lt Col Ronald J. Brown, U.S. Marine Corps Reserve (USMCR) and Maj Charles D. Melson (USMC), U.S. Marine Corps History and Museums Division, 2 Jul 91, Washington, D.C.

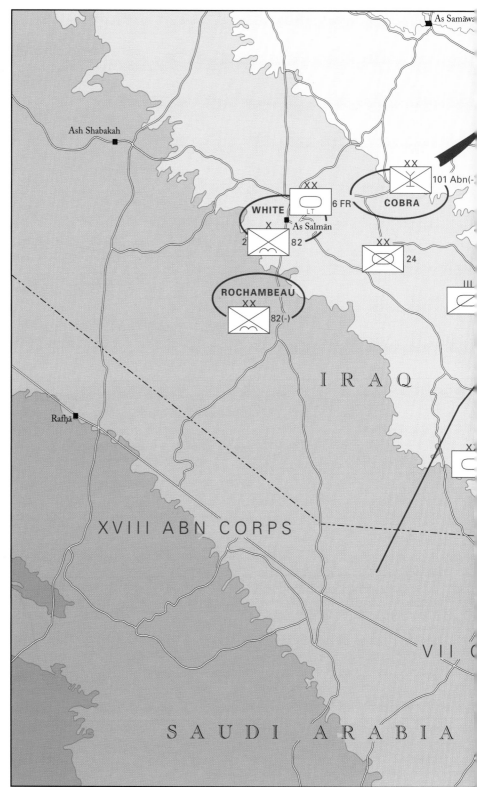

Map 13

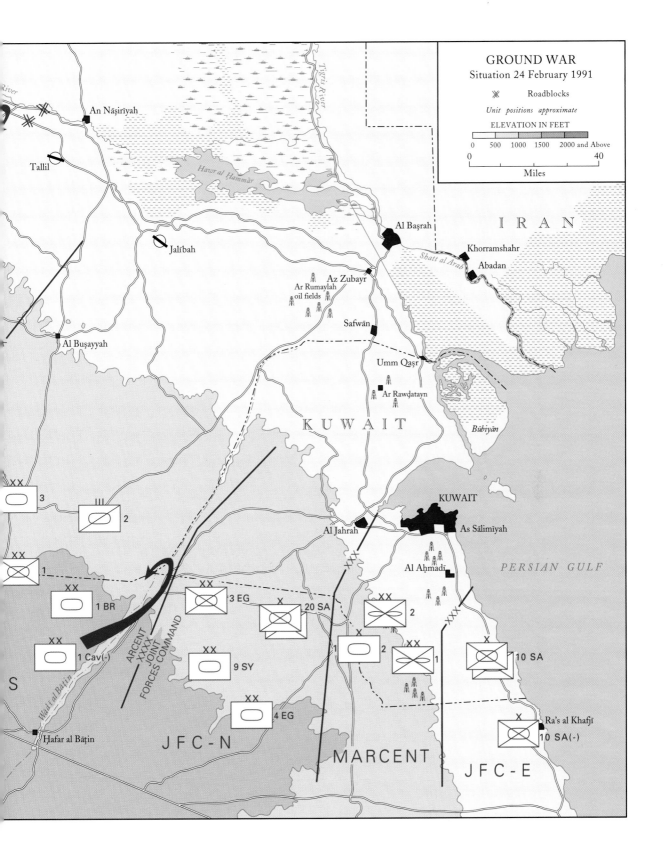

GROUND WAR
Situation 24 February 1991

✕ Roadblocks

Unit positions approximate

ELEVATION IN FEET

0 500 1000 1500 2000 and Above

0   40
Miles

River

An Nāṣirīyah

Tallil

Jalībah

Ḥawr al Ḥammār

Tigris River

IRAN

Al Baṣrah

Khorramshahr

Abadan

Shatt al Arab

Az Zubayr

Ar Rumaylah
oil fields

Safwān

Umm Qaṣr

Ar Rawḍatayn

Al Buṣayyah

K U W A I T

Būbiyān

KUWAIT

As Sālimīyah

Al Jahrah

Al Aḥmadī

PERSIAN GULF

XX
3

III
2

XX
1

XX
1 BR

XX
1 Cav(-)

XX
3 EG

X
20 SA

XX
2

X
2

XX
1

X
10 SA

ARCENT
XXXX
JOINT
FORCES COMMAND

Wādī al Bāṭin

XX
9 SY

XX
4 EG

S

Ḥafar al Bāṭin

J F C - N

M A R C E N T

X
10 SA(-)

Ra's al Khafjī

J F C - E

mine plows to clear six lanes in the division center, between the Umm Qudayr and Al Wafrah oil fields. By 1615 the Tiger Brigade had passed the mine belts. As soon as other units passed through the safe lanes, the 2d Marine Division repositioned to continue the advance north, with regiments on the right and in the center and the Tiger Brigade on the left tying in with the allied forces.[15]

To maintain command and control and to measure progress beyond the mines, Boomer's staff had drawn a series of parallel east-west phase lines, most of which followed power lines or desert trails. Reaching daily objectives on the approach to Kuwait City, the 2d Marine Division would cross phase lines RED, HORSE, WOLF, BEAR, and OX. The last two phase lines were modern multilane highways leading to Kuwait City. Navigation between phase lines became easier after the Iraqis ignited oil fields, for these became reliable landmarks.[16]

Moving ahead a short distance to phase line RED near the end of the day, the 2d Marine Division captured intact the Iraqi *9th Tank Battalion* with thirty-five T–55 tanks and more than 5,000 men. Already on the first day of ground operations the number of captives had become a problem in the Marine sector. After a fight for Al Jaber airfield, during which the 1st Marine Division destroyed twenty-one tanks, another 3,000 prisoners were seized. By the end of the day the I Marine Expeditionary Force had worked its way about 20 miles into Kuwait and taken nearly 10,000 Iraqi prisoners (*see Map 13*).[17]

Day Two: 25 February 1991

On 25 February XVIII Airborne Corps units continued their drive into Iraq. The 82d Airborne Division began its first sustained movement of the war, although, to the disappointment of General Johnson and his troops, the division had to stay on the ground. The 82d followed the French 6th Light Armored Division along phase line SMASH. While the 82d entered As Salmān—Objective WHITE—the 101st Airborne Division sent its 3d Brigade out of COBRA on a jump north to occupy an observation and blocking position on the south bank of the Euphrates River, just west of the town of An Nāṣirīyah.[18]

In the early morning darkness of the same day, General McCaffrey put his 24th Division in motion toward its first major objective. Following close air support and artillery fires, the division's 197th Brigade attacked at 0300 toward Objective BROWN in the western part of the division sector. Instead of determined opposition, the brigade found hungry prisoners, dazed by the heavy artillery preparation. By 0700 the 197th had cleared the area around BROWN and established blocking positions to the east and west along a trail, which was then being improved to serve as XVIII Corps' main supply route VIRGINIA. Six hours later the division's 2d Brigade followed its own artillery fires and attacked Objective GREY on the right, encountering no enemy fire

[15] 1st Brigade, 2d Armored Division, Commander's Summary, n.d.

[16] Brown interview.

[17] Boomer, Command Brief: Persian Gulf Campaign; U.S. Marine Corps Operations, n.d.; *Army Times*, 11 Mar 91, p. 15.

[18] Third U.S. Army, After Action Review, 12 Mar 91.

and taking 300 prisoners. After clearing the area, the brigade set blocking positions to the east.[19]

At 1450, with the 2d Brigade on GREY, the 1st Brigade moved northwest into the center of the division sector and then angled to the division right, attacking Objective RED directly north of GREY. Seven hours later the brigade had cleared the RED area, set blocking positions to the east and north, and processed 200 captives. To the surprise of all, the 24th Division had taken three major objectives and hundreds of men in only nineteen hours while meeting weak resistance from isolated pockets of Iraqi soldiers from the *26th* and *35th Infantry Divisions*. By the end of the day XVIII Airborne Corps had advanced in all division sectors to take important objectives, establish a functioning forward operating base, place brigade-size blocking forces in the Euphrates River valley, and capture thousands of prisoners of war—at a cost of two killed in action and two missing.[20]

In VII Corps General Franks faced two problems. The British 1st Armored Division, one of the units he had to have when he met the *Republican Guard* armored force, had begun passage of the mine breach cut by the 1st Infantry Division at 1200 on the twenty-fifth, and would not be completely through for several hours, possibly not until the next day. With the 1st and 3d Armored Divisions along the western edge of the corps sector, and the British not yet inside Iraq, the 1st Infantry and 1st Cavalry Divisions lay vulnerable to an armored counterattack.

A more troubling situation had developed along VII Corps' right flank. The commitment of some coalition contingents had concerned General Schwarzkopf months before the start of the ground war. Worried about postwar relations with Arab neighbors, some Arab members of the coalition had expressed reluctance to attack Iraq or even enter Kuwait. If enough of their forces sat out the ground phase of the war, the entire mission of liberating Kuwait might fail. To prevent such a disaster, Schwarzkopf had put the 1st Cavalry Division next to coalition units and gave the division the limited mission of conducting holding attacks and standing by to reinforce allies on the other side of the Wādī al Bāṭin. If Joint Forces Command North performed well, the division would be moved from the corps boundary and given an attack mission. Action on the first day of the ground war bore out the wisdom of holding the unit ready to reinforce allies to the east. Syrian and Egyptian forces had not moved forward, and a huge gap had opened in the allied line. Central Command notified the 2d Armored Cavalry to prepare to assist the 1st Cavalry Division in taking over the advance east of the Wādī al Bāṭin.[21]

But Franks could not freeze his advance indefinitely. The VII Corps had to press the attack where possible, and that meant on the left flank. Maj. Gen. Ronald H. Griffith's 1st Armored Division and Maj. Gen. Paul E. Funk's 3d Armored Division resumed their advance north shortly after daybreak. Griffith's troops made contact first, with outpost units of the Iraqi *26th Infantry Division*, and turned on the enemy the tactical sequence that brought success throughout the campaign. With the 1st

[19] Maj Gen Barry R. McCaffrey, 24th Infantry Division (Mech): Operation DESERT STORM Post-Attack Summary, 18 Mar 91.

[20] Ibid.; Interv, Maj William H. Thomas III with Col John Lemoyne, commander, 1st Brigade, 24th Infantry Division (Mech), 7 Mar 91; XVIII Airborne Corps Sitrep, 25 Feb 91.

[21] VII Corps, Desert Sabre Operations Summary.

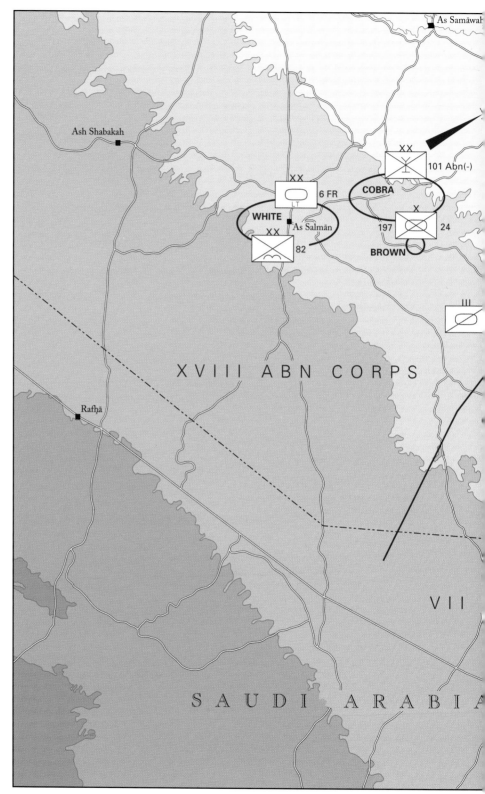

Map 14

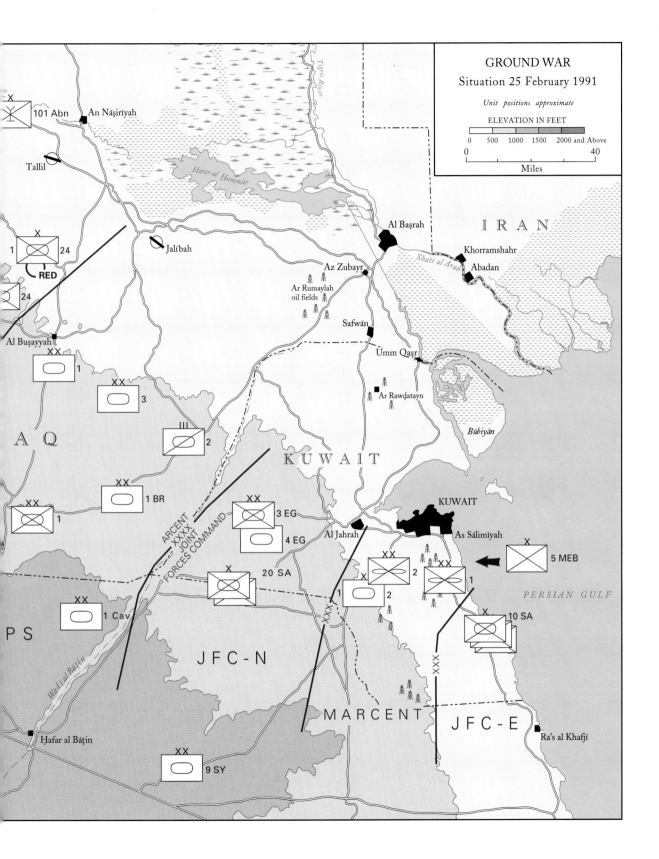

GROUND WAR
Situation 25 February 1991

Unit positions approximate

ELEVATION IN FEET

0   500   1000 1500 2000 and Above

0   40

Miles

An Nāşirīyah

101 Abn

Tallil

Tigris River

Hawr al Hammār

Al Başrah

IRAN

Khorramshahr

Abadan

Shatt al Arab

1   24

RED

Jalībah

Az Zubayr

Ar Rumaylah
oil fields

Safwān

Umm Qaşr

24

Al Buşayyah

Ar Rawdatayn

Būbiyān

A Q

1

3

2

1 BR

KUWAIT

KUWAIT

As Sālimīyah

5 MEB

1

3 EG

4 EG

Al Jahrah

2

1

1 Cav

20 SA

2

1

PERSIAN GULF

P S

10 SA

ARCENT
XXXX
JOINT
FORCES COMMAND

JFC-N

Wadi al Bāţin

MARCENT

JFC-E

Ḥafar al Bāţin

Ra's al Khafjī

9 SY

M1A1 tank of 3d Armored Division advancing north

Armored Division still about 35 to 40 miles away from its objective, close air support strikes began, followed by attack helicopter strikes. As the division closed to about 10 to 15 miles, artillery, rocket launchers, and tactical missile batteries delivered preparatory fires. As division lead elements came into visual range, psychological operations teams broadcast surrender appeals. If the Iraqis fired on the approaching Americans, the attackers repeated artillery, rocket, and missile strikes. In the experience of the 1st Armored Division, that sequence was enough to gain the surrender of most Iraqi Army units in a given objective. Only once did the Iraqis mount an attack after a broadcast, and in that instance a 1st Armored Division brigade destroyed forty to fifty tanks and armored personnel carriers in ten minutes at a range of 1.2 miles.[22]

By late morning of 25 February Joint Forces Command North had made enough progress to allow VII Corps and Marine Central Command on the flanks to resume their advance. That afternoon and night in the 1st Infantry Division sector, the Americans expanded their mine breach and captured two enemy brigade command posts and the *26th Infantry Division* command post, with a brigadier general and complete staff. Behind them, the British 1st Armored Division made good progress through the mine breach and prepared to turn right and attack the Iraqi *52d Armored Division.*[23]

Approaching Al Buṣayyah in early afternoon, the 1st Armored Division directed close air support and attack helicopter sorties on an Iraqi brigade position, destroying artillery pieces, several vehicles, and taking nearly 300 prisoners. That night the 2d Armored Cavalry and 3d Armored Division oriented east and encountered isolated enemy units under conditions of high winds and heavy rains.[24]

With the allied advance well under way all along the line, a U.S. Navy amphibious force made its final effort to convince the Iraqi command authority that Central Command would launch a major over-the-beach assault into Kuwait. Beginning late on 24 February and continuing over the following two days, the Navy landed the 7,500-man 5th Marine Expeditionary Brigade at Al Mish'āb, Saudi Arabia, about 28 miles south of the border with Kuwait. Once ashore, the 5th became the reserve for Joint Forces Command East. Later investigation showed that the presence of the amphibious force in Persian Gulf waters before the ground war had forced the Iraqi command to hold in Kuwait as many as four divisions to meet an amphibious assault that never materialized.[25]

[22] Ltr, Maj Paul J. Jacobsmeyer to Col K. Hamburger, Department of History, USMA, 7 Mar 91.

[23] VII Corps, Desert Sabre Operations Summary; VII Corps Commander's Sitrep (Combat) 39, 25 Feb 91.

[24] MS, Swan, 1st Armored Division in Combat, 21–28 February 1991, p. 1; Ltr, Capt Kevin McKedy to "Dear Mil [sic] Artists," 9 Mar 91.

[25] *Army Times*, 11 Mar 91, p. 14.

At daybreak on 25 February Iraqi units made their first counterattack in the Marine sector, hitting the 2d Marine Division right and center. While Marine regiments fought off an effort that they named the "Reveille Counterattack," troops of the Tiger Brigade raced north on the left. In the morning the brigade cleared one bunker complex and destroyed seven artillery pieces and several armored personnel carriers. After a midday halt, the brigade cleared another bunker complex and captured the Iraqi *116th* brigade commander among a total of 1,100 prisoners of war for the day. In the center of the corps sector the marines overran an agricultural production facility, called the "Ice Cube Tray" because of its appearance to aerial observers.[26]

By the end of operations on 25 February General Schwarzkopf for the second straight day had reports of significant gains in all sectors. But enemy forces could still inflict damage, and in surprising ways and places. The Iraqis continued their puzzling policy of setting oil fires—well over 200 now blazed out of control—as well as their strategy of punishing Saudi Arabia and provoking Israel. They launched four Scuds, one of which slammed into a building housing American troops in Dhahran. That single missile killed 28 and wounded more than 100, causing the highest one-day casualty total for American forces in a war of surprisingly low losses to date (*see Map 14*).[27]

Day Three: 26 February 1991

On 26 February the XVIII Airborne Corps units turned their attack northeast and entered the Euphrates River valley. With the French and the 101st and 82d Airborne Divisions protecting the west and north flanks, the 24th Division spearheaded Luck's attack into the valley. The first obstacle was the weather. An out-of-season *shamal* in the objective area kicked up thick clouds of swirling dust that promised to give thermal-imaging equipment a rigorous field test through the day.

After refueling in the morning, all three brigades of the 24th moved out at 1400 toward the Iraqi airfields at Jalībah and Tallil. The 1st Brigade went north, then east about 40 miles to take a battle position in the northeast corner of the corps sector; the 2d Brigade moved 35 miles north to a position along the eastern corps boundary and then continued its advance another 25 miles until it was only 15 miles south of Jalībah; and the 197th Brigade went northeast about 60 miles to a position just south of Tallil. Meanwhile, the 3d Armored Cavalry screened to the east on the division's south flank.

In these attacks the 24th encountered the heaviest resistance of the war. The Iraqi *47th* and *49th Infantry Divisions*, the *Nebuchadnezzar Division* of the *Republican Guard*, and the *26th Commando Brigade* took heavy fire but stood and fought. The 1st Brigade took direct tank and artillery fire for four hours. For the first time in the advance the terrain gave the enemy a clear advantage. McCaffrey's troops found Iraqi artillery

[26] Brown interview; 1st Brigade, 2d Armored Division, Commander's Summary, n.d.

[27] ODCSINT Intelligence Summaries 404, 25 Feb 91, and 406, 26 Feb 91.

and automatic weapons dug into rocky escarpments reminiscent of the Japanese positions in coral outcroppings on Pacific islands that an earlier generation of 24th Infantry Division soldiers had faced. But Iraqi troops were not as tenacious in defense as the Japanese had been, and the 24th had much better weapons than its predecessors. American artillery crews located enemy batteries with their Firefinder radars and returned between three and six rounds for every round of incoming. With that advantage, American gunners destroyed six full Iraqi artillery battalions.[28]

In the dust storm and darkness American technological advantages became clearer still. Thermal-imaging systems in tanks, Bradleys, and attack helicopters worked so well that crews could spot and hit Iraqi tanks at up to 4,000 meters (2.5 miles) before the Iraqis even saw them. American tank crews were at first surprised at their one-sided success, then exulted in the curious result of their accurate fire: the "pop-top" phenomenon. Because Soviet-made tank turrets were held in place by gravity, a killing hit blew the turret completely off. As the battle wore on, the desert floor became littered with pop-tops. A combination of superior weaponry and technique—precise Abrams tank and Apache helicopter gunnery, 25-mm. automatic cannon fire from the Bradleys, overwhelming artillery and rocket direct support and counterbattery fire, and air superiority—took the 24th Division through enemy armor and artillery units in those "valley battles" and brought Iraqi troops out of their bunkers and vehicles in droves with hands raised in surrender. After a hard but victorious day and night of fighting, the 2d Brigade took its position by 2000 on the twenty-sixth. The other two brigades accomplished their missions by dawn.[29]

In VII Corps' sector on 26 February the 1st Armored Division fired heavy artillery and rocket preparatory fires into Al Buşayyah shortly after dawn, and by noon had advanced through a sandstorm to overrun the small town. In the process, General Griffith's troops completed the destruction of the Iraqi *26th Infantry Division* and, once in the objective area, discovered they had taken the enemy *VII Corps* headquarters and a corps logistical base as well. More than 100 tons of munitions were captured and large numbers of tanks and other vehicles destroyed. The 1st Armored Division pressed on, turning northeast and hitting the *Tawakalna Division* of the *Republican Guard*. Late that night Griffith mounted a night assault on the elite enemy unit and, in fighting that continued the next day, killed 30 to 35 tanks and 10 to 15 other vehicles.[30]

In the 3d Armored Division sector Funk's men crossed the intercorps phase line SMASH just after daylight and attacked Objective COLLINS, east of Al Buşayyah. Through the evening the division fought its toughest battles in defeating elements of the *Tawakalna Division*. With the capture of COLLINS and nearby enemy positions, VII Corps reached the wheeling point in its advance. From here, General Franks' divisions turned east and assaulted *Republican Guard* strongholds. Meanwhile, the 1st Infantry Division was ordered north from its position inside the mine

[28] McCaffrey, 24th Infantry Division (Mech): Operation DESERT STORM Post-Attack Summary, 18 Mar 91; Lemoyne interview.

[29] Ibid.; Wright interview.

[30] VII Corps Sitrep, 27 Feb 91; VII Corps Commander's Sitrep (Combat) 40, 26 Feb 91; 1st Armored Division Executive Summary—Operation DESERT STORM, 19 Apr 91.

1st Armored Division soldiers digging out a heavy equipment transporter

belt breach. As the attack east began, VII Corps presented in the northern part of its sector a front of three divisions and one regiment: the 1st Armored Division on the left (north); the 3d Armored Division, the 2d Armored Cavalry, and the 1st Infantry Division on the right (south). Farther south, the British 1st Armored Division, with over 7,000 vehicles, cleared the mine breach at 0200 and deployed to advance on a separate axis into Objective WATERLOO, and on to the juncture of phase line SMASH and the corps boundary. From ARCENT headquarters came word that General Luck's corps would soon be even stronger. At 0930 the ARCENT commander, Lt. Gen. John J. Yeosock, released 1st Cavalry Division from its theater reserve role to VII Corps.[31]

In the early afternoon Col. Leonard D. Holder, Jr.'s 2d Armored Cavalry advanced east of COLLINS in a *shamal*. The regiment, screening in front of 1st Infantry Division, had just arrived from the mine belt along the Saudi border that it had breached the first day of the ground war. The cavalrymen had only a general idea of the enemy's position. The Iraqis had long expected the American attack to come from the south and east and were now frantically turning hundreds of tanks, towed artillery pieces, and other vehicles to meet the onslaught from the west. On the Iraqi side, unit locations were changing almost by the minute. As Holder's men neared phase line TANGERINE, 20 miles east of COLLINS, one of the cavalry troops received fire from a building on the 69 Easting, a north-south line on military maps. The cavalrymen returned fire and continued east. More enemy fire came in during the next two hours and was immediately returned. Just after 1600 the cavalrymen found T–72 tanks in prepared positions at 73 Easting. The regiment used its thermal-imaging equipment to deadly advantage, killing every tank that appeared in its sights. But this was a different kind of battle than Americans had fought so far. The destruction of the first tanks did not signal the surrender of hundreds of Iraqi soldiers. The tanks kept coming and fighting.[32]

The reason for the unusually determined enemy fire and large number of tanks soon became clear. The cavalrymen had found two Iraqi divisions willing to put up a hard fight, the *12th Armored Division* and the *Tawakalna Division*. Holder's regiment found a seam between the two divisions, and for a time became the only American unit obviously outnumbered and outgunned during the ground campaign. But, as the 24th Division had found in its valley battles, thermal-imaging equipment cut through the dust storm to give gunners a long-range view of enemy vehicles and grant the fatal first-shot advantage. For four hours Holder's men

[31] VII Corps Sitrep, 27 Feb 91; VII Corps Commander's Sitrep (Combat) 40, 26 Feb 91; Third U.S. Army, After Action Review, 12 Mar 91; 1st Infantry Division (Mech), Operations DESERT SHIELD and DESERT STORM Command Rpt, 19 Apr 91, p. 5; 3d Armored Division, Historical Overview of the 3AD in the Persian Gulf War, p. 10.

[32] Memo, Col Michael D. Krause for Gen Gordon R. Sullivan, 19 Apr 91, sub: Battle of 73 Easting.

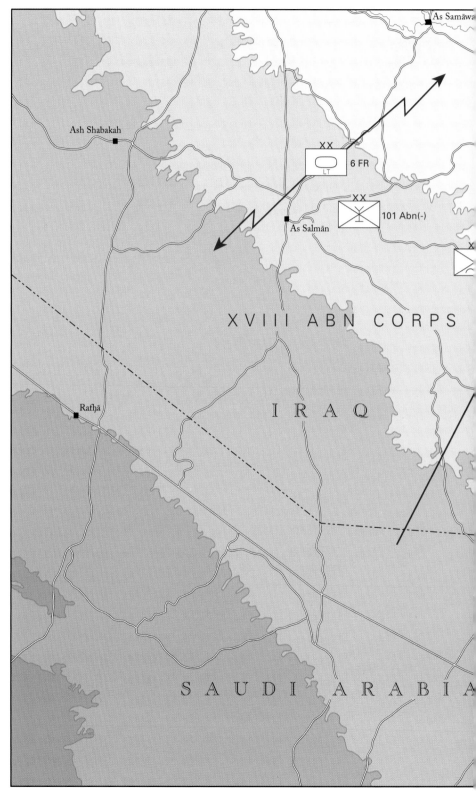

Map 15

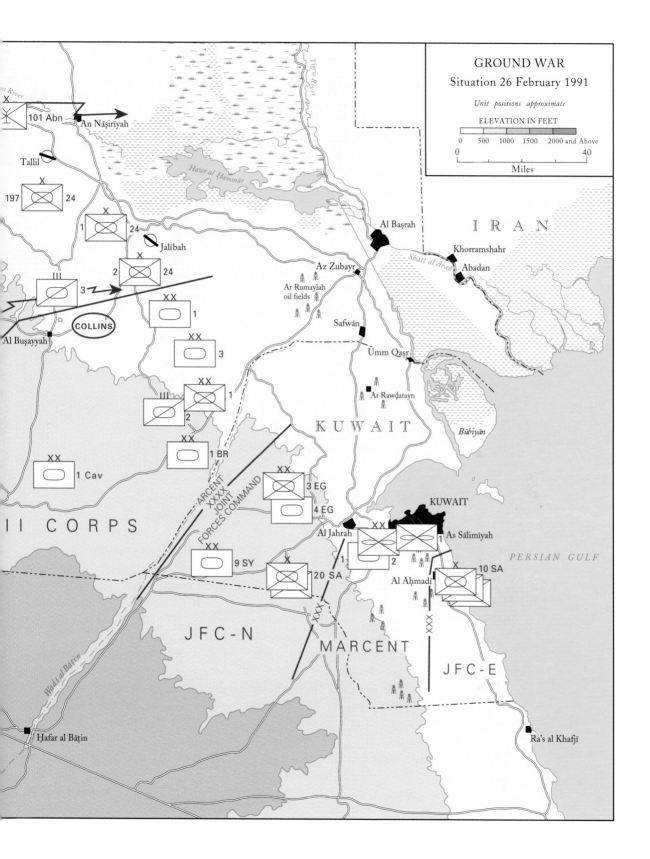

GROUND WAR
Situation 26 February 1991

Unit positions approximate

ELEVATION IN FEET

| 0 | 500 | 1000 | 1500 | 2000 and Above |

0   40

Miles

IRAN

101 Abn
An Nāşiriyah
Tallīl
197   24
1   24
Jalībah
2   24
III   3
COLLINS
Al Buşayyah
1
3
III   1
2
1 BR

1 Cav
3 EG
4 EG
Al Jahrah
1
2
1
9 SY
20 SA
Al Aḥmadī
10 SA

II CORPS

Tigris River
Hawr al Ḥammār
Al Başrah
Khorramshahr
Abadan
Az Zubayr
Shatt al Arab
Ar Rumaylah oil fields
Safwān
Umm Qaşr
Ar Rawḍatayn
KUWAIT
Būbiyān
KUWAIT
As Sālimīyah
PERSIAN GULF

ARCENT
JOINT
FORCES COMMAND

JFC-N

MARCENT

JFC-E

Wadi al Bāţin
Ḥafar al Bāţin
Ra's al Khafjī

killed tanks and armored personnel carriers while attack helicopters knocked out artillery batteries. When the battle of 73 Easting ended at 1715, the 2d Armored Cavalry had destroyed at least 29 tanks and 24 armored personnel carriers, as well as numerous other vehicles and bunkers, and taken 1,300 prisoners. That night, the 1st Infantry Division passed through Holder's cavalrymen and continued the attack east.[33]

Farther to the south, the British 1st Armored Division attacked eastward through the *48th Infantry* and *52d Armored Divisions* and remnants of other Iraqi units trying to withdraw north. This attack marked the start of nearly two days of continuous combat for the British, some of the toughest fighting of the war. In the largest of this series of running battles, the British destroyed 40 tanks and captured an Iraqi division commander.[34]

To the east, the Marine advance resumed on the twenty-sixth with the two Marine divisions diverging from their parallel course of the first two days. The 2d Marine Division and the Army's Tiger Brigade, 2d Armored Division, continued driving directly north, while the 1st Marine Division turned northeast toward Kuwait International Airport. The Army tankers headed toward Mutlā Ridge, an extended upfold only about 25 feet high. The location next to the juncture of two multilane highways in the town of Al Jahrah, a suburb of Kuwait City, rather than the elevation, had caught General Boomer's attention weeks earlier. By occupying the ridge the brigade could seal a major crossroads and slam the door on Iraqi columns escaping north to Baghdad.[35]

The brigade advanced at 1200 with the 3d Battalion, 67th Armor, in the lead. Approaching Mutlā Ridge, the Americans found a minefield and waited for the plows to cut a safety lane. On the move again, the brigade began to find enemy bunker complexes and dug-in armored units. Enemy tanks, almost all of the T–55 type, were destroyed wherever encountered, and most bunkers yielded still more prisoners. During a three-hour running battle in the early evening, Tiger tankers cleared the Mutlā police post and surrounding area. Moving up and over Mutlā Ridge, the 67th's tanks found and destroyed numerous antiaircraft artillery positions. Perimeter consolidation at the end of the day's advance was complicated and delayed by the need to process an even larger number of prisoners of war than the day before: 1,600.[36]

The Tiger Brigade now controlled the highest point for hundreds of miles in any direction. When the troops looked down on the highways from Mutlā Ridge, they saw the largest target an armored brigade had probably ever seen. The previous night Air Force and Navy aircraft had begun destroying all vehicles spotted fleeing from Kuwait. Now the brigade added its firepower to the continuous air strikes. On the "Highway of Death" hundreds of burning and exploding vehicles of all types, including civilian automobiles, were visible. Hundreds more raced west out of Kuwait City unknowingly to join the deadly traffic jam. Here and there knots of drivers, Iraqi soldiers, and refugees fled into the desert because of the inferno of bombs, rockets, and tank fire.

[33] Ibid.; VII Corps Sitrep, 27 Feb 91.

[34] VII Corps Sitrep, 27 Feb 91; VII Corps Commander's Sitrep (Combat) 40, 26 Feb 91; VII Corps, Desert Sabre Operations Summary; VII Corps DESERT SHIELD/DESERT STORM After Action Rpt, 29 May 91.

[35] Brown interview.

[36] Boomer, Command Brief: Persian Gulf Campaign; U.S. Marine Corps Operations, n.d.; 1st Brigade, 2d Armored Division, Commander's Summary, n.d.

These lucky ones managed to escape and join the ranks of the growing army of prisoners.[37]

At the close of allied operations on 26 February a total of twenty-four Iraqi divisions had been defeated. In all sectors the volume of prisoners continued to grow and clog roads and logistical areas. Iraqi soldiers surrendered faster than Central Command could count them, but military police units estimated that the total now exceeded 30,000 (*see Map 15*).[38]

The day ended with at least one other major logistical problem. The 24th Division had moved so fast in two days that fuel trucks had difficulty keeping up. After taking positions on the night of the twenty-sixth, the lead tanks had less than 100 gallons of fuel on board. Brigade commanders had the fuel, but lead elements were not sure where to rendezvous in the desert. The problem was solved by the kind of unplanned actions on which victories often turn. A small number of junior officers took the initiative to lead tank truck convoys across the desert at night with only a vague idea of where either brigade fuel supplies or needy assault units were located. By approaching whatever vehicles came into view and asking for unit identity, those leaders managed to refuel division vehicles by midnight.[39]

Day Four: 27 February 1991

On the morning of 27 February XVIII Airborne Corps prepared to continue its advance east toward Al Baṣrah. But before the assault could be resumed, the 24th Division had to secure its positions in the Euphrates River valley by taking the two airfields toward which it had been moving. Tallil airfield lay about 20 miles south of the town of An Nāṣirīyah; Jalībah airfield lay 40 miles east southeast, near the lake at Hawr al Māliḥ. The task of taking the airfields went to the units that had ended the previous day in positions closest to them. While the 1st Brigade would conduct a fixing attack toward the Jalībah airfield, the 2d Brigade planned to move east about 25 miles and turn north against the same objective. Moving north, the 197th Brigade would take Tallil.

Following a four-hour rest, the 2d Brigade attacked at midnight, seized a position just south of Jalībah by 0200 on the twenty-seventh, and stayed there while preparatory fires continued to fall on the airfield. At 0600 the 1st Brigade moved east toward the airfield, stopped short, and continued firing on Iraqi positions. At the same time, the 2d Brigade resumed the attack with three infantry-armor task forces and crashed through a fence around the runways. Although the airfield had been hit by air strikes for six weeks and a heavy artillery preparation by five battalions of XVIII Corps' 212th Field Artillery Brigade, Iraqi defenders were still willing to fight. Most Iraqi fire was ineffectual small arms, but armor-piercing rounds hit two Bradleys, killing two men of the 1st Battalion, 64th Armor, and wounding several others in the 3d Battalion, 15th Infantry. As nearly 200 American armored vehicles moved across the air-

[37] Brown interview.

[38] ODCSINT Intelligence Summaries 406, 26 Feb 91, and 408, 27 Feb 91.

[39] Interv, S Sgt Warren B. Causey, 317th Military History Detachment, with Lt Col Raymond Barrett, commander, 3/15th Infantry, 2d Brigade, 24th Infantry Division, 1 Mar 91.

Chinook helicopter delivering supplies to XVIII Corps troops on the move

field knocking out tanks, artillery pieces, and even aircraft, Iraqis began to surrender in large numbers. By 1000 the Jalībah airfield was secure.[40]

At midday heavy artillery and rocket launcher preparations, followed by twenty-eight close air sorties, were directed on the Tallil airfield. As the fires lifted, the 197th Brigade advanced across the cratered runways and through weaker resistance than that at Jalībah. But like the 2d Brigade at Jalībah, the 197th killed both armored vehicles and aircraft on the ground and found large numbers of willing prisoners.[41]

As the 197th Brigade assaulted Tallil, General McCaffrey realigned his other units to continue the attack east centering on Highway 8. The 1st Brigade took the division left (north) sector, tying in with the 101st Airborne Division. The 2d Squadron, 4th Cavalry, the 24th's reconnaissance unit, moved east from the Hawr al Mālih lake area to set up a tactical assembly area behind the 1st Brigade. The 2d Brigade left its newly won airfield position and assumed the center sector of the division front. The 3d Armored Cavalry took the right sector, tying in with VII Corps to the south. With the 24th Division now oriented east after its northern advance of the first two days, a new series of phase lines was drawn between the Tallil airfield and the Ar Rumaylah oil fields, just southwest of Al Baṣrah. From the line of departure east of the Jalībah airfield, McCaffrey's units would advance across phase lines Axe, Knife, Victory, and Crush.[42]

The run down the highway showed more clearly than any other episode the weaknesses of Iraqi field forces and the onesidedness of the conflict. Through the afternoon and night of 27 February the tankers, Bradley gunners, and helicopter crews and artillerymen of the 1st and 4th Battalions, 64th Armor, fired at hundreds of vehicles trying to redeploy to meet the new American attack from the west, or simply to escape

[40] Ibid.

[41] McCaffrey, 24th Infantry Division (Mech): Operation DESERT STORM Post-Attack Summary, 18 Mar 91.

[42] Ibid.

north across the Euphrates River valley and west on Highway 8. With no intelligence capability left to judge the size or location of the oncoming American armored wedges and attack helicopter swarms, as well as insufficient communications to coordinate a new defense, Iraqi units stumbled into disaster. Unsuspecting drivers of every type of vehicle, from tanks to artillery prime movers and even commandeered civilian autos, raced randomly across the desert or west on Highway 8 only to run into General McCaffrey's firestorm. Some drivers, seeing vehicles explode and burn, veered off the road in vain attempts to escape. Others stopped, dismounted, and walked toward the Americans with raised hands. When the division staff detected elements of the *Hammurabi Division* of the *Republican Guard* moving across the 24th's front, McCaffrey concentrated the fire of nine artillery battalions and an Apache battalion on the once elite enemy force. At dawn the next day, the twenty-eighth, hundreds of vehicles lay crumpled and smoking on Highway 8 and at scattered points across the desert. The 24th's lead elements, only 30 miles west of Al Başrah, set up a hasty defense along phase line VICTORY.[43]

The 24th Division's valley battles of 25–27 February rendered ineffective all Iraqi units encountered in the division sector and trapped most of the *Republican Guard* divisions to the south while VII Corps bore into them from the west, either blasting units in place or taking their surrender. In its own battles the 24th achieved some of the most impressive results of the ground war. McCaffrey's troops had advanced 190 miles into Iraq to the Euphrates River, then turned east and advanced another 70 miles, all in four days. Along the way they knocked out over 360 tanks and armored personnel carriers, over 300 artillery pieces, over 1,200 trucks, 500 pieces of engineer equipment, 19 missiles, and 25 aircraft, and rounded up over 5,000 enemy soldiers. Just as surprising as these large enemy losses were the small numbers of American casualties: 8 killed in action, 36 wounded in action, and 5 nonbattle injuries. And in the entire XVIII Airborne Corps, combat equipment losses were negligible: only 4 M1A1 tanks, 3 of which were repairable.[44]

In VII Corps' sector the advance rolled east. The battles begun the previous afternoon continued through the morning of 27 February as General Franks' divisions bore into *Republican Guard* units trying to reposition or escape. As the assault gained momentum, Franks for the first time deployed his full combat power. The 1st Cavalry Division made good progress through the 1st Infantry Division breach and up the left side of VII Corps' sector. By midafternoon, after a high-speed 190-mile move north, General Tilelli's brigades were behind 1st Armored Division, tying in with the 24th Division across the corps boundary. Now Franks could send against the *Republican Guard* five full divisions and a separate regiment. From left (north) to right, VII Corps deployed the 1st Armored Division, 1st Cavalry Division, the 3d Armored Division, the 1st Infantry Division, the 2d Armored Cavalry, and the British 1st Armored Division.[45]

[43] Ibid.; Interv, Maj William H. Thomas with Maj Gen Barry R. McCaffrey, 28 Feb 91; Interv, Thomas with Lt Col David Jensen, commander, 3/7th Infantry, 1st Brigade, 24th Infantry Division, 9 Mar 91.

[44] Ibid.; Wright interview.

[45] Third U.S. Army, After Action Review, 12 Mar 91.

1st Armored Division elements passing the burning remnants of an Iraqi tank

The dust storms had cleared early in the day, revealing in VII Corps' sector the most awesome array of armored and mechanized power fielded since World War II. In a panorama extending beyond visual limits 1,500 tanks, another 1,500 Bradleys and armored personnel carriers, 650 artillery pieces, and supply columns of hundreds of vehicles stretching into the dusty brown distance rolled east through Iraqi positions, as inexorable as a lava flow. To Iraqi units, depleted and demoralized by forty-one days of continuous air assault, VII Corps' advance appeared irresistible.

Turning on the enemy the full range of its weapons, VII Corps systematically destroyed Iraqi military power in its sector. About 50 miles east of Al Buşayyah, the 1st and 3d Armored Divisions tore into remnants of the *Tawakalna, Madina,* and *Adnan Divisions* of the *Republican Guard.* In one of several large engagements along the advance the 2d Brigade, 1st Armored Division, received artillery fire and then proceeded to destroy not only those artillery batteries but also 61 tanks and 34 armored personnel carriers of the *Madina Division* in less than one hour. The 1st Infantry Division overran the *12th Armored Division* and scattered the *10th Armored Division* into retreat. On the south flank the British 1st Armored Division destroyed the *52d Armored Division,* then overran three infantry divisions. To finish destruction of the *Republican Guard Forces Command,* General Franks conducted a giant envelopment involving the 1st Cavalry Division on the left and the 1st Infantry Division on the right.

The trap closed on disorganized bands of Iraqis streaming north in full retreat. The only setback for VII Corps during this climactic assault occurred in the British sector. American Air Force A–10 Thunderbolt aircraft supporting the British advance mistakenly fired on 2 infantry fighting vehicles, killing 9 British soldiers.[46]

At 1700 Franks informed his divisions of an imminent theater-wide cease-fire but pressed VII Corps' attack farther east. An hour later the 1st Squadron, 4th Cavalry, 1st Infantry Division, set a blocking position on the north-south highway connecting Al Başrah to Kuwait City. The next morning corps artillery units fired an enormous preparation involving all long-range weapons: 155-mm. and 8-inch (203-mm.) self-propelled pieces, rocket launchers, and tactical missiles. Attack helicopters followed to strike suspected enemy positions. The advance east continued a short time until the cease-fire went into effect at 0800, 28 February, with American armored divisions just inside Kuwait.[47]

In ninety hours of continuous movement and combat, VII Corps had achieved impressive results against the best units of the Iraqi military. Franks' troops destroyed more than a dozen Iraqi divisions, an estimated 1,300 tanks, 1,200 infantry fighting vehicles and armored personnel carriers, 285 artillery pieces, and 100 air defense systems, and captured nearly 22,000 men. At the same time, the best Iraqi divisions destroyed only 7 M1A1 Abrams tanks, 15 Bradleys, 2 armored personnel carriers, and 1 Apache helicopter. And while killing unknown thousands of enemy troops, VII Corps lost 22 soldiers killed in action (*Map 16*).[48]

In the Marine Central Command's sector on 27 February the Tiger Brigade, 2d Armored Division, and the 2d Marine Division began the fourth day of the ground war by holding positions and maintaining close liaison with Joint Forces Command North units on the left flank. The next phase of operations in Kuwait would see Saudi-commanded units pass through General Boomer's sector from west to east and go on to liberate Kuwait City. At 0550 Tiger troops made contact with Egyptian units, and four hours later Joint Forces Command North columns passed through 2d Marine Division. During the rest of the day Tiger troops cleared bunker complexes, the Ali Al Salem Airfield, and the Kuwaiti Royal Summer Palace, while processing a continuous stream of prisoners of war. The Army brigade and the 2d Marine Division remained on Mutlā Ridge and phase line BEAR until the cease-fire went into effect at 0800 on 28 February. Prisoner interrogation during and after combat operations revealed that the Tiger Brigade advance had split the seam between the Iraqi *III* and *IV Corps*, overrunning elements of the *14th*, *7th*, and *36th Infantry Divisions*, as well as brigades of the *3d Armored*, *1st Mechanized*, and *2d Infantry Divisions*. During four days of combat Tiger Brigade task forces destroyed or captured 181 tanks, 148 armored personnel carriers, 40 artillery pieces, and 27 anti-aircraft systems while killing an estimated 263 enemy and capturing 4,051 prisoners of war, all at a cost of 2 killed and 5 wounded.[49]

[46] Ibid.; MS, Swan, 1st Armored Division in Combat, 21–28 February 1991, pp. 2–3; MS, VII Corps Public Affairs Office, VII Corps DESERT STORM History, p. 5; VII Corps, Desert Sabre Operations Summary; VII Corps Commander's Sitrep (Combat) 41, 27 Feb 91; 1st Armored Division Executive Summary—Operation DESERT STORM, 19 Apr 91.

[47] MS, Doughty, War in the Persian Gulf, p. 16; MS, Swan, 1st Armored Division in Combat, 21–28 February 1991, p. 3.

[48] MS, Doughty, War in the Persian Gulf, p. 17; MS, Carver, Narrative of VII Corps in Operation DESERT STORM, p. 7.

[49] Boomer, Command Brief: Persian Gulf Campaign; U.S. Marine Corps Operations, n.d.; 1st Brigade, 2d Armored Division, Commander's Summary, n.d.

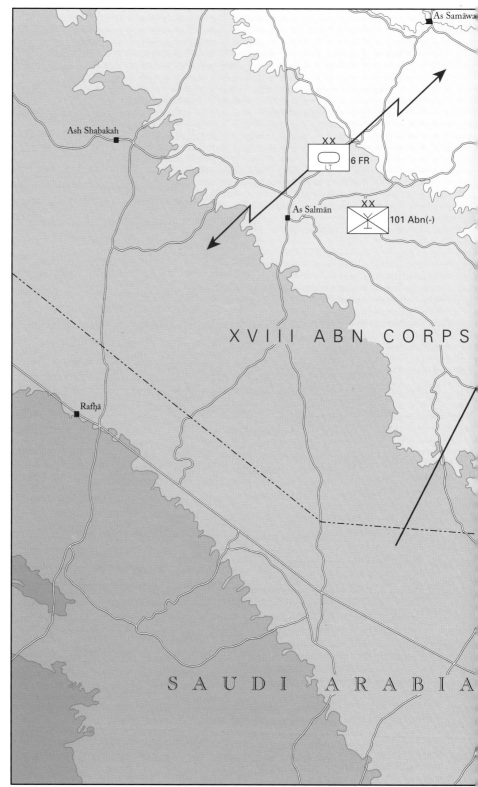

Map 16

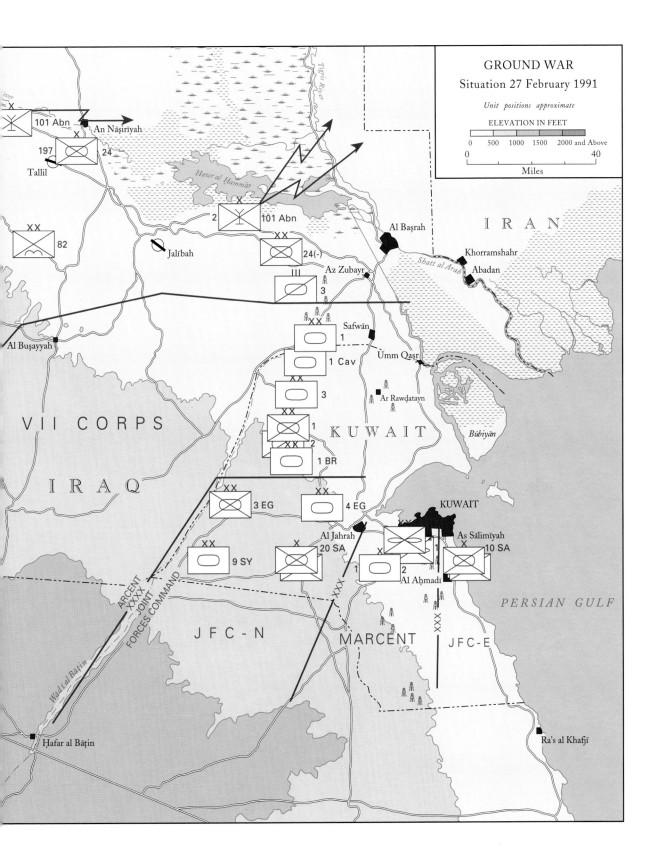

GROUND WAR
Situation 27 February 1991

Unit positions approximate

ELEVATION IN FEET

| 0 | 500 | 1000 | 1500 | 2000 and Above |

0   40

Miles

An Nāṣirīyah

101 Abn

197   24

Tallil

82

2   101 Abn

Jalībah

24(-)

III   Az Zubayr

3

Al Buṣayyah

XX   Safwān

1

1 Cav   Umm Qaṣr

3   Ar Rawḍatayn

1

2

1 BR

VII CORPS

IRAQ

KUWAIT

Būbiyān

3 EG   4 EG

Al Jahrah   KUWAIT

9 SY   20 SA   As Sālimīyah

1   10 SA

1   2   Al Aḥmadī

PERSIAN GULF

ARCENT
XXXX
JOINT
FORCES COMMAND

JFC-N   MARCENT   JFC-E

Wādī al Bāṭin

Ḥafar al Bāṭin   Ra's al Khafjī

An Nāṣirīyah

Al Baṣrah   IRAN

Khorramshahr

Shaṭṭ al Arab   Abadan

Tigris River

Hawr al Hammār

An abandoned Iraqi armored personnel carrier, exterior and interior views

An Iraqi T–72 tank, pene-trated and destroyed by two 120-mm. sabot rounds

Cease-fire

When the cease-fire ordered by President Bush went into effect, ARCENT divisions faced the beaten remnants of a once-formidable force. The U.S. Army had contributed the bulk of the ground combat power that defeated and very nearly destroyed the Iraqi ground forces. The Iraqis lost 3,847 of their 4,280 tanks, over half of their 2,880 armored personnel carriers, and nearly all of their 3,100 artillery pieces. Only five to seven of their forty-three combat divisions remained capable of offensive operations. In the days after the cease-fire the busiest soldiers were those engaged in the monumental task of counting and caring for an estimated 60,000 prisoners. And these surprising results came at the cost of 148 Americans killed in action. In the theater of operations Army Central Command had won the fastest and most complete victory in American military history.[50]

Of the many successful aspects of Army operations in Operation DESERT STORM, three stand out. First, Army units moved so fast that they found their enemy consistently out of position and oriented in the wrong direction. In 100 hours of combat XVIII Airborne Corps moved its lead elements 190 miles north into Iraq and then 70 miles east. Even the armor-heavy VII Corps drove 100 miles into Iraq and then 55 miles east. Iraqi units showed themselves unable to reposition even short distances before Army units were upon them.

Second, American forces enjoyed substantial technological advantages, most notably in night vision and electro-optics. Two types of vision-enhancing technology had been incorporated into Army operations preceding the deployment to the Persian Gulf. One of these aids to vision represented advanced development of a device first field tested during the Vietnam War, the image intensification system known as

[50] Third U.S. Army, After Action Review, 12 Mar 91; ODCSINT Intelligence Summary 412, 1 Mar 91; *Washington Post*, 13 Jun 91.

On the Kuwaiti border moments after the cease-fire

Starlight. Gathering and concentrating the faint light of the moon and stars, Starlight offered a view of terrain out to about 100 yards in shades similar to a photographic negative. It did not depend on a transmitted beam that an adversary could detect. Still, it had drawbacks, among them the system's need for a clear night as well as expense, weight, and size. So the early Starlight scopes had been distributed only to specialized units, such as long-range patrol and sniper teams.

By 1991 image intensification systems had been refined to the point that small lightweight units could be used by individual soldiers, in the forms of night vision goggles and weapon sights. Among an entire family of night vision and electro-optical devices, three particular types showed the wide battlefield applicability of the technology. The AN/PVS–4 individual-served weapon sight could be used with the M16 rifle, the M60 machine gun, the M72 rocket launcher, and the M203 grenade launcher. Detached from these weapons, the sight offered commanders the ability to carry out night surveillance. The AN/PVS–7 night vision goggle was a head-mounted monocular unit for ground vehicle operation, map reading, navigation, maintenance, and first aid. The AN/AVS–6 aviation night vision imaging system was a binocular system that allowed helicopter pilots to conduct nocturnal missions as close to the ground as possible.[51]

Another category of vision enhancement technology—thermal imaging—avoided the need of image intensification systems for clear night skies and retained the advantage of passivity. By reading the heat signatures of vehicle engines and human bodies at distances beyond 2 miles, thermal-imaging systems penetrated visual barriers created by nighttime, dust storms, and rain or snow. These systems proved particularly useful on M1A1 tanks, Bradleys, TOW missile launchers, and Apache

[51] Ibid.; Wright interview.

The day after the war. Soldiers relax at forward operating base COBRA.

helicopters. When combined with laser range-finding systems on armored vehicles, thermal imaging gave crews the ability to fire on targets—the troops called them "hot spots"—before the enemy even knew they were there.[52]

Soldiers at all levels enthusiastically praised all of the imagery devices. American troops were able to carry out night or day combat operations with virtually the same efficiency. This equipment vastly surpassed the obsolescent Soviet equipment used by the Iraqis and overturned the age-old assumption that the force fighting on its own territory had an inherent advantage. By seeing the heat signatures of Iraqi tanks and other vehicles on their thermal-imaging scopes before their own appeared on Iraqi scopes, Americans could engage targets in heavy rain, dust storms, and darkness. So, throughout the ground war the Iraqis, on their own familiar territory, were continually subjected to accurate fire in conditions, at distances, and from directions they did not expect.[53]

Other products of advanced technology contributed significantly to success. Two location and navigation devices, named Trimpack and Magellan by their manufacturers, minimized disorientation on the ground, a perennially serious problem that was magnified by the featureless desert environs of Southwest Asia. Trimpack (officially called the small lightweight global positioning system receiver) was dubbed "Slugger" by the troops. Both devices weighed about six pounds and were small enough to fit in a pack. They had solid-state electronics that read transmissions from orbiting satellites and gave their users precise coordinate locations. Both also determined firing data for artillery units, corrected azimuth bearings to objectives, and measured angles of descent for aircraft heading for landing zones or targets. Magellan and Trimpack rendered the age-old problems of map or terrain-reading errors obsolete.

[52] VII Corps Sitrep, 27 Feb 91.

[53] MS, Lt Col Gregory Fontenot, commander, 2/34th Armor, Attack on Objective NORFOLK, 26 Mar 91, p. 1.

Among weapons, the AH–64A Apache attack helicopter, armed with HELLFIRE missiles, belied its reputation as an overly complex, breakdown-prone system. The Apache proved a highly effective tank killer. The multiple launch rocket system and Army tactical missile system demonstrated great effect against entrenched enemy and in counterbattery missions in their own right. When combined with the Firefinder device to locate the source of enemy fire, the rocket and missile systems suppressed Iraqi artillery fire quickly and permanently. Because of the Firefinder advantage, enemy batteries were rarely heard from in XVIII Airborne Corps' sector after the first two days of the conflict, a great relief to Army commanders concerned about one of the few advantages of the Iraqis—the greater range of their newer artillery. The older mainstays of Army artillery, 155-mm. and 8-inch (203-mm.) pieces, underlined their well-founded reputations as accurate and dependable direct support systems.[54]

Just as impressive as the high-technology Army inventory at the beginning of the crisis in late 1990 was the ability of American defense agencies to answer demands from Central Command for new products. A dramatic example of this response capability came in the days before the ground war. The successful allied counterattack on the city of R'as al Khafjī in the first week of February was marred when American support fire killed several CENTCOM troops. General Schwarzkopf ordered accelerated research on antifratricide methods. A joint research team, coordinated by the Defense Advanced Research Projects Agency, immediately went to work on the problem of making American vehicles and positions visible only to American armored vehicles and aircraft. Just nineteen days later Central Command distributed the results of the agency's work: On the Army side of the research effort the Center for Night Vision and Electro-Optics at Fort Belvoir, Virginia, came up with the Budd Light and over twenty other solutions to the problem, some of which were fielded before the end of the war.[55]

Third, American soldiers outperformed their Iraqi enemies. Particularly gratifying to higher-echelon commanders was the conduct of personnel in the all-important middle-level action positions: junior officers and noncommissioned officers. Those were the lieutenants and sergeants who took the initiative to lead convoys across dangerous desert expanses at night to resupply the advance; found and engaged thousands of enemy tanks and positions in the confusion of heavy rains and blinding dust storms; and, when called for, treated a defeated enemy with dignity and care. As General McCaffrey observed of his junior officers and noncommissioned officers during the 24th Division's dash to the Euphrates River valley, "They could have done it without us."[56]

The impressive overall performance notwithstanding, problems requiring postwar attention did occur. Several types of equipment drew criticism from commanders. American field radios proved unreliable, and commanders who had the opportunity to try British-made Iraqi radios

[54] Wright interview.

[55] John F. Morton, "DARPA, Industry Fielded Antifratricide Device in 19 Days," *Armed Forces Journal International* (May 1991): 58, 60; Interv, Charles R. Anderson with Walter B. Morrow, Center for Night Vision and Electro-Optics, 27 Jun 91, Fort Belvoir, Va.

[56] McCaffrey interview.

pronounced them superior. Fortunately, the initiative of key commissioned and enlisted personnel at the battalion and company levels bridged communications gaps at crucial times. In a curious split decision on a weapon, the M109 155-mm. field artillery piece won praise for fire effect on targets, but its self-propelling component proved underpowered to keep pace with mechanized and armored assaults. One piece of combat engineer equipment earned similar criticism. The M9 armored combat earthmover cut through berms easily but could not keep up with assaults over open terrain.

Despite its brevity, the 100-hour Persian Gulf war lasted long enough to provoke an update of the age-old postwar lament, criticism of the supply effort. This time, the speed of the advance exposed a shortcoming: helicopters, tanks, and Bradleys outdistanced supply trucks. Lifting fuel tanks and ammunition pallets by helicopter provided a quick fix, but choppers carrying fuel gulped it almost as fast as they delivered it. If the ground war had lasted longer, General Schwarzkopf would have had to halt the advance to fill forward operating bases. On the morning of 27 February, as VII Corps prepared to complete the destruction of the *Republican Guard Forces Command*, 1st and 3d Armored Division tanks were almost out of fuel.[57]

After isolating and evaluating various aspects of Army operations and systems, questions remained about the overall course of the war and its outcome. Was the Army really as good as the overwhelming victory and one-sided statistics of the war suggested? Was Iraq's military really that weak? Complete answers awaited more careful analysis of the combatants, but in the immediate aftermath of the ground campaign two conclusions seemed justified.

First, Iraq's military was not prepared for a war of rapid movement over great distances. The Iraqis, in their most recent combat experience against Iran, had developed skills at slow-paced, defense-oriented warfare. Those skills proved inadequate to stop an army with high-speed armor capabilities.

Second, Central Command used its air arm to devastating advantage. With air supremacy established more than a month before the ground war began, the success of General Schwarzkopf's well-conceived and dreadfully misnamed "Hail Mary" play—the huge corps-size envelopment to the west—was assured. The relentless day and night pounding of aerial bombardment made easier the task of coalition units not in the envelopment, for when they attacked straight ahead into Iraqi positions, they found enemy units less than 50-percent effective. The combination of a powerful air offensive, followed by a fast moving armor-reinforced ground campaign, proved extremely effective in the desert environs of Southwest Asia.

[57] Ibid.; Chamberlain interview; Memo, Lt Col Fontenot, 8 Mar 91, sub: Operation DESERT STORM After Action Report; MS, Swan, 1st Armored Division in Combat, 21–28 February 1991, p. 2.

Chapter 9

PROFILE OF THE NEW ARMY

In addition to raising and answering a variety of questions about weapons, doctrine, and organization, the Southwest Asia campaigns also tested the relatively new all-volunteer Army and its corollary, the total force policy. In so doing, the Persian Gulf crisis brought to the fore a wide range of issues concerning sex, race, and family, as well as conscientious objection and employment of civilians in a war zone. Almost as soon as the shooting stopped, political and defense analysts, the press, and the American public all started to scrutinize the performance of Regular Army, Army National Guard, and Army Reserve troops and to ask hard questions about not only the Army's readiness to defend the country on short notice and over the long term but also the monetary cost of this readiness.

The Army of the Persian Gulf war presented a vastly different profile from the Army of the Vietnam War era. While the force of the 1960s consisted mainly of eighteen- and nineteen-year-old male draftees, volunteers, both male and female, comprised the Army of 1990.[1] Moreover, the average soldiers were older, better educated, more highly trained, and had greater skills than soldiers of the immediate past, making them more difficult and expensive to replace. They were also far more likely to be married homeowners with dependent children than were soldiers of the Vietnam years.[2]

In 1973 the United States abolished the draft. Throughout the rest of the decade the Army had difficulty drawing enough volunteers, and the quality of recruits, as measured by the Armed Forces Qualification Test, was low. To obtain the necessary number and quality of volunteers in the 1980s, the Army pursued an aggressive publicity campaign, "Be All That You Can Be," and offered high school graduates substantial education subsidies, job training programs, and potential career advancement. Young people without the money for their education and those in dead-end service jobs found the incentives appealing. The Army College Fund offered potential recruits $17,000 towards college in exchange for two years of active service, $22,800 for three years, and $25,200 for four. That inducement attracted able people. The Army College Fund Plus, designed to attract recruits into hard-to-fill military specialties, offered

[1] Joseph L. Galloway, "Life on the Front Lines," *U.S. News & World Report* (24 December 1990): 28–37; Leslie Dreyfous, "From Teens in Vietnam to Parents in the Gulf," *Philadelphia Inquirer*, 20 Feb 91, p. 11.

[2] Ibid.; Tom Morganthau et al., "The Military's New Image," *Newsweek* (11 March 1991): 50–51.

even greater educational benefits for commitments of two years of active duty, followed by two years in the Army Reserve.[3]

Both programs attracted high-quality recruits. Young men and women from every sector of society, except the poor and illiterate and the extremely wealthy, joined the Army. The recruits were ambitious, intelligent, dedicated, and upwardly mobile. In 1990 almost 98 percent of enlistees had high school diplomas, compared with a graduate rate of 75 percent among civilians of the same age. And although fewer than 3 percent of enlisted soldiers had attended college, two-thirds of those between eighteen and twenty-one years of age expected to do so, compared to 57 percent of their civilian counterparts.[4] In any case, new recruits soon found themselves in the classroom, because all Army military occupational specialties required specific training.[5]

Minorities

The incentives used by the Army to recruit its volunteer force and the philosophy behind that concept remained politically controversial. Critics claimed that many young people entered the Army in response to a so-called poverty draft, joining not because they wanted to serve but because they found no opportunities for advancement in the civilian economy. The Army became a choice of last resort. The poverty draft, insisted critics, resulted in an overrepresentation of minorities in the Persian Gulf. Blacks, who made up between 11 and 12 percent of the population in 1990, comprised 32 percent of the Army's enlisted force

and 28 percent of the troops deployed to Southwest Asia. This fact drew unfavorable publicity and caused concern for some black leaders. Was it fair, they asked, that a disproportionate number of minority youth, lured through opportunities unavailable elsewhere, were required to risk their lives for their country in the desert?[6]

Supporters of the volunteer Army believed that the young blacks who joined the service represented an able and ambitious group. Edwin Dorn of the Brookings Institution reminded critics that "the kind of young men and women going into the military are not the kind that…would (otherwise) end up

Soldier returns home to his child

[3] Robert L. Phillips and John D. Blair, "The All-Volunteer Army: Fifteen Years Later," *Armed Forces and Society* 16:3 (Spring 1990): 329–50; Fred Tasker, "The Military Gets a New Identity," *Orange County Register*, 27 Sep 90, p. J1. For a general background on the establishment of the all-volunteer Army, see Robert K, Griffith, Jr., *The U.S. Army's Transition to the All-Volunteer Force, 1968–1974*, Army Historical Series (Washington, D.C.: U.S. Army Center of Military History, forthcoming).

[4] Doug Bandow, "The Volunteer Army Represents America," *Wall Street Journal*, 27 Nov 90, p. 16; Ronald Brownstein, "Volunteer Force: Is It Truly Fair?," *Los Angeles Times*, 6 Dec 90, p. 1.

[5] David Gergen, "America's New Heroes," *U.S. News & World Report* (11 February 1991): 5.

[6] Juan Williams, "Race and War in the Persian Gulf: Why Are Black Leaders Trying To Divide Blacks From the American Mainstream?," *Washington Post*, 20 Jan 91; "Representative Conyers Says Blacks Are Victims of Economy," *Washington Post*, 14 Feb 91; Information Paper, Maj Plumer, DAPE-HR-L, 19 Mar 91, sub: Racial/Ethnic and Gender Breakdown by CMF.

pushing drugs...." The ones who did well in the Army did so because they had the drive necessary for success in whatever career they chose. Richard L. Fernandez, a Congressional Budget Office analyst, added that "a young man from a community with family incomes 20 percent below average [was] only slightly more likely to enlist than one from an area with incomes 20 percent above the average." Essentially, the Army that went to Southwest Asia was middle class and happened to be both black and white. The black soldiers did not think of themselves as cannon fodder or victims. Instead, they saw themselves as professionals doing the jobs for which they had trained.[7]

Some analysts claimed resumption of the draft would create an Army more representative of the total population. Department of Defense spokesmen reminded critics that the Army did not want a pool of soldiers that was representative of the general population. The Army did not accept men and women who scored in the lowest third of the Armed Forces Qualification Test. Such individuals would be both expensive to train and difficult to place in an organization with very few "unskilled" jobs.[8]

No one denied that many young people, both black and white, entered the military with career advancement rather than warfare in mind. But no evidence has been found that such soldiers were less ready to fulfill their military obligations when called to do so. On the contrary, the well-educated, highly trained Army of the Persian Gulf war consisted of soldiers who were more mature than their cohorts of the past and who had fewer disciplinary problems. Married homeowners with dependent children, they had greater stakes in society and took fewer risks. Research indicated that they made more thoughtful, analytical soldiers who performed exceptionally well under battlefield stress.[9]

Women

The concept of the all-volunteer force required that the Army select the best of those who volunteered, regardless of race, sex, or quotas. When the Army had difficulty recruiting high-quality males into the enlisted ranks in the 1970s, the recruitment of women became crucial to the success of the volunteer force. "Had the Army not expanded the opportunities for women soldiers," noted Martin Binkin, a senior military analyst at the Brookings Institution, "it is doubtful if the All-Volunteer Force could have survived the 1970s."[10]

Sociologist Charles Moskos of Northwestern University agreed. He believed that women provided the "margin of success" for the all-volunteer force. Without women with superior formal education and mental test scores, the Army would have had to rely on less qualified male volunteers. Women, he said, allowed the United States to maintain the quality of its armed forces without conscription.[11]

In 1991 minorities and women constituted 49.1 percent of the Regular Army. The enlisted force was 41.3 percent minorities, with minority

[7] Williams, "Race and War in the Persian Gulf."

[8] David Evans, "Some Urge Draft To Ensure a War Is Classless Struggle," *Chicago Tribune*, 29 Nov 90, p. 1.

[9] Ibid.

[10] Robert K. Landers, "Should Women Be Allowed Into Combat?," *Congressional Quarterly's Editorial Research Reports* 2:14 (October 1989): 577.

[11] Ibid.

women making up 56.4 percent of enlisted females. Black women comprised 49 percent of enlisted females. Minorities made up 16.4 percent of the officer corps, with 25.6 percent of female officers from minority groups. Women accounted for over 11 percent of the Regular Army and 8 percent of the regulars deployed to the Persian Gulf. Women also accounted for 20.5 percent of Army reservists and 17 percent of the reserve soldiers in Saudi Arabia at the height of the conflict. All told, over 26,000 women from active and reserve components went to Southwest Asia. Women represented over 8.6 percent of the Army's deployed force.[12]

Although federal law mandated that the Navy and Air Force prohibit women from serving in direct combat roles, no such law bound the Army to do so. Instead, the Army used its combat exclusion policy to regulate itself to conform to the intent of the federal laws that affected the other services. Thus, the Army's combat exclusion policy limited women from direct combat. That policy defined direct combat as "engaging an enemy with individual or crew-served weapons while being exposed to direct enemy fire, a high probability of direct physical contact with the enemy's personnel, and a substantial risk of capture." According to the Army, "Direct combat takes place while closing with the enemy by fire, maneuver, or shock effect in order to destroy or capture, or while repelling assault by fire, close combat or counterattack."[13]

The Direct Combat Probability Coding System implemented the combat exclusion policy. The coding system evaluated every position in the Army based on its duties and the unit's mission, tactical doctrine, and position on the battlefield. The Army coded each position based on the probability of engaging in direct combat, with P1 representing the highest likelihood and P7 the lowest. Women were prohibited from P1 positions. An entire specialty could be closed to them if the number or grade distribution of positions coded P1 made advancement or development in that area impossible for women. At the time the Persian Gulf crisis occurred, 86 percent of all military occupational specialties in the Army were open to women.[14]

Army officials told the General Accounting Office in 1987 that battlefield location had the greatest impact on the rating of a position. The service generally rated jobs located forward of the brigade's rear boundary as P1, thus making them closed to women. However, women could move forward of the brigade's rear boundary temporarily to deliver supplies or fix equipment. Furthermore, no limit existed on how far forward a woman could travel during a temporary excursion.[15] Throughout the Persian Gulf war women visited the forward-deployed units periodically but were not stationed there.

Prevented by policy from assignments to direct combat positions, women served in jobs generally classified as combat support and combat service support. Combat support assignments, which provided operational help to the combat units, included civil engineering, military police, transporting personnel and equipment via truck or helicopter,

[12] Information Paper, Maj Plumer, DAPE-HR-L, 19 Mar 91, sub: Equal Opportunity Climate; Information Paper, Maj Etchieson, DAPE-HR-S, 19 Mar 91, sub: Women in SWA.

[13] MS, Women's Research and Education Institute, Women in the Military 1980–1990 [Washington, D.C., 1991], p. 9.

[14] Ibid., p. 10; Statement by Lt Gen William H. Reno, Deputy Chief of Staff for Personnel, U.S. Army, before the Subcommittee on Military Personnel and Compensation, Committee on Armed Services, House of Representatives, 102d Cong., 1st sess., 7 March 1991.

[15] MS, Women in the Military 1980–1990, p. 10; Landers, "Should Women Be Allowed Into Combat?," p. 572.

communications, and intelligence support. Combat service support positions provided logistical, technical, and administrative services (such as personnel, postal, medical, and finance) to the combat arm. Female soldiers worked in high concentrations in these areas. Black women, for example, represented a majority of the force in the following career fields: supply and services (55 percent), petroleum and water (58 percent), administration (52 percent), and food services (54 percent).[16]

The concentration of minorities and women behind the front lines in these roles resulted in relatively low casualty rates among these groups. As of 11 April 1991 the casualty count was as follows: whites killed in action—74 (78 percent), blacks killed in action—12 (13 percent), white nonbattle deaths—80, black nonbattle deaths—23, whites wounded in action—247, blacks wounded in action—95, white nonbattle injuries—167, and black nonbattle injuries—57. Eight women were killed, 5 in action and 3 in accidents.[17]

Analysts were concerned about the validity of the combat exclusion policy and reminded policy makers that even the most cursory examination of recent combat experience revealed that all divisional troops could be called on at any time to fight as infantry. That was true at Kasserine Pass in North Africa, in the Battle of the Bulge, in Korea, and in Vietnam. According to this viewpoint, all armies implicitly viewed all of their soldiers except medical personnel as infantrymen. But that notion was becoming outdated. Martin Binkin has contended that "with the growing sophistication of weapons, you can't hand a cook or a clerk a Dragon [an antitank weapon] and send him up there. The only soldiers who will know how to use that weapon are the ones who have spent time training to use it." Still, regardless of the complexity of the equipment, soldiers on the ground were the only ones capable of seizing terrain from an enemy and holding it.[18]

Although U.S. forces sustained relatively few casualties in the Persian Gulf, the combat exclusion policy did not protect women from being among them. Women died while performing their duties just as men did. The Iraqi missile that destroyed a U.S. Army barrack in Dhahran, 200 miles from the Kuwaiti border, killed 3 women along with 25 men. Of the other 2 female soldiers killed in action, 1 died in a helicopter crash and the other in an antipersonnel mine explosion. Nineteen women were wounded in action, while 2 were taken prisoner of war. Three women died in nonbattle deaths and 13 suffered nonbattle injuries.[19]

S. Sgt. Tatiana Dees of the 92d Military Police Company out of Baumholder, Germany, became the first female nonbattle fatality in DESERT SHIELD. On 7 January 1991 she fell from a pier at the port city of Ad Dammām and drowned. She had been on patrol with another military police officer when she noticed an unknown person atop a crane photographing the port. Dees stayed to help after the local police arrived. Looking upward, unaware of the edge of the pier, she accidentally fell into the water. She was pulled out, but attempts to revive her

[16] Information Paper, Plumer, sub: Equal Opportunity Climate; Information Paper, Etchieson, sub: Women in SWA; Landers, "Should Women Be Allowed Into Combat?," p. 572; MS, Women in the Military 1980–1990, pp. 9–10.

[17] Information Paper, Plumer, sub: Equal Opportunity Climate; Information Paper, Etchieson, sub: Women in SWA; Executive Summary, Capt Buckmaster, TAPC-PLF, 11 Apr 91, sub: REDCAT Data on DESERT SHIELD/STORM Casualties; Executive Summary, Lt Col Roberts, CMAOC, 11 Apr 91, sub: DESERT STORM Demographics.

[18] Landers, "Should Women Be Allowed Into Combat?," pp. 578–80.

[19] Information Paper, Etchieson, sub: Women in SWA; List, Maj James C. Trower, TAPC-MOB, 18 Apr 91, sub: In Response to the DCSPER Query Regarding Female KIA/NBD and on the Civilian Death.

failed. Dees was 34 and the mother of a seven-year-old daughter and a son aged five.[20]

Another woman, Sgt. Sheri L. Barbato, worked as a records keeper in a vehicle maintenance unit of the 1st Cavalry Division (Armored). Her unit crossed the border into Iraq on the opening night of the fighting. Barbato later remembered thinking, "I didn't think women were supposed to get this close to the front lines." Thereafter, she was unconvinced of the viability of the exclusion policy. "There wasn't anything over there that happened to the guys that didn't happen to me," she said. "There were times when I would have welcomed the opportunity to fight back."[21]

Lt. Phoebe Jeter, "the first female Scudbuster," led a platoon of fifteen men assigned to a Patriot missile control team. She identified incoming Scuds, ascertained their location on a computer screen, and gave her men orders to destroy them. Her job entailed a great deal of pressure: If she did not destroy the Scuds that she saw on her screen, they could land on her base. Jeter had trained for three years in her assignment. As a result of her performance, she became the first woman in her battalion to earn an Army Commendation Medal while in Saudi Arabia.[22]

Sgt. Barbara Bates, 28, a meteorologist, was the sole woman serving with more than 700 artillerymen in a forward-based self-propelled howitzer artillery unit of the 24th Infantry Division (Mechanized). Bates had a noncombat specialty but was supporting a combat unit. As long as her assigned duties matched her noncombat specialty, her assignment fell within Army policy. She provided the combat troops with swift, precise readouts of local winds, temperature, and other conditions that could make the difference between a killing shot and a wasted round. Combat related or not, Bates was in as much danger as the male soldier standing beside her firing the howitzer. "When the shells start coming downwind, I will be counting on my flak jacket for protection, not my MOS," she laughed.[23]

Sgt. Bonnie Riddell, a 27-year-old military policewoman from Fort Hood, Texas, spent her nights on perimeter duty. Like other guards she worked thirteen-hour shifts on a sandbagged observation post, which she shared with a male soldier. She carried a .45-caliber pistol at her hip, had an M16 rifle at her side, and manned a light machine gun. Riddell told a reporter who interviewed her while on duty that she was nervous and scared, but added: "If it happens while I'm sitting here, and it's a question of me or them, it's going to be them."[24]

The 24th Support Battalion (Forward), 24th Infantry Division, was the most forward-deployed American supply battalion in Saudi Arabia. Women comprised nearly one-quarter of the battalion's 400 troops. The battalion kept tank crews and infantry supplied with food, fuel, medicine, spare parts, and ammunition. To accomplish that, male and female soldiers of the 24th drove trucks and water and gas tankers, manned radios, and stood guard. Both men and women slept with their M16s "right next to us, like part of our bodies." Conditions in the desert were

[20] Memo for the Deputy Chief of Staff of Personnel, 16 Jan 91.

[21] Jon Nordheimer, "Women's Role in Combat: The War Resumes," *New York Times*, 26 May 91, p. 28.

[22] Jeannie Ralston, "Women's Work," *Life* (May 1991): 56.

[23] Colin Nickerson, "Combat Barrier Blurs for Women on the Front Line," *Boston Globe*, 13 Nov 90.

[24] Tony Clifton, "You're Here. They're There. It's Simple," *Newsweek* (12 November 1990): 28.

A military policewoman on patrol, as depicted in the painting "Patrol Duty in Kuwait City"

tough, and the women complained no less than the men. But everyone, men and women alike, did the work they had to do.[25]

The American public saw female troops working side by side with men in the desert on the network news. A woman briefed General Schwarzkopf nightly with the latest military intelligence. Interviewers talked to women who fixed the engines of fighter jets, drove trucks, piloted supply planes, commanded communications centers, stood guard duty, tracked ships and planes on radar, served in secret intelligence units, and performed surgery in field hospitals. They learned that a woman led a company of Chinook helicopters into Iraq on the first day of the ground war.[26]

Although women could not fly combat aircraft during DESERT STORM, they engaged in many activities that exposed them to the same risks as men. Female helicopter pilots, while not participating in direct combat, flew into combat zones to move food, fuel, and soldiers around the battlefield and to evacuate wounded soldiers. Three percent, or 380, of the Army's 13,650 active-duty pilots were women.[27]

[25] Quote from Ibid. Mariam Isa, "Some Female Soldiers Want Out," *Washington Times*, 27 Sep 90, p. 1; James LeMoyne, "Army Women and the Saudis: The Encounter Shocks Both," *New York Times*, 25 Sep 90, p. 1.

[26] Ibid.

[27] Eric Schmitt, "Head of the Army Sees Chance of Female Fliers in Combat," *New York Times*, 31 May 91.

The death of Maj. Marie Rossi, a helicopter pilot interviewed by CNN shortly before her aircraft crashed returning from a supply mission, became a well-publicized tragedy. Rossi, a pilot with the XVIII Airborne Corps, was one of the first female soldiers over the border into Iraq when she led her company of Chinook helicopters in supplying ammunition to combat troops. "What I'm doing is no greater or less than the man who is flying next to me or in back of me," she said during the interview. Major Rossi died with her three crew members when their Chinook crashed into an unlit microwave tower during bad weather the day after the cease-fire.[28]

Two female soldiers were taken prisoner by the Iraqis. Both women received considerable media attention, but Army Spc. Melissa Rathbun-Nealy became a media-inspired instant celebrity because she was captured first and held longer. Rathbun-Nealy, aged 20, and her partner Spc. David Lockett, both of the 233d Transportation Company, were wounded and captured by the Iraqis on 30 January.

As the first American female prisoner of war in fifty years, Rathbun-Nealy rapidly captured the public's imagination. Her company had been in Saudi Arabia since October. She, Lockett, and two other soldiers went to retrieve two heavy equipment vehicles being repaired near Dhahran. On 30 January the vehicles were ready, and the four soldiers set out from Dhahran with maps to return the trucks to their unit. They passed through an intersection, failed to turn west as directed, and mistakenly headed toward R'as al Khafji, where heavy fighting was going on. The two trucks passed through several Saudi checkpoints. As they approached R'as al Khafjī, they came under fire. The driver of the second truck made a U-turn and retreated. Looking back, the soldiers saw the lead truck stuck in the sand. Enemy troops quickly surrounded the vehicle. Rathbun-Nealy and Lockett were held as prisoners of war in Baghdad for over a month before they were released with other U.S. prisoners on 4 March 1991.[29]

The second American female soldier captured by the Iraqis was Maj. Rhonda L. Cornum. Cornum, 36, was an Army flight surgeon with an Apache attack helicopter battalion. She had volunteered for a helicopter search-and-rescue mission and crashed behind enemy lines. Five of the helicopter's eight crew members were killed. Cornum was listed as missing, and it was not known that she was a prisoner until a day or so before her release.[30]

Congresswoman Patricia S. Schroeder of Colorado believed that after the war the American voter was willing for the first time to accept the lifting of the ban on servicewomen in direct combat. Other observers claimed that Desert Storm was not a fair test of the capabilities of female soldiers under pressure, because the war was short and casualties low. So, for some, questions remained about the performance of female soldiers over the long haul.[31]

In an Associated Press poll on women in combat, conducted between 13 and 17 February 1991, with a sample of 1,007 adults from forty-eight states, 56 percent responded that women in the armed forces should par-

[28] Joseph F. Sullivan, "Army Pilot's Death Stuns Her New Jersey Neighbors," *New York Times*, 7 Mar 91, p. B1.

[29] Mary Radigan, "Army Details How Melissa Got Lost, Was Captured by the Iraqis," *Grand Rapids Press*, 25 Feb 91, p. A8.

[30] *Washington Post*, 6 Mar 91.

[31] Lorraine Dushy, "Combat Ban Stops Women's Progress, Not Bullets," *McCall's Magazine* (May 1990): 26.

ticipate in the war and 39 percent believed they should not. While 45 percent would not have objected to women from their family participating, 50 percent did not want to see a female family member deploy as a soldier. This contrasted substantially with the 22 percent who would have objected to a male member of their family fighting in Southwest Asia. Although 35 percent believed men and women were equally suited for combat, 61 percent believed men were better qualified. Thirty-one percent believed it was acceptable to send women with young children to the Persian Gulf; 64 percent found that unacceptable. Only 28 percent thought it was unacceptable to send young fathers, and 68 percent believed it was acceptable.[32]

Charles Moskos observed that female officers wanted the combat exclusion policy abolished, because it inhibited their careers, but that enlisted women felt differently.[33] The difference of opinion may have been due to education levels. The more education women received, the more they believed in equal rights. The vast majority of Army officers had at least bachelor's degrees, and many had higher degrees or planned to pursue them. Most enlisted women had high school diplomas, although many planned to attend college in the future.[34]

Due to the professionalism with which female soldiers did their jobs in the war, Secretary of Defense Richard B. Cheney stated that he "would not be surprised" if women's combat roles were eventually expanded. In fact, during the last week of May 1991 the House of Representatives approved a military budget bill with a provision removing the legislative language that had precluded women in the Navy, Marines, and Air Force from flying aircraft in combat missions. As the Army patterned its combat exclusion policy on the legal restrictions pertaining to the other services, it could follow their lead and open direct combat flying positions to women. Army women themselves were divided on whether they wanted to engage in direct combat, but the vast majority believed they should be given the opportunity to choose.[35]

Postwar Recruiting

Some military analysts believed the war would be followed by a decline in the numbers of volunteers for military duty. They suggested that those tempted to join the Army or the reserve components primarily because of the educational benefits would hesitate now that they might actually be expected to go overseas and fight. Immediate postwar recruitment figures did not confirm that suspicion. During the first quarter of fiscal year 1991, for example, the Regular Army enlisted 26,936 soldiers against a quarterly goal of 25,700. Ninety-six percent of these were high school graduates and 73 percent scored in the top half of the Armed Forces Qualification Test.[36]

Reserve-component recruitment showed a significant overall decline. Army National Guard recruiters achieved 72 percent of their goal and the Army Reserve reached 77 percent in the first quarter of 1991. During the

[32] Associated Press Gulf Poll, 20 Feb 91.

[33] Nordheimer, "Women's Role in Combat"; Landers, "Should Women Be Allowed Into Combat?," p. 2.

[34] MS, Women in the Military 1980–1990, p. 2.

[35] Schmitt, "Head of Army Sees Chance of Female Fliers in Combat."

[36] Statement by Lt Gen William H. Reno, Deputy Chief of Staff for Personnel, U.S. Army, before the Subcommittee on Military Personnel and Compensation, Committee on Armed Services, House of Representatives, 102d Cong., 1st sess., 7 March 1991, p. 8.

crisis the Army's "Stop Loss" program held soldiers who might have completed terms of service, many of whom would have gone into the reserves.[37] In addition, during the first months of DESERT SHIELD reserve units were prevented from recruiting once they were activated, so activated units could not fill vacancies through recruitment. Furthermore, the recruiting services were limited with respect to the units and positions against which they could recruit people. Analysts realized that this practice would create a long-term shortage for reserve units once hostilities ceased and units went home. So the policy was reversed in late November, when reasons for the recruitment shortage became clear. While new enlistees did not deploy with the unit, they were scheduled for training and would be available to man the unit when it returned.[38]

Family Readiness

In early 1991 the Army had 51,849 soldiers with military spouses—33,179 men and 18,670 women. Of this total, 9,000 were deployed to Southwest Asia. Within that 9,000, there were 2,462 couples with dependent children.[39]

The Army required both single and dual military parents to set up care arrangements in the event that they were deployed. Single and dual military parents maintained up-to-date family care plans that included all the provisions necessary for the care of dependents when the soldier deployed, such as powers of attorney for temporary and long-term guardians, notarized certificates of acceptance as guardians, identification card applications, and signed allotment forms or other financial support documentation. Regulations required annual review and validation of the plans. If a commander found a plan to be inadequate, the soldier had to fix it or face separation from the service. The same provisions applied to members of the Selected Reserve, but individual ready reservists did not have to complete the necessary paperwork until activated. Then they either developed an acceptable family care plan or faced separation.[40]

Inevitably, some plans proved unrealistic, and others became outdated because of circumstances beyond the soldier's control. Designated guardians became ill or injured and were unable to care for the children as planned. Some guardians discovered that the strains of caring for dependents were too much for them physically or emotionally. Longer deployments resulted in a higher number of failed plans.[41] The Army could do little about that except continue to replace soldiers who could not remedy family care problems.

When a plan failed, Army regulations required that the soldier attempt to arrange alternate care while remaining on duty. That was not always possible. During the Persian Gulf war the Army permitted soldiers to return home for a maximum of thirty days to resolve family care problems. The Army voluntarily or involuntarily separated any soldier who could not establish a workable alternative plan within that time.[42]

[37] Ibid.; JULLS Long Rpt, JULLS 51760–11293 (00028), Lt Col Dennis Winn, DAPE-MPA, 21 May 91, sub: Recruiting During Hostilities.

[38] Ibid.; DESERT STORM After Action Rpt, Lt Col Winn, DAPE-MPA, 23 May 91.

[39] Information Paper, Lt Col (Chaplain) Jack Anderson, DAPE-HR-S, 19 Mar 91, sub: Single Parents/Dual Military Couples.

[40] Information Paper, Lt Col Anderson, 11 Mar 91, sub: Family Care Plans AR–600–20.

[41] Barbara Kantrowitz and Mike Mason, "The Soldier-Parent Dilemma: Which Comes First, Children or Country?," *Newsweek* (12 November 1990): 84.

[42] Rick Maze, "Immediate Change in Family Policy Unlikely," *Army Times*, 26 Feb 91, p. 8.

Family assistance center, Fort Riley, Kansas, where volunteers provided information and support to the families of lst Infantry Division soldiers during the Persian Gulf crisis

Throughout the crisis, the majority of readiness problems occurred in units unaccustomed to regular deployments. More soldiers in these units turned out to be nondeployable or lost deployment time because of outdated or unrealistic family care plans. In units that practiced deployment regularly, single and dual military parents were generally fully ready to go. The results indicated that the best way to ensure realistic plans and the deployability of the force was to test readiness in all units regularly. After all, the best way to discover if something worked properly was to try it. The maximum number of Forces Command and U.S. Army, Europe, soldier family care plans that proved to be inadequate at any one time was 124. In many of those cases solutions were found in time for the soldiers to deploy.[43]

Studies showed that soldiers who knew that their families experienced difficulties back home performed less efficiently and were more vulnerable to stress-induced mental and physical illness and accidents. Family assistance centers and informal family support groups organized at the unit level helped maintain the morale and efficiency of the deployed

[43] Information Paper, Lt Col Theodore Parukawa, CFSC-AE-R, 24 Jan 90, sub: Soldier Deployability and Family Situation.

force.[44] The 166 Army-sponsored assistance centers functioning in the United States proved particularly valuable to the families of soldiers who went to Southwest Asia. In areas that did not have assistance centers, informal volunteer-run support groups provided information and support to the families of soldiers in the Persian Gulf. Those organizations helped with problems ranging from monetary and legal difficulties through medical and psychological illnesses.[45]

Press reports focused on the various stresses and strains with which the families of soldiers coped. Some families handled the situation better than others. Invariably their experiences were as different as the families themselves. Supply Spc. Michele Brown, a 21-year-old single mother, went to Saudi Arabia with the 202d Military Intelligence Battalion. Brown left her 3-year-old daughter with her own mother. While in the Persian Gulf, Brown learned that her daughter was hospitalized with asthma. "It's hard being a single parent and going to war," said Brown. "I don't want to be here."[46]

Married soldiers had their own problems. Some young wives who remained behind while their husbands deployed had never driven a car, paid a bill, or balanced a checkbook. Young couples without children sometimes made no arrangements to deal with a deployment. Young wives were left without access to bank accounts. Some soldiers put their cars in unit lockups when they left because they did not want their wives to drive them. The women were left with no transportation. One soldier locked his foreign-born wife into their trailer with three weeks' groceries and no plan for a longer deployment. The Inspector General's Office at Fort Hood, Texas, estimated that 28 percent of the young wives of deployed soldiers left the Fort Hood vicinity and returned "home" to live with relatives for the duration of the deployment. Fort Stewart, Georgia, and Fort Bragg, North Carolina, reported similar developments.[47]

More than 14,000 women gave birth without the support of their husband's physical presence. Many spouses with infants and small children felt like single parents and had problems coping with confused and frightened children. Some schools noticed increased truancy rates as the children struggled to deal with their fears. Some spouses who stayed behind developed stress-related illnesses, from insomnia through migraines, ulcers, and changes in weight.[48]

Family assistance centers and support groups gave the families of deployed soldiers the information, advice, and emotional support they needed to help deal with those problems. Those organizations also provided critical information to guardians unfamiliar with standard military services and procedures. For example, some guardians had trouble obtaining military identification cards, which gave the children of military parents access to military services and facilities such as medical care. Although by law military dependents were entitled to medical care, some guardians had trouble obtaining it for the children in their care.[49]

[44] MS, Lt Col David J. Westhuis, Human Factors in Operation DESERT SHIELD: The Role of Family Factors, U.S. Army Community and Family Support Center, 9 Nov 90.

[45] Bulletin 16–90, 28 Nov 90, Directorate of Public Affairs, Headquarters, Forces Command, Fort McPherson, Ga.

[46] Eric Schmitt, "War Puts U.S. Servicewomen Closer Than Ever to Combat," *New York Times*, 22 Jan 91.

[47] MS, Westhuis, Human Factors in Operation DESERT SHIELD: The Role of Family Factors, p. 9; Galloway, "Life on the Front Lines," pp. 28–37.

[48] Ibid.; Lara Marlowe, "Life on the Line," *Time* (25 February 1991): 36–38.

[49] JULLS Long Rpt, JULLS 51669–84605 (00014), DAPE-HR-S, 21 May 91, sub: Secure ID Cards and Agent's Letters by Guardians.

The dependents of Army Reserve and Army National Guard personnel had special problems. As of July 1990, only 22 percent of reserve and 21 percent of guard personnel had pre-enrolled their family members in the Defense Enrollment and Eligibility Reporting System, the program that automatically entitled them to medical care. The paperwork necessary for enrollment often could not be accomplished during the mobilization period.[50]

Soldiers who went to the Persian Gulf from Europe had unique family care problems. Often, the guardians designated by family care plans lived in the United States. In many cases the deployment came so fast that soldiers did not have time to escort dependents home to the United States and return to their units in Europe in time to deploy with them.[51]

Not every family needed an assistance center or a support group. Some spouses accepted and enjoyed the new challenges they faced. Optometrist and Washington State Senator Mike Kreidler, an Army Reserve lieutenant colonel with the 6250th U.S. Army Hospital, was called to active duty for three months early in 1991. According to state law, Kreidler had to give his county commissioners a list of three candidates qualified to carry out his senatorial responsibilities while he was gone. One of the names on his list was that of his wife. Mrs. Kreidler was surprised when chosen to fill in for her husband. She had never been interested in "becoming a public figure and inhabiting the limelight." But she accepted because "she knew how much politics and serving in the legislature meant to her husband, and he needed to be sure that the person inhabiting his position was someone he could trust, someone who shared common views on legislative matters." Enjoying the work more than she expected, she began considering entering politics herself.[52]

The deployment of single and dual military parents caused a great deal of controversy and comment among the press and the public. The concern was inevitably reflected in Congress. Should the services deploy single and dual military parents to a combat area? The image of mothers kissing small children good-bye to march off to war, and the specter of large numbers of war orphans, bothered many politicians as well as their constituents. Congress responded to public concern with several different proposals, all seeking to limit the Defense Department's ability to send parents of dependent children to a combat zone.

Senator John Heinz of Pennsylvania proposed a nonbinding resolution asking the Department of Defense to consider a policy allowing single parents and one member of dual military parents a noncombat zone duty assignment. The bill sponsored by Congresswoman Barbara Boxer of California would have limited the military's ability to send single parents and both military parents into a combat zone. Congressman E. Clay Shaw, Jr., of Florida proposed that mothers of children under six months of age not be assigned to an area subject to hostile fire. Others in Congress who expressed public concern and who proposed changes in

[50] JULLS Long Rpt, JULLS 51671–64420 (00016), Maj Scott Howard, DASG-PSA, 21 May 91, sub: Reserve, NG DEERS Eligibility.

[51] JULLS Long Rpt, JULLS 51671–10083, DAPE-HR-S, 21 May 91, sub: FCP, Single Parents, Dual Military Couples, NEO, Escorts, Guardians, OCONUS.

[52] Bill Timnick, "Reservist Gave Senate Seat to Spouse During DS," *The Ranger* (Army Reserve Newsletter, Fort Lewis, Wash.), n.d.

Department of Defense assignment policies included Senator Herb Kohl from Wisconsin and Congresswoman Jill L. Long of Indiana.[53] The Department of Defense, opposed to all limitations on its ability to deploy soldiers overseas, claimed such restrictions were not needed given the volunteer nature of the force and the overall success of the family care plans.[54] Because large numbers of casualties did not occur, the political pressure to resolve the issue of the deployment of single parents to a combat zone was minimal, and the issue remained unresolved.

The war in Southwest Asia resulted in the deaths of three soldiers with custody of minor children, one woman and two men. In each case, the soldier's family care plan had designated long-term guardians. Two of the designated guardians accepted the children in question. In the third case the soldier's family petitioned a court to make alternative arrangements.[55]

Pregnant Soldiers

Pregnancy became another highly controversial issue related to readiness and deployability. At any time over the past several years, 7 to 8 percent of female soldiers have been pregnant or on maternity leave. That percentage remained static throughout the war.[56] Unit commanders, however, noticed that the percentage of nondeployable female soldiers was significantly higher than that of nondeployable male soldiers. In some units, as many as 18 to 20 percent of females could not go due to disqualifying physical profiles.[57] Pregnancy was the major contributor to the disparity. Nondeployable soldiers had to be replaced before a unit could function at full strength. Commanders had to anticipate a higher rate of nondeployability among female soldiers and plan accordingly.

Another issue revolved around the amount of leave time granted to female soldiers after giving birth. Several highly publicized episodes involving maternity leave led to criticism of existing Army policies. Two Pennsylvania reservists gave birth shortly after receiving their call-up papers. Although one had a Caesarean section, she was originally allowed only a fifteen-day delay. The other initially received a ten-day leave.[58] In both cases the Army resolved the mistake made at the Reserve Call-Up Center and granted the women the standard amount of time they were entitled to by regulation.[59]

Regulation allowed female members of the Regular Army, Army National Guard, and Army Reserve a recovery period after birth of forty-two days, after which they had to return to duty or leave the service. The situation encountered by the two Pennsylvania reservists mentioned above indicated a problem in the Individual Ready Reserve call-up process. The Individual Ready Reserve is a category into which the Army placed active-duty soldiers unable to perform their duties because of health or family problems but who had an unexpired term of service. Both women had left the Regular Army and entered the Individual Ready Reserve because of their pregnancies.[60] In the event of

[53] Maze, "Immediate Change in Family Policy Unlikely," p. 8; Dana Priest, "G.I.'s Left 17,500 Children," *Washington Post*, 15 Feb 91, p. 1; *Washington Post*, 20 Feb 91.

[54] Ltr, Secretary of Defense Cheney and General Powell to George Mitchell, Majority Leader, U.S. Senate, 7 Feb 91.

[55] Briefing to DCSPER, Lt Col Donald Pavlik, DAPE-ZX, 19 Mar 91.

[56] Interv, Judith L. Bellafaire with Maj Marlene Etchieson and Lt Col (Chaplain) Jack Anderson, Apr 91.

[57] "Personnel Service Support," in *Getting to the Desert* (Fort Leavenworth, Kans.: Center for Army Lessons Learned, n.d.), pp. 1–2.

[58] "University of Penn Researcher Says Army Calls New Mothers to Duty Too Soon," *Philadelphia Inquirer*, 12 Feb 91.

[59] Interv, Judith L. Bellafaire with Col Terrence Hulin, DAPE-HR, 14 Nov 91.

[60] Katherine Seelye, "Called to Duty While in Labor," *Philadelphia Inquirer*, 6 Feb 91.

a call-up, the very factors that placed the soldiers into the reserve often made them unavailable for deployment.[61] The call-up process confused many reservists; however, if they could supply a doctor's note describing them as unfit for duty because of a medical condition, they were granted leave. Approximately 430 individual ready reservists eventually obtained leave from their commands through the proper channels due to documented health problems.[62]

Reserve soldiers ordered to duty while in their first trimester of pregnancy were activated but not deployed. They were assigned duties in the United States. The Army dealt with soldiers in their second and third trimesters on a case-by-case basis. Usually the Army retained them with light or even part-time duty. Soldiers in Saudi Arabia found to be pregnant by military physicians were sent to their home base for prenatal care and continued duty. Conditions in the Persian Gulf, from the climate to the weight of chemical protective gear worn by all soldiers, did not meet Army standards for the assigned duties of pregnant soldiers.[63]

Sole Survivors

Another family-related issue that appeared in the press involved the issue of whether the services should deploy sole surviving sons and daughters into a combat area. Those soldiers were the only remaining offspring of a family that had lost a father, mother, or sibling to combat or a duty-related accident during a war. Many soldiers fit into this category.[64]

Army policy allowed eligible soldiers to apply through their units for sole survivor status, which would place them in assignments in the United States or another noncombat area. The services allowed the soldiers to refuse sole survivor status if they desired.[65] The Army believed the policy was fair and that it worked well. Once again, the low level of casualties in the Persian Gulf war prevented this dilemma from remaining in the forefront of public concern.

Personnel Shortages

Throughout the Persian Gulf crisis the Army had to fill critical and unexpected shortages in unusual specialties. For example, the Army had a sudden yet critical need for relatively scarce Arabic linguists specializing in the Iraqi dialect. The Army's language school, the Defense Language Institute, had concentrated for years on training Russian and Eastern European experts. The sudden shift in priorities caught the school unprepared. Arabic, a complicated language, required sixteen weeks of intensive training to acquire only minimal skills. The institute immediately began an accelerated training program for an increased number of candidates, since the attrition rate in Arabic was 28 percent. To answer the Army's immediate need, the institute initiated some stopgap measures, including an abbreviated course in Iraqi Arabic for soldiers conversant in

[61] Discussion Paper, Chaplain Anderson, 13 Mar 90, sub: Single Parents/Dual Military Parents.

[62] Hulin interview.

[63] Etchieson interview.

[64] AR 614–200, *Assignments, Details, and Transfers: Selection of Enlisted Soldiers for Training and Assignment* (1982), sec. IV 3–16.

[65] Ibid.

other dialects, such as Syrian and Egyptian; an Iraqi dialect video crash course in military terminology; and an Iraqi dialect dictionary. The video and dictionary were sent to Saudi Arabia to help intelligence officers already in the field.[66]

The U.S. Total Army Personnel Command found several Arabic linguists at Forts Campbell (Kentucky), Stewart (Georgia), and Devens (Massachusetts), as well as three serving in non-language positions in Germany and two in Hawaii.[67] On 14 January the retraining of about 160 high-caliber German, French, Polish, and Chinese Mandarin linguists began at four sites. Those people were scheduled to be available for deployment to Southwest Asia by mid-July.[68]

The Army also experienced shortages of truck drivers, helicopter pilots, and medical personnel. Additional truck drivers came from the Individual Ready Reserve, and volunteer and involuntary retirees were used as helicopter pilots. The Army also called involuntary retirees to fill medical positions. The twelve-week initial entry training requirement kept the Army from rapidly filling critically needed positions, which required specialized training in medicine, dentistry, and law. That requirement stipulated that no soldier was legally available for deployment overseas before completing a mandatory twelve-week basic training course that taught military survival skills. Although military planners did not seriously consider removing the prohibition, they wanted to modify the requirement so prospective reservists specializing in those fields could undergo their military survival training immediately after joining the Army Reserve.[69]

Army and Other Civilians

The Army as a whole had done little planning for the use of Department of the Army civilians in a war zone. It soon discovered, however, that civilians were needed to fill a number of skilled positions, such as air traffic safety controllers, port safety officers, logistics management specialists, automation and computer specialists, engineers, electricians, equipment repair technicians, and communications specialists. Most civilians in Southwest Asia worked at modifying and maintaining equipment. As of 31 October only 280 Army civilians had deployed, but by 17 December that number had increased to 881. At peak deployment in February 1,500 civilians were in the theater.[70]

Civilians served in temporary assignments that ranged from 30 days with the Corps of Engineers to 179 days in the Army Materiel Command. Those directly supporting a specific military unit served a six-month temporary tour, while those supporting operations in general but not linked to a specific unit served shorter temporary stints or a one-year unaccompanied tour, based on the nature of the assignment and the commander's discretion.[71]

The Engineers and the Army Materiel Command deployed the most civilians. At first, only Forces Command had a civilian personnel office in

[66] Discussion Paper, Col Lipke, DAMI-PII, 18 Mar 91, sub: Arabic Linguists in Support of DESERT SHIELD; Sfc. Tony Nauroth, "Arabic Linguists," *Soldiers* (May 1991): 18.

[67] Executive Summary, Col Dabbieri, TAPC-EPL, 6 Mar 91, sub: Assessment of Arabic Linguists.

[68] Memo, Lt Col Brooks, DAPE-MBI, for the Deputy Chief of Staff for Personnel, 18 Jan 91, sub: Arabic Linguists Training Status.

[69] JULLS Long Rpt, JULLS 51660–70986 (00006), CWO3 R. L. Gray, TAPC-MOB, 21 May 91, sub: Twelve Week Initial Entry Training Requirement.

[70] Deployment of Civilians, tab H, DESERT STORM Special Study Report, General Officer Steering Committee, 9 Jul 91; Interv, Judith L. Bellafaire with Pat Stepper, TAPC-CPF-S; Rpt of the DCSPER/PERSCOM/FORSCOM Mobilization Lessons Learned Workshop, 1–3 May 91.

[71] Rpt of the DCSPER/PERSCOM/FORSCOM Mobilization Lessons Learned Workshop, 1–3 May 91; Memo, James L. Yarrison for Gen Vuono, 8 May 91, sub: DCSPER/PERSCOM/FORSCOM Civilian Personnel Lessons Learned Workshop.

Riyadh. Other Army commands sent civilians to the Persian Gulf but provided no in-theater personnel assistance for them. Eventually, the Army Materiel Command established a position for a civilian personnel adviser in Dhahran, and the Corps of Engineers borrowed a Training and Doctrine Command employee to fill that role. But the Department of the Army provided no overall coordinator and troubleshooter to handle such issues as pay and allowances, benefits, entitlements, training, equipping, and processing with Army Central Command.[72] Although the vast majority of Army civilians performed commendably, a great deal of time, confusion, and aggravation could have been avoided had the deployments been better planned. For example, at the height of civilian deployment the Army belatedly discovered that many civilians had been sent without dental x-rays, a main source of identification in the event of mass casualties.

In retrospect, some analysts thought that future deployments would work better if the use of civilians in specific functions was incorporated into Army plans. That way the functions and the support provided for them would be underpinned with authorization documents, equipment, and personnel slots and training. Civilian personnel positions that were potentially deployable would be clearly designated as such, and the occupants of these positions would be required to meet physical and mental standards comparable to those for military personnel in similar positions.[73] That did not happen in the Persian Gulf war. Although a system existed for designating civilian positions "emergency essential," very few of the people deployed were in positions so designated.[74]

The Army also discovered the need for training programs for civilians in positions identified as deployable so that they could maintain and operate protective chemical equipment and survive on the battlefield if necessary. Moreover, the Army had to realign the benefits and pay of civilian positions designated "emergency essential" so that those civilians sent into a combat theater would get the same type of consideration, including medical, as soldiers.[75] Finally, an Army command had to serve as the authority for the cross-leveling and assignment of civilians to support deployments in a manner similar to that of military personnel. Such action could have prevented problems such as the one that occurred when the commander of U.S. Army, Europe, refused to release a civilian safety officer for duty in Saudi Arabia despite an identified need for one there. Command-and-control issues had to be rectified before Army civilians could be used to full advantage.[76]

Contractor personnel and Red Cross workers also deployed to Southwest Asia to work with the Army. At least 3,000 contractor employees were in the theater during the peak deployment in February. Those men and women went there to service and maintain the complicated equipment used by the Army. For example, contractor capability helped maintain an aircraft availability rate of near 90 percent in the desert. Although the Army assumed minimal responsibility for those people, the issue of the extent of Army responsibility needed clarification for future

[72] JULLS Long Rpt, JULLS 51669–34892 (00013), Patricia Turk, CPMD-DSTF, 21 May 91, sub: Requirement for CP Advisor on Forward PERSCOM MOBTDA.

[73] Memo, Yarrison for Vuono, 8 May 91, sub: DCSPER/PERSCOM/ FORSCOM Civilian Personnel Lessons Learned Workshop.

[74] Deployment of Civilians, tab H, DESERT STORM Special Study Report, General Officer Steering Committee, 9 Jul 91.

[75] Ibid.

[76] Memo, Yarrison for Vuono, 8 May 91, sub: DCSPER/PERSCOM/ FORSCOM Civilian Personnel Lessons Learned Workshop.

deployments. Red Cross workers—men and women alike—also played a part, making sure that emergency messages concerning life-and-death situations at home reached the troops.[77]

Subsistence Allowance

The Army's early mobilization decision to terminate, in accordance with the law, the basic allowance for subsistence caused a great deal of concern among soldiers, their families, the media, and Congress. That supplement, traditionally added to soldiers' paychecks during periods of nondeployment, amounted to $184.50 for enlisted soldiers who lived off post and $129 for officers. Soldiers' who deployed to Southwest Asia, where shelter and rations were provided, were no longer legally entitled to the allowance. However, many families had incorporated the supplement into their household budgets. When the allowance suddenly stopped, some families suffered financial setbacks. The severance of the allowance was roundly criticized until the secretary of defense designated the Arabian Peninsula an area of imminent danger, allowing the soldiers there to receive imminent danger pay of $110 per month and a $60 monthly allowance for families separated over thirty days.[78]

Conscientious Objection

The issue of the conscientious objector in a volunteer Army also received a great deal of publicity. Inevitably, some Regular Army and Army Reserve soldiers ordered to deploy decided to apply for conscientious objector status. The relatively small number of applicants was not surprising, considering that these soldiers had voluntarily entered the military. However, the small number of potential objectors showed that critics, who believed that many young people entered the military for educational benefits and did not intend to go to war, underestimated the sense of responsibility felt by these soldiers.

Active-duty and reserve soldiers who decided to apply for objector status were free to do so, but the Army required them to deploy with their units while it considered their applications. Those who submitted applications were often assigned duties that provided a minimum practicable conflict with their asserted beliefs. Between August 1990 and April 1991 the Department of the Army Conscientious Objector Review Board reviewed 131 requests from soldiers in the Regular Army and 10 from the Army Reserve and Army National Guard. The board approved 89 of the above cases. Seven of the soldiers withdrew their requests.[79]

Several reservists and active-duty soldiers who declared themselves conscientious objectors received a great deal of press coverage. Spc. Stephanie Atkinson was the first reservist who refused to report, claiming objector status. Atkinson held that she had joined the Army Reserve for the educational benefits and claimed that she had never really considered

[77] Ibid.; T. Sgt. Linda L. Mitchell, "American Red Cross in Combat," Associated Press wire service report, 6 Mar 91.

[78] JULLS Long Rpt, JULLS 52063–28207 (00043), Maj Rob Kissel, DAPE-MBB-C, 21 May 91; Memo, Maj Gen Larry D. Budge, Assistant Deputy Chief of Staff for Personnel (ADCSPER), through CSA, for Assistant Secretary of the Army (Manpower & Reserve Affairs) (ASA M&RA), 28 Jan 91, sub: Report to Congress on Basic Allowance for Subsistence.

[79] Information Paper, Lt Col Horne, DAPE-MPA, 7 Feb 91, sub: Conscientious Objectors; Briefing, Lt Col Hanrahan, DAPE-MO, 8 May 91, sub: Mobilization.

the possibility of being sent into a combat zone. She received a notice to report to Fort Benjamin Harrison, Indiana, for training with her unit, the 300th Adjutant General Company (Postal), in October 1990. The unit was scheduled to leave for Saudi Arabia on the twenty-third. When she did not report for duty, she was apprehended and placed in detention. Although she claimed objector status, the Army did not recognize her as such because she had not followed regulations in filing her claim and had refused to deploy with her unit while her claim was being considered. Wanting to avoid a long and expensive court-martial, the Army released her from her Illinois unit under "other than honorable conditions" in early November.[80]

A Black Muslim at Fort Campbell claimed objector status, citing his religion, which forbade him to kill fellow Muslims. A Department of Defense spokesman stated that about 2,700 followers of Islam served in all the U.S. military services and that Muslim soldiers had deployed to Saudi Arabia. One such soldier said that he was "defending the birthplace of his religion" and that he had no problems serving in the allied forces against Iraq. These and similar cases underscored the persistence of the issue despite the transition to an all-volunteer force.[81]

Yellow Ribbons

One of the most remarkable aspects of the war was gradual development of immense public support for U.S. forces that went to Southwest Asia. This support did not appear at the outset. Several days after Iraq invaded Kuwait a public opinion poll showed that over 40 percent of the American public opposed sending troops to the Persian Gulf.[82] But communities across the United States rallied around the Regular Army, Army Reserve, and Army National Guard troops as they deployed to Saudi Arabia. That patriotic support remained high through the buildup and the waiting period, the short decisive war, and the demobilization.

The public showed its support for the troops in many and varied ways. Universities and colleges gave tuition refunds and "incomplete" or "withdrawn passing" grades to deploying students. Large and small businesses provided Army Reserve and Army National Guard employees supplemental salaries, designed to fill the gap between civilian and military paychecks. Chambers of Commerce raised money via bake sales, book sales, and rodeos to send care packages and Christmas stockings to soldiers in the Persian Gulf. Pizza parlors provided free pizzas and soda to family support centers and support groups. Large corporations, such as Walmart, Nabisco, Wendy's, and Proctor and Gamble, donated material for care packages. The National Football League sent 700 footballs and 20,000 pounds of jerseys, towels, hats, sun visors, sunglasses, sweatbands, and trading cards to the troops in the desert.[83]

[80] "Reservist Refuses To Go To Gulf," *Washington Times*, 12 Nov 90, p. 2.

[81] Ibid.; Quote from Information Paper, Maj (Chaplain) Esterline, DACH-PPOT, 21 Feb 91, sub: Islam and Conscientious Objection to War. Laurie Goldstein, "The Other Side of Mobilization: Those Who Don't Want To Go," *Washington Post*, 5 Sep 90, p. 22.

[82] James Bennet, "How They Missed That Story," *Washington Monthly* (December 1990): 8.

[83] MS, Public Affairs Office, 87th Maneuver Area Command, Birmingham, Ala., Home Front Efforts for OPERATION DESERT SHIELD, n.d.

A declaration of public support. Representatives of a Chattanooga radio station present to Secretary of Defense Richard B. Cheney the signatures of 30,000 local residents in support of Persian Gulf operations.

The outpouring of appreciation continued even after the soldiers came home. Soldiers coming home from Vietnam had been greeted by a bewildering combination of hostility and neglect. Those who returned from the Persian Gulf found themselves starring in victory parades and celebrations. Perhaps the abundant support represented a clumsy public apology to the veterans of Southeast Asia. Whatever the case, for the first time in over a generation American servicewomen and men were all, without exception, considered heroes.

Yeosock in the victory parade, as depicted in the painting
"Desert Storm NYC Homecoming Parade"

Chapter 10
THE LEGACY OF WAR

Many years will pass before the geopolitical implications of DESERT SHIELD–DESERT STORM, the first post–Cold War conflict fought outside the context of superpower competition, sort themselves out. The wartime coalition led by the United States included many Arab states, some of which might well have lined up with the Soviet Union under the old framework. The new grouping may yet help to bring about an accommodation between Israel, a long-term American ally, and these Muslim nations. In 1977 President Anwar Sadat of Egypt broke a long-standing impasse with a dramatic visit to Israel that ultimately led to peace between his country and the Jewish state. The Persian Gulf war seemed to have the potential to provide a jolt of the same magnitude and revive the process that has been dormant since then. The recent accord between Israeli and Palestinian leaders promises such an outcome.[1]

Other long-term effects of the war are less certain. To one degree or another, many of the governments in Southwest Asia have begun to examine their own relationships with their populations and are trying to come to terms with pressures for reform. Widespread revulsion against chemical weapons and the use of missiles against noncombatants may also affect the future of warfare, both in the region and elsewhere. At the moment, only the craving for oil by the industrialized world appears impervious to change.

Implications for Southwest Asia

The Southwest Asia campaigns surely halted and deflected the upward spiral of President Saddam Hussein and Iraq toward regional leadership, although perhaps only for the time being. Here too questions remain. Some of those involve the character of Saddam Hussein, whose wars with Iran and then the coalition of DESERT STORM were two of the most egregious blunders ever made by a twentieth-century dictator. Was he a disciple of Joseph Stalin, as suggested in a biography published just after the Persian Gulf war, or a compulsive gambler who kept throwing the dice and losing?[2] Or perhaps the modern incarnation of a traditional Arab warrior-predator?[3]

[1] Thomas L. Friedman, "Whose Pace in Mideast?," *New York Times*, 17 May 91, p. 1.

[2] Efraim Karsch and Inari Rautsi, *Saddam Hussein, A Political Biography* (New York: Free Press, 1991), passim; Thomas L. Friedman, "Explaining Saddam: Hard Gambling," *New York Times*, 28 Sep 91, p. 6.

[3] David Selbourne, "The light that failed, again," *London Times Literary Supplement*, 10 May 91, pp. 7–8.

Beyond questions involving the roots of the dictator's behavior lay those concerning the future of Iraq. In the period immediately after the war Saddam Hussein's regime reasserted its viability. The dictator, who had enhanced his prewar legitimacy by informal appearances throughout his realm, emerged from hiding. After three months away from the camera the visits resumed on 13 April 1991, starting in Irbīl, a town in the country's troubled Kurdistan region.[4]

Saddam Hussein reaffirmed his authority in spite of the crushing economic sanctions imposed after a severe military defeat. Essentially, Iraq lost control of its foreign trade to the United Nations until it paid for the damage it did to Kuwait.[5] Nevertheless, Iraq managed to delay United Nations efforts to inventory and destroy its remaining arsenal of chemical, biological, and nuclear weapons. As of late 1991, with its economy in shambles despite its vast oil reserves, the regime still remained firmly in power, even though its future role in regional affairs was unclear.

In neighboring Kuwait, with its independence restored, the emir returned to power and set about reestablishing his regime. The hundreds of oil well fires in Kuwait, the last one of which was finally capped in November 1991, served as ugly reminders of both Iraqi aggression and of the oil nexus of the conflict. Other less spectacular manifestations of the invader's vandalism and damage directly related to the war created a need for a massive effort to rebuild public facilities and restore services, in which the U.S. Army—particularly the Corps of Engineers—played an important role. But for the short term the prewar political status quo and the flow of oil had been restored.

That result conformed with the goals of the United States. As President George H. Bush noted when asked if he was disappointed about the lack of democratization in Kuwait, "The war wasn't fought about democracy in Kuwait."[6] Instead, the war was about restoration of the status quo, presumably featuring a balance of power in which Iraq still served as a counterweight to the radical regime in Iran. Facing the possibility that the overthrow of Saddam Hussein would disrupt such stability as existed in the Persian Gulf region, the Bush administration stopped short of complete support for any of the Iraqi groups that sought to depose the Ba'th regime.

The issues and conditions in the region that could provide rationales for subsequent rounds of warfare persisted. The border disputes between Iraq and its closest neighbors remained unresolved. Even though it had been thrice defeated in major efforts to expand its access to the Persian Gulf at the expense of Kuwait, Iraq showed no signs of abandoning its aspirations in the area. In August 1991, barely six months after a crushing defeat, journalists reported yet another Iraqi effort to infiltrate Būbiyān island. Whether the incursion actually took place or Kuwaiti sources fabricated the story to convince coalition forces to stay, it was clear that the larger issue was not dead.[7]

Moreover, the huge disparities between rich and poor were a fact of life in Southwest Asia. Saddam Hussein had achieved some success in

[4] Christine Moss Helms, *Iraq: Eastern Flank of the Arab World* (Washington, D.C.: Brookings Institution, 1984), p. 34; *New York Times*, 15 Apr 91, p. 9.

[5] Patrick E. Tyler, "Punished but Hanging On," *New York Times*, 7 Apr 91, p. 1.

[6] Quote from Thomas L. Friedman, "A Rising Sense That Iraq's Hussein Must Go," *New York Times*, Week in Review, 7 Jul 91, pp. 1, 3.

[7] Jerry Gray, "Kuwait Reports Repelling Iraq Force at Gulf Island," *New York Times*, 29 Aug 91, p. A10.

exploiting regional antipathies and jealousies of the enormous wealth of Kuwait and other sheikhdoms. The war destroyed the livelihoods of countless thousands, many of them Palestinians who were no longer welcome in Kuwait. It also displaced huge numbers of Iraqis. So the war only widened the chasm between the region's rich and poor.

The gap was obvious to all, among them the men of Col. William L. Nash's 1st Brigade, 3d Armored Division. They were the last American soldiers to pull out of Safwān, the town that became famous as the location of the truce tent in which General Schwarzkopf had dictated the terms of the cease-fire in February 1991. Even as the men of the 3d Armored Division departed on 7 May, after providing nearly 1 million meals, over 1 million gallons of water, and 28,000 medical visits, they saw the children "by the sand track, one hand tapping their teeth, another their stomachs in the universal refugee sign language for 'Give me food.'" Then, seconds later, came "a blindingly white Mercedes-Benz," which "shussed by, its windows tastefully curtained, its driver shrouded in his white gutra, or headdress." The contrast was stark. As a watching American officer wryly observed, "That is what we fought for."[8]

Implications for the United States

DESERT STORM ended with the United States achieving its aims. The restoration of the prewar status quo seemed assured. However, Washington appeared inclined to go beyond its original goals and encourage the overthrow of the Iraqi dictator, provided that an alternative could be found that would not upset the regional balance of power. The situation that unfolded immediately after the war, with a Kurdish rebellion in the north and a Shiite uprising in the south, seemed capable of significantly altering that balance and leaving a weakened and truncated Iraq that might not be strong enough to serve as a counterweight to Iranian ambitions. Under those circumstances the United States backed away from assuring Saddam Hussein's downfall. War was frequently "a seedbed for revolution."[9] Perhaps the situation would take care of itself, and a suitable group of rebels could bring about the fall of Saddam Hussein without direct American involvement or the fragmentation of Iraq.[10]

The cautious approach prompted some critics to argue that the administration lacked specific strategies for attaining its objectives in Iraq. President Bush seemed wary of the forces that such a result might unleash. William B. Quandt, a Middle East expert at the Brookings Institution and a former member of President Jimmy Carter's national security staff, assessed the Bush policy as "being made on the run." "We didn't have a grand design going in," he observed, "and we don't have a grand design coming out."[11]

The wartime coalition had also met its objectives. It had no mandate to end Saddam Hussein's despotism over Iraq and could only prevent him from tyrannizing other parts of Southwest Asia. With Saddam Hussein still

[8] Edward A. Gargan, "Last G.I.'s Leave a Major Iraq-Kuwait Border Post," *New York Times*, 8 May 91, p. 16.

[9] Robert W. Stookey, *America & the Arab States: An Uneasy Encounter* (New York: John Wiley and Sons, 1975), p. 161.

[10] Andrew Rosenthal, "What the U.S. Wants to Happen in Iraq Remains Unclear," *New York Times*, Week in Review, 24 Mar 91, p. 1.

[11] Ibid.

in power, the world had no guarantee that a similar aggression would not occur sometime in the future. That fact seemed to make it necessary for the United States to maintain a close watch over the region.

After the war, the United States appeared prudently reluctant to maintain a presence in the region. The government of Saudi Arabia, still the largest and most formidable nation bordering the Persian Gulf that tended to side with the United States, continued to shy away from an explicit alliance or an invitation to station troops on its territory. Moreover, the whole history of Western military intervention in Middle Eastern affairs—from the Crusades to the 1983 destruction of the U.S. Marine barracks in Beirut—was replete with examples of failure and disaster.[12] If a vacuum existed there, perhaps it was best left unfilled.

The American reluctance to maintain a presence was offset to a degree by efforts to prepare for a return to the region if necessary. Postwar negotiations dealt with a wide range of possibilities, involving pre-positioning of equipment, joint training exercises, and arms sales. The Bush administration discussed these options with all six Gulf Cooperation Council members, deciding not to press for a permanent American ground force in Southwest Asia. Still, it seemed plain in the aftermath of the war that some sort of stable strategic relationship was necessary to protect the interests of the Persian Gulf countries and those of the United States.[13]

Worldwide attention to the plight of the hundreds of thousands who were uprooted by the war and subsequent efforts by the Iraqi government to crush rebellions forced Bush to act. The result was Operation PROVIDE COMFORT. On 5 April 1991 the president ordered American forces to provide relief for the half million Kurdish refugees who fled into Turkey after the Iraqi government quashed the uprising in northern Iraq.[14]

The day after relief operations began, Iraq accepted United Nations terms for a permanent cease-fire. The terms provided for the destruction of Iraq's most dangerous weapons and established procedures for reparations to Kuwait and for the lifting of trade sanctions. Iraqi acceptance of the resolution marked the formal abandonment by the United States of any possible action by the large force still in southern Iraq to topple Saddam Hussein's government.[15]

While troops under Lt. Gen. John M. Shalikashvili moved into northern Iraq to provide humanitarian assistance to the Kurds, other Americans gradually left the southern part of the country. By early May United Nations observers took over from Central Command posts in Iraq along the border with Kuwait. Colonel Nash's 1st Brigade was the last to go. Finally, in the middle of July, Shalikashvili's troops left too, ending one of the largest military relief operations. A small eight-nation rapid deployment force remained behind in southeast Turkey.[16]

As the operation in northern Iraq ended, it became clear that Iraq was not complying with United Nations mandates for the destruction of its unconventional arsenal and nuclear materials. Reports warned that Iraq had enough uranium to produce twenty or more nuclear weapons

[12] Robert Fisk, "History Haunts the New 'Crusaders,'" *London Independent*, 9 Aug 90, p. 7.

[13] Eric Schmitt, "U.S. Negotiating New Security Pacts in Gulf," *New York Times*, 1 Aug 91, p. A6; Anthony H. Cordesman, *The Gulf and the West: Strategic Relations and Military Realities* (Boulder, Colo.: Westview Press, 1988), p. 456.

[14] Paul Lewis, "Iraq Approval Starts Peace Schedule," *New York Times*, 7 Apr 91, p. 14.

[15] Ibid.; Patrick E. Tyler, "Main U.S. Forces Begin Withdrawal," *New York Times*, 9 Apr 91, p. A14; Eric Schmitt, "Last U.S. and Allied Troops Begin Withdrawal From Northern Iraq," *New York Times*, 13 Jul 91, p. 3.

[16] Schmitt, "Last U.S. and Allied Troops Begin Withdrawal From Northern Iraq," p. 3.

within a decade. President Bush responded by approving a list of Iraqi targets that might be attacked if Iraq did not carry out its commitments. Despite such threats, no air strike was imminent. The United Nations merely increased its surveillance of Iraq by air.[17]

Implications for the U.S. Army

Operations DESERT SHIELD and DESERT STORM presented the most important test of the U.S. armed forces since the Vietnam War. Victory initially appeared neither certain nor easy. President Bush and his advisers avoided the common mistake generally made when planning for low-level wars: focusing on the potential for success and underestimating the full range of risks. If anything, the Bush administration may have taken an overly cautious approach to the Iraqi invasion of Kuwait. The administration's oft-repeated observations on the size and power of Iraqi forces, the formidable nature of their defenses, and the serious possibility of chemical and biological warfare, prepared the American public and the deployed military forces for a long and costly conflict. As one defense analyst observed, "In Vietnam, the United States overestimated its own power and prowess and underestimated that of the enemy. Here, it was just the opposite."[18]

Although it may be premature to draw conclusions about the war or the U.S. Army's performance in the battle, some preliminary assessments are possible. The Southwest Asia campaigns provided a major test for the Army forces that were involved. In the course of the decade leading up to the war, the Army had overhauled much of its training, doctrine, structure, and materiel. The changes all contributed to the emergence of a combat force capable of waging a modern conflict. In just 100 hours of intense warfare, the Army's soldiers, equipment, and doctrine were put to the test and emerged successfully.

The victory validated a revamped politico-military structure based on the reorganization of the Department of Defense under the 1986 Goldwater-Nichols Act. That legislation had clarified the unified commander-in-chief's relationship with the individual services and the National Command Authority. During DESERT SHIELD and DESERT STORM the president designated General Schwarzkopf as the unified commander for the operation, supported by the other unified and specified commands and the services. President Bush concentrated on the larger diplomatic and strategic issues, leaving Schwarzkopf to concentrate on operational concerns. The president provided the necessary guidance, giving his military leader sufficient latitude to accomplish the mission.

In the same manner, the military plans were adequate for the task. The plans, as executed, reflected sound strategic judgment. General Schwarzkopf and his component commanders forced Iraq to fight their kind of war. They matched American military strengths against Iraqi

[17] Eric Schmitt, "U.S. Tries to Intimidate Iraq With Military Targets List," *New York Times*, 12 Jul 91, p. A3; Jerry Gray, "U.N. Using U.S. Spy Planes to Monitor Iraqi Arms," *New York Times*, 13 Aug 91.

[18] R. W. Apple, Jr., "Done. A Short, Persuasive Lesson in Warfare," *New York Times*, Week in Review, 3 Mar 91, p. 1.

weaknesses. The coalition effort frustrated Iraqi attempts to inflict large numbers of casualties on the opposing military forces, as well as on Saudi Arabian and Israeli civilians, and thwarted Iraqi efforts to draw Israel into the war. As the Department of Defense report on the war noted, "We defeated his [Saddam Hussein's] strategy as well as his forces."[19]

On a broader level, the Persian Gulf conflict ushered in an era of more diffuse threats. The United States had to focus on regional developments that could ultimately menace its interests, rather than on global confrontation with the Soviet Union. The campaigns and their aftermath proved that the armed forces were capable of addressing this new situation and reaffirmed their ability to move quickly from combat operations into emergency relief work in northern Iraq and into nation-building in Kuwait.

The war may also have presaged a future marked by a tendency toward coalition warfare. In regional conflicts the United States would not be able to stand alone. It would need the approval and support of other governments before it could intervene in a regional crisis. And it would need help sustaining its forces in a foreign country and in a hostile environment, such as the Arabian desert. Although coalition warfare is inherently ad hoc and complex, the U.S. Army showed that it had the requisite depth of professional training, flexibility, and experience to handle the Persian Gulf operations.

DESERT SHIELD and DESERT STORM revealed a continued need for well-trained and ready forces that could be dispatched abroad quickly to counter threats to American interests. In an era of shrinking budgets, base closures, withdrawals from forward deployments, and reductions in the size of the force, the Army successfully completed a massive deployment and buildup and defeated a formidable army. Furthermore, that success came amidst intense psychological pressure caused by Iraq's seizure of hostages and threats of chemical warfare.

The Persian Gulf crisis also marked the dawn of a new technological age and proved that the most advanced equipment gave a vital edge to an army. Precision-guided munitions were immensely effective. The war witnessed the first—and successful—use of cruise missiles, antiballistic missile defenses, and advanced reconnaissance systems, as well as unprecedented large-scale night-fighting. As the Defense Department after-action report stated, "American technology saved Coalition lives and contributed greatly to victory."[20]

Logistics played a critical role in success. Because of coalition air superiority, logistics specialists were able to work unhindered.[21] Despite long supply lines and severe desert conditions, U.S. and coalition forces were adequately sustained, enabling the combat forces to complete their job. The logistical problems involved in delivering the troops and their equipment to Saudi Arabia seemed, at times, almost insurmountable to Army planners. But they found sufficient transportation assets to move the troops almost 8,000 miles by air and equipment 12,000 miles by sea. Yet, once in the theater, supplies did not always move forward as fast as

[19] U.S. Department of Defense, *Conduct of the Persian Gulf Conflict: An Interim Report to Congress* (Washington, D.C.: Government Printing Office, 1991), p. I-2. Hereafter cited as *Interim Report*.

[20] Ibid.

[21] Apple, "Done. A Short, Persuasive Lesson in Warfare," p. 1.

those who waited for them thought they should. One artillery battalion commander complained that "our logistics systems and people are not user friendly or customer-oriented." Other combat commanders agreed.[22]

Although DESERT STORM demonstrated that the Army could conduct maneuver and fire support in a very intense battle, that its small-unit leadership was sound, and that its weapon systems worked, the military operation left some questions. The defeat of a large but tactically incompetent and poorly led Third World army did not constitute a definitive test for doctrine, personnel, or equipment. Such a challenge could be provided only by an enemy force capable of maneuvering, of using its armor and artillery intelligently, and of employing a credible air force.

For example, the Abrams tank did not have to fight against a comparable modern tank. The T–55 and T–72 used by Iraq were obsolescent. The few hits on M1A1s showed that the armor was good but did not indicate how it would have fared against the T–80. The Bradley also did well, but did not have to operate against the type of artillery and antitank fire of a comparable foe. Initial results showed that the Bradley was too small internally to carry the squad and all of its equipment and still allow for quick dismounts. Overall questions remained about the effectiveness of the Bradley-Abrams team as well as the Patriot. The Patriot, so critical to the success of the coalition, shot down a number of the Scuds sent aloft by the enemy, one at a time. No salvos of missiles tested the system. Any overall assessment would have to consider carefully "why we were successful, what worked and what did not, and what is important to protect and preserve in our military capability."[23]

These issues were still emerging when the war became a tool in interservice budgetary competition. With the overall military budget declining in the wake of the Cold War, some individual services were quick to use the Persian Gulf war to justify their claims for larger portions of defense allocations. The Air Force, asserting that its success in the war validated strategic bombing theory and proved the primacy of its own role, sought more and newer aircraft.[24] The Navy, too, claiming it was the most readily deployable force when hostilities began, urged Congress to fund more ships. In their eagerness to win the largest possible share of the defense budget, the services sometimes lost sight of the specific circumstances of the victory in Southwest Asia. For all of its modernizing efforts, Iraq remained a Third World enemy, with no navy, a modest air force that largely did not stay for the fight, and a huge ground force armed with obsolescent weapons. Victory against such an enemy, as gratifying as it was, did not constitute a definitive test for any theory or doctrine.

Beyond the fight for money and operational considerations of doctrine, leadership, and equipment, Operations DESERT SHIELD and DESERT STORM were perhaps most important for what they gave to America. The overwhelming victory reaffirmed America's faith in its armed forces. And in some small measure, DESERT STORM also helped reaffirm America's faith in itself, in its products, performance, purpose, and dedication.[25]

[22] Ltr, Lt Col Harry M. Emerson, "Letters," *Military Review* 71 (August 1991): 99. See also Memo, Lt Col Gregory Fontenot, 8 Mar 91, sub: Operation DESERT STORM After Action Report.

[23] *Interim Report*, p. I-3.

[24] See U.S. Air Force, *Reaching Globally, Reaching Powerfully: The United States Air Force in the Gulf War, A Report* (N.p., 1991), pp. 11–14, 54–58.

[25] *Interim Report*, p. I-3.

Appendix A

THE PATRIOT AIR DEFENSE SYSTEM

Of all the weapons the U.S. Army used during Operations DESERT SHIELD and DESERT STORM, none became more instantly recognizable than the boxy Patriot air defense missile system. Sometimes described as a dumpster on hydraulic lifters, it contributed to the coalition's victory in the war in the Persian Gulf on several levels. Lauding the Patriot's military and diplomatic achievements, General Schwarzkopf predicted that "when the history of DESERT STORM is written, the Patriot system will be singled out as the key" and that the "Patriot's success has ensured [U.N.] coalition solidarity." Despite its achievements, the Patriot had its weaknesses, and as a weapon system it was almost not available in time.[1]

Development of the Patriot

The Patriot was a product of the Cold War confrontation between the United States and the Soviet Union. Both nations employed German rocket scientists captured at the end of World War II to develop ballistic missiles. These missiles were derived from the V–2 rocket and from the lesser-known German surface-to-air missile called *Wasserfall* (Waterfall), which the Germans flight-tested in early 1944 but were unable to field before the war ended. The research and development effort that eventually produced the Patriot system began in 1965 due to similar work in the Soviet Union that resulted in the fielding of the first Russian tactical ballistic missile in the early 1960s.

The Army awarded a contract to the Massachusetts-based Raytheon Company in 1967 for a new air defense missile to be called Surface-to-Air Missile-Developmental (SAM-D), which was to carry either a nuclear or a conventional warhead. In 1969 an American missile scored its first success against a tactical ballistic missile. The Nike-Hercules, the successor to the first operational American surface-to-air missile, the Nike-Ajax, intercepted first an Army Corporal ballistic missile and later the same year another Nike-Hercules. The Nike-Hercules used a nuclear warhead to assure destruction of the incoming nuclear device. But the SAM-D program languished until the mid-1970s.

[1] "Thunder and Lightning: ADA Plays a Crucial Diplomatic, as well as a Key Tactical, Role in Operation DESERT STORM," 1991 *Air Defense Artillery Yearbook*, p. 29.

The Patriot missile launcher, referred to by some as the dumpster on hydraulic lifters

The SAM-D experimental flights impressed the incoming administration of President Jimmy Carter, who decided to continue funding and even hastened development. Moreover, the project's adherents, responding to the excitement of the 1976 bicentennial celebration of the American Revolution, dropped the prosaic label of SAM-D and applied the catchier tag of "Patriot." In what was reputed to be a political ploy to achieve the backing of House of Representatives Speaker Thomas P. "Tip" O'Neill of Massachusetts, the Carter administration approved the Army's production contract with Raytheon on the eve of the 1980 election. Though Carter's bid for reelection failed, the Patriot was well placed to take advantage of the generous defense funding policies of the newly elected administration of President Ronald W. Reagan.

During Reagan's first term the Pentagon had a large budget, and work on fielding and improving the Patriot accelerated. After overcoming some reliability problems, the Patriot was issued in 1985 to units of the 32d Army Air Defense Command, a major subordinate command of U.S. Army, Europe. At this point, the Patriot was capable only of shooting

2 Interv, J. Britt McCarley with Col Joseph G. Garrett III, 2 Jul 91, Fort Bliss, Tex.; Interv, McCarley with Col David K. Heebner, 6 Jun 91, Fort Bliss, Tex.; Interv, McCarley with Lt Col Charles W. Simpson, 23 Jul 91, Fort Bliss, Tex.; Christopher Chant, *Air Defense Systems and Weapons: World AAA and SAM Systems in the 1990s* (New York: Brassey's Defense Publishers, 1989), pp. 92–96, 133–38; Ted Nicholas and Rita Rossi, *U.S. Missile Data Book, 1990* (Fountain Valley, Calif.: Data Search Associates, 1989), pp. 3-3, 3-6; "Thunder and Lightning," pp. 19–20; Wolf Prow, "Gulf War Weaponry Spawned in World War II," *Air Defense Artillery* (March–April 1991): 41–43; "Team Patriot: Patriot's 'Lesser Heroes' Glory in Dazzling DESERT STORM Showing," *Air Defense Artillery* (March–April 1991): 15; "Patriot Missile Test," *Army* (January 1988): 67; "Army's Patriot: High-Tech Superstar of DESERT STORM," *Army* (March 1991): 40–42; Wayne Biddle, "The Untold Story of the Patriot," *Discover* (June 1991): 74–77; "Patriot's ATBM Improvements Show Their Mettle," *International Defense Review* (February 1991): 103; Joerg Bahnemann and Thomas Enders, "Reconsidering Ballistic Missile Defense," *Military Technology* (April 1991): 46–52; Sheldon S. Herskovitz, "High Marks for Military Radar: The Patriot Missile System," *Journal of Electronic Defense* (May 1991): 55–56; Ralph Kinney Bennett, "The Vision Behind the Patriot," *Reader's Digest* (May 1991): 76–80; *Aviation Week & Space Technology* (15 October 1990): 101, (28 January 1991): 26–28, and (4 February 1991): 63; *Jane's Defense Weekly* (12 January 1991): 53; *Congressional Quarterly Weekly Report*

down aircraft, including helicopters. A major effort to improve the capabilities of the Patriot system was already under way.

President Reagan soon announced his intention to build a space- and ground-based missile defense for the United States called the Strategic Defense Initiative or, more commonly, Star Wars. Riding on the coattails and enjoying the benefits of the program, work on upgrading the Patriot began in earnest in 1984 under the aegis of the U.S. Army Missile Command. The United States did not consider the project in violation of the 1972 Anti-Ballistic Missile Treaty because the resulting enhanced Patriot would not be able to destroy a Soviet Intercontinental Ballistic Missile. The Missile Command's effort was built on a foundation of research and development laid down during the later Carter years that had taken advantage of advances in microchip technology and that had aimed toward adding an antiballistic missile capability to the Patriot.

The Missile Command's work began to bear fruit in the mid- to late 1980s. Important modifications to the system's software sharpened the missile's tracking ability, and changes in the fuzing and warhead of the missile itself increased the probability of a "warhead kill," destroying the incoming missile's offensive power. Labeled Patriot antitactical ballistic missile capability, phase 1 (PAC–1), the first of the software upgrades was tested by the Army at White Sands Missile Range, New Mexico, in 1986. In that year a Patriot missile, guided by special developmental software, intercepted an Army Lance surface-to-surface tactical missile. The test showed that a Patriot missile was capable of knocking a tactical missile off course, making a "mission kill," but was not likely to achieve a warhead kill. During 1987, in the first PAC–1 missile firing, the Patriot intercepted another Patriot configured to mimic the performance of recent tactical missiles. Early limitations notwithstanding, the Army let a contract for production of the improved software. In 1988 the first Patriot units were ready to operate with the PAC–1 software, while modifications to the missile's warhead and fuze were to follow.

When DESERT SHIELD began in August 1990, the production contract for the improved PAC–2 missile had been let, but actual production had not begun. Furthermore, the PAC–2 software upgrade, called Post Deployment Build–3 (PDB–3), had already been produced and was about to be introduced to Patriot units, beginning with the 11th Air Defense Artillery Brigade at Fort Bliss, Texas, but that effort had not started either. This relatively short but intense attempt to provide the Army with an effective defense against tactical ballistic missiles was due to the accelerated missile development by the Soviet Union and the simultaneous spread of such weapons, often provided by the Soviets, among Third World military forces. Even through the period of DESERT SHIELD and DESERT STORM, research never ended. The Army produced and installed six different new versions of PDB–3 software in its ongoing effort to assure a warhead kill.[2]

Development of the Scud

In the early 1960s the Soviets fielded their first tactical missile, known within the North Atlantic Treaty Organization as the Surface-to-Surface–1A (SS–1A) Scunner or, more commonly, the Scud. The second production model, with extended range, was the Scud-B, which the Soviets began to phase out of their own inventories by the early 1970s but which they continued to produce and deliver to client states, such as Iraq in the early 1980s. Over the years the Iraqis upgraded their Scud-Bs, and of the two most commonly developed variants, the *Al-Abbas* and the *Al-Hussein*, the latter one was fired at targets in Israel and Saudi Arabia.

The *Al-Hussein* missile itself was about 37 feet long and was carried on a multiwheeled, heavy-duty transporter-erector-launcher and supported by several additional vehicles to provide command and control, weather information, and fueling. Unlike the Soviet Scud-B, which had a range of about 175 miles, the *Al-Hussein* could travel about 400 miles. The Iraqis paid a price in effectiveness to extend the range of the *Al-Hussein*, which had been accomplished by reducing the weight of the warhead, lengthening the fuselage, and increasing the size of the rocket motor and the amount of fuel. The *Al-Hussein's* reduced payload of 350 pounds was less than that of the Scud-B, and its accuracy was also less than its Soviet progenitor. Moreover, the modifications had compromised the structural integrity of the rocket, so it often broke apart on the plunge toward its target. The separation of Scuds into three parts—warhead, fuel tanks, and rocket motor—as they descended, known to the missile crews as the blossoming effect, meant that five incoming Scuds could appear on radar screens as fifteen. Although intelligence estimates varied, the Iraqis had five hundred to one thousand *Al-Hussein* Scuds when the Persian Gulf crisis began and about thirty-two fixed and thirty-six mobile launchers.[3]

Patriot Battery Organization

Although there were numerous organizational permutations during DESERT SHIELD and DESERT STORM, the standard Patriot missile system fire unit (analogous to "battery" in more standard military lexicon) that deployed to the field contained several major pieces of materiel. The functional center of the battery was the engagement control station, an air-conditioned van outfitted with sophisticated, computer-driven equipment. This station received information concerning the location of targets and dispatched launch commands to the battery's missiles.

The battery searched for and tracked the targets with its radar set, the most important part of which was the multifunction phased-array radar. The fixed, trailer-mounted system contained over five thousand radiating elements that searched the sky in a broad left to right arc from the horizon to nearly straight overhead, depending on the target. The radar could

(26 January 1991): 248–49; *U.S. News & World Report* (4 February 1991): 48; *New York Times*, 5 and 10 Feb 91.

3 Martin Navias, *Ballistic Missile Proliferation in the Third World*, Adelphi Papers no. 252 (London: International Institute for Strategic Studies, 1990), pp. 16, 20, 29–33, 39; Otto Friedrich, ed., *DESERT STORM: The War in the Persian Gulf* (Boston: Little, Brown and Co., 1991), p. 158; Pete Olson, "Winds of Change," *Air Defense Artillery* (July–August 1991): 6; Mary E. Peterson, "SRBMs and ADA: Point Counterpoint," *Air Defense Artillery* (January–February 1991): 20–22; Bernard Blake, ed., *Jane's Weapon Systems*, 1988–1989 (Alexandria, Va.: Jane's Information Group, 1988), p. 127; *Aviation Week & Space Technology* (28 January 1991): 28; *Time* (28 January 1991): 23; *U.S. News & World Report* (11 February 1991): 15; *New York Times*, 20 Jan 91.

Starting one of two Patriot generators

[4] Interv, J. Britt McCarley with Maj Daniel R. Kirby, 26 Jul 91, Fort Bliss, Tex.; Abe Dane, "Report From Charlie Battery," *Popular Mechanics* (April 1991): 23–28, 126; *Aviation Week & Space Technology* (28 January 1991): 26–28.

track many missiles and aircraft out to great ranges simultaneously. Connected to the operators' screens in the engagement control station, the phased-array radar was the "eyes of the battery."

The offensive power of the battery was embodied in the launcher stations, with as many as eight arrayed around the engagement control station according to the situation. Every launcher station contained four missiles, each in its own canister, aimed skyward in the direction of a potentially threatening missile or aircraft. The Patriot missiles were fired by electronic command from the engagement control station. During the Persian Gulf crisis, Patriot batteries were often equipped with a mixed load of PAC–1 and PAC–2 missiles, which could be fired simultaneously during an engagement at different targets.

The remaining major components of a Patriot battery were the antenna mast group, used for ultra–high frequency communications between batteries and with battalion headquarters; the command post, from which the captain commanding the battery directed operations; and the electric power plant, which consisted of two truck-mounted 150-kilowatt generators operated in rotation to provide electrical power for the battery. A Gulf crisis Patriot battery operated with an authorized strength of about eighty-eight operators and maintainers.[4]

Patriot System Operation

With its excellent phased-array radar, a Patriot battery could search for, detect, identify, track, engage, and destroy a missile without external help, even from the battalion's information coordination center that normally controlled the Patriot's participation in a battle against conventional aircraft. However, no such encounter occurred during the Gulf crisis. Rather in the case of an incoming projectile, approaching about six times the speed of sound in the case of an Iraqi Scud, the Patriot radar picked it up as it started to descend toward its target in the final minutes of flight, known as the terminal phase. Because of the late moment at which the Patriot engaged its targets, it was designated a "terminal defense" system.

Less than a minute before impact, the Patriot system's weapon control computer fired or gave the signal to fire PAC–2 missiles less than two seconds apart. The seventeen-foot PAC–2 consisted of upgraded components—fuze, warhead, solid propellant, and control fins—and incorporated the unique, semiactive track-via-missile guidance system. Originally designed in the 1950s to guide antitank missiles to their targets, the system was adapted to the Patriot research and development effort and flight-tested during the mid-1970s. The test at White Sands showed the remarkable accuracy of track-via-missile guidance, even against a maneuvering target drone.

The Iraqi Scud variants were really rockets, rather than missiles. They employed inertial guidance, which meant that once they had been emplaced, aligned, and fired, their flight to the target could not be controlled and was subject to the vagaries of winds and weather aloft. The trajectory of most such projectiles was highly predictable: they ascended to a height of about 160,000 feet above ground level, outside the earth's atmosphere, and then plummeted directly onto their target.

When a Scud appeared on a Patriot operator's radar screen and was identified, the system fired its missiles at it, activating the track-via-missile guidance system. As the Patriot neared its target, only seconds away from interception, the semiactive tracking component began to receive phased-array radar emissions reflected off the incoming projectile. The guidance system then relayed this information to the weapon control computer, which transmitted mid-course correction data back to the missile. As the Patriot neared its target, traveling about three times the speed of sound and within milliseconds of interception, the guidance system took over guidance from the weapon control computer. Using ever-stronger phased-array radar emissions reflected off the incoming rocket, the Patriot's own steering commands, now directing the control fins, in theory almost ensured an interception.

The longer-range Patriot PAC–2 had both fuze and warhead improvements over its PAC–1 predecessor. When the PAC–2 and the target were within microseconds of each other, hurtling along at a closing velocity of almost ten times the speed of sound, the Patriot's upgraded proximity fuze exploded its enhanced fragmentation warhead, creating a veil of shrapnel that destroyed the target's warhead or at least knocked it off course and away from its intended target area. Once a successful engagement was over and nuclear-biological-chemical survey and monitoring teams determined that no hazards were present, the battery signaled "all clear," dispatched damage inspection teams, and began the process of reloading its missile launcher stations with the million-dollar-a-copy PAC–2s. Such was the manner in which Patriot missile systems engaged and destroyed Iraqi Scuds.[5]

Deployment of Patriot Units and PAC–2s

One part of the June and July 1990 command post exercise known as INTERNAL LOOK involved the 11th Air Defense Artillery Brigade, which was attached to the XVIII Airborne Corps' rapid deployment force. The 11th Brigade's part in the exercise involved briefings in late July by the newly installed brigade commander, Col. Joseph G. Garrett III, to the Central Command and ARCENT commanders and staffs on the capabilities of his brigade. Garrett highlighted the deployment and operational potential of the Patriot air defense missile system in his briefings.[6]

Shortly afterward, General Schwarzkopf, at the request of Joint Chiefs of Staff Chairman Powell, briefed the military service chiefs in the Pentagon and other defense leaders at Camp David on the situation in and around Kuwait and the options for a response. After the invasion, Schwarzkopf's briefings centered on executing his operations plan for driving Iraqi forces from Kuwait. Schwarzkopf's discussion focused on two threats: Iraq's chemical weapons and its large ground force, which had the capability to invade Saudi Arabia. Saddam Hussein was known to have moved a number of his Scuds to the desert of western Iraq in April 1990 and had said he would launch the chemical ones at Israel. General Powell's response to Schwarzkopf at Camp David was that "there's a deterrence piece and a warfighting piece. The sooner we put something in place to deter, the better we are. What we can get there most quickly is air power." The Patriot was part of both the deterrent and war-fighting capability that Central Command would have to assemble.[7]

Apparently, Garrett's air defense message to Central Command had registered. As soon as President George H. Bush decided to send American forces to Saudi Arabia, Central Command asked for a Patriot unit from Fort Bliss as an additional demonstration of U.S. resolve in the crisis. The request, however, did not indicate what size unit, a battery or a whole battalion, would be sent, and the post staff at Fort Bliss, home of Air Defense Artillery and Garrett's 11th Air Defense Artillery Brigade, opened the fort's emergency operations center and began to plan for deploying the Patriot missile system.

Army Central Command had already alerted the 11th Brigade to deploy as much as a Patriot battalion. So the post and brigade staffs

[5] Garrett interview; Heebner interview; Simpson interview; Kirby interview; Chant, *Air Defense Systems and Weapons*, pp. 133–38; "Thunder and Lightning," p. 18; Friedrich, ed., *DESERT STORM*, pp. 175, 199; Dane, "Report From Charlie Battery," pp. 23–28, 126; Bennett, "The Vision Behind the Patriot," pp. 76–80; *Aviation Week & Space Technology* (3 December 1990): 22, (28 January 1991): 26–28, and (18 February 1991): 49–51; *Jane's Defense Weekly* (12 January 1991): 52; *New York Times*, 24 and 27 Jan 91.

[6] Bob Woodward, *The Commanders* (New York: Simon and Schuster, 1991), pp. 208–09; Garrett interview; "Desert Victory: ADA Protects Maneuver Forces During 100 Hours of DESERT STORM's Ground Campaign," *1991 Air Defense Artillery Yearbook*, p. 38; *U.S. News & World Report* (18 March 1991): 34–35.

[7] Garrett interview; Kirby interview. Quote from Woodward, *Commanders*, p. 248 but see also pp. 220–21, 227–28, 248–51, 285. Friedrich, ed., *DESERT STORM*, p. 19; "Thunder and Lightning," p. 20; *New York Times*, 23 Jan 91.

began to sort out the details of airlifting the Patriot to Saudi Arabia, which was the only practical way of quickly getting the missile system there. While reviewing load plans for Air Force C–5 Galaxies and C–141 Starlifters, the brigade staff asked White Sands for a count of Patriot missiles on hand. The 11th Brigade had only less capable PAC–1 missiles in its inventory, because PAC–2 production had not started yet. The initial mission of the deploying Patriot unit, to provide air defense for ports, airfields, logistical bases, and command and control centers, demanded PAC–2s to fend off the Scuds that Iraq could launch at these valuable and vulnerable targets.

White Sands had a total of three PAC–2 missiles, which were all being used in testing. Moreover, these were the only three PAC–2s in existence. Within a few days Fort Bliss had received permission from Missile Command to ship the White Sands missiles with the 11th Brigade's first Patriot unit. The post's resident ordnance battalion sent elements of a heavy truck company to White Sands. The three PAC–2s were disconnected from their testing instruments and carried back to Biggs Army Air Field, adjacent to Fort Bliss, to be prepared for shipment. So hurried was the retrieval of the missiles that they still bore the word *experimental* stenciled on their sides.

Around midnight on 11 August 1990, with none of the usual fanfare accorded deploying soldiers because of the need for secrecy, Battery B, 2d Battalion, 7th Air Defense Artillery, from one of the 11th Brigade's two Patriot battalions, loaded personnel and equipment aboard three C–5s for the flight to Saudi Arabia. Because of the uncertainty of what lay ahead, Battery B had been augmented with shorter-range air defense weapon systems, but almost nothing beyond the soldiers and the unit's firing components was on board the aircraft. Battery B landed at the airport in Dhahran, unloaded, and set up to fire, all within forty-eight hours after leaving Fort Bliss. Had Saddam Hussein then decided to start an invasion of Saudi Arabia with a saturation barrage of Scud missiles, the battery would have been unable to prevent it.

With the PAC–2s not scheduled for delivery until January 1991, the Army's air defense community tried to rectify the situation. Uniformed leaders, in conjunction with Raytheon, put the existing PAC–2 missile production contract into operation. They achieved quick success. Martin Marietta Corporation, the subcontractor that actually built the missiles, shipped five of them in September directly from its Orlando, Florida, factory to Saudi Arabia. Production continued around the clock through September. The accelerating flow of PAC–2s to the increasing number of Patriot units in Southwest Asia was sufficient by the time DESERT STORM began to conduct wartime operations with some confidence. A total of 158 PAC–2 missiles were launched at Scuds during the war, but about 3,000 Patriot missiles of all kinds were on hand at the end of the conflict.[8]

Deployment of Battery B, as well as the air defense components of the 82d Airborne Division's 1st Brigade, signaled the beginning of a

[8] Garrett interview; Interv, J. Britt McCarley with Lt Col Elmer J. Polk and Maj Marco E. Vialpando, 28 Jun 91, Fort Bliss, Tex.; Woodward, *Commanders*, pp. 264, 267–68; Friedrich, ed., *DESERT STORM*, p. 199; "Thunder and Lightning," pp. 20–21; "Desert Victory," p. 39; Maj. Gen. Donald M. Lionetti, "Intercept Point," *Air Defense Artillery* (November–December 1990): 1, 34–35; "Waiting Is the Hardest Part: Operation DESERT SHIELD Air Defense Units Prepare for Action as the Persian Gulf Crisis Sizzles on the Anvil of the Sun," *Air Defense Artillery* (November–December 1990): 22–23; Mark Hewish, "War-Winning Technologies: Patriot Shows Its Mettle," *International Defense Review* (May 1991): 457; *Aviation Week & Space Technology* (28 January 1991): 26–28, 34.

A portion of a Patriot battery deployed in the Saudi desert during DESERT SHIELD

steady flow of air defense units to Saudi Arabia, a significant number of which were equipped with the Patriot. Deployment continued into the air campaign phase of DESERT STORM and included the repositioning of individual Patriot batteries and whole battalions from the Persian Gulf island emirate of Bahrain to significant portions of Saudi Arabia and Turkey but initially not to Israel. In addition to protecting the normal range of strategic targets, Patriot units, often in task forces with HAWK antiaircraft missile units, provided air defense for the major ground forces. For example, Task Force SCORPION, made up of the HAWK batteries comprising 2d Battalion, 1st Air Defense Artillery, as well as three Patriot batteries from 3d Battalion, 43d Air Defense Artillery, all with the 11th Brigade, provided mobile air defense for the XVIII Airborne Corps. All of the American Patriot units that fought in DESERT STORM were drawn from the 11th Brigade and from several similar brigades of U.S. Army, Europe's 32d Army Air Defense Command.

The primary, higher-level air defense unit during DESERT SHIELD and DESERT STORM was the 11th Brigade. Its commander, Colonel Garrett, was the senior Army air defense officer in the theater of operations. He commanded his brigade from its headquarters, first in Dhahran and later at King Khalid Military City, and functioned as the primary air defense artillery officer at Central Command and Army Central Command.

When deployment of his brigade and additional air defense units was completed in February 1991, the geographic area over which Garrett exercised command and control was enormous, extending from the Persian Gulf coast across the Arabian Peninsula about 1,000 miles to the city of Tabūk, near the northern end of the Red Sea. Within that vast space, every

Patriot battery defended a "footprint," a programmable and variable geographic area of about 6 to 12 miles in diameter around the battery itself. Operating over such a massive area that covered thousands of square miles created acute problems in maintaining communications and providing a logistical lifeline between Garrett's various air defense units.

"Cuing" and "Gizmos"

The problem of maintaining communications was especially serious for the Patriot units because of the nature of their potential targets. They had to defend against attacks by Iraq's plentiful arsenal of Scud missiles. Patriot ultra–high frequency communications lacked the range to allow the brigade command post, or even in some cases the individual battalion headquarters, to pass on information from the Air Force or other sources to alert the individual batteries in case of a Scud launch. With the Scuds reaching a terminal velocity of Mach 6, time was of the absolute essence in launching Patriots against them.[9]

Two sources of information on potential targets supplemented the Patriot's phased-array radar by providing very early warning or "cuing." One was geared to conventional Iraqi aircraft and the other to Scud missiles. Schwarzkopf's Air Force component included the 552d Airborne Warning and Control System Wing. The wing's E–3 Sentry aircraft, an Air Force version of the Boeing 707 commercial airliner that had a large radar dish, contained the electronic surveillance and communications equipment to track and identify Iraqi aircraft, including helicopters. The E–3s relayed data electronically to an Air Force ground station known as the control and reporting center. From there, the information went to Army air defense units, beginning with the brigade headquarters, then a battalion information control center, and finally a battery engagement control station. While this form of early warning was useful to Patriot units during DESERT SHIELD and DESERT STORM, especially in clarifying identification of allied aircraft, it was not tested in battle.

The other source of cuing was tried and proved in combat. The United States Space Command, headquartered in Cheyenne Mountain, near Colorado Springs, Colorado, had Defense Support Program missile warning satellites, originally designed and emplaced to detect Soviet intercontinental ballistic missile launches. These spacecraft were in geosynchronous orbit high above the earth's surface and able frequently to point their infrared telescopes toward Iraq.[10]

When the Iraqis launched a Scud, the thermal signature from the plume of flame, created when the rocket motor burned its liquid fuel, was detected by a Defense Support Program satellite. The satellite relayed the information through a ground station in the Pacific to Cheyenne Mountain. From there the data were retransmitted through a communications satellite to a Patriot battalion information control center. Because time was at a premium in defending against Scuds, Patriot batteries were

[9] Garrett interview; Kirby interview; "Thunder and Lightning," pp. 21–22.

[10] "USAF Missile Warning Satellites Providing 90-Sec. Scud Attack Alert," *Aviation Week & Space Technology* (21 January 1991): 60–61.

themselves occasionally connected to a communications satellite. While a Scud stayed in the air about seven minutes from launch to impact, the satellite warning took less time after detection to get to a Patriot battery. A number of so-called gizmos enabled the generally incompatible Air Force and Army communications equipment to function together. In many cases these were prototype pieces of hardware that took Air Force communications information and translated it so that similar Army equipment could read and display it. The remaining minute or two gave enough time to bring the battery, or batteries, to full operational status, and then detect, identify, track, engage, and destroy the incoming Scud or Scuds.

Much appreciated by air defense crews, cuing from satellites provided the Patriot units with the knowledge that a Scud launch had taken place and the missile's general direction of flight. That information kept battery and battalion commanders from having to keep all of their radars and missile launchers at full alert around the clock. With space-based cuing, crews and equipment were rested and maintained more systematically, improving their effectiveness.[11]

Operation DESERT STORM

With nearly six months to deploy, train, and generally prepare, the Patriot systems and their crews in Saudi Arabia achieved a finely tuned state of readiness by the time Operation DESERT STORM's air campaign started. In the predawn hours of 17 January 1991, after the last American hostages had been evacuated from Iraq and the United Nations ultimatum for Saddam Hussein to leave Kuwait had expired, coalition aircraft began a massive air assault against Iraq, focusing primarily on command and control centers, air defense sites, and fixed Scud launchers. After declaring that "Iraq will never surrender," Saddam Hussein lobbed several Scuds at Israel. The Patriot missile system was already scheduled for delivery to Israel, but the equipment did not actually arrive until just a few weeks before DESERT STORM began. Meanwhile, the crews trained at the Air Defense Artillery School at Fort Bliss and were not due to complete the Patriot course until early in 1991.[12]

On 17 January and again two days later, Iraqi Scuds, fired from fixed sites and mobile launchers in the desert of far western Iraq, fell on the Israeli cities of Tel Aviv and Haifa, causing locally heavy damage and killing and wounding relatively few Israelis but bringing potentially enormous political ramifications. The natural and historic reaction of the State of Israel and its people to such a direct military challenge was retaliation. Israeli Prime Minister Yitzhak Shamir resisted pressure to strike back from the Israeli military and a hard-line faction within his ruling Likud Party. Retaliation could have transformed the fight over Kuwait into another Arab-Israeli conflict, which could have shattered the fragile coalition.

[11] Garrett interview; Kirby interview; Simpson interview; *Jane's Defense Weekly* (2 February 1991): 134; "USAF Missile Warning Satellites Providing 90-Sec. Scud Attack Alert," pp. 60–61; *Time* (4 February 1991): 47.

[12] Heebner interview. Quote from Friedrich, ed., *DESERT STORM*, p. 158. "Thunder and Lightning," p. 26.

Realizing the risk at hand, the Bush administration pressed Israel for restraint. President Bush himself called Prime Minister Shamir and urged such a course. Shamir was already so inclined but needed a gesture that would add substance to American diplomatic efforts. Deputy Secretary of State Lawrence S. Eagleburger had gone to Israel just before DESERT STORM began and offered to have two American Patriot PAC–2 batteries sent to Israel. After the opening round of Scud attacks on Tel Aviv and Haifa, against which the Israelis had no defense, Secretary of Defense Cheney also offered to airlift two American Patriot batteries to Israel. Never before had Israel used any foreign military force to strengthen its own defenses, but Israeli Defense Minister Moshe Arens accepted the offer. Quickly the call went out to the 32d Army Air Defense Command in Europe to alert and prepare Patriot units for airlift to Israel.[13]

Meanwhile, Saddam Hussein launched yet more Scuds, this time from mobile launchers in Kuwait and southern Iraq toward targets in Saudi Arabia. At about half past four on the morning of 17 January, shortly after the air campaign began, the on-duty crew of Battery A, 2d Battalion, 7th Air Defense Artillery, 11th Brigade, a Patriot unit located to protect the Dhahran airport, was alerted and signaled to don gas masks and chemical warfare suits. Without satellite cuing, Battery A loosed two Patriot missiles into the sky over the airport. Looking from a distance like Roman candles but with a thunderous clap indicating something far mightier, the Patriots leaped skyward, maneuvered, and apparently engaged their target. It was over in a matter of seconds. In the process, history's first wartime engagement of a tactical rocket by an antitactical ballistic missile seemed to have occurred.[14]

During the night of 21–22 January, the so-called battle of Riyadh featured numerous apparent Scuds descending on the Saudi Arabian capital. The blossoming effect produced far more targets than were actually there, but the Patriot crews weeded through the radar clutter and engaged every legitimate target. Destruction of a Scud sometimes produced a small-scale version of the blossoming effect. A new PDB–3 software version was produced to help the overall system track, identify, engage, and destroy "real" targets. In addition, many Patriot batteries began to operate in manual mode. The weapon control computer performed its normal functions, but the actual launching of the Patriot missiles was executed manually by a crew member in the engagement control station, prompted by the system.

Two Patriot batteries from the 32d Army Air Defense Command's 10th Air Defense Artillery Brigade were designated for the airlift to Israel. The 10th Brigade had not trained for airborne deployment for a contingency operation outside Europe. Inexperience notwithstanding, the task began, assisted by the 32d Army Air Defense Command staff, which had already arranged the seaborne deployment of some of the command's units to Saudi Arabia. The batteries were equipped with the PAC–2 missile, and the crews had learned the PDB–3 software in November 1990. Using air-

[13] Heebner interview; Woodward, *Commanders*, pp. 211, 363; Friedrich, ed., DESERT STORM, pp. 41–42, 158–59, 161, 164; "Thunder and Lightning," p. 26; *Newsweek* (28 January 1991): 16, and (11 February 1991): 33; *Time* (28 January 1991): 23–24; *New York Times*, 19, 26, 29, and 30 Jan, and 10 and 12 Feb 91; *USA Today*, 21 Jan 91.

[14] "Thunder and Lightning," pp. 19, 27; Blair Case, "'Scud Busters': Patriot Outduels Iraqi Scuds in Dramatic DESERT STORM Combat Debut," *Air Defense Artillery* (January–February 1991): 5–8; Donna Miles, "DESERT STORM Rises," *Soldiers* (March 1991): 6, 8–9; William H. McMichael, "Patriot Passes the Combat Test," *Soldiers* (April 1991): 19–20; *New York Times*, 19 Jan 91.

craft from the Israeli state airline, El Al, as well as Air Force C–5s and C–141s, the batteries began to arrive at Tel Aviv's Ben Gurion Airport on 19 January, barely a day after receiving notification to deploy from Germany. Time was clearly short. The same day that the first Patriot battery landed and became minimally operational, Scuds again attacked Tel Aviv. About seventeen Israelis were injured, and Israel vowed to defend itself. In only three days from their arrival, both 10th Brigade Patriot batteries were fully operational, in time to receive another salvo of Scuds.

On that day, 22 January, an Iraqi Scud penetrated the U.S. Patriot missile defenses at Tel Aviv and landed in one of the city's suburbs, where three people died of heart attacks, about one hundred were injured, and around nine hundred were forced to evacuate their damaged homes. With Scud missiles now falling regularly on Israel's cities, the Israeli Air Force had summoned its Patriot system operators home on 18 January from Fort Bliss, where they had nearly completed their training. Leaving behind the system's maintainers to finish their course work, the operators were strengthened with about twenty fully trained American maintainers from Fort Bliss. These cobbled-together, international crews arrived in Israel on 20 January, received a further augmentation of American Patriot soldiers, and were ready to operate within twenty-four hours. The two Israeli Patriot batteries came under the operational control, but not the command, of Col. David K. Heebner, commander of the 10th Brigade.

Though the four American and Israeli Patriot batteries did well, some Scuds got through. The diplomatically explosive situation called for extra measures, because four batteries alone were not enough to defend the sprawling urban areas of Tel Aviv and Haifa. Two additional batteries from the 32d Army Air Defense Command's 94th Air Defense Artillery Brigade flew to Israel to enhance the defense, and in time the Dutch contributed a battery of their own to the effort. The Dutch battery defended Jerusalem and communicated with the American and Israeli Patriot crews by secure telephone.[15]

After the first two weeks of DESERT STORM, Scud attacks on Israel and Saudi Arabia virtually ceased. During that time, the various Patriot battalion and brigade headquarters in Saudi Arabia and Israel had established a variety of means of collecting, analyzing, and sharing data from Scud attacks. Among these were training and testing teams, checklists, and seminars. In effect, the Patriot crews studied the experience as they lived it, and their increased proficiency may have helped deter further launches.

The air campaign had a more direct effect on the declining number of Scud launches. The combination of air attacks against targets such as early warning radar sites and the failure of the Iraqi air force to come up and fight for control of the skies led General Schwarzkopf on 30 January to announce that the allies had achieved air supremacy, meaning their aircraft could roam the skies over Iraq with virtual impunity. Without a full-fledged air battle to wage, allied ground attack aircraft turned to the task of destroying Iraq's Scud launchers. Though enjoying more success

[15] Heebner interview; "Thunder and Lightning," pp. 26–27; Friedrich, ed., *DESERT STORM*, p. 159; *New York Times*, 20, 23, and 24 Jan 91.

Task Force 8/43 soldier emplacing a Patriot launcher in Iraq during Desert Storm

against fixed sites than against mobile launchers, which often used overcast weather to shield their firings from satellites and aircraft-borne telescopes and radars, allied tactical airplanes kept the mobile Scuds on the move, reducing their effectiveness and even destroying some of them. By the time the ground campaign began, the Scud threat against Israel and Saudi Arabia seemed to have passed.[16]

Two Patriot task forces supported Army troops in the ground offensive. Task Force Scorpion, the oversized HAWK-Patriot battalion, provided air defense for the XVIII Airborne Corps. The VII Corps, which had no air defense brigade attached as part of its force structure to go with the air defense battalions that served with each of its maneuver divisions, formed another mixed HAWK-Patriot battalion from units of the 32d Army Air Defense Command's 69th Air Defense Artillery Brigade. Dubbed Task Force 8/43, it had four Patriot batteries from the 8th Battalion, 43d Air Defense Artillery, and two HAWK batteries from the 6th Battalion, 52d Air Defense Artillery. Task Force Scorpion and elements of Task Force 8/43, as well as air defense units positioned along the northwest-running main supply route Dodge, or Tapline Road, provided air defense for the long march of the XVIII Airborne Corps to its jumping-off points out in the desert along the Iraqi-Saudi border.

None of the Patriot missiles of Task Force Scorpion made it into Iraq, but 8/43 furnished air defense against aircraft and Scud missiles while elements of VII Corps breached the Iraqi defensive berm in their front. Then as VII Corps surged through the breach and wheeled to the

[16] Garrett interview; Heebner interview; Simpson interview; Kirby interview; Woodward, *Commanders*, pp. 309, 330–31; *Aviation Week & Space Technology* (4 February 1991): 63; *New York Times*, 17, 20, 21, and 25 Jan 91; *USA Today*, 8 Mar 91.

[17] Garrett interview; "Thunder and Lightning," pp. 21–22, 26; "Desert Victory," pp. 39–46; Edward M. Flanagan, Jr., "The 100-Hour War," *Army* (April 1991): 18, 21, 24–26.

[18] Garrett interview; Simpson interview; Kirby interview; "Team Patriot," p. 14; "Thunder and Lightning," pp. 21, 29; Friedrich, ed., *DESERT STORM*, p. 165; Heike Hasenauer, "Theater Missile Defense: Improved Patriot," *Soldiers* (June 1991): 25; *U.S. News & World Report* (11 February 1991): 15; *Army Times*, 11 Mar 91, p. 8, and 13 May 91, pp. 3, 25, 61; *New York Times*, 20 May 91; *El Paso* (Texas) *Times*, 6 Jun 91; *El Paso* (Texas) *Herald-Post*, 15 Aug 91.

[19] Garrett interview; Heebner interview; Simpson interview; Kirby interview; "Thunder and Lightning," pp. 20, 29; "Desert Victory," p. 47; *New York Times*, 26 Jan, 3 Feb, and 7 Mar 91.

east with the rest of the allied force, the vehicles of 8/43 carried their HAWK and Patriot air defense missile systems along with the advance.[17]

While the United Nations forces outmaneuvered and began destroying the Iraqi army, Saddam Hussein turned once more to his Scuds. On 24 February the Iraqis lofted several Scuds in the direction of Israel's Dimona nuclear facility. The Scuds missed and impacted harmlessly in the nearby desert. On the night of 25 February a lone Scud got by the Patriot defenses in Saudi Arabia, slamming into a metal warehouse near Dhahran at Al Khubar. The warehouse had been converted into transient billets to house over one hundred soldiers from several commands. With the Scud's detonation, the entire structure collapsed and turned instantly into a pile of twisted girders and sheet metal. In all, 28 American soldiers were killed and 97 wounded. Thirteen of the dead and 37 of the injured were from a western Pennsylvania Army National Guard unit, the 14th Quartermaster Detachment. On no other occasion during all of Operations DESERT SHIELD and DESERT STORM were more U.S. military personnel killed or wounded.

Less than two full days later, with the Iraqi army nearly in ruins and Kuwait at last liberated, President Bush suspended military operations and laid out the terms for a permanent cease-fire. An informal end to the fighting soon went into effect.[18]

In the final analysis, the Patriot missile made major contributions to the success of Operation DESERT STORM. Though some allied tactical aircraft were diverted to hunt for the elusive mobile Scud launchers, the air phase stayed on track and on schedule in large part because the Patriots were able to deal with the Scuds, which were employed in a piecemeal fashion by an unimaginative enemy. The Patriot also helped keep preparation and execution of the land campaign on schedule by eliminating the need to divert maneuver units to the task of searching for mobile Scuds. In short, the Patriot reduced the Scud to a minor operational irritant. And last, Saddam Hussein's use of Scuds as a terror weapon to goad the Israelis into a reprisal that would possibly unravel the fragile coalition or to panic the Saudis and crush their will to resist came to naught. Overall, the Patriot blunted the foe's only truly effective offensive weapon.[19]

Appendix B

U.S. Equipment

This appendix provides general, unofficial information on the characteristics and armament of selected equipment, to include data on four munitions, used by the U.S. Army during the war in Southwest Asia. For additional technical information, readers should consult the following: the Army publication *Weapon Systems: United States Army, 1991*, issued annually and sold by the Government Printing Office; the magazine *Army*, especially the October issue known as the "Green Book," published by the Association of the United States Army (2425 Wilson Blvd., Arlington, Va. 22201); and the many reference books produced by Jane's Information Group (1340 Braddock Place, Suite 300, Alexandria, Va. 22314), among them *Jane's Armour and Artillery*, *Jane's Infantry Weapons*, and *Jane's Weapon Systems*.

The line drawings are provided for identification and are not drawn to a standard scale. Statistical data is approximate.

AH–1 Series Cobra Attack Helicopter

The AH–1 Cobra is the Army's older attack helicopter. The version deployed to Southwest Asia was the AH–1F. Most systems of the AH–1F have been upgraded to about the level of the AH–64A Apache. Improvements include a more powerful engine and new or enhanced systems for fire control, thermal imaging, radar jamming, and infrared countermeasures.

CHARACTERISTICS

Length: 53.1 feet with rotors
Wingspan: 10.8 feet
Width: 3.3 feet
Height: 13.4 feet
Weight: 5 tons
Speed: 195 miles per hour
Range: 315 miles
Crew: 2

ARMAMENT (various combinations)

Types: TOW missiles
         Hydra 70 rockets
         20-mm. cannon

AH–1F

AH–64A Apache Attack Helicopter

The AH–64A Apache is the Army's principal attack helicopter. Built to endure front-line environments, it can operate during the day or night and in adverse weather utilizing the integrated helmet and display sight system. The AH–64A is also equipped with some of the latest avionics and electronics, such as the target acquisition designation sight, pilot night vision system, radar jammer, infrared countermeasures, and nap-of-earth navigation. The Apaches employed in Southwest Asia also had the global positioning system.

CHARACTERISTICS

Length: 58.3 feet with rotors
Wingspan: 16.3 feet
Width: 6.5 feet
Height: 12.7 feet
Weight: 10.5 tons
Speed: 227 miles per hour
Range: 300 miles
Crew: 2

ARMAMENT

Types: HELLFIRE missiles
         Hydra 70 rockets
         30-mm. chain gun

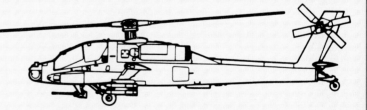

CH–47D Chinook Transport Helicopter

The CH–47D Chinook is a highly versatile heavy-lift helicopter. Its primary missions range from troop movements and artillery emplacement to battlefield resupply. With its triple-hook cargo system, the CH–47D is able to carry heavy payloads—for example, bulldozers and forty-foot containers—and still travel at speeds over 155 miles per hour. In air assault operations it often serves as the principal mover of the 155-mm. M198 howitzer, thirty rounds of ammunition, and an eleven-man crew. Like most Army helicopters, the Chinook is equipped with advanced avionics and electronics, including the global positioning system.

CHARACTERISTICS

Length:	98.9 feet with rotors
Width:	12.4 feet
Height:	18.9 feet
Weight:	27 tons
Payload:	12.5 tons (internal)
	12.5–17 tons (external)
Speed:	177 miles per hour
Range:	706 miles
Crew:	4

OH–58 Series Kiowa Scout Helicopter

The OH–58 Kiowa, as a scout helicopter, has the primary missions of reconnaissance, surveillance, and intelligence gathering. The latest version is the OH–58D Kiowa Warrior, which has the additional mission capability of target acquisition and/or laser designation. It can operate during the day or night and in adverse weather. Under a program designated Prime Chance, some OH–58Ds have been retrofitted to carry air-to-air and air-to-ground weapons.

CHARACTERISTICS

Length:	42.2 feet with rotors
Width:	7.9 feet
Height:	12.9 feet
Weight:	2.8 tons
	2.3 tons (unarmed)
Speed:	149 miles per hour
Range:	288 miles
Crew:	2

ARMAMENT UNDER PRIME CHANCE (various combinations)

Types:	Stinger missiles
	HELLFIRE missiles
	Hydra 70 rockets
	.50-caliber machine gun
	7.62-mm. machine gun

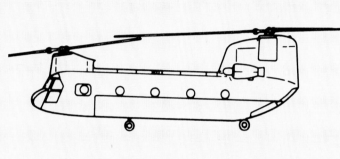

OH-58D

UH–1H Iroquois Utility Helicopter

The UH–1 Iroquois, or "Huey," is a Vietnam-vintage multipurpose helicopter that is being phased out by the introduction of the UH–60 Black Hawk. The latest version, the UH–1H, was deployed to Southwest Asia. Primary missions include general support, air assault, cargo transport, aeromedical evacuation, search and rescue, and electronic warfare.

CHARACTERISTICS

Length:	57.1 feet with rotors
Width:	8.6 feet
Height:	14.5 feet
Weight:	4.7 tons
Payload:	1.5 tons (internal)
	2 tons (external)
Speed:	127 miles per hour
Range:	318 miles
Crew:	3–4
Passengers:	11–14

ARMAMENT

Type:	7.62-mm. machine gun

UH–60A Black Hawk Utility Helicopter

The UH–60A Black Hawk is the Army's primary utility/assault helicopter. It can perform a wide array of missions, to include air cavalry, electronic warfare, and aeromedical evacuation. In air assault operations it can move a squad of eleven combat troops and equipment or carry the 105-mm. M102 howitzer, thirty rounds of ammunition, and a six-man crew. The Black Hawk is equipped with advanced avionics and electronics, such as the global positioning system.

CHARACTERISTICS

Length:	64.9 feet with rotors
Width:	7.8 feet
Height:	12.3 feet
Weight:	10.1 tons
Payload:	2 tons (internal)
	4 tons (external)
Speed:	184 miles per hour
Range:	368 miles
	1,012–1,380 miles with auxiliary tanks
Crew:	3–4

ARMAMENT

Type:	7.62-mm. machine gun

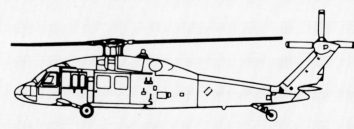

M1 Series Abrams Main Battle Tank

The M1 series Abrams, the Army's principal combat tank, can operate in all climate and light conditions. Several versions were deployed to Southwest Asia, primarily the M1A1. The M1A1's advanced armor, superior maneuverability, low profile, chemical overpressure system, and compartmentalized fuel and ammunition stores provide the crew with levels of battlefield protection that surpass any other tank, and its main gun is capable of making catastrophic kills in excess of 3,000 meters. During Operations DESERT SHIELD–DESERT STORM some M1A1s were modified with add-on armor and others were equipped with mine rollers and mine plows for breaching obstacles and clearing minefields.

CHARACTERISTICS

Length:	32.3 feet with gun
Width:	12 feet
Height:	8 feet
Weight:	62.9 tons
Speed:	41 miles per hour
Range:	288 miles
Crew:	4

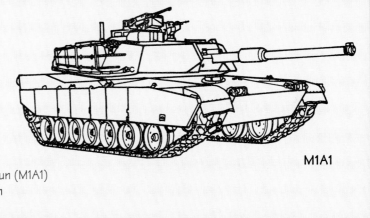

M1A1

ARMAMENT

Primary:	105-mm. gun (M1)
	120-mm. smoothbore gun (M1A1)
Secondary:	.50-caliber machine gun
	7.62-mm. machine gun

M551A1 Sheridan Armored Reconnaissance Vehicle

The M551A1 Sheridan was one of the first pieces of equipment rushed into Saudi Arabia during Operation DESERT SHIELD. Unlike main battle tanks, the Sheridan can be dropped by parachute, making it an important part of the combat power of the 82d Airborne Division. Most systems have been upgraded and improved since the Sheridan was introduced in the 1960s. For example, the M551A1 has enhanced thermal-imaging and targeting sights. Its gun-launcher fires both conventional munitions and Shillelagh missiles.

CHARACTERISTICS

Length:	20.6 feet
Width:	9.2 feet
Height:	7.6 feet
Weight:	17.5 tons
Speed:	43 miles per hour
Range:	372 miles
Crew:	4

ARMAMENT

Primary:	152-mm. gun-launcher
Secondary:	.50-caliber machine gun
	7.62-mm. machine gun

M2/M3 Series Bradley Fighting Vehicle

The M2 and M3 Bradley fighting vehicles are designed to operate in combat with the same speed as the M1A1 Abrams and with a greater degree of protection than the M113 armored personnel carrier. The M2 provides infantry squads with a light armored fighting vehicle. The M3 provides scout and armored cavalry units with a vehicle for reconnaissance, screening, and security missions. The infantry version has firing ports for modified M16 rifles. Other modifications include enhanced armor. In addition to the M2 and M3 configurations, the A1 and A2 versions of both models were deployed to Southwest Asia.

CHARACTERISTICS

Length:	20.5 feet
Width:	10.5 feet
Height:	9.7 feet
Weight:	24.8 tons (M2)
	24.7 tons (M3)
Speed:	41 miles per hour
Range:	300 miles
Crew:	3
Passengers:	6 (M2)
	2 (M3)

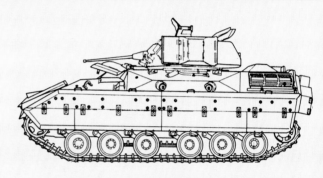

M2

ARMAMENT

Primary:	25-mm. cannon
Secondary:	7.62-mm. machine gun
	TOW missiles (two launch tubes)

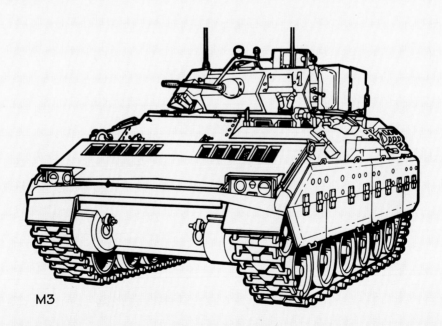

M3

M113 Series Armored Personnel Carrier

The M113 series was used widely by the U.S. Army and coalition forces during Operations DESERT SHIELD–DESERT STORM as an infantry and engineer squad carrier, a medical evacuation carrier, and a maintenance support vehicle. Other variations include an add-on dozer blade, a Vulcan weapon system (M163) for antiaircraft defense, a TOW launch assembly (M901), and a command-and-control vehicle (M577). The upgraded M113A3 has added spall suppression liners, armored external fuel tanks, a more powerful engine and transmission, and mounting plates for the optional bolt-on aluminum armor.

CHARACTERISTICS

Length:	25.8 feet
Width:	8.7 feet
Height:	8.3 feet
Weight:	13.3 tons
Speed:	41 miles per hour
Range:	300 miles
Crew:	2
Passengers:	7

ARMAMENT

Type:	.50-caliber machine gun

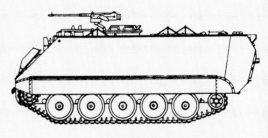

M113A3

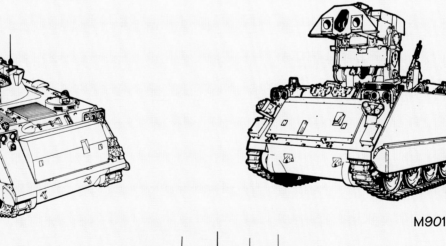

M163

M901

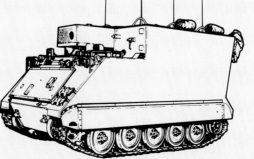

M577

M728 Combat Engineer Vehicle

The M728 is based on the hull of the M60 tank. A dozer blade is mounted to the front of the hull and an A-frame crane is hinged to either side of the turret. In traveling mode the crane is folded down around the rear of the turret. The main gun fires several types of ammunition, to include antipersonnel rounds. During Operation DESERT STORM M728s were used to augment M1A1s equipped with mine rollers and mine plows.

CHARACTERISTICS

Length:	29.3 feet (crane folded)
Width:	12 feet
	12.2 feet with blade
Height:	10.5 feet
Weight:	58.5 tons
Speed:	30 miles per hour
Range:	279 miles
Crew:	4

ARMAMENT

Primary:	165-mm. demolition gun
Secondary:	.50-caliber machine gun
	7.62-mm. machine gun

M9 Armored Combat Earthmover

The M9 ACE is a highly mobile armored tracked vehicle that provides combat engineer support to front-line forces. Its tasks include eliminating enemy obstacles, maintenance and repair of roads and supply routes, and construction of fighting positions.

CHARACTERISTICS

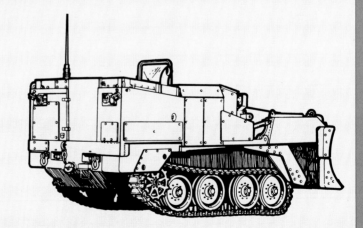

Length:	20.5 feet
Width:	9.2 feet
	10.5 feet with dozer wings
Height:	8.9 feet (windshield down)
	9.9 feet (windshield up)
Weight:	26.9 tons
Speed:	30 miles per hour
Range:	200 miles
Crew:	1

105-mm. M102 Howitzer

First introduced during the Vietnam War, the M102 was the light-towed artillery piece used in Operations DESERT SHIELD–DESERT STORM. It fires a variety of conventional munitions and traverses rapidly through 360 degrees. M102s can be dropped by parachute or transported by utility helicopters for normal movement or air assault operations.

CHARACTERISTICS
Length: 17.1 feet
Width: 6.4 feet
Height: 5.2 feet
Weight: 1.6 tons
Crew: 8
Rate of fire: 10 rounds per minute (maximum)
              3 rounds per minute (sustained)
Range: 11,500 meters
              15,100 meters with rocket-assisted projectile

155-mm. M198 Howitzer

The M198 is a medium-towed artillery piece. It can be dropped by parachute or transported by a CH–47D Chinook. The M198 is deployed in separate corps- and Army-level field artillery units, as well as in artillery battalions of light and airborne divisions.

CHARACTERISTICS
Length: 40.7 feet
Width: 9.2 feet
Height: 9.5 feet
Weight: 7.9 tons
Crew: 11
Rate of fire: 4 rounds per minute (maximum)
              1 round per minute (sustained)
Range: 18,150 meters
              30,000 meters with
                  rocket-assisted projectile

155-mm. M109 Series Self-Propelled Howitzer

The M109 was first introduced in the early 1960s. Continually upgraded and improved, it is still the primary indirect fire support weapon of maneuver brigades of armored and mechanized infantry divisions. The versions deployed to Southwest Asia were the M109A2 or later models with a longer gun tube.

CHARACTERISTICS

Length:	30 feet
Width:	10.3 feet
Height:	10.7 feet
Weight:	27.4 tons
Speed:	35 miles per hour
Range:	216 miles
Crew:	6

ARMAMENT

Primary:	155-mm. howitzer
Secondary:	.50-caliber or 7.62-mm. machine gun
Rate of fire:	3 rounds per minute (maximum)
	1 round per minute (sustained)
Range:	18,000 meters
	23,500 meters with rocket-assisted projectile

M109A2

8-inch M110A2 Self-Propelled Howitzer

The M110A2 is the largest available self-propelled howitzer in the Army's inventory. It is deployed in division artillery of general support battalions and in separate corps- and Army-level battalions. Missions include general support, counterbattery fire, and suppression of enemy air defense systems.

CHARACTERISTICS

Length:	35.3 feet
Width:	10.3 feet
Height:	10.3 feet
Weight:	31.2 tons
Speed:	34 miles per hour
Range:	324 miles
Crew:	5

ARMAMENT

Type:	8-inch howitzer
Rate of fire:	2 rounds per minute (maximum)
	1 round per 2 minutes (sustained)
Range:	16,800 meters
	30,000 meters with rocket-assisted projectile

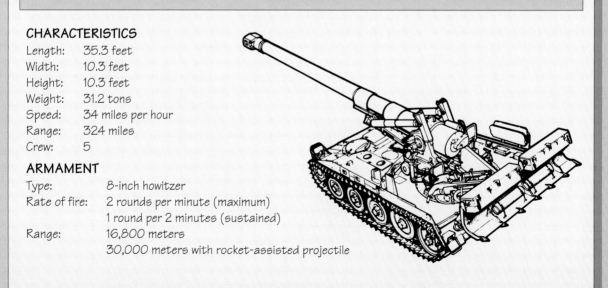

Multiple Launch Rocket System

The multiple launch rocket system (MLRS) delivers extreme firepower in a short time. The MLRS consists of a launcher that holds two six-rocket canisters. Primary missions are counterbattery fire and suppression of enemy air defense systems. Each MLRS artillery rocket disperses 644 fragmentation bomblets over the target. These munitions are both antiarmor and antipersonnel.

CHARACTERISTICS

Length:	23 feet
Width:	9.8 feet
Height:	8.5 feet
Weight:	26.6 tons
Speed:	40 miles per hour
Range:	300 miles
Crew:	3

ARMAMENT

Type:	twelve 227-mm. rockets (six per canister)
Length:	13.7 feet (canister)
Width:	3.3 feet (canister)
Height:	2.7 feet (canister)
Weight:	2.5 tons (armed canister)
Rate of fire:	12 rockets in less than 1 minute
Range:	32 kilometers
Warhead:	dual-purpose improved conventional munitions

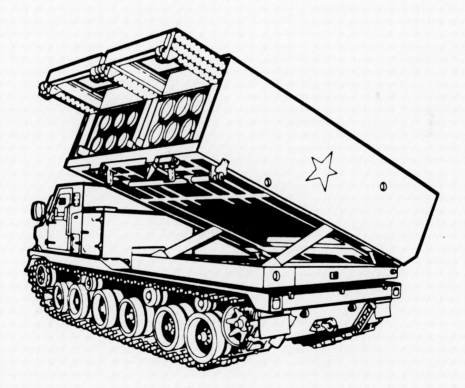

Army Tactical Missile System

The Army tactical missile system (ATACMS) provides artillery units with a long-range capability for destroying high-priority targets. It can operate in all climate and light conditions while remaining beyond the range of most conventional weapons. The system uses the launcher originally designed for the MLRS. The launcher holds two modified canisters, each with one missile. The exterior of ATACMS and MLRS launchers appear similar; however, ATACMS missiles are much larger and have a much greater range than MLRS artillery rockets.

CHARACTERISTICS
Length:	23 feet
Width:	9.8 feet
Height:	8.5 feet
Weight:	26.6 tons
Speed:	40 miles per hour
Range:	300 miles
Crew:	3

ARMAMENT
Type:	two surface-to-surface missiles (one per canister)
Length:	13.7 feet (canister)
Width:	3.3 feet (canister)
Height:	2.7 feet (canister)
Weight:	1.8 tons (armed canister)
Diameter:	2 feet (missile)
Range:	in excess of 100 kilometers
Warhead:	dual-purpose improved conventional munitions

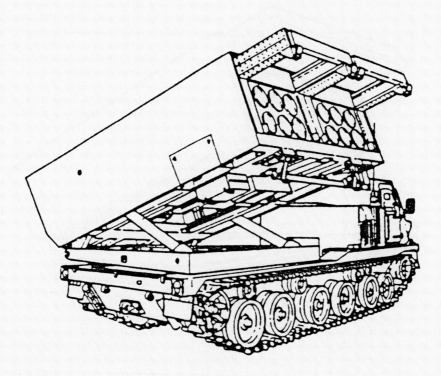

Firefinder Radars

The highly mobile Firefinder radars AN/TPQ–36 and larger AN/TPQ–37 can immediately locate enemy fire. When hostile projectiles penetrate the scanned area(s) but before they even reach the target(s), the Firefinder radar back-plots and transmits enemy artillery and mortar positions, in precise coordinates, to friendly artillery fire centers to allow for counterbattery fire. The radar uses separate tracking channels and traverses in sector increments through 360 degrees. An operations shelter is set up on a cargo truck. A generator and a radar antenna, which has lightweight Kevlar armor added for protection against small-arms fire and shrapnel, are towed behind the truck. Once emplaced, a single soldier can operate the Firefinder system.

CHARACTERISTICS

Type:	artillery-, rocket-, and mortar-locating radars
Radar range:	30,000 meters (AN/TPQ–36)
	50,000 meters (AN/TPQ–37)
Sector:	90 degrees
Transporter:	2.5-ton cargo truck (AN/TPQ–36)
	5-ton cargo truck (AN/TPQ–37)
Emplacement:	15 minutes
Displacement:	5 minutes
Crew:	8–12

AN/TPQ–36

AN/TPQ–37

Patriot Air Defense System

The Patriot provides protection against enemy planes and tactical ballistic missiles. The system consists of the M901 launch station, a remotely operated four-canister unit mounted on an M860 semi-trailer, with its own electronics pack, data link cable, and generator. The prime mover of the M901 is either the M818 tractor or the M983 HEMTT (heavy expanded mobility tactical truck). The Patriot usually is deployed in a battery of five to eight launchers, in conjunction with an electric power plant, an OE–349/MRC antenna mast group, an AN/MPQ–53 radar unit, and an AN/MSQ–116 engagement control center. In addition, each battery has other dedicated support vehicles, to include missile reload trailer transporters and maintenance trucks.

CHARACTERISTICS

Length: 33.3 feet
Width: 9.5 feet (outriggers up)
21.5 feet (outriggers down)
Height: 10.8 feet
Weight: 11.2 tons
Range: transporter dependent

ARMAMENT

Type: four surface-to-air missiles
(one per canister)
Length: 20.1 feet (canister)
Width: 3.5 feet (canister)
Height: 3.2 feet (canister)
Weight: 1.8 tons (armed canister)
Velocity: Mach 3.7
Altitude: 24,240 meters
Range: 160 kilometers
Warhead: high explosive

M901

OE–349/MRC

AN/MPQ–53

AN/MSQ–116

Heavy Expanded Mobility Tactical Truck

The heavy expanded mobility tactical truck (HEMTT) comes in five configurations, designed for different combat-support missions. The M978 tanker refuels tactical vehicles and helicopters in forward locations. The M983 tractor tows the trailer-mounted Pershing and Patriot missile systems. The M984 recovery vehicle uses a lift-and-tow system to recover disabled vehicles in two–three minutes. The M977 and M985 cargo trucks carry all types of equipment, especially ammunition. All but the tanker have optional material-handling cranes at the rear of the vehicle.

CHARACTERISTICS

Length: 33.4 feet (M977, M978, M985)
          32.8 feet (M984)
          29.2 feet (M983)
Width: 8.5 feet
Height: 7.8 feet
Weight: 31 tons (M977, M978, M983)
          34 tons (M985)
          49 tons (M984)
Speed: 55 miles per hour
Range: 300 miles
Crew: 2

M977

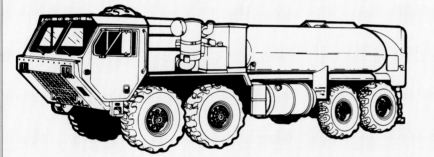

M978

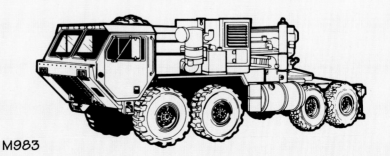

M983

Heavy Equipment Transporter System

The heavy equipment transporter system (HETS) is used to transport, deploy, and evacuate tanks and other heavy vehicles. It consists of either the M746 or the M911 truck tractor, with the M747 semi-trailer. During Operations DESERT SHIELD–DESERT STORM the HETS vehicles were employed primarily to haul M1A1 series tanks. However, they demonstrated poor durability when loads exceeded 60 tons.

CHARACTERISTICS

	M911	M746	M747
Length:	30 feet	27 feet	48.2 feet
Width:	9.5 feet	10 feet	11.5 feet
Height:	11.8 feet	10 feet	6.8 feet
Weight:	26.3 tons	25.8 tons	17.1 tons
Speed:	43 miles per hour	38 miles per hour	
Range:	614 miles	200 miles	
Crew:	2	2	

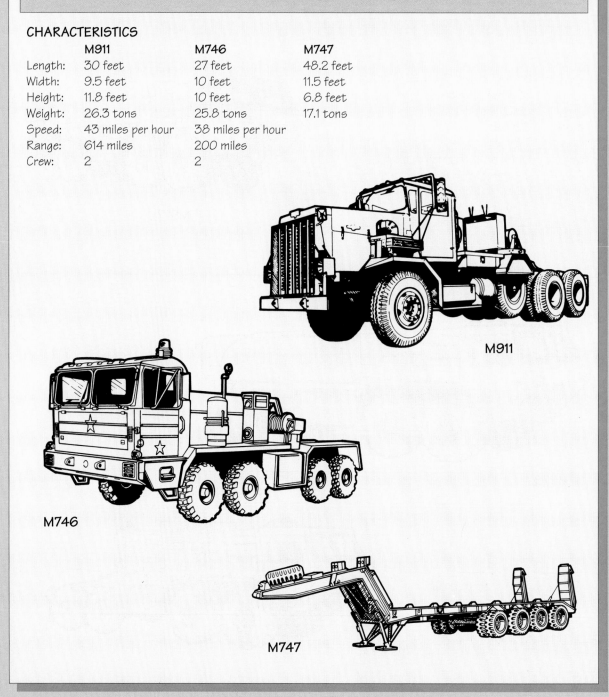

M911

M746

M747

High Mobility Multipurpose Wheeled Vehicle

The high mobility multipurpose wheeled vehicle (HMMWV), or "Hummer," is a highly versatile four-wheel-drive tactical vehicle. Based on the M998 chassis, it comes with various modules and kits that allow for a number of configurations, to include armament carrier for the TOW missile system (M966), ambulance (M997), and cargo-and-troop carrier. Overall, the HMMWV is an adaptable system that lends itself to many field-expedient modifications.

CHARACTERISTICS

Length: 15 feet
Width: 7.1 feet
Height: 6 feet
Weight: 3.8 tons
Speed: 65 miles per hour
Range: 300 miles
Crew: 2–4

ARMAMENT

Type: Configuration dependent (for example, TOW missiles,
          .50-caliber or 7.62-mm machine gun, 40-mm. Mark
          19 automatic grenade launcher)

M998

M997

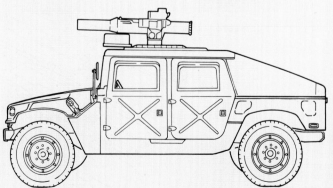

M966

XM93 Fox NBC Reconnaissance System

The Fox is the Army's first reconnaissance vehicle whose primary missions are nuclear-biological-chemical detection, warning, identification, and analysis. Contamination hazards to the crew are minimized by the vehicle's built-in chemical overpressure system. In support of Operations DESERT SHIELD–DESERT STORM the German government donated sixty XM93s, of which fifty were employed by the Army.

CHARACTERISTICS

Length: 22.3 feet
Width: 9.8 feet
Height: 8.1 feet
Weight: 18.7 tons
Speed: 65 miles per hour
Range: 500 miles
Crew: 4

ARMAMENT

Type: 7.62-mm. machine gun

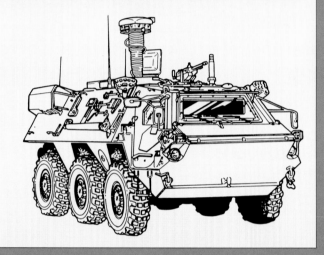

HELLFIRE

The helicopter-launched fire and forget (HELLFIRE) missile system is a laser-guided munition capable of catastrophic kills against armored vehicles and hard-ground targets, such as bunkers. HELLFIRE missiles can be fired while the helicopter is hovering or flying up to maximum speed. The laser designator from either the launch aircraft, an accompanying aircraft, or a ground source illuminates the target. A sensor in the nose of the HELLFIRE guides the missile to the laser beam on the target. A HELLFIRE missile weighs 100 pounds and measures 5.3 feet long and 7 inches in diameter.

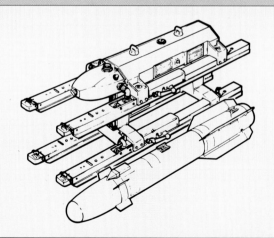

TOW

The tube-launched, optically tracked, wire command-link guided (TOW) missile system is a long-range antitank weapon designed to destroy armored vehicles and other hard-ground targets, such as fortifications. Encased in its launch tube, the TOW missile can be fired from various ground vehicles, from helicopters, or from a ground mount. Once launched, the gunner tracks the target with his sight. Directional changes are sent to the missile from the sight via two very fine wires that trail behind the missile. The TOW missile weighs 62.4 pounds, measures 3.8 feet long and 6 inches in diameter, and has a maximum range of 3,750 meters.

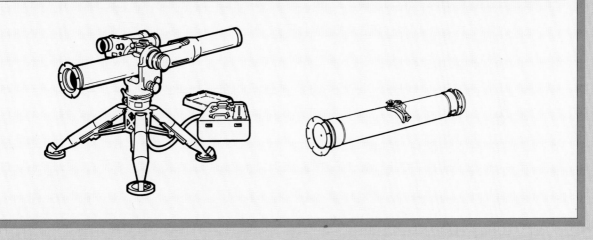

Copperhead

The Copperhead is a high explosive antitank round fired from a 155-mm. howitzer in the same manner as a conventional round. While the round is in flight, a laser designator from either a helicopter or a ground source illuminates the target. A sensor in the nose of the Copperhead guides the missile to the laser beam on the target. The Copperhead round weighs 137 pounds and has a range of 16,000 meters.

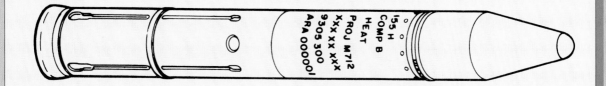

Appendix C

IRAQI EQUIPMENT

This appendix provides general, unofficial information on the characteristics and armament of selected equipment used by the Iraqi forces during the war in Southwest Asia. The Iraqis employed items captured from Iran and Kuwait as well as those purchased on the international arms market. Their practice of battlefield reclamation, together with their upgrades and modifications, produced an assortment of unique equipment made from mix-and-match parts. Many variants by country of origin and diverse specialty vehicles are not covered. For additional technical information, readers should consult the following: reference books published by Jane's Information Group (1340 Braddock Place, Suite 300, Alexandria, Va. 22314), among them *Jane's Armour and Artillery*, *Jane's Infantry Weapons*, and *Jane's Weapon Systems*; and selected training publications prepared by Army organizations, such as *Identifying the Iraqi Threat and How They Fight* (August 1990), *How They Fight: Desert Shield Order of Battle Handbook* (September 1990), the *Aviator's Recognition Manual* (FM 1–402, August 1984), and the *Field Order of Battle Handbook* (May 1989).

The line drawings are provided for identification and are not drawn to a standard scale. Statistical data is approximate.

T–54/T–55 Series Main Battle Tank

CHARACTERISTICS

Length: 30.3 feet with gun
Width: 10.7 feet
Height: 7.9 feet
Weight: 39 tons
Speed: 27 miles per hour
Range: 310 miles
           372 miles with auxiliary tanks
Crew: 4

ARMAMENT

Primary: 100-mm. gun
Secondary: 12.7-mm. machine gun
            two 7.62-mm. machine guns

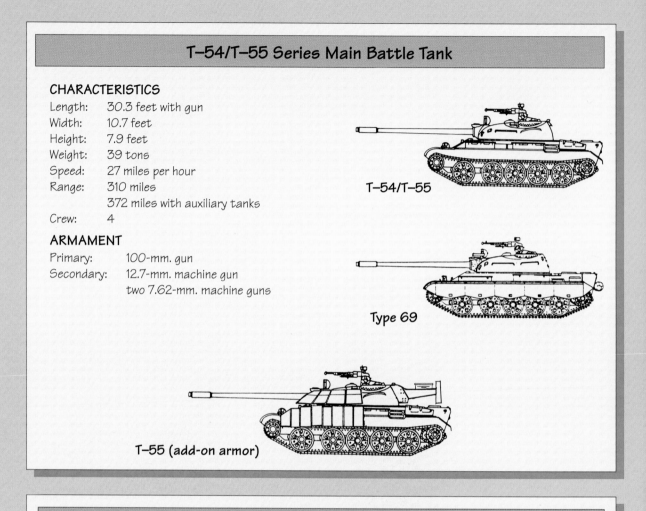

T–54/T–55

Type 69

T–55 (add-on armor)

T–62 Main Battle Tank

CHARACTERISTICS

Length: 30.6 feet with gun
Width: 10.8 feet
Height: 7.9 feet
Weight: 44 tons
Speed: 31 miles per hour
Range: 279 miles
           403 miles with auxiliary tanks
Crew: 4

ARMAMENT

Primary: 115-mm. gun
Secondary: 12.7-mm. machine gun
            7.62-mm. machine gun

T–72 Series Main Battle Tank

CHARACTERISTICS

Length:	30.3 feet with gun
Width:	11.8 feet
	15.5 feet with skirts
Height:	7.8 feet
Weight:	48.9 tons
Speed:	50 miles per hour
Range:	298 miles
	410 miles with auxiliary tanks
Crew:	3

ARMAMENT

Primary:	125-mm. gun
Secondary:	12.7-mm. machine gun
	7.62-mm. machine gun

BMD–1 Airborne Combat Vehicle

CHARACTERISTICS

Length:	17.8 feet
Width:	8.5 feet
Height:	5.3–6.5 feet
Weight:	8.2 tons
Speed:	43 miles per hour
Range:	200 miles
Crew:	3
Passengers:	4

ARMAMENT

Primary:	73-mm. gun
Secondary:	three 7.62-mm. machine guns
	AT–3 SAGGER or AT–4 SPIGOT antitank guided weapons

BMP–1 Infantry Fighting Vehicle

CHARACTERISTICS

Length:	22 feet
Width:	9.5 feet
Height:	7.2 feet
Weight:	14.8 tons
Speed:	50 miles per hour
Range:	310 miles
Crew:	3
Passengers:	8

ARMAMENT

Primary:	73-mm. smoothbore cannon
Secondary:	7.62-mm. machine gun
	AT–3 SAGGER antitank guided weapons

BMP–2 Infantry Fighting Vehicle

CHARACTERISTICS

Length:	22 feet
Width:	10.1 feet
Height:	6.9 feet
Weight:	15.7 tons
Speed:	40 miles per hour
Range:	341–72 miles
Crew:	3
Passengers:	7

ARMAMENT

Primary: 30-mm. cannon
Secondary: 7.62-mm. machine gun
AT–4 SPIGOT or AT–5 SPANDREL antitank guided weapons

M–1974 Series Artillery Command and Reconnaissance Vehicle

CHARACTERISTICS

Length:	23.6 feet
Width:	9.3 feet
Height:	7.5 feet
Weight:	15.4 tons
Speed:	50 miles per hour
Range:	325 miles
Crew:	5

ARMAMENT

Type: 12.7-mm. machine gun

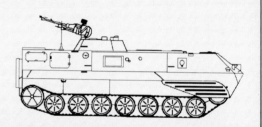

BRDM–2 Scout Vehicle

CHARACTERISTICS

Length:	18.9 feet
Width:	7.9 feet
Height:	7.6 feet
Weight:	7.2 tons
Speed:	62 miles per hour
Range:	465 miles
Crew:	2–4

ARMAMENT

Primary: 14.5-mm. machine gun or 23-mm. cannon or AT–3 SAGGER, AT–4 SPIGOT, and AT–5 SPANDREL antitank guided weapons
Secondary: 7.62-mm. machine gun

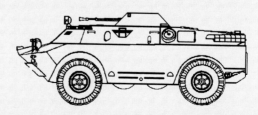

BTR–50P/BTR–50PK Armored Personnel Carrier

CHARACTERISTICS

Length:	23.2 feet
Width:	10.3 feet
Height:	6.5 feet
Weight:	15.6 tons
Speed:	27 miles per hour
Range:	248 miles
Crew:	2
Passengers:	20

ARMAMENT

Type: 7.62-mm. machine gun

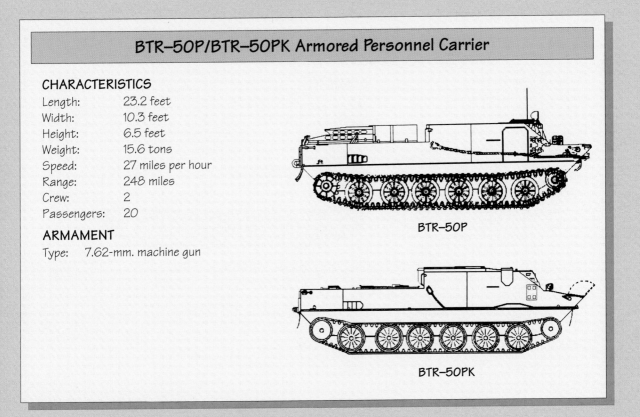

BTR–50P

BTR–50PK

BTR–60PB Armored Personnel Carrier

CHARACTERISTICS

Length:	24.8 feet
Width:	9.3 feet
Height:	7.6 feet
Weight:	11.4 tons
Speed:	50 miles per hour
Range:	310 miles
Crew:	2
Passengers:	8–14

ARMAMENT

Primary: 14.5-mm. machine gun
Secondary: 7.62-mm. machine gun

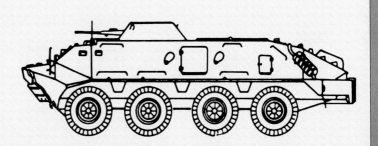

MT–LB Series Armored Personnel Carrier

CHARACTERISTICS

Length:	21.3 feet
Width:	9.5 feet
Height:	6.2 feet
Weight:	12 tons
Speed:	37 miles per hour
Range:	310 miles
Crew:	2
Passengers:	11

ARMAMENT

Type:	7.62-mm. machine gun

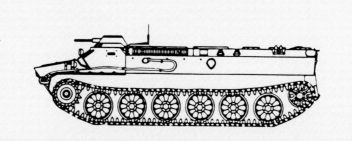

YW–531 Series Armored Personnel Carrier

CHARACTERISTICS

Length:	18 feet
Width:	9.8 feet
Height:	8.5 feet
Weight:	13.9 tons
Speed:	40 miles per hour
Range:	310 miles
Crew:	2
Passengers:	13

ARMAMENT

Type:	12.7-mm. machine gun

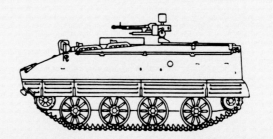

EE–9 Cascavel Armored Car

CHARACTERISTICS

Length:	20.4 feet with gun
Width:	8.7 feet
Height:	7.5 feet
Weight:	14.8 tons
Speed:	62 miles per hour
Range:	545 miles
Crew:	3

ARMAMENT

Primary:	90-mm. gun
Secondary:	7.62-mm. machine gun
	7.62-mm. machine gun or 12.7-mm. machine gun

EE–11 Urutu Armored Personnel Carrier

CHARACTERISTICS

Length:	20 feet
Width:	8.7 feet
Height:	9.5 feet
Weight:	15.4 tons
Speed:	65 miles per hour
Range:	527 miles
Crew:	1
Passengers:	12

ARMAMENT

Type: Configuration dependent (for example, 14.5-mm. machine gun, 12.7-mm. machine gun, 7.62-mm. machine gun)

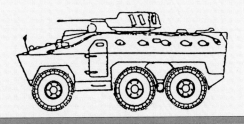

AML 90 Light Car

CHARACTERISTICS

Length:	16.8 feet with gun
Width:	6.5 feet
Height:	6.8 feet
Weight:	6 tons
Speed:	55 miles per hour
Range:	372 miles
Crew:	3

ARMAMENT

Primary:	90-mm. gun
Secondary:	7.62-mm. machine gun

VCR Armored Personnel Carrier

CHARACTERISTICS

Length:	16 feet
Width:	8.2 feet
Height:	8.4 feet
Weight:	8.7 tons
Speed:	62 miles per hour
Range:	496 miles
Crew:	3
Passengers:	9

ARMAMENT

Primary:	12.7-mm. machine gun or HOT antitank guided weapons
Secondary:	7.62-mm. machine gun

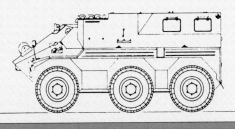

M–3 Armored Personnel Carrier

CHARACTERISTICS

Length:	14.6 feet
Width:	7.9 feet
Height:	7.2 feet
Weight:	6.7 tons
Speed:	55 miles per hour
Range:	372 miles
Crew:	2
Passengers:	10

ARMAMENT

Type: 7.62-mm. machine gun

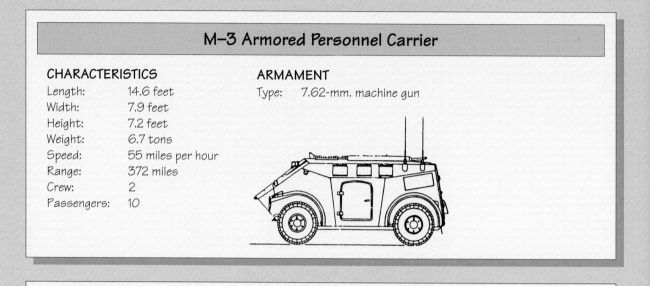

105-mm. Model 56 Pack Howitzer

CHARACTERISTICS

Length:	11.8 feet
Width:	9.5 feet
Height:	6.2 feet
Weight:	1.4 tons
Crew:	7
Rate of fire:	8 rounds per minute (maximum)
	3–4 rounds per minute (sustained)
Range:	10,575 meters

122-mm. D–30 Howitzer

CHARACTERISTICS

Length:	17.8 feet
Width:	6.2 feet
Height:	4.2 feet
Weight:	3.5 tons
Crew:	7
Rate of fire:	7–8 rounds per minute (maximum)
	1 round per minute (sustained)
Range:	15,400 meters
	21,900 meters with rocket-assisted projectile

130-mm. M–46 Field Gun

CHARACTERISTICS

Length:	38.6 feet
Width:	7.9 feet
Height:	8.2 feet
Weight:	9.2 tons
Crew:	8
Rate of fire:	5–6 rounds per minute (maximum)
	1 round per minute (sustained)
Range:	27,150 meters

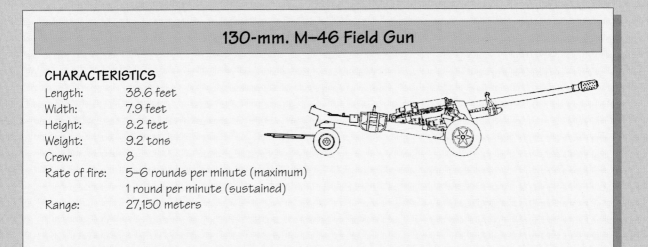

152-mm. D–20 Gun-Howitzer

CHARACTERISTICS

Length:	28.3 feet
Width:	7.5 feet
Height:	6.2 feet
Weight:	6.2 tons
Crew:	10
Rate of fire:	5–6 rounds per minute (maximum)
	1 round per minute (sustained)
Range:	17,410 meters

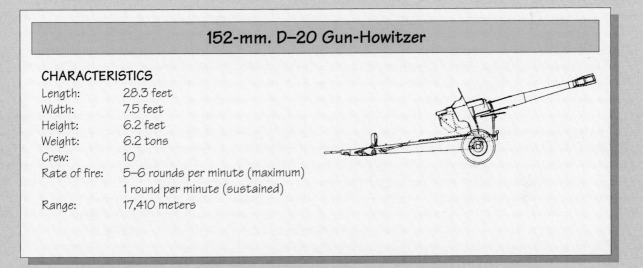

155-mm. G5 Gun-Howitzer

CHARACTERISTICS

Length:	31.3 feet
Width:	10.8 feet
Height:	7.5 feet
Weight:	15.1 tons
Crew:	5
Rate of fire:	3 rounds per minute (maximum)
	1 round per minute (sustained)
Range:	30,000 meters
	39,000 meters with base bleed

155-mm. GH N–45 Gun Howitzer

CHARACTERISTICS

Length:	45.8 feet
Width:	8.2 feet
Height:	6.7 feet
Weight:	11 tons
Crew:	6
Rate of fire:	7 rounds per minute (maximum)
	2 rounds per minute (sustained)
Range:	30,300 meters
	39,600 meters with base bleed

8-inch M115 Howitzer

CHARACTERISTICS

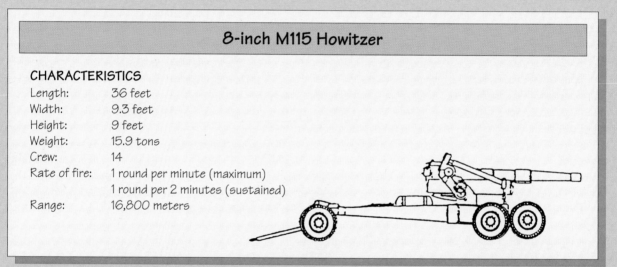

Length:	36 feet
Width:	9.3 feet
Height:	9 feet
Weight:	15.9 tons
Crew:	14
Rate of fire:	1 round per minute (maximum)
	1 round per 2 minutes (sustained)
Range:	16,800 meters

100-mm. T–12/MT–12 Antitank Gun

CHARACTERISTICS

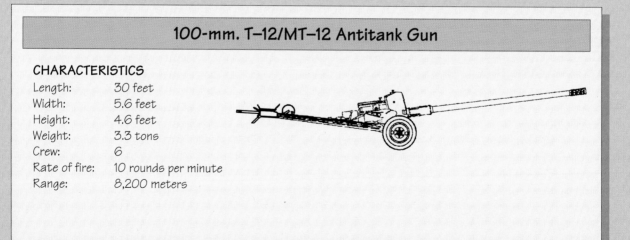

Length:	30 feet
Width:	5.6 feet
Height:	4.6 feet
Weight:	3.3 tons
Crew:	6
Rate of fire:	10 rounds per minute
Range:	8,200 meters

105-mm. M–56 Howitzer

CHARACTERISTICS

Length:	20.1 feet
Width:	6.9 feet
Height:	4.9 feet
Weight:	2.3 tons
Crew:	7
Rate of fire:	16 rounds per minute
Range:	13,000 meters

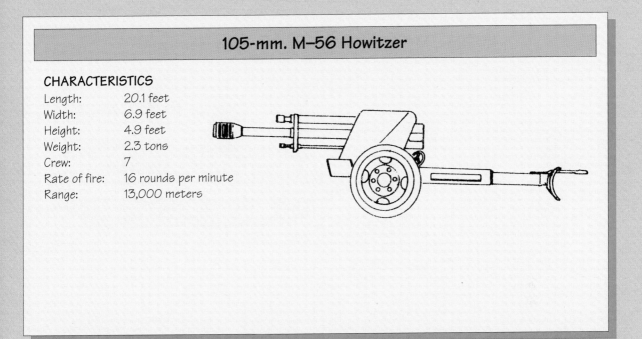

122-mm. M–1974 (2S1) Self-Propelled Howitzer

CHARACTERISTICS

Length:	23.7 feet
Width:	9.3 feet
Height:	8.9 feet
Weight:	17.2 tons
Speed:	38 miles per hour
Range:	310 miles
Crew:	4

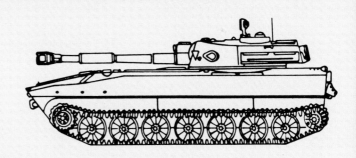

ARMAMENT

Type:	122-mm. howitzer
Rate of fire:	5–8 rounds per minute (maximum)
	1 round per minute (sustained)
Range:	15,300 meters
	21,900 meters with rocket-assisted projectile

152-mm. M–1973 (2S3) Self-Propelled Howitzer

CHARACTERISTICS

Length:	27.7 feet
Width:	10.5 feet
Height:	9.3 feet
Weight:	33 tons
Speed:	38 miles per hour
Range:	310 miles
Crew:	4

ARMAMENT

Primary:	152-mm. howitzer
Secondary:	7.62-mm. machine gun
Rate of fire:	4 rounds per minute (maximum)
	1 round per minute (sustained)
Range:	18,500 meters
	24,000 meters with rocket-assisted projectile

155-mm. GCT Self-Propelled Gun

CHARACTERISTICS

Length:	33.8 feet
Width:	10.3 feet
Height:	9.7 feet
Weight:	47.8 tons
Speed:	37 miles per hour
Range:	279 miles
Crew:	4

ARMAMENT

Primary:	155-mm. gun
Secondary:	7.62-mm. or 12.7-mm. machine gun
Rate of fire:	2–3 rounds per minute (maximum)
	1.5 rounds per minute (sustained)
Range:	29,000 meters

107-mm. Type 63 Multiple Rocket Launcher

CHARACTERISTICS

Length: 8.5 feet
Width: 4.6 feet
Height: 3.9 feet
Weight: 1,344 pounds
Crew: 5

ARMAMENT

Type: 107-mm. rockets (twelve launch tubes)
Rate of fire: 12 rounds per 7–9 seconds
Range: 7,800–10,000 meters
Warhead: high explosive (various types)

BM–21 Multiple Rocket Launcher System*

CHARACTERISTICS

Length: 24.1 feet
Width: 8.9 feet
Height: 9.3 feet
Weight: 14.6 tons
Speed: 46 miles per hour
Range: 251 miles
Crew: 5

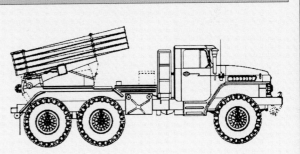

ARMAMENT

Type: 122-mm. rockets (forty launch tubes)
Rate of fire: 40 rounds per 6 seconds
Range: 20,380 meters
Warhead: high explosive–fragmentation, chemical

*Normally mounted on a URAL–375 truck

FROG–7 Artillery Rocket System

CHARACTERISTICS

Length:	35.4 feet
Width:	9.3 feet
Height:	11.5 feet
Weight:	25.3 tons
Speed:	40 miles per hour
Range:	248 miles
Crew:	4

ARMAMENT

Type:	free rocket over ground
Length:	30 feet (7A)
	31.3 feet (7B)
Diameter:	1.8 feet
Weight:	2.5–2.8 tons
Range:	70,000 meters
Warhead:	high explosive, chemical, nuclear-capable

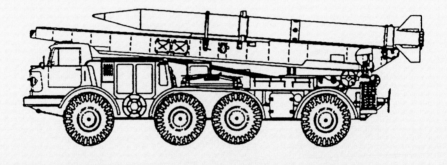

SS–1C Scud-B System

CHARACTERISTICS

Length:	39.6 feet
Width:	9.9 feet
Height:	8.5 feet
Weight:	32 tons
Speed:	43 miles per hour
Range:	341 miles
Crew:	8

ARMAMENT

Type:	surface-to-surface missile
Length:	37.1 feet
Diameter:	1.9 feet
Weight:	7 tons
Range:	300 kilometers
Warhead:	high explosive, chemical, nuclear-capable

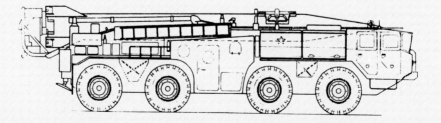

14.5-mm. ZPU–1 Antiaircraft Gun

CHARACTERISTICS
Length: 11.2 feet
Width: 5.31 feet
Height: 4.3 feet
Weight: 909 pounds
Crew: 4

ARMAMENT
Type: 14.5-mm. machine gun
Rate of fire: 150 rounds per minute (practical)
               600 rounds per minute (cyclic)
Range: 1,400 meters

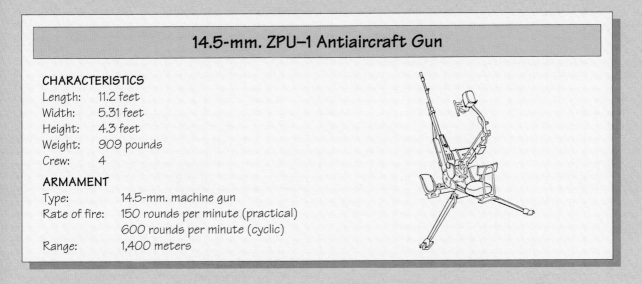

14.5-mm. ZPU–2 Antiaircraft Gun

CHARACTERISTICS
Length: 11.6 feet
Width: 6.3 feet
Height: 6 feet
Weight: 1,370 pounds
Crew: 5

ARMAMENT
Type: two 14.5-mm. machine guns
Rate of fire: 300 rounds per minute (practical)
               1,200 rounds per minute (cyclic)
Range: 1,400 meters

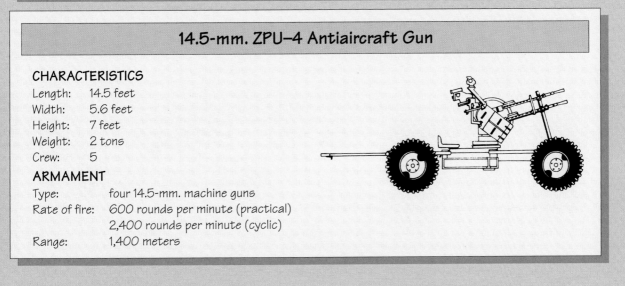

14.5-mm. ZPU–4 Antiaircraft Gun

CHARACTERISTICS
Length: 14.5 feet
Width: 5.6 feet
Height: 7 feet
Weight: 2 tons
Crew: 5

ARMAMENT
Type: four 14.5-mm. machine guns
Rate of fire: 600 rounds per minute (practical)
               2,400 rounds per minute (cyclic)
Range: 1,400 meters

23-mm. ZU–23–2 Antiaircraft Gun

CHARACTERISTICS

Length: 15 feet
Width: 6 feet
Height: 6.1 feet
Weight: 1 ton
Crew: 5

ARMAMENT

Type: two 23-mm. air-cooled cannons
Rate of fire: 400 rounds per minute (practical)
               2,000 rounds per minute (cyclic)
Range: 2,012 meters

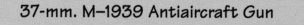

37-mm. M–1939 Antiaircraft Gun

CHARACTERISTICS

Length: 19.9 feet
Width: 6.3 feet
Height: 6.9 feet
Weight: 2.3 tons
Crew: 8

ARMAMENT

Type: 37-mm. antiaircraft gun
Rate of fire: 80 rounds per minute (practical)
               180 rounds per minute (cyclic)
Range: 3,000 meters

57-mm. S–60 Antiaircraft Gun

CHARACTERISTICS

Length: 28.3 feet
Width: 6.8 feet
Height: 8.1 feet
Weight: 5.1 tons
Crew: 7

ARMAMENT

Type: 57-mm. antiaircraft gun
Rate of fire: 70 rounds per minute (practical)
               120 rounds per minute (cyclic)
Range: 4,000 meters with on-carriage fire control
               6,000 meters with off-carriage fire control

23-mm. ZU–23–4 Self-Propelled Antiaircraft Gun

CHARACTERISTICS

Length: 21.5 feet
Width: 9.7 feet
Height: 7.4 feet
Weight: 23.5 tons
Speed: 27 miles per hour
Range: 279 miles
Crew: 4

ARMAMENT

Type: four 23-mm. water-cooled cannons
Rate of fire: 800 rounds per minute (practical)
                4,000 rounds per minute (cyclic)
Range: 2,500 meters

57-mm. ZSU–57–2 Self-Propelled Antiaircraft Gun

CHARACTERISTICS

Length: 28.3 feet
Width: 10.8 feet
Height: 8.9 feet
Weight: 30.9 tons
Speed: 31 miles per hour
Range: 260 miles
            369 miles with auxiliary tanks
Crew: 6

ARMAMENT

Type: two 57-mm. water-cooled cannons
Rate of fire: 140 rounds per minute (practical)
                240 rounds per minute (cyclic)
Range: 4,000 meters

SA–6 (GAINFUL) System

CHARACTERISTICS
Length: 24.3 feet
Width: 10.5 feet
Height: 11.3 feet
Weight: 15.4 tons
Range: 161 miles
Crew: 3

ARMAMENT
Type: three surface-to-air missiles
Length: 18 feet
Diameter: 1 foot
Weight: 1,317 pounds
Velocity: Mach 2.8
Altitude: 100–15,000 meters
Range: 3,000–24,000 meters
Warhead: high explosive–fragmentation

SA–8 (GECKO) System

CHARACTERISTICS
Length: 30.2 feet
Width: 9.2 feet
Height: 13.8 feet
Weight: 19.2 tons
Range: 310 miles
Crew: 5

ARMAMENT
Type: six surface-to-air missiles (one per canister)
Length: 10.8 feet (canister)
Width: 1.1 feet (canister)
Height: 1.3 feet (canister)
Weight: 340 pounds (armed canister)
Velocity: Mach 2.4
Altitude: 25–5,000 meters
Range: 1,500–10,000 meters
Warhead: high explosive

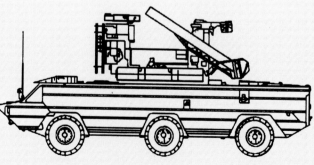

SA–9 (GASKIN) System

CHARACTERISTICS
Length: 19.1 feet
Width: 7.9 feet
Height: 7.5 feet
Weight: 7.7 tons
Range: 465 miles
Crew: 3

ARMAMENT
Type: four surface-to-air missiles (one per canister)
Length: 7 feet (canister)
Width: 1 foot (canister)
Height: 1 foot (canister)
Weight: 110 pounds (armed canister)
Velocity: Mach 2
Altitude: 15–5,200 meters
Range: 800–6,000 meters
Warhead: high explosive

SA–13 (GOPHER) System

CHARACTERISTICS
Length: 21.7 feet
Width: 9.4 feet
Height: 7.5 feet
Weight: 13.5 tons
Range: 410 miles
Crew: 3

ARMAMENT
Type: four surface-to-air missiles (one per canister)
Length: 7.5 feet (canister)
Width: 1 foot (canister)
Height: 1 foot (canister)
Weight: 160 pounds (armed canister)
Velocity: Mach 2
Altitude: 10–3,500 meters
Range: 500–5,000 meters
Warhead: high explosive

ACKNOWLEDGMENTS

Many individuals—military and civilians—provided unstinting assistance and support in the overall preparation of this work.

For aiding the contributors in their research and the collection of photographs, we wish to thank Lt. Col. Richard D. Adamczyk, Lt. Col. (Chaplain) Jack Anderson, Dr. Alfred M. Beck, Sfc. Renalda A. Blount, Howell C. Brewer, Sgt. (USMC) Leviston N. Brisolla, Lt. Col. (USMCR) Ronald J. Brown, Col. James Buchanan, Dr. Susan Canedy, Dr. Albert E. Cowdrey, James T. Currie, Aaron A. Danis, Lt. Col. Steve E. Dietrich, Col. W. Scott Dillard, Capt. (USNR) Larry Douglas, Dr. Edward J. Drea, Robert D. Duckworth, Maj. Marlene Etchieson, Stephen E. Everett, Lt. Col. (USAR) Carolyn Feller, Dr. John P. Finnegan, Lt. Col. Gregory Fontenot, Lt. Col. Mary Frank, Lt. Col. (USA, Ret.) Robert Frank, Stephen L. Y. Gammons, M. Sgt. (USA, Ret.) Gregory R. Gilchrist, Dr. Martin K. Gordon, Dr. John T. Greenwood, Dr. William M. Hammond, Lt. Col. Henry H. Hanraham, Col. (USA, Ret.) Ann M. Hartwick, Geraldine K. Harcarik, Douglas Harvey, Maj. Larry Heystek, Col. (ARNG) Douglas B. Hollenbeck, Capt. Sarah Hood, Col. Terry Hulin, Maj. Stephen Holley, Col. Harold E. Holloway, Dr. Richard A. Hunt, Dr. Perry D. Jamieson, James B. Knight, Col. H. D. Kuhl, Col. Ronald A. Kutka, Maj. William McCoy, Dr. Janet A. McDonnell, Michael P. McHugh, Don E. McLeod, Dr. H. O. Malone, Maj. (USMC) Charles D. Melson, Dr. Joel D. Meyerson, Col. Gene L. Miller, Lt. Col. John Moncure, Walter B. Morrow, Lt. Col. (USA, Ret.) Clayton R. Newell, Gordon L. Olson, Russell J. Parkinson, Hans S. Pawlisch, Frank Pew, Wanda R. Radcliffe, Dr. Edgar F. Raines, Jr., Lt. Col. Richard St. Denis, Col. (USAR) Arthur Samuel, Lt. Col. Joseph Serio, Amy Shimamura, William E. Stacy, Patricia A. Stepper, Dr. Richard W. Stewart, Maj. (USAR) William H. Thomas III, Dr. Wayne W. Thompson, Mark A. Wilner, John B. Wilson, Lt. Col. Patricia B. Wise, Maj. (ARNG) Robert K. Wright, Jr., Dr. James L. Yarrison, and Hannah M. Zeidlik.

In addition, we owe our gratitude to Dr. Jeffery J. Clarke, Lt. Col. Steve E. Dietrich, Dr. George W. Gawrych, Lt. Col. Douglas V. Johnson II, Col. Richard M. Swain, and Col. (USA, Ret.) Raoul H. Alcala for reviewing and critiquing the manuscript. For contributing their diverse talents during the various production phases, we also are indebted to Center of Military History staff members Diane S. Arms, John Birmingham, Joanne M. Brignolo, Joycelyn M. Canery, Sherry L. Dowdy, John W. Elsberg, Marylou Gjernes, Melissa D. Hackett, Arthur S. Hardyman, Catherine A. Heerin, and Adrienne M. Jennings.

Finally, for the use of their photographs, we wish to thank Pfc. (later Spc.) Randall R. Anderson, Sfc. Bob Crockett, Capt. Michael Edrington, Maj. (USA, Ret.) William W. Epley, Pfc. (ARNG) John F. Freund, Sgt. Michele R. Hammonds, Maj. (USA, Ret.) Glen R. Hawkins, Sgt. Howard Johnston, S. Sgt. (ARNG) LaDona S. Kirkland, Spc. Jerry Klotz, Maj. (ARNG) Dennis P. Levin, Maj. Kevin McKedy, Spc. Jackson M. Powell, Spc. K. Benjamin Quigley, Sgt. Raymond Roman, Sgt. M. Martin L. Shupe, S. Sgt. (ARNG) James A. Speraw, Spc. Scott A. Tackett, Spc. James Thompson, Sgt. Nathan Webster, PH2 (USN) Thomas E. Witham, and Sgt. Randall M. Yackiel. The paintings were executed by Capt. Mario H. Acevedo and Sfc. Peter G. Varisano.

ILLUSTRATION CREDITS

INDEX